Access, Management and Usage of Electronic Resources

Access, Management and Usage of Electronic Resources

Edited By
Anil Kumar Siwach
Maharshi Dayanand University, Rohtak, Haryana (India)
Seema Parmar
CCS Haryana Agricultural University, Hisar, Haryana (India)

Ess Ess Publications
New Delhi

Access, Management and Usage of Electronic Resources

ISBN: 978-81-7000-701-2

₹ 1450/-

First Published 2013

Published by:
Ess Ess Publications
4831/24, Ansari Road,
Darya Ganj,
New Delhi-110 002.
INDIA
Phones: 23260807, 41563444
Fax: 41563334
E-mail: info@essessreference.com
www.essessreference.com

Cover Design by *Patch Creative Unit*

Printed and bound in India at Salasar Imaging Systems.

Contents

Foreword

The developments in Information and Communication Technologies (ICT) have induced revolutionary changes in all fields of knowledge, and libraries being "the reservoirs of knowledge" are no exception. The shift to technology-driven library operations and the advent of information and knowledge resources in electronic form has re-invented the library services. The librarians, until a decade back, have been the custodians of library resources, providing traditional library services to their clienteles. They, now, have modern tools at their disposal to accomplish the objectives enshrined in Ranganathan's Five Laws of Library Science.

The modern libraries are witnessing mind-boggling and astonishing changes in the methods of collection, organization, archiving, and dissemination of knowledge. There is a tremendous shift from the print to the electronic media in terms of number and variety in the past decade. The advantages offered by electronic information like exhaustive, pin-pointed and instantaneous access, up-to-dateness, interactivity, economical storage and maintenance, and ease of usability make them an obvious choice in the libraries. The librarians, therefore, need to be more technology savvy and good information managers to exploit full potential of the ICT for the benefit of their patrons—the library users.

The present book, organized in four sections, focuses on electronic resources and the impact they have on the library services.

The changes occurring in the digital environment have been highlighted in the first section of the book. The second section is devoted to topics related to collection development, access modes, service delivery and sustenance of electronic resources. The third section addresses the issues relating to management and subscription, while the fourth deals with marketing, utilization and usage pattern of electronic resources. The book will undoubtedly be of great value to the librarians, consultants, IT specialists, executives, managers, teachers, students and other academic community who need to keep themselves abreast with the latest trends in ICT in general and electronic resources in particular.

The editors and all the contributors deserve commendation for the hard work they have put in. I feel extremely happy to write this foreword and congratulate the editors for bringing out this volume.

Prof. Prem Singh

Advisor (E-governance, University Library and Guest Faculty in Dept. of Lib. & Inf. Sc.), M.D. University, Rohtak Former Deputy Director (Lib. & Inf.), L.B.S. National Academy of Administration, Mussoorie; University Librarian, C.C.S. Haryana Agricultural University, Hisar; and University Librarian and Prof. & Head, Dept. of Lib. & Inf. Sc., M.D. University, Rohtak; Fulbright Fellow in 1992-93

Preface

The developments in Information, Communication and Web technologies have had a profound impact on every sphere of life and libraries are no exceptions. With the advent of Information and Communication Technology (ICT) in general and the Internet in particular, there has been a paradigm shift from print to electronic information resources. In the recent past electronic information resources have grown tremendously and their usage is gaining momentum day by day. The reasons for actually embarking on the purchasing of electronic resources are generally accepted because of the advantages offered by these resources over the print resources.

The main motto of libraries is to endow with better access to information to its users. Libraries are now acquiring various electronic resources for providing easy, reliable and required information to its users. However, to provide better e-resources in this digital environment, there is a need to select, evaluate and organize the e-resources in best possible way to ensure maximum use by both the users and the staff. The resources available on internet, the increased complexity of web based tools and campus networks within the organizations have changed the role of libraries. The concern is how to integrate and handle this information and how quickly and seemingly access can be provided. The library and information professionals need to acquire greater knowledge and information management skills if they are to provide information services to support the pedagogic needs of modern learning and instruction.

The book "Access, Management and Usage of Electronic Resources" have a collection of articles from the library and information professionals at national as well as at international level. It is divided into four sections.

Section I - The Digital Environment is composed of the following chapters:

- Emerging trends in libraries services in the perspective of electronic resources
- Design and development of e-publications: Trends, issues and challenges
- Changing Library services in perspective of Electronic Resources
- E-books – issues and concern of different stake holders in India
- Emerging Non-conventional Publishing Channels: Revolution in scholarly and street Publishing
- Changing Scenario in Information world: Lib 2.0
- Major online databases available in social sciences
- Evolution of libraries in the digital era- from physical to virtual
- Status of electronic & ICT infrastructure in public libraries in Chandigarh city

Section II – Collection Development and Access of e-Resources consists of the following chapters:

- Collection Development of Electronic Resources
- Preserving the Bits for Future: Need, Objectives, Issues and Challenges
- Online Journal: Access and Delivery Models
- Consortia: A back bone for the library users in electronic era

Section III – e-Resource Management have the following contributions:

- Biometrics – Management and use of online journals in Jaykar Library, University of Pune, India
- Electronic resource management: Emerging trends and challenging issues
- E-journal management in libraries
- Electronic resource management
- Electronic Resources: Management and Access
- E-journal and their management in libraries
- Electronic information resources management in academic library in Nigeria
- Management of electronic resources in Nigerian university libraries

Section IV – Publicity, Usage is having the following six chapters:

- Marketing of e-resource for academic libraries
- e-Databases with special reference to National Library of Veterinary Sciences, Indian Veterinary Research Institute, Izatnagar (U.P.)
- Use of electronic resources by the research scholars of the Panjab University Chandigarh: A study
- Usage Pattern of Online Dictionaries among Research Scholars
- Availability and utilization of electronic resources by lecturers at the engineering & environmental campus of the Olabisi Onabanjo University Ogun state, Nigeria
- An assessment of the collection and use of electronic resources in university libraries in Kwara State, Nigeria

The book tries to bring to the fore the major relevant issues related to electronic resources, their access, management, collection development, preservation, marketing and usage. Although it is not claimed that the book is carrying very nascent information in it but professionals have shown their fair and comprehensive contribution to the existing knowledge in the field.

Anil Kumar Siwach
Seema Parmar

Acknowledgements

First and the foremost, we are thankful to our respective organizations where we have been working during the editing of this book. Appreciation is to be given to all the contributors of the present book who have shown their timely interest and response to the book by imparting their thoughts and ideas through their articles. Further, we are thankful to our seniors and colleagues for inspiring us to give contribution in the field in form of the present book. We are indebted to Dr. Manoj K. Joshi, Professor, Kurukshetra University, Kurukshetra and Dr. Satish Malik, Deputy Librarian, M.D. University, Rohtak who have always been the source of inspiration. We also acknowledge M/s Ess Ess Publications and their team for undertaking this publication.

— Editors

Contents in Detail

The central purpose of libraries is to provide access to information. The shift to computer-based technical operations and, more especially, the advent of library materials in electronic form indicate the prospect of radical changes in the means of library service. The library needs to sustain its high motivation by providing just-in-time services that will meet user's needs for relevant information resources. Electronic resources offer creative possibilities for expanding access as well as changing learning behaviour and academic research. The new emerging roles of librarians require that they acquire greater knowledge and information management skills if they are to provide information services to support the pedagogic needs of modern learning and instruction.

With the emergence of ICT applications in libraries in general and with the advent of Internet in particular, there is a paradigm shift from traditional print information resources to electronic information resources. The chapter discusses the future trends in design and development of e-publications, types of e-publications and their advantages and disadvantages. It also discusses the impact of electronic publishing on libraries along with issues associated with e-publications. The major developments of e-publishing have been described especially with an impact of electronic media and Internet. After study the different issues related with e-publications and e-publishing, it has come out that print form is still popular in peer groups and retained by libraries. Development of electronic publications in India has also being discussed.

Chapter 3 : Changing Library Services in Perspective of Electronic Resources — *Jacintha U. Eze*

Over the past few years, library and information centres, and their services have been greatly affected by the emergence and use of electronic resources and facilities in the search, retrieval, organization and dissemination of information. The flow of information through the superhighways –the Internet and the use of information and communication technology, ICT have made the library not just a building but a virtual entity that can provide more information than is available in its physical collections. This chapter intends to delve into how the contemporary library and information services are changing and being modeled to integrate e-resources. The meaning, types/forms of electronic resources, usefulness and effect on traditional library and information services, acquisition of these resources, challenges posed by these electronic resources to libraries and librarians especially in the developing countries and the way forward in changing library services in the perspective of these resources are all examined.

Chapter 4 : E-Books – Issues and Concern of Different Stake Holders in India — *Rakesh Mani Sharma*

The chapter describes the e-books, its development, design, merits, demerits, and issues and concerns of different stake holders like users, authors, publishers, libraries and vendors of e-books in Indian perspectives. Many feel that the current usability of e-books is too poor to offer a genuine alternative to printed resources for serious research and academic study but it is not true. The emergence of e-books is going to supplement the contents of printed books instead of replacing them. The quality of the content and users' abilities to assess that quality influences their use of e-books within academic and research community. There are huge concerns and issues of different stake holder in e-book production, marketing and use, but the advantages offered by e-books like easy to carry, saving space, convenience, saving money and time, and ease-of-use will put forward the e-book alongside of printed books just like printed journals with their electronic versions. However to promote the usage of e-books while librarians need to educate users as well as staff about the benefits in use of e-books, the users require a paradigm shift in their attitude away from the current perception that everything must be on the printed page to the varied better possibilities offered by e-books. Further the publishers, vendors and librarians need to work together on more mutually congenial and beneficial business models for greater e-book usage.

Chapter 5 : Emerging Non-conventional Publishing Channels: Revolution in scholarly and Street Publishing

— Tabasum Maqbool

The web resources are becoming more powerful than they were in 1990's and are developing at a very fast rate in the various subjects. With the success of web 2.0 and its various tools especially wikis and blogs have given easy and far-reaching coverage not only to scholars but also to ordinary beings to express their ideas, thoughts, imagination and a power to improve each other's understanding of various concepts, ideas, improving and updating knowledge due to collaborative intelligence.

Chapter 6 : Changing Scenario in Information World: Lib 2.0

— Anvita Shrivastava

Internet's rapid growth and broad penetration, along with affordable enabling Web 2.0 technologies, has not only democratized access to information but also catalyzed open access publishing which has contributed marjory to the explosion of freely available digital information. This phenomenon poses tremendous challenges, and opportunities, for Libraries and Information officers. The present chapter is an attempt to describe the various elements of lib 2.0 i.e. technology, social networking and innovativeness as well as different components on which, principles of the lib 2.0 are lying. It also tries to explain the diverse tools of the web 2.0 which helps to convert traditional libraries in to modern information center and finally it tells about the role and responsibility of the information officers to adopt the modern technology for providing better users services through breaking the different barriers.

Chapter 7 : Major Online Database Available in Social Sciences
—Satwinderpal Kaur Gill

Considering the plethora of information available on the internet, it becomes necessary that some agencies act towards filtering and providing relevant information to users. Database is one of such services which aim to save the valuable time of the researchers and provide them quality information. This chapter discusses some of the major online databases in social sciences including International Political Science Abstracts, Bibliography of Asian Studies, Sociological abstracts, LISA, LISTA, Dissertation Abstracts Online, Population Index, DARE, PsycINFO and Social Sciences Citation Index.

Chapter 8 : Evolution of Libraries in the Digital Era- From Physical to Virtual
— Y. Gautam

The transformation of collections from print to electronic media, increasing involvement with digitization of local library materials and the development of new services to accommodate new generations of library users has led to many technological advancements and the functioning of a library and the day is not far when physical library will give way to a virtual one. To some, the virtual library connotes the ultimate fear: obsolescence of the librarian. To others, the virtual library offers the promised land: the utopia of information access to all. Carried to its ultimate end, the virtual library offers a universe of information to any user, anywhere in the world, at any time of the day or night through the power of a personal computer with telecommunication capabilities. The Internet is an information free-for-all, with no standardized organizational structure or defined mandate. While libraries are quintessential examples of information order.

Chapter 9 : Status of Electronic & ICT Infrastructure in Public Libraries in Chandigarh City — *Parveen Kumar*

Information and Communication Technology (ICT) has brought revolutionary changes in the concept of collection, organization and dissemination of information in library and information systems throughout the world. The impact of these changes is pervasive and affecting all the aspects of library operations, information resources & services and user expectations. There is growing need to investigate the present state of public libraries in this ICT era. The chapter provides an insight into the current state of information and communication technology (ICT), infrastructure, automation/computerization and available skilled ICT staff in the public libraries of Chandigarh City.

SECTION II : COLLECTION DEVELOPMENT AND ACCESS OF E-RESOURCES

Chapter 10 : Collection Development of Electronic Resources — *Anil Kumar Siwach*

In the recent past electronic information resources have grown tremendously and their usage is gaining momentum day by day. The reasons for actually embarking on the purchasing of electronic resources are generally accepted because of the advantages offered by these resources over the print resources. The electronic resources present a number of challenges not encountered with the selection and acquisition of traditional analogue materials and it is advisable for the library to develop clear policies and processes for the selection and management of such resources. The chapter highlights some of the important steps and considerations for building an e-resource collection.

Chapter 11 : Preserving the Bits for Future: Need, Objectives, Issues

and Challenges — *Sunder Singh Tanwar*

Digital preservation is the active management of digital contents over time to ensure ongoing access and awfully significant to our social, cultural, intellectual, technological and economical growth. Though the preservation issues are not new, however, the perspective has changed with the Information Revolution. The volume of information is increasing swiftly which exists in digital form. It may be digitized non-digital collections, born digital, or created as part of the day-to-day business of an organisation, more and more information is being created digitally and the velocity at which it is being created is accelerating. This chapter states about the need of digital preservation, its objectives, issues involved, challenges, strategies and implications in library environment. Extended benefits of digitization over traditional approach are also discussed.

Chapter 12 : Online Journal: Access and Delivery Models

— *Prakash Dongardive*

Electronic transition of information mostly in the context of online journals provide superior way of having current and concern information to academic science community, with wide opportunities to satisfy their information needs. The chapter discusses the access and delivery models which are available for the online journals.

Chapter 13 : Consortia: A Back Bone for the Library Users in Electronic Era — *Chandresh A. Shah*

Library Consortium is the latest buzzword of today's electronic environment. Due to increase in the cost of journals, dwindling library budgets and proliferation of electronic information resources, libraries have been involved in cooperation, coordination and collaboration in resource sharing. Consortium is all about sharing resources and improving access to information. There resources are shared among libraries that have common mission, goals and clients (users) and act on those commonalties. This chapter highlights the concept, need, objectives, models, features, advantages, disadvantages of library consortia, etc.

SECTION III : E-RESOURCE MANAGEMENT

Chapter 14 : Biometrics – Management and Use of Online Journals in Jaykar Library, University of Pune, India

— *Prakash Dongardive*

Internet, especially its nature of technology and utility is a remote access model. Seamless access possible through linking information resources like databases and online journals distributed at various sites. Internet and its secured cousin intranet have however, thrown up different access models that fit into the convenience of libraries. Information technology has changed the world and has become the important tool for retrieving information. Now a day, library collections are not limited to printed document only but also electronic resources such as CD ROM resources, Web resources such as, E-journals, e-books etc. the format of document has changed from paper to digital form. The electronic information resources have became the important part of today's libraries. Importance of information resources increasing day by day, so it is an important to know the utilization of the e-resources, by using electronic information resources Academic community can update their knowledge and pursuing their currier. There are different purposes for the academic community in using the electronic resources. The present study is an attempt to investigate the use of online journals by the science faculty members in University of Pune.

Chapter 15 : Electronic Resource Management: Emerging Trends and Challenging Issues

— *Madan Kumar Stanley*

Knowledge-based information and its flow has to be streamlined to be made available to the user community. The advances in ICT have transformed traditional libraries from mere static store houses of print documents to a dynamic powerhouse of information. The way librarian acquires, processes, stores and disseminates information to the user community has undergone radical changes. This chapter presents the impact of increasing production of digital information resources and discusses the advantages and challenges of electronic information resource management.

Chapter 16 : E-journal management in libraries

— Seema Parmar

In the era of ICT, e-journals are keeping a special place among all electronic resources, thus their management in libraries is a very vital issue. It involves various technical, legal and such other issues. Subscribing e-journals in libraries is a costly affair and one library cannot independently purchase all e-journals within their restricted library budget. So libraries are moving towards e-journals consortia to meet their users' informational needs. Librarians are required to be more competent to tackle with managing issues' of e-journals. They are required to welcome existing and new coming challenges and be technology familiar.

Chapter 17 : Electronic Resource Management

— Oghenovo Kelvin Onoriode

The purpose of this chapter is to provide in-depth overview of E-resources management. It takes a vivid coverage of what E-resources are, why manage E-resources and discussed the types of E-resources. The chapter also covers Management of E-Resources in this era, E-Resources Management LifeCycle, Software for management of E-resources and Issues in Management of electronic Resources.

Chapter 18 : Electronic Resources: Management and Access

— Sandhya Aggarwal

Electronic publishing has led to new era of communications and information sharing .It creates opportunities for users as well as authors and publishers. Moreover, as the popularity of e-resources increases, the librarians and staff are also concerned about e-resources, their methods accessing, evaluation, selection, organization etc. The present chapter is an aim to know how to manage e-resources in the modern LIS for better digital information services and challenges facing with e-resources.

Chapter 19 : E-Journal and their Management in Libraries
— *Ivwighreghweta Oghenetega*

In most libraries of the world, the concept of e-journals and their management of digital collections is a very important issue. In certain ways, digital materials are incredibly fragile, dependent for their continued utility upon technologies that undergo rapid and continual change. Keeping and managing the e-journal resources accessible for use by future generations will require conscious effort and continual investment. No library is self sufficient to purchase all the books, Journals and other library documents with in their library budget. So customers belonging to different academic institutions or university may purchase e-journals and sharing its cost through consortia. E- Journal management requires librarians to acquire new competence on technological know-how, how to deal with licensing, copyright implications and new purchasing methods such as consortia etc.

Chapter 20 : Electronic Information Resources Management in Academic Library in Nigeria — *Olatokunbo Christopher Okiki*

The main aim of this chapter is to examine the availability, importance, implications, and opportunities available to Nigerian libraries in the current Information Age in relation to the evolution of electronic information resources globally. This chapter attempts to address possible areas of importance and advantages that can propel Nigerian universities especially academic libraries to embrace global e-revolution and in order to enhance students and faculty members' success. This chapter reviewed available academic electronic resources, and stresses the necessity for Nigerian academic libraries to acquire and promote users awareness and use of e-resources. It further examines the role played by organization other than government in providing a stronger library development as well as charts the way forward in dealing with identified problems.

Chapter 21 : Management of Electronic Resources in Nigerian University Libraries — *Janet Onomeh Ubogu*

The study examines management of e-resources in Nigerian University Libraries in South-South. The population of the study consist of 290 respondents. Data was collected from 290 librarians of sampled libraries through questionnaire. 212 (73.1%) valid questionnaire were used for the analysis, simple percentage and frequency counts were used in analyzing the data. The study revealed the following; that management of e-resources is necessary, experts are required in managing e-resources, in-service training is necessary in managing e-resources, planning and policies serve as guidelines in the management of e-resources, Google and ebscohost are the most used search engines. Communication gap between librarian and vendors, and inadequate personnel to handled e-tools are some of the problems militating against the management of e-resources in the university libraries. The study will bridge communication gap between librarian and vendors for the effectiveness of e-resources management. The findings of this study will also move the university authorities in Nigeria to see need to employ adequate qualify personnel to manage these e-resources.

SECTION IV : PUBLICITY, USAGE

Chapter 22 : Marketing of e-resource for academic libraries — *Sanjiv Kadyan*

The article focuses on marketing of e-resource in libraries. Marketing of e-resource plays an essential role in today's era. Scholarly journals have almost completely converted to electronic formats accessed from a remotely located publisher or aggregators. This article concentrates e-resource for Academic libraries and how it can be applied for marketing and beneficial for the library professionals.

Chapter 23 : E-Databases with Special Reference to National Library of Veterinary Sciences, Indian Veterinary Research Institute, Izatnagar (U.P.) — *S.S.Rawat and K.N.Kandpal*

e-Databases are necessary for providing quick, better, and accurate information services to the researcher. Consortium for e-Resources in Agriculture (CeRA), is an e-consortium of Agricultural Libraries under Indian council of Agricultural Research. e-Resources are the need of hour for fast development of research in agricultural sector in India.. The Indian Council of Agricultural Research (ICAR) appointed many committees to meet the challenges for providing agricultural information to the users. To help in the development of research activities, budgetary support has been provided through NATP and NAIP under NARS (National Agricultural Research System). The Indian Veterinary Research Institute (IVRI) is the first premier scientific research Institute and oldest Institute in India. National Library of Veterinary Sciences (NLVS), IVRI, Izatnagar also participates actively in fulfilling the information need of the scientists and students of the institute. Various e-databases under the projects Krishi Prabha, CeRA, AGRIS and e-Granth are being maintained, created, updated and provided in NLVS as well as in NARS.

Chapter 24 : Use of Electronic Resources by the Research Scholars of the Panjab University Chandigarh: A Study

— *Kiran Chopra and Rajveer Kaur*

E-resources are resources in which information is stored electronically and it can be accessible through electronic systems and network environment. The chapter discusses utilization of digital resources by the research scholars of Panjab University, Chandigarh. Questionnaire method was employed to gather data from researchers of humanities disciplines in Panjab University. Responses received from 90 research scholars shows that in general the research scholars prefer print resources and there exists significant difference in the preference of print and electronic resources among various disciplines. Study reveals that the electronic resources have created a positive hope among the research community in searching the information.

Chapter 25 : Usage Pattern of Online Dictionaries among Research Scholars — *Devendra Singh*

This study investigated various aspects related to the use of online dictionaries among fifty three research scholars at Kurukshetra University. Two-third scholars were found using the online dictionaries but nearly all of them were using the free ones only. However, 11.3 percent scholars also reported to have their own e-dictionaries in the CD/DVD format. Use of online dictionaries, definitions in the free online dictionaries considered to be authentic, and satisfaction with the free online dictionaries by research scholars were found statistically significant with Chi-Square.

Chapter 26 : Availability and Utilization of Electronic Resources by Lecturers at the Engineering & Environmental Campus of the Olabisi Onabanjo University Ogun State, Nigeria — *M. A. Adeniji*

The level of awareness of electronic resources and its utilization by academic staff of the Ibogun Campus of the Olabisi Onabanjo University Ogun state, Nigeria was the main focused of this work. The profile of the college was presented showing that the College has thirty lecturers cutting across the seven departments of the College. The e-resources annexed by the lecturers for their research and teaching function was described, pointing out constraints that the lecturers faced in the course of duties while utilizing the resources. The Challenges against the usage of electronic resources by the lecturer were categorized. Recurrent power outages topping the list, followed by limited bandwidth, insufficient funds, inability to download information facilities and network problems. The e-resources as a booster to their work were used for more than one purpose either for research or teaching function to aid the work of these professionals of the college. For better utilization of these resources for teaching function. All the stakeholders in Education industry has one role or the others to play in order to promote effective utilization of e-resources in Nigerian Universities. The government should provide enough resources for effective teaching and learning in Nigerian Higher institutions. The College management and the lecturers should address the constraints that hindered the usage of the e –resources in their various campuses. The, University management should invest greater part of its fund into the issue of learning resources for a better service. Individual lecturers should reciprocate the government gesture by using the e –resources for the purpose it was meant for However, with the above been put in place the College will make a positive contribution to the development of the society and nation at large.

Chapter 27 : An Assessment of the Collection and Use of Electronic Resources in University Libraries in Kwara State, Nigeria

— Abdulwahab Olanrewaju Issa, Shuaib Agboola Larongbe and Sunday Adebisi Oguntayo

There is no doubt that the library, its collections as well as its collection building process have changed dramatically from what they used to be. Today, books are no longer just physical objects as they have transformed into audio, video, Braille, large print, paper back and indeed electronics. This means that the same content had been repurposed and reformatted, especially in the developed countries. However, research evidence has not suggested that academic libraries in developing countries like Nigeria are fast joining the positive given its obvious advantages. Their level of involvement in the building of e-resources is still largely a subject of conjecture and against which background this study investigated the collection building of the electronic resources in the four university libraries in Kwara State, Nigeria. The study adopted the survey research method with the Questionnaire (Library Users) and Interview (University Librarians) were used for the data collection exercise. The results indicate that daily and weekly library visits were highest (58.2% and 31.6%) at UI as against the low rates from KWASU and LU; textbooks were the main purpose of the visits, which for AU is 76.7%, LU and KWASU, 68.8% each, and the UI (62.3%). However, the textbook needs were unmet substantially, as confirmed by 73.5% response from UI, 64.6% from KWASU, 56.2% from LU and 46.7% from AU. Provision of more print resources was suggested by respondents from UI (51.0%), AU (46.7%), KWASU (45.8%) and LU (68.8%). Findings also revealed that only UI is in a purposefully built accommodation; while only KWASU and LU have automated library systems, using KOHA and ALEXANDRIA LIBRARIAN as software. Although UI has the largest print collections of 87,134 book titles and 2,458 periodical titles, LU holds an impressive and unmatched over 30000 e-periodical titles. Instead, UI only has an NUC subscription to five databases. Lack of awareness, leading to limited/non use of e-resources were major challenges found while automation of the remaining two libraries, separate budgets for print and e-resources collection building, training library staff in e-resources management and a sustained user education programme were recommended.

List of Contributors

1. **Abdulwahab Olanrewaju Issa**
Head & Senior Lecturer
Department of Library and Information Science
Faculty of Communication and Information Sciences
University of Ilorin, Ilorin
Kwara State, Nigeria

2. **Anil Kumar Siwach**
Assistant Professor
Department of Library & Information Science
M.D. University, Rohtak
Haryana, India

3. **Anvita Shrivastava**
Department of Library & Information Science
Banaras Hindu University
U.P., India

4. **Bhanu Partap**
Librarian, T.S. Central State Library
Sector-17, Chandigarh, India

5. **Chandresh A. Shah**
Library Assistant, Junagadh Agricultural University
Junagadh, Gujarat, India

6. **Devendra Singh**
PhD Scholar, Department of Library & Information Science
Kurukshetra University, Kurukshetra
Haryana, India

7. **Ivwighreghweta Oghenetega**
Readers Service Librarian
Western Delta University
Oghara, Delta State, Nigeria

8. **Jacintha U. Eze**
Senior Librarian, Enugu State Library Board
Enugu, Nigeria

9. **Janet Onomeh Ubogu**
Assistant Librarian
Cataloguing and Classification Unit
Delta State University Library
Abraka, Nigeria.

10. **K.N.Kandpal**
Technical Officer, National Library of Veterinary Sciences
Indian Veterinary Research Institute
Izatnagar, Uttar Pradesh, India.

11. **Kiran Chopra**
T.S. Central State Library
Sector 17, Chandigarh, India

12. **M. A. Adeniji**
College Librarian, Engineering and Environmental Campus
Olabisi Onabanjo University
Ogun State, Nigeria

13. **Madan Kumar Stanley**
University Librarian (Retd.)
No. 80, "Sri Ranga".
2A Main, 10th Cross
Laxmaiah Block, Ganganagar
Bangalore, Karnataka, India

14. **Oghenovo Kelvin Onoriode**
Cataloging/ICT Librarian
Western Delta University
Oghara, Delta State, Nigeria

15. **Olatokunbo Christopher Okiki**
Serials Librarian
University of Lagos Library, Nigeria

16. **Oluwatoyin Oyeyemi Obinyan**
Graduate Student, Delta State University, Abraka
Delta State, Nigeria

17. **Parveen Kumar**
Librarian, T.S. Central State Library
Sector-17, Chandigarh, India

18. **Prakash Dongardive**
Deptt. of Library and Information Science,
College of Natural and Computational Sciences,
University of Mekelle,
Mekelle, Tigray, Ethiopia

19. **Rajveer Kaur**
Librarian, T.S. Central State Library
Sector-17, Chandigarh, India

20. **Rakesh Mani Sharma**
Senior Librarian, Central Potato Research Institute
Shimla, Himachal Pradesh, India

21. **S.S. Rawat**
Officer-in-Charge
National Library of Veterinary Sciences
Indian Veterinary Research Institute
Izatnagar, Uttar Pradesh, India.

22. **Sanjiv Kadyan**
Assistant Professor
Department of Library & Information Science
M.D. University, Rohtak, Haryana, India.

23. **Sandhya Aggarwal**
Librarian, M.M.P.G.College
Fatehabad, Haryana, India

24. **Satwinderpal Kaur Gill**
Assistant Professor
Department of Library and Information Science
Guru Nanak Dev University
Amritsar, Punjab, India

25. **Seema Parmar**
Assistant Librarian
Nehru Library, CCS Haryana Agricultural University
Hisar, Haryana, India

26. **Shuaib Agboola Larongbe**
Lecturer, Department of Library and Information Science
Faculty of Communication and Information Sciences
University of Ilorin, Ilorin
Kwara State, Nigeria

27. **Sunday Adebisi Oguntayo**
Resource Officer I, Centre for Learning Resources
Landmark University, Omu-Aran
Kwara State, Nigeria

28. **Sunder Singh Tanwar**
Information Scientist
M.D. University
Rohtak, Haryana, India

29. **Tabasum Maqbool**
Librarian, DIET
Ganderbal, J&K, India

30. **Y. Gautam**
Scientist, Indian Agricultural Statistics Research Institute
New Delhi, India

SECTION - I
THE DIGITAL ENVIRONMENT

1

Emerging Trends in Libraries Services in the Perspective of Electronic Resources

Oluwatoyin Oyeyemi Obinyan

INTRODUCTION

Libraries form the bedrock and corner-stone for every intellectual advancement. Nwofor and Ilorah (2006) assert that reading is indispensable in the life of man; it is the most important of all subjects and the road to learning. This invariably underscores the role of libraries in the provision of adequate information services via the resources acquired to meet users' needs vis-à-vis creating enabling environment needed for learning. Library is a strong educational force in achieving any developmental goals (Okeke 2000). Good and well organised library links the past, present and the future knowledge through the works of past and present writers. The library today is a pivot on which all academic activities in any educational institution revolve and education is a societal instrument of change and consequently it is affected by social, political, economic, scientific and technological changes.

Culturally, libraries as home of knowledge are both creation and servants of society. They exist for the acquisition, conservation and advancement of knowledge as well as dissemination of same through learning, teaching and research. As a focal point in education, it is expected to provide standard information resources. Today, libraries are struggling to keep their place as the major source of inquiry in the face of emerging digital technology. Digital technology has revolutionized not only the way information is packaged, processed, stored, and disseminated, but also how users seek and access information. Libraries no longer restrict themselves to print services such as collection development, cataloguing and classification, circulation and reference services, current awareness, selective dissemination, and other bibliographic services, but have extended their efforts to interdisciplinary concepts and computer software and hardware and telecommunication engineering and technology. Since advances in technology have changed how librarians do their work so also the business of libraries- connecting people to information has changed. Librarians have assumed the role of educators, to teach their users how to find information both in the library and over electronic networks. Libraries have always played vital roles as social institutions and served as tangible structures where books, journals, magazines, and all kinds of information sources are kept and made available for end users.

SERVICES PROVIDED FOR LIBRARY USERS

1. Reference services
2. Reprographic services
3. Lending services
4. Bibliographic services
5. Referral services
6. Bindery
7. Information search

LIBRARY COLLECTIONS

Today, library collections no longer mean just what a library physically owns but increasingly, what they provide access to regardless of the format. Collections now consist of hard-copy books, periodicals, videos, CDs, CD-ROMs and DVD along with free and subscription-based documents available electronically to patrons of modern day library and this has increased the global dissemination of information. Electronic resources can be accessed electronically through networked facilities in the library and are easily accessible in the remote area. Electronic resources are many and carried and they include e-books, e-journals, online databases, CD-ROMs to mention just a few. Prior to the advent of the acquisition of electronic resources in the libraries, the services rendered by libraries were limited to their wall.

Laguardia et al (1996) described how the new electronic catalogue has rescue patrons from what they termed "Nightmare" having to know the insides of the catalogue. Nowadays, electronic catalogue gives more headings to include table of contents and even abstract to the material as such users can access the resources easily.

FOUNDATIONS OF LIBRARY SERVICE

The central purpose of libraries is to provide access to information. The purpose being pursued in library service is the provision of access to books, journals, and other informative materials. Library service is a busy, service-oriented activity, with a deeply-rooted emphasis, reflected in the professional literature, on practical and technical matters, on means, rather than on ends, and tactics rather than strategy.

Library services have two bases :

I. the role of library service is to facilitate access to documents; and

II. the mission of a library is to support the mission of the institution or the interests of the population served.

Interpreting these two general statements for any given situation provides the foundations for effective library service. Most library survey, however, find that few users are aware of existing libraries services, let alone new services whey they are introduced. The problem lies in the fact that little emphasis has been placed upon the understanding of users and their new needs.

CHANGING LIBRARIES SERVICES IN PERSPECTIVE OF ELECTRONIC RESOURCES

World Wide Web (WWW) technology had been described as an innovation that suddenly altered expectations and behaviour to such a degree that the existing competing institutions within its ecosystem are simply incapable of adapting. Library collections changed from what is available within the library wall to information population which includes owned and accessed resources available to the library users. The impact of all these changes gave the impression of putting information at your fingertips just as Bill Gate noted.

The shift to computer-based technical operations and, more especially, the advent of library materials in electronic form indicate the prospect of radical changes in the means of library service. Lancaster (1997) states that in order to justify library existence in the electronic world "the library must continue to perform one of the most important functions its performs in the print-on-paper world: to organise the universe of resources in such a way that those most likely to be of value to the user community are made most accessible to this community, physically and intellectually". Traditionally, library services were originally tried to print resources usually expensive reference resources but in electronic form now. Library materials in electronic form differ significantly from traditional media. In particular, unlike paper and microform, it is possible to make electronic media available so that they can be used from a distance, used by more than one person at a time, and used in more different ways.

Library services have to do with support for learning, both the study of what others have discovered, and research to discover what is apparently not yet known. There is considerable increase in the publishing output of scholarly resources which are readily accessible remotely via global electronic networks. This has resulted in new, faster and more effective ways of information access and delivery. Information can now be passed directly to the user through cyberspace without any intermediary, the skills of cataloguing and classification in print-based library can now be used to improve the end users experience of networked information retrieval and creation of catalogues to ensure access, authenticity, reliability and validity of networked resources.

The library therefore needs to sustain its high motivation by providing Just-in-time services that will meet user's needs for relevant information resources. Electronic resource services that include the provision of Internet access not only to the bibliography of the library holdings but also to its full text is now being offered in libraries as a result electronic resources. As observed in literatures, numerous creative and useful services have evolved within libraries system in this age such as providing quality learning spaces, creating metadata, offering virtual reference services, teaching information literacy, choosing resources and managing resource licenses, collecting and digitizing archival materials, and maintaining digital repositories.

Online Instruction

Online instruction similar to library orientation services is part of the services provided by the libraries as a result of inclusion of electronic resources in the library's collections. Creth (1996) noted that offering instruction in a variety of formats (including web based instruction and online tutorials) are part of the new services in libraries. This is to make full use of information and multimedia technology available outside the library wall and this form part of the services that libraries are expected to provide to their users.

Creating web pages

Information professionals within libraries according to Hashim & Mokhtar (2005) are playing an increasing role in dealing with information in electronic formats by creating web pages to promote their services to external customers and choosing automated library management systems. Other services include:

- Online/offline access to digital information resources~
- Database searching~
- Public access services ~
- Electronic reference services~
- Public relations services~
- Library promotion and marketing~
- E-publishing~
- Information literacy programmes~
- Online circulation activities, such as electronic reserves~
- User Services, and queries~ and
- Online access to library catalogues, databases and the Internet.

Off-sight reference questions and answers

Through the use of e-mail reference questions are emailed to library, the responses are sent by email after sometimes.

COLLECTION DEVELOPMENT OF ELECTRONIC RESOURCES

Collecting the materials and making it available to all current and future users is another core value of librarianship. The challenge is for the librarian to contribute to establish realistic collection-development policies covering acquisition of and provision of access to electronic resources for users now and in the future. With the increase in electronic resources, librarians and libraries are no longer just collecting and caring for print materials. Payment for a product covered by a license is a payment to use the information product for a period of time that is usually specified in a contract. This payment is not for the outright purchase of the product or for ownership of all the rights to that product.

PRESERVATION/ARCHIVING OF ELECTRONIC RESOURCES

To preserve the e-resources for access would be a great task for librarians however Roes (2005) suggested two strategies for preservation electronic resources: migration and emulation.

1. Migration may not work for specialized, proprietary formats. It may save the content of a file but lose or diminish the internal relationships or contexts of the information.
2. Emulation, assumes future access to multiple data objects. If one or more of the components were missing, this complex environment would most likely fail.

Digitization of Library Resources

Distribution and archiving through digital repositories will insure that the library has a viable system for sustaining digital content. Digital repositories also will facilitate the long term conversion and preservation of print materials, and create new opportunities to structure learning activities around the content. If we need to preserve electronic resources/documents, we need to preserve all the software and hardware also to read the documents that we create.

BENEFITS OF ICT BASED PRODUCTS AND SERVICES IN LIBRARIES

Electronic resources offer creative possibilities for expanding access as well as changing learning behaviour and academic research. Content can always be accessed regardless of time and place. Electronic resources offer Library clients potential solutions to information shortages. Parvez (2011) noted the following benefits:

1. It provides efficient and accurate services;
2. It saves the time, space, energy and resources;
3. It helps for controlling the tremendous escalation of information;
4. It assists to provide high quality of services and increases the range of services;
5. It has invented the ways of resource sharing by co-operation and co-ordination;
6. It helps for the betterment of library image by providing better services in modern ways.

USERS AND THEIR NEW INFORMATION NEEDS AND SERVICES

Libraries are facing new challenges such as a changing clients-based, multiple information formats, multiple information and communication technologies and change in methods of teaching and learning. In providing improved libraries service there is need to understand the users and their new information needs and thus new services.

The users want basic services - competency, reliability, responsively, timeliness, honestly and a caring approach (Titangos and Jan, 2007). They further assert that users now want assistance with information access and to be able to read materials in both print and online formats. They want to use library resources effectively with minimum effort and in a timely manner. Library Services includes Reference Services, Multimedia Suites, Photocopying Services, circulation services and Research Services, Really Simple Syndication (RSS), instant messaging, streaming media etc. The introduction and use of social networking services e.g. Facebook, Twitter, web site interface for mobile devices and reference service via SMS form the major service with the new trend in library services via electronic resources. .

a. Information Access & Retrieval Services

In the current information environment, libraries are recognizing that providing access to resources is a complex multi-dimensional phenomenon.

b. Selective Dissemination of Information (SDI)

Selective Dissemination of Information (SDI) refers to tools and resources used by the Library to keep a Client informed of resources on specified topics. SDI involves selecting from a flow of new documents, those of interest to individual or group of Library Clients. SDI also includes information already in the collection that the Library might deem necessary to individuals as at that time for study or research purposes. This process may be thought of as the inverse of information retrieval.

c. Current Awareness Services (CAS)

A current awareness system alerts Library Clients on a periodic basis to the latest publications in their specified field(s) of interest, keeping one's research up-to-date. In other word, it involves making Library clients aware of new acquisitions available in the Library that may be of interest to them. In addition, CAS provides non-bibliographic information such as news on meetings, training courses and other events of interest to users. CAS is also provided through routing of journals and circulation of new arrival lists to Clients by way of enhancing ability of locate useful information sources. This is akin to information literacy.

d. Information Literacy Skills

Information Literacy is a set of abilities requiring individuals to "recognize when information is needed and have the ability to locate, evaluate, and use effectively the needed information". Information Literacy is increasingly becoming important in the contemporary environment due to technological change and proliferating of information resources. Resultantly individuals are faced with diverse, abundant information choices in their academic studies, in the workplace, and in their personal lives due to the escalating complexity of this environment. Increasingly information comes to individuals in unfiltered formats, raising questions about its authenticity, validity, and reliability. Above all, the uncertain quality and expanding quantity of information pose large challenges for society hence the need for Information Literacy Skills.

CHANGING ROLES OF LIBRARIANS IN THE FACE OF ELECTRONIC RESOURCES

The changing role of librarians and library professional implies a set of updated skills needed to face the challenges created by technological advancement. It is in the context of the changing teaching and learning environment and the complexities in the acquisition, usage and dissemination of information and knowledge that librarians are embracing new roles which are melting down the boundary that exists between the library and the academic departments. The learning environment has become hybrid and distributed, so also is the librarian. Librarians now create powerful web sites e.g. (National Library of Medicine's PubMed database). They create their own website as an easier way to share with others what they know. They gather electronic information and create electronic pathfinders and front-end search tools to help users for accessing the required information. Part of library services is to collaborate with publishers and IT companies and other content providers in negotiating the cost of content and access.

All these changes are major drivers calling for modern library services and greater librarians' involvement in the learning process. The new roles require that librarians acquire greater knowledge and information management skills if they are to provide information services to support the pedagogic needs of modern learning and instruction. The skills to teach information competency skills and facilitate problem analysis using information communication technologies form part of the skills that is needed by the librarians and information professionals in this era. The emphasis will be on communication, training, management and interpersonal skills that will make librarians more effective managers of networked resources and services. Skills in information organisation are more needed in managing electronic resources in libraries. They have to acquire skills that will contribute to success of information dissemination in electronic environment.

Librarians are essential in managing electronic resources by responding with a sense of urgency to critical information needs as they provide the information edge for the knowledge-based organisation. In order to fulfill this key information role librarians require professional competencies and personal competencies (Hashim and Mokhtar, 2005)

CONCLUSION

Library has to rethink its services and provide more flexible user-centred services. Such flexibility should be manifested in the abundant provision of information resources that are boundless, virtual, multimedia as well as timeless services to meet the information needs of users. Resources today occur in hybridized form: print and electronic, and therefore services provided and skills possessed by professionals in these libraries should reflect that trend. This includes providing easy, convenient, rapid and increased access to valuable information that already exists within the library walls to patrons outside those walls, and also provide remote access to resources outside the library walls.

REFERENCES

Breeding, Marshall. (2007). We need to go beyond Web 2.0. *Computers in Libraries,* 27(5), 22-26.

Creth, S.D. (1996). The electronic library: Slouching toward the future or creating a new information environment. *Fellett Lecture series.* Retrieved from http://www.ukoln.ac.uk/services/papers/follett/creth/paper.html

Fourie, D.K. & Dowell, D.R. (2002). *Libraries in the information age: An introduction and career exploration* . Colorade: Libraries Unlimited.

Gates, Bill (1990). *Information at your fingertip.* Keynote address. Fall comdex.

Gerolimos, M. & Konsta, R. (2011). Services for Academic Libraries in the New Era. *D-Lib Magazine,* 17(7/8). doi: 10.1045/july2011-gerolimos.

Hashim, L. & Mokhtar, W. N. W. (2005). *Trends and issues in preparing new era librarians and information professionals.* Retrieved from http://www.lib.usm.my/.../ICOL%202005%20Paper%203%20Laili%20Has...

Kanjilal, Uma. (1998). *Migrating to the electronic learning environment: Prospects for LIS distance learners in India.* 64th IFLA General Conference-August16-August 21, 1998.

LaGuardia, C., Blake M., Dowler, L., Laura, F., Kent, C.M. & Tallent, E. (1996). *Teaching the new library: A how-to-do-it manual for planning and designing instructional programs.* New York: Neal-Schuman.

Lancaster, F.W. (1997). Artificial intelligence and expert system technologies: prospects. In: *Libraries for the new millennium: implications for managers* (pp. 19-37). London: Library Association Publishing.

Nesta, F. & Jia, M. (2011). Library 2.0 or Library III: Returning to leadership. *Library Management,* 32 (1/2), 85-97.

Nwofor, F. A. & Ilorah, H.C. (2006). School media resource centre: A tool for developing good reading habits in children. *Nigerian Library Link,* 4(1), 7-95.

Okeke, I.E. (2000). *The library as a research institution.* Onitsha: Elite publication.

Parvez, A. (2011). Development in library services with the advent of ICT based products & services: A continuous process. *International Journal of Digital Library Services, 1(2).*

Roes, H. (2001). Digital libraries and education: Trends and opportunities. *D-Lib Magazine*, 7 (7/8 July/August).

Thamaraiselvi, G. (2009). Vision and the changing roles of the future academic library professional in the e-learning environment: Challenges and issues. *ICAL 2009 – Vision and roles of the future academic libraries*, pg 141-145.

Titangos, H. & Jan, D. (2007). Library innovations in the 21st century: An international perspective. *Chinese librarianship: An international electronic journal,* 23. Retrieved from http//www.iclc.us/cliej/c123TitangosJan.htm.

2

Design and Development of E-publications : Trends, Issues and Challenges

Bhanu Partap

INTRODUCTION

From greetings to governance, from cards to commerce every aspects of life is becoming 'e' or electronic. The current development and advances in information and communication technologies, networking and Internet, increasing trends in use of electronic resources has provided electronic publishing with new explosive growth opportunities. Electronic publications affect virtually all areas of library and information management processes, e.g. selection, acquisition and information transfer process. The concept of archiving and using-making of publications has also been changed by the growth in new ways of using the ICT. The technology is mainly being used for communication, database searching, bibliographic and full text searching.

Computers and networks have changed society and our way of thinking and living. The Internet, handheld computers, liquid crystal displays and enhanced font rendering are the technological basis for the development of e-publications. The development of e-publications has changed the whole publication industry. These are a new, self-contained medium that will have an enormous impact in time on society.

The dynamic world changes the publishing industries to the new technology. With the development of World Wide Web and Internet, this industries change their traditional databases to electronic form. Electronic publishing such as e-journals, e-abstract and e-indexes, bibliographies and still e-books have found space in almost all the libraries of modern age. E-journals and e-books are accesses into the form of CD-ROMs and through online databases. Publishers disseminate their resource up-to-date publication in various fields as well as of specialized interest in electronic form. Electronic delivery of information is not limited to books and journals, but it also begun to publishing e-magazines, newspapers, reference sources etc. E-publishing is appearing in a number of different formats like PDF (Portable Document Format). It can be viewing or read through by using Adobe Acrobat Reader software, HTML (Hypertext Markup Language) used for web pages, Internet explorer. ASCII (American Standard Code for Information Interchange) used for text file or images in graphics such as GIF. E-publishing can be search by search engine or through URL involves the use of keywords, authors, or by title with search box available into the screen of databases and always available with use of Boolean operator (AND, OR, NOT). Today libraries and information professional started subscribing and using two important publications are e-journal and e-books.

IT has provided several new media, new modes of studies, organizing retrieving and communicating information to users of the same. This ability to communicate has opened up the emergence of new modes of publication from authorship to digital system for information access which is easily movable and transferable to any point on the globe. The developments that are emerged during the present century have brought many opportunities and challenges for the libraries in general and library professionals in particular. The most important issues or realities are electronic publishing and networking of libraries, changing concept from ownership to access, and commercial availability of databases, etc. These realities have a direct impact on libraries. Hence, library professionals must cope up with these realities to meet the challenges.

ERA OF E-PUBLICATIONS

Electronic publications are the information resources in which information or contents are stored in electronic format instead on paper or print form. Electronic publication is emerging rapidly due to the recent advances in ICT technology. Changes in the publishing industry have a direct impact on the information systems and services. The IT has altered the mode of publication in such a way that the traditional sources of information continued to be flooded with the electronic form of publications. Thus the era of e-publishing or e-publication has begun affecting the library and information centers and user community. New technologies have transformed the process of publishing and distribution of information.

E-PUBLISHING

E-publishing is short for electronic publishing, referring to a type of publishing that does not include printed books. E-publishing instead takes the format of works published online, on a compact disk, emailed, or provided in a file format compatible with handheld electronic readers. E-publishing is an alternate form of publication especially attractive to new writers.

E-publishing refers to the use of computer technology in publishing or distributing information. The impact of e-publishing on library collections, services and administration is complex. There are no simple solutions of managing the collection, archiving and access to e-publications, as well as their use in library services. Electronic publishing includes the digital publication of e-books, e-journals and e-articles, and the development of digital libraries and catalogues. Electronic publishing has become common in scientific publishing where it has been argued that peer-reviewed scientific journals are in the process of being replaced by electronic publishing. Although distribution via the Internet is nowadays strongly associated with electronic publishing.

So we can say that electronic publishing refers to the application of computing software by a publisher to information content created and packaged for a specific audience, and the distribution of the final product publishing is an integrated electronic means. As such, publishing is an integrated process aimed at providing information in different quantities and with different qualities to different categories of end-users.

Electronic publication is arranged computer information. In electronic publishing, material is produced and stored electronically rather than in print. Whenever users display, present or "post" any written, auditory or visual media on to the World Wide Web, it can be said they are "publishing" electronic content. Advances made in networking technologies has resulted in e-publications increasingly being used to refer to information content distributed over network environments such as the Internet (Ludwick & Glazer, 2000; Burk, Roberta (2001). Electronic publishing can therefore be categorized broadly into offline and online publishing. Offline publishing utilizes different types of storage and delivery media such as CD-ROM, CD-I, DVD, memory card, and diskettes, while online publishing uses communication networks such as the Internet, Intranets and extranets as the delivery platforms.

IN TERMS OF DEFINITION

"E-publishing term is define that publishing techniques are changed from paper printing media to electronic format, and refer to the current offering of online and web based publication on the Internet and also available into CD-ROMs".

"E-publishing has been defined as any non-print media material that is published in digitized form to an identifiable user's community. The media in an e-publishing can be text, numeric, graphic, still or motion pictures, video, sound or a combination of any or all of these."

Nowadays, most publications are written, edited and formatted using word processors and desktop publishing software. Electronic publications can be original publications, but they can also be the digitized version of a written or printed document. For many collections, most of the electronic publications will be the digitized version of a written or printed document in their possession. The electronic publishing can enable any individual member to select exactly what he or she wants-potentially it is possible to appeal to an audience of one.

So, the term electronic publications or , as they are sometimes called, Virtual Information, refers to the modern methods of transmitting documents between individuals, primarily text-based documents-the equivalents of letters and memoranda-by electronic means i.e. without the use of paper.

OBJECTIVES

- To know about what is electronic publishing and electronic publications.
- To know about the nature and categories of e-publications.
- To know about the availability of e-publications.
- To know about the problems & prospects of e-publications.
- To know about the major trends of e-publishing.
- To know about the e-publishing models.
- To know about the technology associated with e-publishing.

NEEDS OF E-PUBLICATIONS

- Electronic technologies are emerged into every field. An e-publishing is one of them, which need for this technology for distribution their own material more effectively then the traditional publishing houses.
- Increasing into number of publishing industries, information need of the users are also increase.
- The rising cost of publication is also need for e-publication

because it has made it impossible for the users to purchase all the information for their research works.

- The speed of e-publication will focus to the users to search or access information faster than print media and save the time.
- The scientist's need for new information for their research work. Interdisciplinary research and new fields of research has increased.
- E-publishing is very ease to access than the paper publication and access at any time with the connectivity of Internet.

TYPOLOGY OF E-PUBLICATIONS

I. Off-line publications : An off-line publication is an electronic document which is bibliographically identifiable, which is stored in machine readable form on an electronic storage medium. CD-ROM, diskettes and magnetic tapes are examples.

(a) Off-line monograph; e.g. a CD-ROM encyclopaedia.

(b) Off-line serial; e.g. a CD-ROM journal.

II. On-line publications : An on-line publication is an electronic document which is bibliographically identifiable, which is stored in machine readable form on an electronic storage medium and which is available on-line. For example – an electronic journal, a World Wide Web page or an on-line database.

(a) On-line monograph; e.g. a dictionary on the web.

(b) On-line serial; e.g. an electronic journal on the web.

(c) On-line resource; e.g. an organization's home page.

MAJOR TYPES OF E-PUBLICATIONS

(a) E-books : E-books are electronic versions of books which are delivered to consumers in digital formats. Electronic –books available anywhere through the Internet accessed any hour of the day. An e-book can be stored in one or several digital files. These books are distributed via storage media such as disk and CD-ROM's and online. There are a large number of devices being developed to make reading e-books easier for consumers. E-books offer creative possibilities for expanding access as well as changing learning behavior and research in libraries. E-books provide a lot of enhanced features such as full text searching, changeable font size, mark-up, citation creation, and note taking will enhance usability. Print text can be integrated with multi dimensional objects, sound, and film to create a whole new kind of monograph work. Due to slow pace of e-books penetration in libraries, it is still not clear that e-books will be able to replace print as a long-term collection goal. As more content becomes available, it is believed e-book usage in education will start to increase.

(b) E-Journals: An electronic journal is a publication issued at regular intervals and available electronically. E-journals may be defined very broadly as any journals, magazines, newsletter or type of electronic serial publication which is available over the Internet and can be accessed using different technologies such as www, e-mail, telnet, or list serve. An e-journal is a journal available online or offline containing research papers, review articles, scholarly communications etc. Gail Macmillan defines e-journals as "any serials produced, published and distributed nationally and internationally via electronic network such as Bitnet and Internet." E-journals have become an increasingly important parts of library collection, especially academic and special libraries It is assumed that approximately 60% of the active peer reviewed journals are available in electronic form.

(c) E-databases : Electronic database is a computerized collection of information, organized so that it can be expanded, manipulated and retrieved rapidly for various uses. E-databases have helped in improving information, accessibility, research scholars, technologies etc. can access the relevant information with quite ease & quickness. The information both bibliographic and full text is made available on CD-ROMs or online by the e-database publishers. According to its content, databases have different kinds, such as bibliographic databases, directory databases, databanks, full text databases, abstracts databases, pictorial or image databases, etc. ERIC, EEVLXTRA, Ingenta.com, EBSCO and DIALOG are prominent examples of electronic databases. EBSCO host, DIALOG are the prominent publishers in the field e-databases.

(d) E-Link : Electronic link is a developing technology that could have a huge impact on the media and publishing industries. E-link could be used to create a newspaper or book that updates itself. The technology could also be used on billboards, clothing, walls and homes to allow content to appear. For media companies, the possibilities are almost endless. It may be possible, someday our e-newspaper will simply update itself every day. E-Ink Corporation and Xerox are two major companies currently developing this technology.

(e) CD-ROMS : Computer bases information storage and retrieval medium of e-publishing that contains data text of multimedia formats. The contents of CD-ROMs vary from database to digital documents or electronic journals. The usability of CD-ROMs in networking environment have made this technology more attractive and acceptable to library community as they have good storage capacity, save shelf space and data is easy to retrieve.

(f) Digital content : Digital content generally refers to the electronic delivery of fiction which is shorter than book-length, non-fiction, documents and other written works of shorter length. Publishers of digital content deliver shorter sized works to the consumer via download to handheld and other wireless devices. Technology used for delivering digital content includes Adobe PDF, XML, HTML, WAP (Wireless Application Protocol) and other technologies.

(g) POD (Print-on-Demand) : Print-on-Demand is a new method for printing books and other contents which allow books to be printed one at a time, or on demand. This method helps free publishers from the process of doing a traditional print run of several thousand books at a time. The technology involves complex laser printing systems and electronically formatted text, which the printers can read. POD is very hot right now; in a sense, it is a good intermediary step between the regular method of printing paper books and electronic books.

(h) Email publishing : Email publishing, or newsletter

publishing, is a popular choice among readers who enjoy the ease of receiving news items, articles and short newsletters in their email box. Newsletters are also widely used by media companies to complement their web and print offerings. Many authors and writers publish their own newsletters in order to attract new readers and to inform their fans about new books and book signings.

(i) Web publishing : Web publishing is not a novel practice any longer, but it continues to change and develop with the introduction of new programming languages. HTML is still the most widely used web programming language, but XML is also making headway. XML is valuable because it allows publishers to create content and data that is portable to other devices.

(j) Indexes : An index is a reference source which provides bibliographic information about journal articles, as well as other types of materials. While indexes have long existed in print, online indexes have expanded the type of work done by researches. Online indexes allow you to look beyond subject, author, or title.

(k) Catalogues : Most libraries now provide access to their catalogues from their web sites, known as Web catalogue or Web OPAC. Many others provide information about their holdings into larger databases such as WorldCat or the RLG union catalogue. The libraries provide links to these catalogues under the "Catalogues" section on its web site.

(l) Sound recordings : There are only a few library databases which provide access to sound recordings. If you are looking for music online, start at the music subject guide for the resources that are available to the library patterns.

(m) Image databases : Some databases include graphics or images, such as photos, paintings or maps. You can use the Database Finder page to locate these. The Art Subject Guide also provides extensive information about location images.

(n) Electronic theses and dissertations as e-reference tools : Electronic Theses & Dissertations are important resources of primary information. These are valuable resources for the academic and research communities. In universities and colleges, the students, faculty & researchers contribute immensely in terms of content to the online repositories in the form of theses & dissertations.

ISSUES RELATED WITH E-PUBLICATIONS

Electronic publishing inherits the difficulties that are common to all applications of electronic commerce. Beyond mere electronic publishing, the current and near-future phases of cross-media publishing and interactive publishing raise some issues.

(a) The Risk of Appropriation of Works : Traditional publishing houses are very wary about the security of their intellectual property. The costs of replication are negligible, and little or no trail is left by an infringer. Hence they fear that reticulation of bootleg copies by third parties will deny them revenue that they, particularly as IP-owners in their own right, but also as agents for IP-owners, believe they would otherwise achieve. Some authors are successful in making portions of works, and even entire works, available gratis over the Internet. Only a miniscule proportion of authors earn enough from authorship to survive, let alone prosper.

(b) Content Discovery: Discovering what information exists, and where it is to be found has always been a challenge. Techniques have been developed and articulated, and an infrastructure and professions have grown up around them, which enable skilled researchers to navigate around physical collections, and around the catalogues that document them.

(c) Content Quality and Availability: The publishing industry value chain incorporates a series of filters, and content quality. Self-publishing and other forms of disintermediation tend to remove those filters. On the other hand, at least in the more academic market segments, the primary quality contribution of the publishing industry value chain has been in format and presentation. Content quality assurance has been largely performed outside the paid sector, and there is no reason to expect that peer-review and honorary editorship will be undermined by the disappearance of, or substantial change in the operations of, journal and text-book publishers. The functions of resource duplication, resource retention, and resource archival have been performed through the production of many copies, the storage of a proportion of them in private and public collections, and compulsory deposit in National and State Libraries.

(d) Archiving and preservation: Archiving responsibilities are a major problem in e-publishing. Publishers and aggregators offer solutions for this problem by creating on CD-ROMs for e-journals backsets. However, only point of consideration is whether it will support the rapidly changing technology in the coming years. Libraries are reluctant to accept the credibility of publishers towards preservation because of the threats to publisher continuity in changing markets.

(e) Rights in Licensing Agreements: Licenses are negotiated between the copyright owner (*The Licensor*) and the organization that wishes to exploit the material (*The Licensee*). Among the different type of arrangements are: selling the work up front to the user, the user buying a subscription for an unlimited number of uses without ownership, the user paying for each use of copyright-protected works, or the user paying for use of a work at a particular site. When a reader pays a subscription to a website for accessing and reading online. When he/she stops paying the subscription, he/she loses all access to the content, although when he/she stopped subscribing to a printed magazine, he/she still had the old back issues.

(f) Rights in Copy Protection: Publishers and authors have been using copyright and the courts to protect their print investment and are relying on the same concept to protect e-publications and works. This is problematic as copy protection is more like putting a lock on each copy then selling a key with each locked e-resource. The attempt to equate intellectual properties with tangible properties or rights on tangible properties is too limiting and cumbersome, generating legal expenses and causing annoyance to legitimate users.

(g) Fair Use: The concept of fair use permits copying or excerpting of copyrighted material in the course of education, scholarship, commentary, advancing learning or for other societal goals (Harper, 2001; Basek, 2003). It has been said that the principle of public access can only be safeguarded and not limited by the exclusive rights given to authors and producers when the existing practices in libraries are also valid in the electronic environment.

In general, governments should regulate the application of copyright provisions in libraries and other educational and cultural institutions in order to ensure the general public, scholars and students can have free access to electronic copyright content. It is important to continue the tradition of making knowledge (in all forms or mediums) universally accessible to all members of society.

(h) Legal Deposits and Public Access: Legal deposits have been legislated and established for printed documents and have been extended to audio-visual documents, films, microfilms and other categories of non-print materials. The same should be done for e-publications. Many websites that provide valuable information move or delete information (or parts of it) when it is no longer current. Legal deposits legislation should cater for the public to be allowed access to deposited electronic materials, for example, having unrestricted local access to e-publications at public institutions.

(i) Economics of e-publishing: This is also a major issue as in many cases electronic access is costlier than the traditional resources of publication. The pricing for electronic research material is not standardized. Different publishers have different system for pricing of their e-publications. Some publishers sell the entire packages to consortia which in turn offers wide dissemination while some charge flat rates for web services, while some other offer print + online packages for their publications. E-collections development includes heavy costs for implementation, licensing, training, promotion and the development and support of a technical infrastructure.

(j) Censorship Laws: Content may be subject to censorship on many different grounds. In some countries, substantial constraints are imposed on freedom of speech in relation to political, religious, or racial topics. Many countries ban instruction in, and incitement to, violence. In virtually all jurisdictions, bans apply to sexually explicit material of various kinds, although the thresholds vary enormously.

Electronically published materials are made available in one jurisdiction, but in such a manner that they are very widely accessible. This creates great difficulties for countries with relatively restrictive censorship laws, whose populace can readily gain access to banned materials.

(k) Confidentiality and Trade Secrets: The law of confidence imposes responsibilities on a recipient of information, if it was communicated with an expectation that care would be taken with it. It applies especially to particular relationships, but also more generally. Internet technologies make it very simple to accidentally breach confidence. Although the body of law originally developed in the context of personal relationships, disclosure of 'commercial in confidence' information can be much more expensive for the person or organization that makes the mistake. The law of trade secrets also imposes responsibilities on individuals and organizations that are in possession of valuable information.

LATEST TRENDS

Without a doubt, the e-publication is practically the biggest thing that's hit the publishing industry since the invention of movable type. Publishers and e-resources resellers are reporting astronomical growth. Recent developments in ICT have enabled higher bandwidth to be made available to support online multimedia applications. Wireless networking allows online access to information and content by mobile users on the move or in the field. Cheaper and higher capacity storage technology provides a means to contain large amounts of multimedia content. Written, audio and visual works are no longer a book, a record, a film, or a television programme when transmitted through the Internet but instead they become content or knowledge. This is the consequence of the convergence of media forms in e-publications or e-publishing, which blurs the previous distinction among works created with different media.

Electronic publishing is expected to create an environment where authors can circulate their works widely, producers can see their investments rewarded by high profits and information providers and librarians can make cheap information widely available to all. However, many publications are still being produced conventionally and in conventional formats. Where electronic products do exist, they complement rather than replace print, resulting in few benefits because publishers, distributors and users must sustain both the printed and the electronic forms of production, distribution and use. E-Ink and E-Paper is expected to be the future for electronic publishing.

E-Ink combines the look of ink on paper with the dynamic capability of an electronic display. E-Ink displays are being designed for many applications, including handheld devices, outdoor billboards, e-books and e-newspapers (Sheridon, Howard & Richley, 1997; Desmarais, Norman 2003; McKernzie, 2001). Current handheld devices with LCD displays are expected to be replaced by a new generation of mobile devices with e-Ink displays and highly graphical mobile applications using 3G technologies that are lighter, thinner, more readable and yet require much lower power consumption.

SOME TRENDS THAT WILL CHANGE THE FUTURE OF PUBLISHING

(a) Enhanced E-books are coming and will only get better: Consumers have already shown that they love e-resources today are the same as print, just in digital form. The e-resource especially e-book of the not-too-distant future will be much more than text. Interactivity has arrived and will change the nature of the e-book. Imagine video that shows how to fix a leaky faucet or solve complex math problems in statistics; audio that pronounces foreign language words as you read them, and assessment that lets you check what you remember and comprehend what you just read. Publishers are already conjuring up designs for the enhanced e-book or e-publication of the future.

(b) The Device War is nearly over: Devices are proliferating to the point of confusion. Does a consumer buy a Nook, Kindle, Sony e-reader, an iLex or any one of 20 other dedicated e-readers? Or do they buy an iPad, Galaxy Tab, or other Android tablet? Or do they buy an e-reader at all? As far as devices go, consumer confusion is likely to drive quick consolidation around a few winners in the market-no one wants to own the next "Betamax for books". Because most developers are developing e-reader software that will work on multiple other devices, consumers will care less about the device and more about the user experience of the e-reader software, portability of titles from on device to another, and access to a full catalog of titles.

(c) The $9.99 E-book won't last forever: Amazon popularized the $9.99 price point for best-seller trade titles, driving the widespread consumer adoption of the Kindle and consumption of e-books. This has caused confusion among many consumers who simply think every e-book should be $9.99 or less. But majority of titles offered on Amazon are priced above $9.99, especially those with unique interactive features. The real opportunity for publishers will be develop e-book or e-resources that offer the kind of interactive features.

(d) The Contextual Upsell Will be a Business Model to Watch: E-publications allow publishers to interact with their customers in new ways. Imagine customers who are trying to learn statistics and get stuck on a particular formula. They ask friends but no one can explain it well. They're stuck. They click a help button, which points them to the publisher site where they can choose the one they need and get a new learning tool. It becomes an interesting new marketing opportunity.

(e) Publishers Will be More Important than Ever: Despite the hype around self-publishing via the web, publishing houses will play an even greater role in an e-book/e-resource world. Commodity content is everywhere, so high-quality vetted, edited content-which takes a staff of experts-will be worth a premium. In the digital world, the role of publishers will be larger as new technologies provide for an even greater user and learning experience. Furthermore, with the skyrocketing amount of content being served on the web, customers will seek and pay expert content providers that aggregate and contextualize information for tem efficiency and provide highly accurate and specific search options. Publishers with expertise and resources in these and emerging areas will be the ones that write the new rules of e-publishing.

ADVANTAGES OF E-PUBLISHING/E-PUBLICATIONS

Speed : It takes little time to browse or search, to extract information, and reached quickly from information generator to the retrieval of information.

Dissemination : The major advantage of e-publication are distribution, their hypertext link the ability to access from different web sites and the ability to search.

Functionality : An electronic version will allow the user to approach the publication and to analyse its content in new ways.

Information Retrieval : To retrieve essential and useful information, user can search with available numbers of search engines and URL on the Internet. Search box are provide by the e-publisher on the screen, for different types of search such as keywords, authors and title wise.

Saving Time : E-resources save the time of users and also not need to physical boundary for accessing these publications. E-publications are accesses by users at any place, at any time with the connectivity of Internet.

Multi-User Access : Same copy of the article or page can be accessed by more than two users sitting on their desktops through LAN connectivity.

Storage : It is becoming very cheap to store data with the dramatic reduction in the costs of computer hardware.

Easily manageable : E-publications can easily manage for storage, conservation and preservation than print paper. Electronic resources can be managed effectively by appropriate software.

Content : E-resources consist with the multimedia effect, i.e. images, video, audio and animation, which could not be replicated in print.

Less publishing cost : The costs in publishing and distributing of these publications are much less as compare to print format.

Inter-operability : With the advent of such standards as open

URL we are increasingly witnessing the linking together of systems so that one item within an electronic resource can directly link to another elsewhere.

Re-Use : E-resources can be repackaged and re-used in such systems as Virtual Learning Environments, or resource/reading list tools.

ISBN Number : Works published electronically have an ISBN number, just like printed books. This means anyone can walk into a storefront bookstore and order an electronic copy of the book.

Royalty Issue: Authors or writers get a higher percentage of royalties through e-publishing because the initial financial layout for the publisher is so much less than for a paper publisher.

DISADVANTAGES OF E-PUBLISHING/E-PUBLICATIONS

(a) The saleability of e-publications is far less than of printed ones. Most readers still prefer to read the printed versions. Many people are not aware of e-publications.

(b) Books are not available in book stores. The publicity and marketing of e-publications depends entirely on writers. A book might be great, but if nobody knows about it, it won't sell.

(c) Authors/Writers who go for e-publishing don't get an advance.

(d) If interested in building credentials, e-published works do not carry the same weight as traditional paper publishers.

(e) Piracy becomes a major concern in the e-publishing industry.

(f) Prices being similar or more than the printed ones, people tend to prefer the paper publications more than the electronic ones.

LIBRARIANS AND E-PUBLICATIONS - CHALLENGES

On promotion of e-journals, e-books, e-databases, e-portals the publishers have designed their products in such a way that these products will help the librarian thus:

- IP based access for full-text journals, books, databases through web site

- Help desk support for the librarian
- Comprehensive user support materials
- Periodical usage reports
- Registering users interest through mail-box
- Regular information update to the user through e-mail
- Complementary mimeographed print issues, where possible.

"The current developments in information and communication technology have great impact on every aspect of library operations and information services. The paper or print publishing is slowly shifting towards electronic publishing. As a result libraries need to develop electronic documents selectively, and get access to electronic information resources using network facilities to serve the users (Zink, 1991). Keeping in view all these changes the library professionals have to accept and adapt the phenomena of change. Thus, some of the challenges before library professionals can be summarized as follows:

- Information professionals should have expertise in total management of information.
- Mind-set of the library professionals has to be changed in order to enter into the electronic era by revising professional methods, techniques and tools.
- The information professional needs specific training to understand the implications of the new working conditions.
- The collection development librarians have to be more proactive by becoming familiar with the environmental changes so that they could adapt better as the changes unfold (Zhou, 1994).
- It is important for library professionals to focus on the capabilities enabled by the networked environment rather than the complications brought forth by the complexity of network based information resources and services.
- Information professionals require to become knowledge managers rather than collection managers in order to manage the intersection of the print and the electronic information

systems by applying the skills of collection planning, selection, analysis and co-operation (Branin, 1994).

- Library and information professionals need to rethink their approaches to marketing when it comes to online resources, details that were incidental to marketing print resources may be crucial to how well an online product is received by users."

Above all the information professionals have to concentrate more and more on such challenges and to overcome these challenges is the real problem of the professionals working in different types of library and information centers in the developing countries like India (Kumbar and Hadagali, 2005).

CONCLUDING REMARKS

With all the advances in technology and the emergence of the digital library, it is easy to assume the conventional library will be completely left behind. Traditionally the libraries and information centres are dealing with information resources and providing information through information identification, location acquisition and dissemination mechanisms. In view of on-going changes in libraries and changing information seeking patterns of information users, the challenge before library professionals is to obtain understanding of the new technologies for information and knowledge management and continually change as per changes in the information landscape in which they are expected to do their jobs.

Change is the only static thing in this world. We've to keep pace with the changing scenario in the field of information technology. Limitations imposed by print documents are being overcome with the help of electronic resources, which changed the information scenario all over the world. There is a major challenge before librarians and publishers to understand the expectations of the user community. Both of them should evolve some methods to understand the changes in use of the information by the readers because in the current electronic era, change is occurring very fast and some sectors are more prone to changes. Besides all these, the importance of print cannot be ignored. E-publications cannot completely replace the print publications but both will supplement each other to meet the needs of the users. Libraries and publishers are finding themselves in a transition phase of print and electronic only documents or information resources.

Electronic publications affect all areas of library management, and traditional collection management needs to be enhanced to remain effective. The electronic environment has initiated a much more market-oriented approach in evaluating information resources than we have been used to up to now. Librarians usually can choose among a variety of access conditions when dealing with e-publications. The libraries are now in the digital age so it is necessary to reshape or re-design these libraries in such a way that they will be able to improve the services they provide to the teachers, scholars and students both for the present and the future.

Many issues in electronic publishing are still open to discussion. Often publishers have not yet abandoned the phase of experimenting with possible solutions, and most of them are willing to cooperate with and listen to librarians. E-publishing provides fast and easy access to the information contained in objective publication with simple, powerful search and retrieval capabilities. The main role of the library and information centres are the selection, the storage, the retrieval of ultimately the dissemination of information to the users' community should remain what they have always been. Dealing with electronic publications needs thoughtful and fair solutions; only these will be advantageous for the entire community of information providers, mediators, and users.

REFERENCES

Arora, R.L. and Pradeep Kumar (2008). *Major trends of e-publishing in social sciences: An overview*, pp 153-160, Proceedings of the ICSSR Sponsored Seminar on Trends and Strategic Issues for Libraries in Global Information Society, held on March 18-19, 2008 at Panjab University, Chandigarh.

Babbar, Parveen (2007). *The future of e-books in academic libraries*, pp 74-81. Proceedings of the UGC Sponsored National Seminar on Managing College Libraries in the Digital Environment: Opportunities and Challenges held on August 03-04, 2007 at Dev Samaj College for Women, Sector 45-B,

Chandigarh.

Branin, J.J. (1994). Fighting back once again from collection management to knowledge management. In Johnson, P. and MacEwan, B. (Eds.) *Collection management and development issues in an electronic era.* Chicago: American Library Association.

Chennupati, K.R., Foo, S., and Heng, P.C. (2006). Trends in electronic publishing. In Ching, H.S., Poon, P.W.T., & McNaught, C. (Eds.) *eLearning and Digital Publishing* (pp. 111-132). Springer.

Desmarais, N. (2003). E ink and digital paper. *Against the grain,* 14 (Dec-Jan), 88-90.

Grothkopf, Uta (1998). *Electronic publications and collection management- Issues to consider.* ASP Conference Series, Vol. 153, 1998.

Heath, Malcolm, Jubb, Michael and Robey, David. (2008). E-Publication and Open Access in the Arts and Humanities in the UK. *Aridane,* Issue 54. Retrieved from http://www.ariadne.ac.uk/issue54/heath-et-al

http://mashable.com/2010/12/27/e-book-publishing-trends/

http://michaelhyatt.com/six-e-book-trends-to-watch-in-2011.html

http://www.chillibreeze.com/articles_various/epublishing/Electronic-Publishing.asp#a

http://www.rogerclarke.com/EC/issues98.html

http://www.sanathsolutions.com/src/serices/epub.html

http://www.wikipedia.org/wiki/publishing

http://www.wisegeek.com/what-is-e-publishing.htm

Kovacs, Diane K. (1999). Electronic publishing in libraries: Introduction. *Library Hi-Tech,* 17 (1), 8-9.

Kumbar, B.D. and Hadagali, Gururaj S. (2005). *Collection development in the electronic environment: Challenges before library professionals,* pp 72-82, 3rd Convention PLANNER-2005, Assam University, Silchar, November 10-11, 2005.

Ludwick, R. & Glazer, G. (2000). Electronic publishing: The movement from print to digital publication. *Online journal of issues in Nursing,* 5 (5). Retrieved from http://www.nursingworld.org/ojin/topic11/tpc11_2.htm

McDonough, B. (2001). Think 'e-ink' if you like paper. *Wireless News factor.* Retrieved from http://wirelessnewsfactor.com/perl/story/10301.html

McKenzie, M. (2001). *Electronic paper still on the horizon, but getting closer,* Seybold Report Analyzing Publishing Technologies, 1(6), pp 4-6.

Nandi, Subodh Gopal (2007). *E-publications as helpful resources for researchers of Indian libraries: An overview,* pp 22-27, Proceedings of National Conference on Recent Trends in Library and Information Science, held on November 15-16, 2007 at NIT Hamirpur (H.P).

Peek, R.P. (1994). Where is publishing going? A perspective on change, *Journal of the American Society for Information Science*, 45(10), 730-736.

Sheridon, N., Howard, M. & Richley, E. (1997). *Gyricon displays and electric paper.* Proceedings of SID, May 1997. San Jose, California: Society of Information Display.

Sukhwinder Kaur and Rekha (2007). *New era of publishing industries: E-journals & e-books*, pp 203-209, Proceedings of National Conference on Recent Trends in Library and Information Science, held on November 15-16, 2007 at NIT Hamirpur (H.P).

Vijayakumar, J.K. and Vijayakumar, Manju (2001). *E-journals in a networked environment: It's impact on academic libraries in the digital millennium*, Proceedings of National Seminar on Library Co-Operation in a Networked World, University of Calicut, Kozhikode, India. May 25-26, 2001.New Delhi, ESS ESS, 2002: pp 75-82.

Vohra, Ranjana and Bhatia, Neeru (2008). *Perspectives in electronic publishing.* Proceedings of the ICSSR Sponsored Seminar on Trends and Strategic Issues for Libraries in Global Information Society, held on March 18-19, 2008 at Panjab University, Chandigarh, pp 146-152.

Wayatt, Jeremy C. (1997). Commentary: Measuring quality and impact of the World Wide Web. *BNJ.* Ol. 314 (7078), Retrieved from http://bmjjournals;com/archive/7078ip2htm

Zhou. Yuan (1994). From smart guesser to smart navigator: Changes in collection development for research libraries in a networked environment. *Library Trends,* 42 (4), spring, 649-651.

Zink, S.D. (1991). Will libraries have a place in the information society? *Reference Service Review.* 19 (1), 76-77.

3

Changing Library Services in Perspective of Electronic Resources

Jacintha U. Eze

INTRODUCTION

The recent development in the information age has affected all spheres of human life and endeavour. Over the past few years, libraries and information centres have been greatly affected by changes in information technology (IT) and the rate of changes is still accelerating in this era. Through Information Technology, certain new inventions in information are being created. Such things as customized information packages, video cassettes, home information products, personal computers and reprographic equipments; external dependents, database online information systems; cooperative library information networks and electronic information processing system which has given birth to various electronic resources like e books, e journals, e databases and consortia of such. Libraries and librarians were in the past seen as keepers and custodians of knowledge embedded in physical library collections mainly in print format. In the new information era we are in, the shift from print to electronic information media and resources has added a new phase to the perception of libraries and librarians (Kaur and Sharda 2010).

In order to cope with the present development in IT, modern libraries are now adopting various electronic resources for its collection development to fulfill the requirements of different users in a better way. The migration of information from paper to electronic format is supposed to redirect the services and resources of the libraries to be able to adapt to the new information environment. Even the mode of information seeking of users is changing in the face of e resources. Users now prefer faster information access (both in the library and from remote access) to long browsing through the books on the shelves. According to Obuh (2009) more recently, focus of inquiry has been on those factors that play a role in deciding to use the library's e resources as opposed to just surfing the Internet. However to achieve the goals of ideal library and information services of the 21st Century, there is a need to select, evaluate and organize the e-resources in the best possible way as to provide maximum ease, both to the users and the staff for its accessibility and retrieval at all times.

WHAT ARE E RESOURCES?

Electronic resources usually called e-resources in short form are those electronic products that deliver a collection of data, be it in text referring to full text basis, e journals, image collection, other multimedia products and numerical, graphical or time based as a commercial available till that has been published with an aim to being marketed (Devi and Devi; n.d). E-resources could be said to be all the information resources that are available and can be accessed and retrieved through electronic means.

There are three main types of documents used in digital or e resources:

(a) **Static :** Static are the most basic - they contain fixed information and never change their form (such as traditional online data)

(b) **Dynamic :** Dynamic documents also contain fixed information but also able to change their outward form, the way embedded material is presented to users (such as multimedia CD-ROMs).

(c) **Living** : Living documents are able to change both their form (outward appearance) and the embedded information (such as information contained on the web.)

Electronic resources consist of data (information represented by numbers, text, graphics, images, maps, moving images, music, sound, and many others), programs (instructions that process data for use) or a combination of data and programs. The material is usually available in monograph, serial, e-book and sometimes on a website (Rule 9.0A1 of AACR2, 1988).

The collection and relevance of electronic resources has given rise to the concept of E- library. According to Achebe (2008), an e-library is an electronic library, a kind of bookless space that facilitates the provision of information resources predominantly by electronic means. Okoro (2008) illustrated the different types of e- resources as including Databases (such as EBSCO host, OARE, AGORA, HINARI, JSTOR NEXUS, Keesings, Mathsci – Net, Research pro, Sabinet); Search engines (e.g. Yahoo!, Google, Oracle, Jetspeed, Metalib, Zportal, Encompass) and Electronic database in-house (e.g. e-library, e-journal, e-zines etc.). When library resources are electronically generated, they are called e resources. Obviously, there is currently a paradigm shift from library services based on print resources to those based on electronic resources.

RATIONALE FOR E-RESOURCES IN LIBRARIES

Electronic library resources are computer readable file that occupies lesser space compared to the traditional library resources. Ease of access to information is major contribution brought about by the emergence of e-resources. According to (Tenopir, 2003), microcomputers, mainframe, mobile phones and many others are the various means through which individuals or group could use and or access electronic resources via a local or remote area network even outside the library. The traditional and print resources these days face challenges from their electronic counterparts in faster and timely delivery of information as well as easier accessibility. According to Obuh (2009), among various resources for learning, workers and users of the library throughout the world can retrieve seemingly endless volumes of information from all over the globe in a short span of time.

LIBRARY SERVICES AFFECTED AND RE-DEFINED BY E RESOURCES

Technology is driving change across the entire range of library responsibilities and services. Youngman (1999) noted that, librarians are moving into dramatically different roles as new services are implemented. The age of technology is driving change across the entire range of librarians' responsibilities. Traditionally, librarians have been information providers for centuries. They now have the opportunity to use modern tools and not only print but electronic resources to provide quicker, more complete and more sophisticated services to the users. Acquisition librarian for instance according to Grodzin-Lipow (1997) still selects and purchase books and traditional journals but they must also deal with many "access without ownership issues involving leased electronic databases, full-text journal article and other services to integrate e resources. Cataloguers in this age also now process not only books, but also CD-ROMs, computer discs and multi-format items. As technology advances, the reference librarians as Osorio (1997) puts it, are increasingly involved as teachers of "information literacy" providing reference services through various electronic means.

Crosby (2001) also noted that the work of librarians and library services are increasingly varied as it expands to keep up with the flow of information following the use of electronic resources. She remarked that the core of librarianship remains the same but their work is increasingly varied as it expands to keep up with the flow of information. Librarians still develop ways to make information useful. They still teach patrons how to evaluate sources and introduce children to reading and research; but now they use new tools, handle more varied responsibilities, and have more opportunities to see their work reach beyond library walls through electronic resources. Librarians, she said answer reference questions, and now do it more efficiently and completely. She discussed how technology of information age reflected in the emergence of electronic resources has impacted on the various services of the library.

Readers services

The information age has changed the definition of "the reader" in readers services. Modern electronic resources enable librarians help people from around the globe. Librarians still find ways to make information useful, but now technology gives them more options. In every library, the work of readers' services department – reference, reader advisory, teaching and collection development according to Youngman (1999) and Crosby (2001) has changed dramatically over the last decade.

Just as the reference service is vital in the internet era when searches can bury people under mountain of unfiltered data, librarians are there to help patrons sharpen their questions, pinpoint their needs and access the right electronic resources. Technological tools and e-resources have made the hunt for information more interesting. Librarians still scour materials in their own collections, but now they also search private, on – line databases, the texts of hundreds of magazines and journals, the World Wide Web and the on-line catalogues of other libraries. Internet is not the only new tool in reference librarians arsenals. Learning about other new innovations like the one noted by Crosby, the Geographic Information System (GIS), which combines digital satellite maps with data about population, demographics, natural resources, and other factors that vary from place to place. Librarians might use GIS to help businesses choose new locations or families choose new neighbourhoods. Many coperate librarians now use electronic information sources almost exclusively - search on-line databases, newswires, journals and associations' websites.

Reference librarians have recently been experiencing double

jeopardy. Rettig (1999) noted that, while continuing to serve patrons from service points in the library, many reference librarians are now also supporting a growing clientele of remote – access patrons using e resources. Grodzins-Lipow (1997) believes that reference department may be experiencing the greatest variety of new roles. In the words of Osorio (1999), as technology advances in the direction of e resources, reference librarians are increasingly involved as teachers of information literacy. Today we are living in virtual realities as captured by Omekwu and Echezona (2008) where library services are now in cyberspace and are not affected by time of opening and closing hours. This was corroborated by Ajigboye (2010), who found that users have control of what they want to learn and from which location they want to learn and at any time of their choice.

(i) **Readers' advisory service** : Readers advisory service which is a reference work with a more personal touch, traditionally involves helping readers to decide and choose which books to read. This is a long-standing role for librarians especially in the public and school libraries. This has taken on new dimensions as librarians create web pages as well as provided access to other electronic resources to advice from afar.

(ii) **Teaching** : Just as Osorio (1997) noted that, librarians in the information age are now teachers of information literacy, Crosby maintained that librarians are bringing the information revolution to the public. Often a person's first exposure to the internet she said, is at a library – in a public library or school media resource centre. Fishel (2000) agreed that one of the jobs that come with technology of which the emergence of e resources is part of has to do with training people to use it. This involves teaching computer basics; like how to use a mouse to more complex subjects and also teaching library users and researchers how to source and synthesize information from the e-resources. In the words of Francis-Swanson (2010), the teaching of information literacy skills by the librarians is one of the roles that come with technology and e resources. The growth of electronic resources has added new challenges to the librarians in all these.

(iii) **Collection development :** Readers services librarians decide what types of materials a library should buy. Technology reflected in the availability of electronic resource according to Youngman (1999) and Crosby (2001) has given librarians more choices in materials' selection and acquisition. They not only consider print materials but also select and buy audio-visuals, CD-ROMs, and the right to use professionally maintained databases and other related and relevant e-resources. In some libraries in advanced places, especially those in businesses, databases and on-line information are the primary materials librarians buy. Electronic materials are acquired via purchase, subscription or freely from their source. Just as they would when buying a book, librarians analyze the publishers to decide which are most trustworthy; they also decide which databases are sufficiently current and which will fit with the library's existing computer systems and software.

Selection of e-resources

Selection is not a new term to librarians as they have been doing it since the libraries started acquiring printed materials. However libraries are now focusing to adopt e-resources rather than printed materials in line with advancement in technology. In fact, the emergence of Internet, particularly, the www (World Wide Web) has a triggered proliferation of web based full text online resources as a new media of information delivery. As the web has grown, not just in popularity and use, but also in content, librarians are trying to meet the needs of the user and identify new resources, such as online databases, web based resources, collections in digital library, e books, e-journals etc. The selection process should be done in relevance with the demands of the users and other related factors; taking into consideration the following steps:

- identify library needs;
- identify content and scope of the e-resources;

- evaluate quality of that particular resource and search capabilities;
- estimate the cost;
- check either subscription based or web based when acquiring;
- evaluate the systems and technical support;
- review licensing agreements;
- evaluate application software and installation, updated sporadically or in regular schedule; and
- check the facilities for educational support and training.

After due selection of types of e resources, the next very important thing is the evaluation of these resources. This involves checking the authority of the material, currency, the audience for which it is meant for, ease of use and so on. Evaluation is very important more so now that there is kind of information explosion especially over the Internet. After selection, evaluation and collection of these e- resources, another important task is the proper organization for the users to access them.

Technical Services

Technical services librarians organize and manage information. They form the backbone of the library. If they do not do their job well, the public services librarians cannot do theirs. Technical services workers identify and classify books and materials in print. The invention of e-resources has carried technical work out of the shadows into the limelight. Information management is more visible as people search digital databases and on-line collections. The technical services most affected by new technology of e-resources are cataloguing and information architecture.

Cataloguing : Cataloguers classify books, videos, CD-ROMS, and other materials so as to enable users find what they are looking for. Cataloguing has grown more important as searchers log on to on-line catalogues and other related e-resources from anywhere. Technology has made cataloguing more efficient. In the words of Youngman (1999), cataloguers are moving into new roles as they attempt to provide enhanced access to the new resources. They now process not only books, but also CD-ROMs, computer discs, and multi-format items. Cataloguers are required to add the records they create to a shared international database. It is known that librarians have been sharing catalogues for a long time, but electronic resources, sources, gadgets and the internet have made it easier. As a result of on-line access, making catalogues easy to use is more critical and more possible. Crosby (2001) affirmed that using computers, librarians are starting to create different catalogues for different kinds of readers. A catalogue designed for casual browsers for instance, she said, might display summaries of each book while the one designed for preschoolers might use more graphics or might not rely as heavily on putting things in alphabetical order.

Cataloguers in the present day information age are required to and must make informed decisions on matters such as linking to electronic journals and managing holdings "hooks" to various databases. Cataloguers today create records that accommodate multiple means of accessing a particular resource. Library patrons are coming to expect records that include print holdings, microforms, and direct links to an electronic version of the item. Cataloguing the internet itself (the various information resources therein) is a task that has fallen on librarians.

Application of the Dublin Core metadata tag systems is a skill that did not exist just a few years ago but is now rapidly growing in importance as an additional role for librarians. As Chepesuik (1999) earlier noted, "it is not a metadata element set to replace MARC, rather it is going to evolve alongside it". Crosby (2001) further confirmed this, by saying that some librarians are helping to organize the internet as they are setting their sights on digital information. Many pieces of electronic materials on the internet have digital tags that describe them so that search engines can find them more easily. These tags – (metadata tags) might say who wrote the material or what it is about. So they organize books, but that is rarely done with card catalogues rather they use databases and digital metadata tags. Francis-Swanson (2010) presenting the current status and in more common terms was of the opinion that a feature of today's library is the Online Public Access Catalogue which is a database containing the library's collections that can be accessed by anyone on-line. She added that academic libraries now have offer full text electronic subscription-based journals to their users that can be accessed via the library's web page in addition to supplying a user name and pass word.

Information architecture : Some technical services librarians according to Crosby now work with computer experts to create websites and intranets. This is information architecture. According to a study by the Association of Special Library, librarians now use information architecture to organize their library services.

Library management : Librarians do not just staff libraries, they manage them too. Like most other library jobs, supervisory roles have been changed by technology. New work assignments involving new technologies can be motivating to experienced librarians and an excellent means of avoiding stagnation and burnout. In managing the library material resources, paper cards and ink stamps were the primary way books were tracked but now, most librarians in advanced places use automated circulation systems to simplify book management.

The need for faster, more accurate and personalized services in libraries is at hand. As Lison and Lunden (2004) said, the technology for the e-library is here; and must be integrated into the classic work of libraries. They brought up the concept of the "hybrid library" to be a library using all the instruments – be they electronic, virtual or traditional to produce good and appropriate services corresponding to customer needs. The hybrid library is characterized by new ways of meeting today's customer demands, new Net services, new communication lines with the customer, intelligent building, new concepts of work and a new orientation of the values of the job.

CHALLENGES POSED BY E-RESOURCES TO LIBRARIES

Information professionals and users both suffer from the problem of exhaustive information, from a wide range of sources and shortage of time to find, manage and evaluate (Kaur and Sharda, 2010). Sometimes users search internet indiscriminately without knowing the facts. Here librarian plays an important role by making the users aware of the importance of the evaluation of the retrieved information by guiding them on how to retrieve, what to retrieve and how to further use that retrieved information (which is called evaluation of information).

The very nature of electronic resources

One obstacle to the use of a library's electronic resources is that they are not seen as being straightforward (Obuh, 2009). In contrast to an Internet search engine, where a single keyword search will usually result in thousands of hits, no matter what the topic, in the library, library users have to choose a particular database and be more selective in the search words they use. Moreover, database subjects often overlap, with differences in dates, journal and subjects covered, and whether the material is full text or not.

Furthermore, in addition, the library may have a print subscription to a certain title that is not full-text electronically, or the title may be accessible full-text through another database than the one originally searched. Therefore, not only do library users have to find the relevant citations, but they also have to know how to locate the article after that. This means juggling many screens, many technologies, multi-tasking electronic jobs, and of course, knowing where to look for all this necessary information.

Also, there is the additional confusion that more and more library databases use web-based technologies. Because the interface is seamless there does not seem to be a visible, on the screen, difference between web-based library resources and general web-based resources.

Level of electronic and computer skills of the users

Making electronic resources available to users assumes that the library user is proficient in the use of computers. It is quite clear that searching for information has become inexorably linked to computer technology. The fact that there may be a good number of library users who do not have adequate computer skills to manipulate and utilize e-resources on their own creates additional challenges to libraries and librarians. Libraries now deal with electronic library resources that use computer and other closely related devices to access and use the information content. Aina (2003) opines that access and usage of e-resources can only be from computer and/or a closely related device.

Inadequate funding

This is a major problem faced by libraries coupled with material cost of electronic resources and facilities. With the emergence of electronic library resources, libraries are faced with the challenge of acquiring sophisticated materials needed to access and use these materials. The cost of acquiring this set of material is really a problem in the face of inadequate fund.

It is obvious that every library especially in the developing parts of the world and its librarians will like to adapt to the new ways of handling and providing information in the face of e-resources, but most of them lack the means to do so. Libraries in advanced places may have less of this problem of funding, but for the fact that wants are always insatiable especially with the recent global economic crisis. Funding still remains one of the outstanding problems hindering the growth of libraries in many parts of the world especially the underdeveloped cuntries. Lack of fund hampers the adequate continuous training of the library staff. Also Nwokocha (2002) and Eze (2012) stressed that inadequate funding is a major hindrance to the development and maintenance of electronic facilities and resources especially in developing countries. Fund is needed to ensure that the effect and benefits of the information age are felt in the libraries. Computerization and automation of library services and subsequent acquisition of e-resources can only be facilitated when there is adequate fund to do so.

Lack of manpower and necessary technical know-how

This is another major factor hindering the full accessibility, acquisition, organization, evaluation and the utilization of electronic resources in libraries of the developing parts of the world as it has been in advanced countries. This requires increased and continuous skills acquisition. As Oshilalu (2011) put it, aside having knowledge of librarianship, librarians now require computer knowledge to be able to handle electronic library resources conveniently. Also, since some electronic library resources have unique access means, librarians cannot but keep updating their computer use skills. Just as Ademodi and Adepoju (2009) lamented, that most librarians still lack the required computer skills and competencies to join the trend in the new information age. This is in line with what Oduwole (2005) earlier observed, that lack of required ICT infrastructure and poor ICT skills among staff are the major problems faced by most libraries in this age. Acquisition of skills and competencies required of librarians to effectively utilize e-resources in serving the library users is not well covered in library school curriculum and the technology needed to teach the little covered is inadequate (cases of few computers for many students).

Another major factor that causes setback is the unstable power supply and related poor infrastructures especially in the developing countries. For instance, many of our Nigerian libraries still do not have computers at all while some have very few which are used for administrative purposes and not for library services and routine work. Some of these libraries do not have any electronic resources at all but only hear of them. To be able to join the libraries in developed countries and adapt to the new information environment, not only the libraries and librarians alone will be involved, the government, Non-governmental Organizations (NGOs) and other stakeholders in the information industry will pull resources together. This is to develop both the human and material resources of the libraries to be in line with what is obtainable in other places.

The challenge posed by the information explosion is being successfully met by electronic information sources. Further this information explosion, diversity of user need, financial crunch and impossibility of self-sufficiency has led to the formation of consortia at local, regional, national and international level.

Increase workload

With the emergence of electronic library resources, librarians now have additional work load. Aside having to add electronic resources to their library collections, they have lots and loads of electronic resources to treat. Electronic publishing has obviously led to information overload and explosion. Because of this, librarians are now charged with the task of ensuring that the right information gets to those that need it at the right time and at the desired place. In this case, it challenges the professionalism of librarians to ascertaining the quality of lots of materials to meet the numerous tastes of their users. Tenopir (2003) affirms that not all that is published electronically is credible for inclusion into library collection. But, one has to note that, every publisher has a target audience in mind.

Unstable power supply

This is a major problem to the acquisition and utilization of e-resources especially in developing countries like in of Africa. Since access to electronic library resources is with the aid of computer or such like devices, it becomes a problem to libraries to ensure that the library has constant supply of power to facilitate access and usage of electronic resources.

Way forward

To ensure an effective change in library services in line with electronic resources which has become the order of the day, there is need for the libraries to acquire, organize and utilize the growing range of electronic resources. To achieve this, the library workers as well as the users must have to acquire and practice the skills necessary to exploit these resources. (Blandy & Libutti, 1995) cited by Obuh (2009) stressed that, "for the library using a variety of on-line databases, it is as though they were parking lot attendants, where every vehicle is not only a different make and model but has a different configuration". The skills required to maximize the potential of electronic resources are much greater than those required for searching printed sources. These skills include knowledge of the structure of the database and the necessary instructions required in searching, accessing and retrieving needed information, as well as an understanding of the ways in which the instructions are linked with one another. The ability to find and retrieve information effectively is a skill needed by any library user and worker.

Training and retraining of library workers

To meet up with the challenges of e-resources and the supposed changes reflected on library and information services, there is dire need for providing avenues for the training and retraining of the librarians and other library workers to acquire the necessary computer and electronic skills. As new e-resources emerge, new ways of accessing and utilizing even the already existing ones emerge as well. For the library and the librarians to serve their users satisfactorily in the face of such developments, there has to be training and retraining programmes to this effect. This is needed more so in the developing parts of the world where Ademodi and Adepoju (2009) saw as having many librarians who still carry out a lot of library and information services manually and with mainly non-electronic resources.

In addition to the training of the librarians, there is need for educating and training the users as well in the accessing, retrieval and utilization of e-resources. It is only when the librarians are conversant with such skills that they can effectively carry the users along.

REFERENCES

Achebe, N.E. (2008). Concept of library. In Achebe, N.E. (Ed.) *Library and information literacy for higher education* (pp. 1-15). Enugu: Nigerian Library Association.

Ademodi, D.T and Adepoju E.O (2009). Computer skills among librarians in academic libraries in Ondo and Ekiti states, Nigeria. *Library Philosophy and Practice*. Retrieved from http://unlib.unl.edu/lpp/ademodi-adepoju.htm. on 4/6/2010.

Aina, L.O. (2003). *Library and information science text for Africa*. Ibadan: Third World Information Services.

Ajigboye, S. (2010) *Mobile Learning: Exploring Partnership between Education and Communication Platforms*. Being a paper delivered at the 2nd Professional Summit on Information and Technology held at the Nnamdi Azikwe Library, University of Nigeria Nsukka 3rd -7th May, 2010. Pp. 49.

Blandy, S.G. & Libutti, P. (1995). As the cursor blinks: Electronic scholarship and undergraduates in the library. *Library Trends, 44* (2), 279-305.

Crosby, O. (2001). Information experts in the information age. *Occupational Outlook Quarterly*. Retrieved from www.bls.gov/opub/ooq/2000/winter/art01.pdf.

Devi, T.S. & K.S. Devi (n.d). Management of e-resources in the modern library information system: an outlook. Retrieved from irinflibnet.ac.in/dxml/bitstream/handle/1944/1409/49.pdf

Eze, J.U. (2012). Cataloguing in the era of ICT: What is happening in public libraries of South-East Nigeria. *Library Philosophy and Practice,* June 2012.

Fishel, F (2000). Training on use of technology in libraries. Oral interview. In Crosby, O. (2001). Information experts in the information age. *Occupational Outlook Quarterly* (winter, 2001). Retrieved from www.bls.gov/opub/ooq/2000/winter/art01.pdf.

Francis-Swanson, S (2010). *Information for a new age: Redefining the roles of libraries and librarians.* Retrieved from http://www.thevoiceslu.com/features/2010/april/17-04-10/Information-for-a-new-a. on June 10, 2009.

Grodzins-Lipow, A (1997). Who will give reference service in the digital environment? *Reference & User Services Quarterly,* 37 (Winter 1997), 125-129.

Joint Steering Committee for Revision of AACR (1988). Anglo-American Cataloguing Rules. 2nd ed. Chicago: American Library Association, p. 677.

Kaur, H. and Sharda, P. (2010). Technological innovations in improving library services. *International Journal of Library and Information Science,* 2(1), 11-16. Retrieved from www.academicjournals.org/ijlis/pdf/.../HarkaurandShardap.

Lison, B and Lunden, I. (2004). *Staffing the hybrid library: Innovative strategies in the field of staff development.* Guterslo: Bertelsmann Stiftung. Retrieved from www.publi-libraries.net/html-media/pdf/staffing-engl-haselhorst-040923.pdf.

Nwokocha, U. (2002). Public libraries in Nigeria: Decades of persisting problem. *International Info Library Review,* 30 (2), 97-104.

Obuh, A.O. (2009). Use of electronic resources by postgraduate students of the department of library and information science of Delta State University, Abraka, Nigeria. *Library Philosophy and Practice.*

Oduwole, A.A. (2005). Information technology applications to cataloguing in Nigerian libraries. *The Electronic Library,* 23 (3), 289-291.

Okoro, H.C. (2008). Virtual library services. In Achebe, N.E. (Ed.) *Library and information literacy for higher education* (pp. 16-29). Enugu: Nigerian Library Association.

Omekwu C. and Echezona, R.I (2008). *Emerging challenges and opportunities for Nigerian libraries in a global service.* Paper delivered at the Nigerian Library

Association 46th Annual National Conference and AGM Held at Arewa House Conference Centre Kaduna 1-6 June, 2008 HEBN Publishers PLC, Ibadan:Pp.63-76

Oshilalu, H. A. (2011). Emergence of electronic library resources: a threat to librarians? *International Journal of Library and Information Science,* 3(2), 29-33.

Osorio, N (1997). In distance learning, is there a role*? Issues in Science and Technology Librarianship*. Retrieved from http://www.library.ucsb.edu/istl/97-spring/article3.html.

Rettig, J.R. (1993). Academic reference service: Astride a fault line. *Wilson Library Bulletin,* 67 (1), 53-54.

Tenopir, C. (2003). Use and Users of Electronic Library Resources: An overview and analysis of recent research studies. Washington D.C.: Council on Library and Information Resources.

Youngman, D.C. (1999) Staffing considerations in an age of age: Basic elements for managing change. *Issues in science and Technology Librarianship*. Retrieved from www.istl-org/99-fall/article-5.html-20k

4

E-books – Issues and Concern of Different Stake Holders in India

Rakesh Mani Sharma

INTRODUCTION

The development in Information Technology (IT) enabling devices and services have made inroads for fundamental change in the way we think and do the things of our daily life – be it keeping our self informed, taking decision, seeking and using information for knowledge up-gradation, entertainment, business, marketing, purchasing, decision making, career selection, education or research. This has amply been reflected in our approach to find and use everything and anything in 24X7 modes. Perhaps this approach and availability of enabling technologies have resulted in development of many IT based application and services. Out of many such applications and services the concept of e-books emerged.

An e-book also known as electronic book, ebook, digital book, is a book-length publication in digital form, consisting of text, images, or both, and produced on, published through, and readable on computers or other electronic devices (Gardiner & Musto, 2010).

The *Oxford Dictionary of English* defines the e-book as "an electronic version of a printed book," but e-books can and even do exist without its any printed equivalent. It's a digital equivalent of a traditional (printed) book, where information is organized and structured in a manner that facilitate consultation and use on dedicated devices like e-book reader, or personal computers and some on mobile phone.

Although it has been anticipated that e-books will gain wide spread use but this has not yet come actually true (Armstrong, 2001; Abram, 2004; Chu, 2003) unlike e-journals. In fact after the emergence of e-books/e-journals the library users have become more demanding expecting information at their fingertips. Like many developed countries the library users in India also uses e-journals more in comparison of the use of e-books due to various reasons (Ramaiah, 2012).

DEVELOPMENT OF E-BOOKS

The concept of e-book first surfaced in 1945 when Vannevar Bush published his seminal article titled "As we may think" in the "Atlantic Monthly" (Ramaiah, 2012). Since then many development took place in the hardware/ software technology of the e-books. But with a limited magnitude except the Project Gutten Berg in 1970 that claimed to store nearly 40, 000 titles electronically covering English and other languages books falling outside of copyright act and or having been explicitly licensed for use (Lebert, n.d.).

Despite of project Gutten Berg, the development in e-book remained in low profile as compared to e-journals till the dawn of internet in 1990. The Internet popularity forced many publishers to think over making the e-books available to users who were already accustomed to the use of digital content in the form of e-journals particularly in Science, Technology and Medicine (STM). Perhaps the comfortability of users in STM subject wherein articles could be scanned on computers screen without much difficulty has paved the way for development of e-books production. Some publishers started publishing and selling e-books with their print version that enables OCLC to make available approximately 2000 e-books commercially to libraries through its Net Library services in 1999. Latter on e-book providing commercial companies like Questia and ebrary entered in the market in the year 2000 with different access and business modules. Now a days almost every renowned publishers like Springer, Taylor & Francis, Academic Press, CRC Press, Elsevier, CABI, Humana, Oxford University Press and many more do publish e-books and made them available for use through various access and pricing modules.

DESIGN OF E-BOOKS

The design of e-books needs to take into account the advantages and disadvantages of e-books in terms of legibility, portability and autonomy of the medium by which they are hosted (Wilson, Landoni & Gibb, 2003). The main idea that has inspired the design of e-books has taken its starting point from paper books in terms of its physical appearance, logical structure and usage. This motivated the designers of e-books to include the desirable modifications like lower numbers of words per page, title headings on each page, clearer page layouts, typographical clues and tools for searching and browsing.

Despite of inclusion of these desirable characteristics in e-books, the e-book reading devices created specifically for storing and reading e-books have been a continuous concern for e-book users. Because it draws only one aspect of the paper book metaphor is its portability. The screen resolution of e-book readers neither was at par with that of the paper printed book resolution nor even today. This has stirred the designers of e-books for research in the area of technical quality and improving the screen resolution of e-books reading devices.

Although electronic books have been around us for a quite long time, but with a different understanding to different stake holders like publishers, library users, authors etc. As a result there is lot of confusion about e-books with regard to its basic definition and meaning, but this could be understood with a simple four connect of e-books i.e. Content, Format, Purpose and Use.

E-book: Content

The famous saying of printed books/information world that "Content is King" is equally true for e-book also. By drawing the parallel with paper books, it becomes clear that content is crucial in dictating for whom and how an e-book should be designed, and that the format should be dictated by purpose, not vice versa. E-book design then becomes a two- step process, in which an analysis of user requirements yields a user profile that may then be utilized to develop the optimum format.

E-book: Format

There is a variety of e-book formats used to create and publish e-books. Some supported by major software companies such as Adobe with its PDF format, and others supported by independent and open source programmers. Multiple e-book readers followed multiple formats and most of them specializing in only one format leading to fragmentation of e-book markets. Due to exclusiveness and limited readerships of e-books, the fractured market of independent and specialty authors lacked consensus regarding a standard for packaging and selling e-books. A writer or publisher has many options to choosing a format for production of E-book. Although every format has its own proponents and champions, the major formats available as of now in the market are as under.

1. Amazon Kindle : The amazon.com created the proprietary format AZW and launched a reading device Kindle eBook reader. It is based on the Mobipocket standard, with a slightly different serial number scheme (it uses an * instead of a $ sign) and its own Digital Rights Management (DRM) formatting. Since the e-Books bought on the Kindle are delivered over its wireless system called Whispernet, the user does not see the AZW files while downloading for use. The Kindle format is now available on a variety of platforms.

2. Archos Diffusion : The AEH format is an XML-based proprietary format developed by the French firm Archos Diffusion. AEH files use a proprietary DRM and encryption method and are readable only in the Archos Player. It supports various input formats for text, audio or video, such as PDF, WMA, MP3, WMV, and allows multiple interactive functions such as bookmarking, advanced plain-text searching, dynamic text highlighting, etc.

3. Comic Book Archive file : A Comic Book Archive file or Comic Book Reader File consists of a series of image files, typically PNG (lossless compression) or JPEG (lossy compression) and stored as a single archive file for the purpose of sequential viewing of images, especially comic books.

4. Compiled HM : The CHM format is a proprietary format based on HTML. While in this format multiple pages and embedded graphics are distributed along with proprietary metadata as a single compressed file, in HTML, a site consists of multiple HTML files and associated image files in standardized formats.

5. DAISY – ANSI/NISO Z39.86 : The Digital Accessible Information System (DAISY) format is an XML based open standard format maintained by the DAISY Consortium for people with print disabilities. DAISY has wide international support with features for multimedia, navigation, and synchronization.

6. Desktop Author : Desktop Author is an electronic publishing suite that allows creation of digital web books with virtual turning pages. Digital web books of any publication type can be written in this format, including brochures, e-books, digital photo albums, e-cards, digital diaries, online resumes, quizzes, exams, tests, forms and surveys. Desktop Author packages the e-book into a ".dnl" or ".exe" book.

7. EPUB : The .epub or OEBPS format is an open standard for e-books created by the International Digital Publishing Forum (IDPF). It combines three IDPF open standards viz. Open Publication Structure (OPS) 2.0 for content description, Open Packaging Format (OPF) 2.0 for structure of an .epub file in XML and OEBPS Container Format (OCF) 1.0, which bundles files together (as a renamed ZIP file). The EPUB format is rapidly gaining popularity and has been reported as the most widely supported vendor-independent XML-based e-book format in the year 2011. This format can be read by the e-book readers like Kobo eReader, Blackberry Playbook, Apple's iBooks app running on iOS devices such as the iPhone, iPOD Touch and iPad, Barnes and Noble Nook, Sony Reader etc.

8. eReader : The eReader format (formerly known as Palm Digital Media/Peanut Press) is a freeware program for viewing Palm Digital Media electronic books which use the pdb format used by many Palm applications. In this format the e-book reader shows text one page at a time, as paper books do.

9. Hypertext Markup Language : HTML is a markup language used for most web pages. E-books using HTML can be read using a Web browser. The specifications for the format are available without charge from the World Wide Web Consortium (W3C). HTML adds specially marked meta-elements to otherwise plain text encoded using character sets like ASCAII or UTF-8. Though HTML on its own is not a particularly efficient format to store information and requires more storage space for a given work than many other formats. Still, several e-Book formats including the Amazon Kindle, Open eBook, Compressed HM, Mobipocket and EPUB store each book chapter in HTML format and then use ZIP compression to compress the HTML data, images, metadata and style sheets into a single, significantly smaller, file.

10. Mobipocket : The Mobipocket e-book format is based on the Open eBook standard using XHTML and can include Java Script and frames. It also supports native SQL queries to be used with embedded databases. The Mobipocket Reader has a home page library with full screen facility for reading and supports many PDAs, Communicators, and Smartphones.

11. Newton eBook : The Newton e-book commonly known as an Apple Newton e-book can contain multiple books. All systems running the Newton operating system have built-in support for viewing Newton books. Newton books have no support for DRM or encryption. They do support internal links, potentially multiple tables of contents and indexes, embedded gray scale images, and even some scripting capability. Newton books utilize Unicode and are thus available in numerous languages.

12. Portable Document Format : PDF the widely used file format was initially created by Adobe Systems to provide a standard form for storing printable documents containing a set of page images. The format derives from PostScript, but without language features like loops, and with added support for features like compression, passwords and DRM. Because PDF documents can easily be viewed and printed by users on a variety of computer platforms, they are very common on the World Wide Web. The PDF files are supported on many e-book readers including Mobipocket, iRex iLiad, DR1000, Sony Readers, and Barnes & Noble Nook, the iPad, PocketBook Reader, Bebook Neo and the Kobo eReader.

The aforesaid formats are only indicative and not exhaustive. There are many more formats already available for e-book publishing and many more would may come in future in view of rapid development in hardware and software technology.

E-book: Purpose and Use

The purpose and use are the twin factors influencing a lot to designers of the e-books. This can be explained by adopting a user centric approach. To take the obvious parallel with publishing of printed book, it would be useful to look at how paper books have evolved in format (both in appearance and functionality) to fulfill the need and purpose of individual category of different user groups. For example, the books written for children are different from that of adults' scientific books (in terms of contents and presentation), which are again different from novels. Likewise the encyclopedias are differed from monographs, and monographs from textbooks and so on. There are subtle differences within each group of users. Sometimes the same title can be produced in different editions with different formats in order to target a specific reader group. That is why there are separate edition of Harry Potter books for children and adults, which contain the same content in a different packaging (the font, size, title page and overall presentation style have been changed according to readership). Therefore, the purpose and user groups for whom the e-book is proposed to be written and published, should be at the core of e-book design.

After understanding the e-books, it's desirable to see what are the advantages and drawbacks of e-books in comparison of printed books.

ADVANTAGES OF E-BOOKS

The e-books have many advantages over the printed books. Say -

- An e-book can be offered indefinitely, without ever going "out of print".
- The e-book took very little space for storage as compared to printed book. Even an e-reader can potentially contain thousands of e-books, limited only by its memory capacity as such an e-book collection takes up negligible physical space and weight.
- E-book websites can extend the facility to translate the e-books contents into many different languages, making the works available to speakers of languages not covered by printed translations.
- Depending on the device, an e-book may be readable in low light or even in total darkness. Many newer readers have the ability to display motion, enlarge or change fonts, (Harris, n.d.) use speech software to read the text aloud for visually impaired, partially sighted, elderly, dyslectic or just lazy people.
- Devices that utilize E Ink can imitate the look and ease of readability of a printed book while consuming very little power, allowing continuous reading for weeks together.
- While an e-book reader costs much more than one book, the electronic texts are quite cheaper. Moreover, great shares of e-books are available online for free, minus the minimal costs of the electronics required. Over 2 million books are freely

available for download as of August 2009. This number must swelling and increasing day by day.

- E-books can be printed for less than the price of traditional new books using new on-demand book printers.
- An e-book can be purchased/ borrowed, downloaded, and used immediately, whereas when one buys or borrows a printed book, one must go to a bookshop, a personal collection library, or public library during limited hours, or wait for a delivery.
- The production of e-books does not consume paper and ink. The necessary computer or e-reader uses less material as compared to printed books which needs to use 3 times more raw materials and 78 times more water for being produced.
- Depending on possible digital rights management, e-books can be backed up to recover them in the case of loss or damage and it may be possible to recover a new copy without cost from the distributor.
- Compared to print publishing, it is cheaper and easier for authors to self-publish e-books. Also, the dispersal of a free e-book copy can stimulate the sales of the printed version.

DRAWBACKS OF E-BOOKS

- The advances and developments made in information technology or the introduction of new proprietary formats of e-book made them quickly incompatible with new e-book reading devices.
- While printed books remain readable for many years, e-books may need to be copied or converted to a new carrier or file type over time. Because of proprietary formats or lack of file support, formatted e-books may be unusable on certain readers.
- While paper books can provide visual appeal and touch feel, the digital nature of e-books makes them non-visible and intangible. E-books cannot provide the physical feel of the cover, paper, and binding of the original printed work.
- While e-Books with large pictures (such as children's books)

or diagrams are more inconvenient for viewing and reading on e-book reading devices, the printed books don't have such problems.

- A book will never turn off and would be unusable only if damaged or after many decades time when it become unfit for use. The shelf life of a printed book exceeds that of an e-book reader, as over time the reader's battery will drain and require recharging.
- Further, there is no guarantee that electronic copies will last for ever because bits become degraded over time and hardware and software become extinct at a distressing rate.[14] Thereby rendering e-book unusable.
- The e-book readers are more susceptible to damage from being dropped or hit than a print book. Moreover the faults in hardware or software may cause e-book readers to malfunction and thereby causing loss of data.
- Just like any electronic items, the e-book reader must be protected from the extreme weather conditions like extreme cold, heat, water, etc. otherwise they don't work properly.
- The e-books and its reading electronic devices are very much susceptible to damage from electromagnetic pulses, surges, impacts and temperatures typically found on a hot day.
- The cost of an e-book reader far exceeds that of a single book, and e-books often cost the same as their print versions. Due to the high cost of the initial investment in some form of e-reader, e-books are cost prohibitive for much of the world's population.
- There is no market of used e-books, so consumers will neither be able to recoup some of their costs by selling an unwanted e-book or the titles they have finished, nor will they be able to buy used copies at significant discounts, as they can now easily do with printed books.
- Because of the high-tech appeal of the e-reader, they are a greater target for theft than an individual print book. Along with the theft of the physical device, any e-books it contains

also become a soft target for stolen.

- Although e-books purchased from vendors like Amazon or Barnes & Noble.com are stored "in the cloud" on servers and "digital lockers" and have the benefit of being easily retrieved if an e-reading device is lost. But then not all e-booksellers are cloud based and in such cases if an e-book is stolen or accidentally lost or deleted, then in the absence of a backup copy it may have to be repurchased.
- The display resolutions of reading devices are currently lower than those of printed materials and may cause discomfort due to glare on the screen or difficulty of holding the device.
- Due to digital rights management, customers typically cannot resell or loan their e-books to other readers.
- E-book readers produces many toxic substances which are non-biodegradable, and their disposal particularly batteries raises environmental concerns. As technologies rapidly change and old devices become obsolete, there will be larger amounts of toxic wastes that are not easily biodegradable like paper.
- Reading devices for e-books in a re-flowable format such as EPUB may display page numbers, but these numbers change from device to device depending on factors such as the size of the display and the selected font size. This makes them unsuitable for citations purposes.

In making the e-book popularity for access and use, it's imperative to under stand what are the major issues and implications for different stake holders in e-book production, marketing and use cycle.

MAJOR ISSUES OF E-BOOKS

The Digital Rights Management (DRM) and e-book readers are the two major issues in provisioning of e-book for access and use.

1. Digital rights management

Digital Rights Management is a major issue in provisioning of e-books. Digital rights management is meant to prevent copying of the e-book. This includes restricting the copying and distribution of works in the public domain through the use of "click wrap" licensing, effectively limiting the rights of the public to distribute, sell or use texts in the public domain freely. However in many cases it is also possible that digital rights management will result in the complete denial of access by the purchaser of the e-book. In the cases where the e-book is tied with some formats of DRM to a specific computer or device, the DRM will usually let the purchaser to move the book to a limited number of times after which they cannot use it on any additional devices. If the purchaser upgrades or replaces their devices eventually they may lose access to their purchase.

2. e-Readers

An e-book reader, also called an e-book device or e-reader, is a mobile electronic device that is designed primarily for the purpose of reading digital e-books and periodicals. To a greater extent it is similar in form and function to that of a tablet computer. A tablet computer is more versatile having a faster screen capable of higher refresh rates is more suitable for interaction, consumption and creation of multiple types of content, but with poor readability. The e-book reader may not be very versatile and interactive as tablet computers but they are equipped with better readability by virtue of their screens resolution and function especially in bright sunlight and longer battery life. This is achieved by using electronic paper technology to display contents to readers.

Besides, the aforesaid two majour issues, it has also been reported in many studies that there are differing levels of dissatisfaction among owners of different e-book readers due to their inconsistent availability for sought after e-book titles. The other important issues that work as impediment to promote the usage of e-books are as under.

- The wide diversity of software and hardware products associated with e-books is a cause of confusion and therefore works as barrier to uptake of e-books.
- Currently there are significant differences between the print

book and e-book physical form and information supply chains. The e-book information supply chain is imperfect. The awareness of the e-books among the main user groups, especially of academics, lecturers, students and researchers, and in some cases even in librarians, is low.

- Many publishers are reluctant to make their publications available in e-book format and / or to promote them too seriously, because they are afraid of the effect on their revenues. This is especially true of the major textbook publishers, who have invested heavily in producing/publishing print books.
- Both publishers and aggregators and sometimes vendors have developed a wide range of pricing models for e-books, some of which are really very difficult to understand.
- Booksellers have been slow to experiment with selling e-books. Therefore the important roles of information providers that they fulfill in the traditional supply chain of printed books are missing from the e-book supply chain.
- Assessing potential demand for e-books is difficult, because of the imperfect supply chain and inadequate usage statistics provided by publishers and aggregators. Therefore, invariably it becomes difficult to understand and determine the quality and usage extent of e-books.

Despite of these issues, many who have knowledge of e-books see them as potentially useful tools for research and education. However, we should not forget that everyone do not have access to computers or e-book reading devices. While this is a much bigger issue than just for e-books, it is important within the e-book context that libraries should continue to improve computer access on campus and librarians must also be careful to provide simple, clear and comprehensive e-book training for all library users.

IMPLICATION FOR DIFFERENT STAKE HOLDERS

The choice for switching over from printed books to e-books by different stake holders determined by their different perceptions and reasons. For example while librarians and library users see e-books as supplement to their reading materials and also to address some extent budgetary issues, the publishers and book vendors see it as threat to their profit. The author whose manuscript does not accepted by the publishers for publications sees it as a freedom of publications and expression. If e-books are to be widely used, the funding and revenue issues of the two main groups of stakeholders, i.e., librarians and academics on the one hand, and publishers and aggregators on the other, will have to be intelligently resolved. One of the main ways that this can be achieved is by increasing the "added value" qualities to e-books like keyword searching in e-book, or e-book collection. This is obviously a major advantage, and is one of the reasons why e-journals have become such an indispensable tool for many researchers using online facilities. Since all stake holders like librarians, publishers, authors and users have different understanding and perspective of e-books, the implications also differs for them.

Users : The cost of hardware, Internet access, quality content and pricing modules are the majour concern of the users that influences their choices for e-books use. In one of the e-book user's perceptions study made in India, has reported that majourity of the users indicated that they make less use of e-books because they found that e-books have not yet become as portable, flexible, and readable as their print counterparts and still they are much more costly than of printed books (Ramaiah, 2012).

The users' current reliance on printed books negates the benefits that e-books offers in addition to additional costs of e-books. There are copyright and technological issues that have yet to be resolved. The problem of reading from a low resolution screen has not yet been resolved completely. Till it resolved to an accepted level, it is important that the use of e-books on the computer screen should be promoted.

Libraries : The problems of making sure that new e-resource like e-books are available for use is more than just a marketing issue for libraries. Libraries have tight budgets so it is important that the resources they buy are justifiable and well-used by its clientele. For libraries it's not the "one time" purchases, but to continue to fund annual access fees also. Inspite of this, librarians should understand that whatever purchase models they propose for purchase of e-books, it must accommodate the commercial viability of the publisher also. This will go a long way to promote the usage of e-books offering high quality reading material in a mutually acceptable sales model.

In addition the e-books require cataloguing and integration with other library resources and easy location by users. The borrowers, particularly those who are currently not very avid e-book users, will look to the library as their main source for e-books. So it is important for libraries to see that the e-books should be easily retrievable from their online library catalogue. There is much works needed to be done on this front, besides, on metadata and interoperability of e-books.

Publishers : Publishers and vendors are the big stake holders and play an important role in the adoption of e-books in libraries particular and public in general. The publishers and other e-book vendors should work on developing a method for preservation and continued future access of e-books. Until these developments take place, academics, librarians, students and researchers may find it difficult to convince themselves that e-books offer a benefit beyond providing additional copies of existing printed texts.

Publishers now have fully recognized the significance of the move from printed books to e-books, but they are reluctant to pass on the savings to users which electronic publishing and handling provides. This is providing motivation for authors and their institutions to examine other channels for handling and distributing electronic texts.

Authors : Authors whose books are not accepted by publishers for publications, the e-book offers a great opportunity to them to put their works online and publish, so it could be seen by others. As such it looks very lucrative, but it brings extra burden on authors to maintain the content quality. Otherwise their e-books would not going to fetch them any benefit whether monetary or otherwise.

CONCLUSIONS

At the moment, there is no suggestion that the emergent resource of e-books will replace existing information resources, rather than it will just supplement them. Many feel that currently the usability of e-books is too poor to offer a genuine alternative to printed resources for serious research and academic study. The quality of the content is also huge issue, and the ability of users to assess the quality influences their use, particularly within the academic and research community. If the production and review of e-books got done by reputed academics, academic and library journals, publishers and booksellers, just like printed books, then it will ensure increased user confidence in the quality of the e-book contents.

Despite of different concern and issues of stake holders, the advantages offered by e-books like easy to carry, saving space, convenience, saving money and time, and ease-of-use will put forward the e-book alongside of printed books just like printed journals with their electronic versions. Nowadays, storage space has become cheap so it is easy to take good number of e-books on any portable device so that entire collection can be accessed at one's fingertips. In today's world, physical space is very expensive, particularly libraries need lots of space irrespective of their category and that problems keep increasing with the size of the library. It is one of the problems faced by all libraries in the world and for that e-books are the best answer as there is no run out of space, to add any number of books, because disc space is becoming cheaper day by day.

However to take the usage of e-books to a new height, while librarians need to educate users as well as staff about the benefits in use of e-books, the users require a paradigm shift in their attitude away from the current perception that everything must be on the printed page to the varied better possibilities offered by e-books. Further the publishers, vendors and librarians need to work together on more mutually congenial and beneficial business models for greater e-book usage.

REFERENCES

Abram, S. (2004). e-Books: Rumors of our death are greatly exaggerated. *Information Outlook*, 8(2), 14-15.

Armstrong, C.J., et al. (2001). A study of the use of electronic information systems by higher education students in the UK. *Program*, 35(3), 239-60.

Buchanan, Matt (2008). Amazon Kindle and Sony Reader Locked Up: Why Your Books Are No Longer Yours. Retrieved from http://gizmodo.com/369235/amazon-kindle-and-sony-reader-locked-up-why-your-books-are-no-longer-yours

Chu, H. (2003). Electronic books: Viewpoints from users and potential users. *Lib Tech*, 21(3), 340-46.

Gardiner, Eileen & Ronald G. Musto. (2010). The Electronic Book. In Suarez, Michael Felix, and H. R. Woudhuysen (Eds.) *The Oxford Companion to the Book*. (p. 164). Oxford: Oxford University Press.

Goleman, Daniel & Norris, Gregory (2010, April 4). How green is my iPad? *The New York Times*. Retrieved from http://www.nytimes.com/interactive/2010/04/04/opinion/04opchart.html

Harris, Christopher (2009). The truth about ebooks. *School Library Journal*. Retrieved from http://www.schoollibraryjournal.com/article/CA6660883.html

http://liblog.law.stanford.edu/tag/2-million-free-ebooks/

http://pogue.blogs.nytimes.com/2009/07/17/some-e-books-are-more-equal-than-others/

http://www.nybooks.com/articles/archives/2008/jun/12/the-library-in-the-new-age/?pagination=false

Lebert, M. (n.d.). *A short history of ebooks*. Retrieved from http://www.etudes-francaises.net/dossiers/ebookEN.pdf

Oxford Dictionaries. E-book. Oxford: Oxford University Press.

Ramaiah, Chennupati K. (2012). E-books, past, present and future. *DESIDOC Journal of Library & Information Technology*, 32(2), 77-82.

Ramaiah, Chennupati K. (2012). Users' perception about e-books in India. *DESIDOC Journal of Library & Information Technology*, 32(2), 86-94.

Siegle, Lucy. (2009, August 30). Should we switch to reading books online? *The Observer*. Retrieved from http://www.guardian.co.uk/environment/2009/aug/30/reading-books-online-eco-friendly

Wilson R., Landoni M. and Gibb F. (2003). The WEB Book experiments in electronic textbook design. *Journal of Documentation*, 59(4), 454-477.

5

Emerging Non-conventional Publishing Channels: Revolution in Scholarly and Street Publishing

Tabasum Maqbool

Web technologies have changed the whole scenario of information access right from their origin. Before the inception of the Web, access to the information was either through the traditional means of visiting a library or browsing a document or accessing it in an offline manner. But the web publishing made the access to documents easy. The importance of the web resources in day-to-day life continues to grow. An increasing number of institutes associated with education research, business and entertainment all over the world are opting for web resources over traditional formats. With the initiatives like consortia systems, archives, databases etc. the importance of web resources in distance learning, higher education and research programmes are getting more popular. Web resources are becoming more powerful than they were in 1990's and are developing at a very fast rate in the various subjects. With the success of web 2.0 and its various tools especially wikis and blogs have given easy and far-reaching coverage not only to scholars but also to ordinary beings to express their ideas, thoughts, imagination and a power to improve each other's understanding of various concepts, ideas, improving and updating knowledge due to collaborative intelligence. Keeping these unique features in view an endeavour is made to discuss different facets of wikis and blogs in detail.

Wiki

Wiki has brought fruition to the earliest hopes for the internet. That is, a democratic, accessible community of users responsible for its own content, supported by an open model of knowledge creation and communication. Wikis in particular embodies the highest attainable information sharing dream of an organization where a group of its members is voluntarily and unselfishly collaborating and creating knowledge and working towards a common goal to benefit the organization. This has implications on the management, culture, technology and knowledge base of the organizations and will also inadvertently change the dynamics of organization communication.

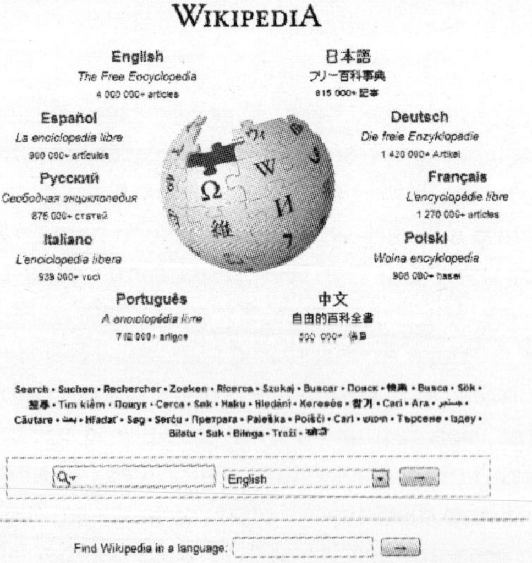

An illustration of most popular wiki site (Wikipedia)

It was Ward Cunningham in 1994 who in order to facilitate communication between software developers, and also to experiment with the new hypertext capabilities, created the first wiki, as a supplement to the *Portland Pattern Repository*, a website containing documentation about design patterns, a particular approach to object-oriented programming, which he called "*WikiWikiWeb*" (using the Hawaiian word "wiki" meaning "quick"). Cunningham went public with the first wiki in early 1995, inviting a selected group of programmers to participate in the experiment. Wiki met with immediate success, and quickly spawned "*wiki clones*," alternative versions of the wiki software. The use of wiki websites was rapidly adopted by communities of free software developers, but at first remained confined to these specialised groups (Ebersbach*et al.*, 2006). In the meantime the *WikiWikiWeb* evolved rapidly as features were added to the software and as the growing body of users developed a unique "*wiki culture*." By year 2000 the number of contributors to *Cunningham's* website had grown so large that conflicts developed between those who wanted to restrict the discussion to computer programming and those who wanted to discuss issues relating to the functioning of the wiki itself. The conflict was resolved by the creation the "SisterSites" *MeatballWiki*and *WhyClublet* as separate forums for discussion.

Yet, wikis remained largely unknown outside of circles of software developers until around 2001, when the success of the free content encyclopaedia *Wikipedia* introduced wikis to the general public. After 2001 the number of wiki websites and the varieties of wiki engines (software implementations) increased exponentially. There now exist thousands of wiki websites and hundreds of wiki engines. Wikipedia's popular success has meant that the concept of the wiki, as a collaborative tool that facilitates the production of a group work, is widely understood.

Thus Wiki is a collective website where a large number of participants are allowed to modify any page or create a new page using their Web browser. Wiki has introduced ground-breaking innovations at the level of technology for supporting collaborative web-authoring.

Like many simple concepts, "open editing" has some profound and subtle effects on Wiki usage. It allows all users to create and edit any page in a website and encourages democratic use of the Web and helps less IT-competent users to contribute content. Wikis are often used to create collaborative websites, to power community websites, and for note taking. A wiki provides an extremely fast and efficient way to collaborate and communicate knowledge among virtually anyone interested without the constraints of place or time. Wikis are, transforming the way corporate world works. Due to advent of wiki there is no longer need for countless conference calls, meetings and emails back-and-forth to resolve issues and understand requirements (Krause, 2004). Wikis are one example of what is coming to be known as "Social Software" a type of software that makes it easy for groups of people to work together in a virtual environment.

Wikis being of recent origin and technology is still in evolving phase, yet various authorities and researchers have defined "Wiki" in their own right. Some of the well-known definitions are given below.

In words of Ward Cunningham, the father of the wiki, it is

"... . a freely-expandable collection of interlinked web "pages", a hypertext system for storing and modifying information – a database, where each page is easily editable by any user ..." (Leuf and Cunningham, 2001).

While as Chawner and Lewis (2004) describe it

"Atype of software that makes it easy for groups of people to work in a virtual environment"

According to Encyclopaedia Britannica, wiki (2009) is

"A website that allows the easy creation and editing of any number of interlinked Web pages, using a simplified markup language or a WYSIWYG text editor, within the browser"

Therefore, it can be concluded that the wiki is social or

organizational web platform where every member or a person can use, contribute and improve the resources.

Salient Features

Various salient features of "Wikis" are

(a) A unique characteristic of "wiki" technology is the ease with which pages can be created and updated.

(b) Most wikis provide the user with a set of navigation or utility tools such as the ability to edit a page; view recently changed pages; use a 'history' feature to view or roll back to a previous version of a page; 'discuss' offline changes or proposed changes to a page; use a 'backlinks' function (view all the pages that link to the page currently displayed); search the wiki; and others" (Peterson, 2004).

(c) Most wikis provide a "sandbox" where user can test and experiment with the wiki syntax, editing conventions, and other features and functionalities.

(d) Some wiki implementations provide the ability to register users and restrict editing capabilities to a particular set of users (Peterson, 2004).

Reliability and validity

There is a continuous debate over the authenticity of wiki content. The recent studies by Wilkinson and Huberman (2007); Giles (2005) and Anthony *et al.* (2005) provide evidence that articles contained within Wikipedia are reliable and valid. Research conducted by Stvilia *et al.* (2005) shows that the Wikipedia community takes issues of quality seriously. While as counter argument given by John Seigenthaler, a journalist and a former official in the Kennedy administration, who determined that Wikipedia contained an inaccurate and defamatory biography article about him in 2005 (Ramasastry, 2005; Helm, 2005). Another extensively reported event in 2006 involved senatorial staffers altering factual information about political rivals.

Furthermore, unlike other reference sources, individual

Wikipedia entries do not list authors' full or even real names, and authors do not post their credentials in terms of expertise in the field of their contributions. Without full disclosure of authorship, readers cannot verify the expertise of the author or even conduct further research on his/her credentials. Although anyone can participate in editing articles, the results are carefully reviewed and discussed in ways very similar to open-source programming projects (McGuinness *et al.*, 2006) that makes its contents reasonably authentic and reliable.

Blog

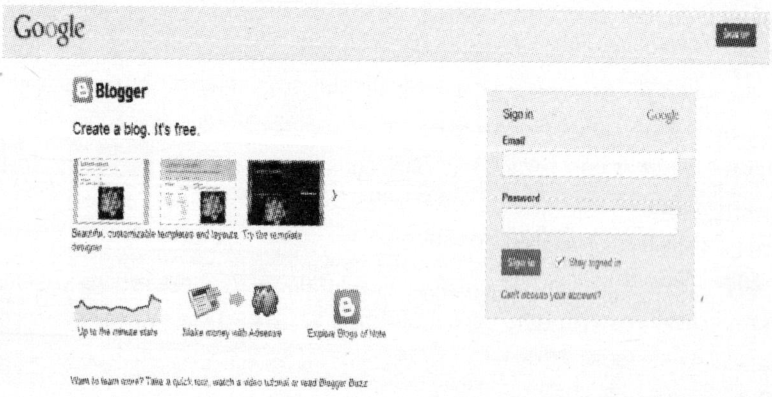

An illustration of most popular blog hosting site (Blogger)

Blog had already been around for several years by 1997, when Robert Wisdoms Jorn Borger coined the term "weblog" (Wired, 2009). He described a weblog as "a webpage where a weblogger (sometimes called blogger or a pre-surfer) logs all other webpages he finds interesting. And Peter Merholz shortened it to 'blog' in May of 1999 when he "broke the word weblog into the phrase *"we blog"* on his site (*Merholz, 1999*). The first website with blog like features was the National Centre for Supercomputing Applications (NCSA) "*What's New page"*. From 1993 to 1996 NCSA's website was keeping track of new websites and provided links to new pages on web in reverse chronological order. By 1996 so many new websites had appeared that it was impossible to keep track of them all in one place. A number of notable weblogs sprang up in the late 1990's, designed to point bloggers' friends to new websites of interest. At the beginning of1999, only about 23 weblogs existed. That year, the world of weblogs would be forever changed with the advent of "*Blogger*" the blog software unveiled by Pyra Labs (American Dialect Society Mailing List, 2008). Before 1999, anyone who wanted to create a blog had to build it from scratch. It was complicated to develop a simple HTML page for people who knew nothing about the design, networking or software development fields. Its popularity helped spread the term across the Web and to solidify the look and feel of blogs.

To draw a description from its historical use, it can be said that a blog or weblog is a type of website, usually maintained by an individual with regular entries of commentary, descriptions of events, or other material such as graphics or video. The items of information are constantly updated with new information, personal experiences, analysis, hyperlinks and comments. Entries are commonly displayed in reverse-chronological order.

A typical blog combines text, images, and links to other blogs, Web pages, and other media related to its topic. The ability for readers to leave comments in an interactive format is an important part of many blogs. Most blogs are primarily textual, although some focus on art (artlog), photographs (photoblog), sketches (sketchblog), videos (vlog), music (MP3 blog), audio (podcasting), which are part of a wider network of social media. As of June 2009, blog search engine Technorati was tracking more than 262 million blogs (*Technorati, 2009).* With the advent of video blogging, the word blog has taken on an even looser meaning — that of any bit of media wherein the subject expresses his opinion or simply talks about something.

Blogging systems are so easy to use that many organisations use them as a web publishing system. It's easy to take a blogging template, rework it to remove the "blog" features such as date and author listings, and set up a reasonable stylesheet. The result looks like a regular web site, but it's much easier to use than traditional

HTML editors. The blogging system allows the easy addition of new items and automatically creates the RSS feed, and the result doesn't look like a traditional blog. Libraries can use blogs to promote and publicise different events and services and activities of library. Blog can act as a channel to get feedback from users regards its various activities and services this way it would be easy for them to improve shortcoming in a more efficient and spontaneous manner than possible earlier.

Different interested persons have attempted to define blog and blogging, including practitioners, academics and authoritative information resources.

> Rebecca (2005) defines it
>
> *"The original Weblogs were link-driven sites containing a mixture in unique proportion of links, commentary, and personal thoughts and essays".*
>
> Salon (1999) describes it
>
> *"...personal websites operated by individuals who compile chronological lists of links to stuff that interests them, interspersed with information, editorializing and personal asides".*
>
> According to Wijnia (2004) blog is
>
> *"A webpage on which authors publish their thoughts with the intention of starting a conversation"*
>
> ODLIS defines blog (2009) as
>
> *"A webpage that provides frequent, continuing publication of weblinks and/ or comments on a specific topic or often in the form of short entries arranged in reverse chronological order, the most recently added information appearing first"*
>
> In words of Scott (2001) a blog is
>
> *"A web page containing brief, chronologically arranged items of information".*

OED (2003) defines it as

"A frequently updated web site consisting of personal observations, excerpts from other sources, etc., typically run by a single person, and usually with hyperlinks to other sites; an online journal or diary"

Miriam-Webster (2005) call it

"A web site that contains an online personal journal with reflections, comments, and often hyperlinks provided by the writer"

From above definitions it can be inferred that blog is a very broad concept. People use it for range of purpose like personal diaries, forum to discuss socio, political and economic issues and also acts as an interface between the people and the new web resources published every now and then on the Web.

Salient Features

Some of the unique features associated with blogs are discussed below:

- Easy for users to write and upload posts and edit them later if needed
- Allows users to save drafts prior to final posting – so a post doesn't have to be completed in one go
- Easy for users to embed images and videos and provide optimised alt text
- Allows full coding rather than just plain text so that posts can have hyperlinks to other pages in the main website or to other posts, or to another website or blog, etc.
- Allows the addition of multiple widgets for extra visual functionality
- Can add very valuable plugins for enhancement and extra functionality
- Can provide visitor statistics
- Customisable themes

- Can show links to other favourite blogs or websites
- Everything is self-contained – no need for other programs like an HTML editor
- The ability to summarise posts with an automatically generated page which contains the whole post and a link to this page from the main blog.
- The ability to assign multiple tags to any post and be able to display archives by category.
- Easy for visitors to navigate and find things of interest to them
- Allows comments on individual posts by visitors (user interactivity)
- Shows recent posts in the sidebar and previous posts easy to find in the sidebar
- Has an RSS feed so visitors are encouraged to subscribe to all posts via email or newsfeed system
- Has a tag cloud so visitors can see the most popular topics
- Has archived posts listed by months in the sidebar

Types of Blogs

There are many types of blogs, differing in the type of content and style

I. Personal blogs : The personal blog is an on-going diary or commentary by an individual, is the traditional and most common blog.

II. Corporate blogs : A blog can be private, as in most cases, or it can be for business purposes. Blogs either used internally to enhance the communication and culture in a corporation or externally for marketing, branding or public relations purposes are called corporate blogs.

III. Question blogging : It is a type of **blog** that answers questions. Questions can be submitted in the form of a submittal form, or through email or other means such as telephone or VOIP. Qlogs can be used to display show-notes from podcasts or the means of conveying information through the internet. Many question logs use syndication such as RSS as a means of conveying answers to questions.

IV. By Content : A blog comprising videos is called a vlog, one comprising links is called a linklog, a site containing a portfolio of sketches is called a sketchblog or one comprising photos is called a photoblog. Blogs with shorter posts and mixed media types are called tumblelogs.

Some of the well-known blog hosting sites are:

- Blogger
- WordPress
- Technorati Blogging
- Blog.com
- Squarespace
- HubPages
- Blogsome
- BlogHer
- LiveJournal
- Weebly

CONCLUSION

The two main big advantages of wikis and blogs are their ease of use and the availability of many Open Source/free or low-cost software and hosting options to run them. Examples of the latter include MediaWiki (Open Source – the same software package that runs Wikipedia) and Google Blogger. Wikis and blogs also use RSS, which means users can easily set up/subscribe to 'feeds' to automatically receive content updates from their favourite services. With blogs hosting audio it has the potential of offering superior support for auditory learners and also for visual learners in case of vlog.

If effectively deployed, wikis and blogs could offer a way to enhance users learning experiences, and deepen levels of learners' engagement and collaboration within digital learning environments. With these varieties of web 2.0 publishing modes available, the future looks all for the Web enabled information resources for every sort of information and knowledge. With every passing year the organization of these publishing channels is expected to be more systematic and meaningful for all the stakeholders. It will help users to make maximum use of them in their pursuit of knowledge and scholarship.

REFERENCES

American Dialect Society Mailing List. (2008). *Origins of "Blog" and "Blogger".* Retrieved from http://listserv.linguistlist.org/cgi-bin/wa?A2=ind0804C&L=ADS-L&P=R16795&I=-3

Anthony, D. et al. (2005). *Explaining quality in internet collective goods: zealots and good samaritans in the case of Wikipedia.* Paper presented at the Fall 2005 Innovation and Entrepreneurship Seminar at MIT, Retrieved from http://web.mit.edu/iandeseminar/Papers/Fall2005/anthony-pdf

ODLIS (2009). *Blog.* ODLIS- Online Dictionary for Library and Information Science. Retrieved from http://lu.com/odlis/odlis_w.cfm#weblog

Chawner, B. & Lewis P.H. (2004). *WikiWikiWebs: New ways of interacting in a web environment.* Paper presented at the ALA (American Library Association) LITA National Forum, October. Retrieved from http://www.ala.org/ala/mgrps/divs/lita/litaevents/2004forum/CS_WikiWikiWebs.pdf

Ebersbach, A. et al (2006). *Wiki: Web Collaboration.* Germany: Springer-Verlag.

Giles, J. (2005). Internet encyclopedias go head to head. *Nature,* 438, 900-901. Retrieved from http://www.nature.com/nature/journal/v438/n7070/full/438900a.htm

Helm, B. (2005). Wikipedia: a work in progress. *Businessweek,* 14 December, Retrieved from www.businessweek.com/technology/content/dec2005/tc20051214_441708.htm?chan=db

Krause, J. (2004). A wiki-wiki way to work. *ABA Journal,* 90(12), 61. Retrieved from http://www.abajournal.com/magazine/article/a_wiki_wiki_way_to_work/

Leuf, B., & Cunningham, W. (2001). The WIKI WAY. Quick Collaboration on the Web. Boston: Addison-Wesley.

McGuinness, D. et al (2006). *Investigations into trust for collaborative information. Repositories: a Wikipedia case study. Proceedings of Workshops on Models of Trust for the Web (MTW06), 22 May 2006, Edinburgh.* Retrieved from http://citeseerx.ist.psu.edu/viewdoc/download?doi=10.1.1.62.1991&rep=rep1&type=pdf#page=51

Merholz, Peter. (1999). Peterme.com.The internet archive. Retrieved from http://web.archive.org/web/19991013021124/http://peterme.com/index.html.

Mirriam-Webster. (2005). Merriam-Webster's Words of the Year 2004. Retrieved from http://www.m-w.com/info/04words.htm

OED: The Oxford English Dictionary (2003). Blog and Web log.

Peterson, B. (2004), Tech talk: Wiki. *Library Instruction Round Table News,* 27(1), 13-15 Retrieved from www.baylor.edu/LIRT/lirtnews/2004/sep04.pdf

Ramasastry, A. (2005). Is an online encyclopedia, such as Wikipedia, immune from libel suits?" *Findlaw Legal News and Commentary,* Retrieved from http://writ.news.findlaw.com/ramasastry/20051212.html

Rebecca. (2005). *Weblogs.* Retrieved from www.rebeccablood.net/essays/weblog_history.html.

Salon (1999). Fear of links. Retrieved from http://www.salon.com/technology/col/rose/1999/05/28/weblogs/index.html

Scott, Peter. (2001). Blogging: Creating Instant Content for the Web. Retrieved from http://www.library.usask.ca/~scottp/il2001/definitions.html

Technorati (2009). Welcome to Technorati. Retrieved from http://technorati.com/about/.

Wijnia, E. (2004). Understanding weblogs: a communicative perspective. In T. Burg (Ed.) *BlogTalks 2.0: The European Conference on Weblogs* (pp.38-82).Retrieved from http://elmine.wijnia.com/weblog/archives/wijnia_understandingweblogs.pdf

Wiki (2009). Encyclopaedia Britannica. Retrieved from http://www.britannica.com/EBchecked/topic/1192819/wiki.

Wilkinson, D.M. & Huberman, B.A. (2007). Assessing the value of cooperation in Wikipedia, *First Monday,* 12(4). Retrieved from www.firstmonday.org/issues/issue12_4/wilkinson/index.html.

Wired.com (2009). After 10 years of blogs, the future's brighter than ever. Retrieved from http://www.wired.com/entertainment/theweb/news/2007/12/blog_anniversary.

6

Changing Scenario in Information World: Lib 2.0

Anvita Shrivastava

INTRODUCTION

Due to tremendous growth in the field of information & communication technology Lib 2.0 concept came into existence. We all know that the rise of internet services like Google, Yahoo and others posed a serious challenge before Information officers. These services offer easy access to find out the desired information at a short call. Now the users are independent enough to browse the information round the clock and most of them are free of cost. It's a hassle free service in which users is not require moving to library premises and confined to working hours of library.

Are these conditions not a big challenge for the very existence of the information officers? Are they compatible enough to face it and last but most important as to whether they are really ready to equipped to transform themselves under altered circumstances? There is no doubt Lib 2.0 is answer of all the questions. Now information officers have started to use Web 2.0 applications to prove themselves equivalent to other information providers, and start delivering experiences that completely fulfill the user's expectations.

It is a revolution in the field of user services; it changes the entire scenario to interact with the library users. It endow with a set of new space were users can interact more collectively and collaboratively. It facilitates two way communications between users and library staff, which ensures user participation and relative feedback of the services provided by the library. Lib 2.0 concept is not new one as it has been derived from the very philosophy on which Web 2.0 operates, whereby different online interactive services are used for wider communication. The concept of Lib 2.0 is more user centered in which they are the prime focus of the organisation.

Lib 2.0 came into the existence just because users get weary of the static implementation of the concept web 1.0. Initially libraries started Online Public Access Catalogue (OPAC), which provides only one way communication from the organizational side. Under the circumstances users are unable to provide feedback which is a pre-requisite for improvement of any system. As we see that many online book sellers on the website specially emphasis the feedback and review column and encourage user to fill it. The feedback provided by the users gives tremendous opportunity to improve the system on ground level.

In view of variety of system process and attitudinal mind set of users, Lib 2.0 system requires to be further looked into. In fact this system is easily available at any point of time and requirement. It is visually available on a number of devises, other integrated services apart from traditional library system, e.g. portals, distant learning, audio visual programmes and other learning mechanism connected with e-learning system These are some areas where information officer are required to address themselves and evolve ways and means for adoption and popularization of these facilities to give it larger spectrum

LIB 2.0

As we all know that Lib 2.0 is practical implication of web 2.0 technology in the field of information science which provides interactive platform to the users. Lib 2.0 encourages users not just to search or retrieve information on the responding database, but also contribute the information and play the role as good as author or creator. Lib 2.0 is a loosely defined term which modernized the information centers in a way where users enjoy the real time interaction with the staff and the can get different view of other users

According to Michael Casey (2005), *"Lib 2.0 is a user-centered model for library services that encourages user participation in the creation of both the physical and digital services, supported by the consistently evaluating services"*

According to Ken Chad and Paul Miller (2006), *"Lib 2.0 is a concept of a very different library service that operates according to the expectations of today's library users in which, library makes information available wherever the user requires it"*

It came into the existence following the path of social networking website where users can communicate each other exploiting the different services, i.e. collaborative tagging, RSS feeds, wikis, synchronous messaging, tagging Streaming media, blogs and Mashup. There are certain elements which must be considered by Information officers before practical implementation of web 2.0 concept in information centers. These elements are shown in Fig. 1.

Eventually if information officer want to convert their traditional library system in to Lib 2.0 he/she must concentrate on users. As library science discipline is basically a service industry, services provided by the information Officers is of utmost importance for research Scholars Information seekers and its users. For Sustained survival and compete with other search engines one must anticipate needs of the users and provide an opportunity to user to come forward, contribute for enrichment of library study materials. In such condition Information Officer is not solely responsible for content creation but users should equally share responsibility for deriving best results out of it.

With the introduction of Multimedia Technology society has witnessed tremendous changes. It has proved to be a boon for challenged human beings as audio-visual facilities derived through this technology enables them to perform their duties efficiently with a little effort and it also help other segments of the society.

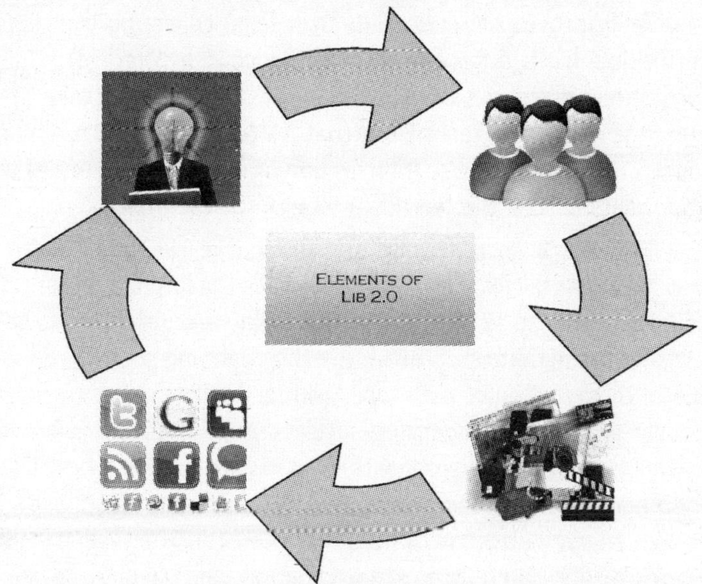

Fig. 1. Elements of Lib 2.0

Social networking is an important tool to effectively interact with others and take out the maximum information from different sources and provide to the users as the spectrum of this facility is wide enough. Therefore Lib 2.0 is a point around witch the entire efforts for seeking information and its dissemination smoothly revolve. Information officers must use this technology to provide better services.

In the past Libraries is the place of gathering where different prominent comes and share their views in various topics and make detail discussion on it. As a results different innovative ideas come across which enhance the entire community as a whole. The same old wine come in to the new bottle. Innovativeness is a continuous process with are the sole responsible for development of any society and as well as the most basic element s of the Lib 2.0. Information Officers must prepare themselves for these changes and play their role accordingly.

COMPOSITION OF LIB 2.0

Lib 2.0 means brought out from the physical wall of the libraries and offer improved services to its user from collecting the required information from different sources (Resource Sharing). But yet information officers are not fully prepared themselves to take the full advantage of the new technology that is Web 2.0. Lib 2.0 is a mixture of different components so information officers must aware of these components to take the full advantage of the technology

There are so many things which are responsible for the constituent of the Lib 2.0. Users are always the important part of the discussion because all the things are moving around them, to satisfy them and make them comfortable in the changing scenario of library service. Introduction of new tools and technology defiantly improve the user expectation regarding services and libraries are bound to provide better services to retain its users in open market where Google, yahoo and other proving round the clock information services. In a gist we can say "Lib 2.0 is a change in interaction between users and libraries in a new culture of participation catalyzed by social web technologies"

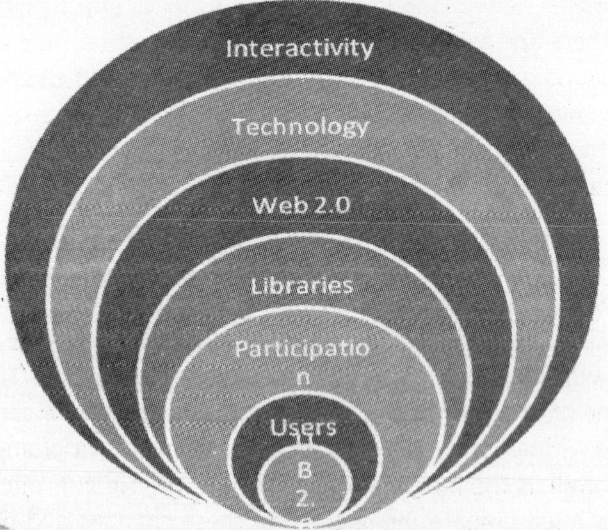

Fig. 2. Components of Lib 2.0

Miller defines Lib 2.0 as an order to re-imagine data as content through the transformational power of Web-based services and data 'mash-ups'.

Users

Libraries are come into the existence just because of its user. Users are the central peripheral on which libraries rotates. Lib 2.0 changes the entire way of interaction with the users. Now users don't need to walk in to libraries to read but libraries moved accordingly with the help of communication technology to the users.

Participation

Introduction on Web 2.0 promotes the participation from the user. The transformation in web technology such as wikis, blogging, social networks, RSS feed collectively allowed extremely easy content creation and sharing by anyone. These technologies allow users to add and edit the things according to their needs. It allow two way communication as compare to one way communication in web 1.0 Now the readers/users are encourage to give feedback. With the help of fruitful suggestions came from users libraries change themselves according to the need of the users.

Decentralisation

The best part of Lib 2.0 is it decentralization in nature, i.e. participation, architecture and usage. The benefit of decentralization can be seen in the way of control where single authority is solely not responsible for up gradation or changes but the user as whole can participate and improve the content which benefit others.

Libraries and Library Service

Lib 2.0 can't come in to the reality without the existence of libraries or it can say Lib 2.0 concept is a modified form of libraries dedicated to best user services.

Web 2.0

No one can imagine the Lib 2.0 without Web 2.0. As it consider earlier Lib 2.0 is a technological application of Web 2.0 in the libraries to enhance its services and maximise the satisfaction of the user interact with the same.

Technology

As mention earlier Lib 2.0 is fusion of two components i.e. libraries and application of technology and its tool. So without the help of technology it is quite impossible for the libraries to implement web 2.0 techniques in real practice.

Interactivity

Lib 2 has provide the interaction with the user, library service Web 2.0 and technology, basically it provides the interface with all the basic services and technologies which help user. Lib 2.0 is about a change in interaction between users and libraries in a culture of new social participation.

No matter which aspects are emphasizing, it is clear that Lib 2.0 is about a change in interaction that has been made possible by technological developments in user-friendly social aspects in web-based services.

TOOLS OF WEB 2.0 FOR CONVERSION OF LIB INTO LIB 2.0

Wikis

A wiki is a set of webpages that can be easily modified by user have a register account. It can also be called as "electronic chalks" Wikis are open access pages on which user have to create an account for publishing, editing and modification etc. Wikis could be useful in internal Libraries activities to create Knowledge base, to support work that moves quickly from discussion to collaborative writing to create a place for writing, editing and storing meeting notes and reports, or it could even become the platform for the library intranet. Wikis can also be used to support various courses, subject gateways, planning and delivering subject content and organizing conferences and seminars as well as connecting users have a similar interest.

Blogs

A blog is a website where library users can enter their thoughts, ideas, suggestions, and comments. Blogs are the most popular tool of publishing subject content over the internet. Martin and Zannier (2007, pp. 90-92) mention that blogs are diaries or on varying topics posted online so that others can read and reply to them. Information officers can use blogs to share thoughts and ideas in the library community and to get feedback from library y users. Information officers can blog about library events and activities, or write book reviews. Higginbottom (2008, p. 271) said that "blogs are useful for marketing". Several libraries use blogs to disseminate information about their library news, new book new resources and others. The information officers however should ensure that posts are kept on topic and relevant to the blogs scope. Xu, et al. (2009) found that blogs' popularity as a Web 2.0 application in academic library is only second to IM.

Social Networking

Social networking is the boon in the field of Web 2.0, which enables blogging, messaging, and tagging. Facebook, Twitter, LinkedIn are networks that cater the massive number of users. All these networks work on the principle of sharing with each other upload Social networking enables information officers to interact with the users and share the library resources electronically. For this library users just have to create an account with the library network, find the users have similar kind of interest and share the data between each other. A library can use social networking as a tool that permit users to share their own collection of data online over the network and not just to share with each other but also recommend other connect users regarding good material for the same area of interest.

Really Simple Syndication

RSS is a web feed format which is used to make user aware regarding the updates of the site such as news headlines audio and video, which is changed frequently with time, RSS is a technology which provide users a way to syndicate and regenerate content on the Web. Such kind of content syndication is another Web 2.0 application that provides great impact on Information centers.

RSS feeds allows subscriber to avoid manual checking of update for their interested sites instead of this RSS reader collect the information regarding the users most access site and pused new content of the same in to their browser when it becomes available. Most of the Information centers. are building RSS feeds for users to inform regarding updates of their library holdings, new services and content in subscription databases.

Instant Messaging (IM)

Instant Messaging is popularly known as synchronous messaging. It is a form of real-time direct text-based communication between two or more people using system or other devices, along with shared clients. The user's text is conveyed over a network, such as the Internet.

The implication of Instant Messaging in the library is very useful. With the help of IM, Information Officer directly interacts with the user and tries to find out the better way to serve the users. With the introduction of advanced technology now the information officer has more empowered. Now with the help of audio-visual messaging user can experiences multi-way effect.

Time is not too far away when the IM can become a essential part of the Library network for providing great user experience.

CONVERSION OF LIBRARIES INTO LIB 2.0

Library is an integral part of the nerve centre of any institution, which imparting its services to students, faculty members and other staff members. The traditional way of library is changing into the modern context. Now Lib 2.0 came into existence. Lib 2.0 is independent of technology has given the fact that every library activity designed with active participation and feedback of its user community qualifies to the concept of Lib 2.0.

In traditional libraries people have to visit the library which takes extra time from their busy schedule, with Lib 2.0, libraries move beyond the notion of "libraries without walls", in which they offered a destination web site that attempted to reproduce the total library experience online. Instead relevant aspects of that library experience should be reproduced wherever and whenever the user requires them, without any need to visit a separate web site for the library. Previously libraries have closed stacks which creates problem for the users, it might be unsatisfied them with the accessioning of the relevant documents or information, but in changing era "open-stacks" are there, users are free to access their relevant documents, which will satisfies them.

Earlier, collection development is the only aim of libraries and information centers, but with Lib 2.0 "library suggestion box" have taken places in the library services where people are free to suggest their demand or any other suggestion to the library improvement. The traditional library read only catalogues will become Amazon style comments where the user comments, reviews and feedbacks will be used for enhancing the catalogue. Traditional library's operation is to provide the library and information service and its mission focus is the mere output but on the outcome of an organization. To summarize, Lib 2.0 focuses on user and how to attract the user as information consumer as well as contributor. Traditional libraries maintain their resources, authorities, information on the shelves or behind a login that are known by the libraries, but today libraries maintain their records in such a way through which users can explore the resources easily.

CONCLUSION

Lib 2.0 put great challenges in front of Information officer to redefine their traditional services and approach. It's time for him to come out from the cell of Information gatekeeper and play proactive role and provide pinpointed information to the users. Now-a-days information officers are ready to adopt the change and implementing the Lib 2.0 functionalities in their Information centers.

In the words of Ian Davis said "Web 2.0 is an attitude, not a technology" the same is true of Lib 2.0. Libraries merely offer us a means by which we can realize a set of goals shared across the library sectors. The concept of Lib 2.0 builds upon all that has been best about libraries to date, harnesses technological potential and community capability in order to deliver valuable, valued and World-class services directly to those who stand to benefit from them, whether they physically enter a library building or not.

It's duty of an information officer to connect people and technology and information in context. He doesn't hesitate to adopt tagging, tag clouds and user-driven content descriptions and classifications instead of traditional cataloging and classification. He try to connects the users to expert discussions, conversations, and communities of practice and participates there as well and uses the latest tools of communication to connect content, expertise, information coaching, and people. He encourages user has driven metadata and user developed content and commentary and understands the wisdom of crowds. It is, finally, also necessary to consider that the Web will continue to change rapidly with time, and information centers must adapt to it, much as they did the Web originally, and must continually adapt for the foreseeable future.

REFERENCES

Alexander, B. (2006). Web 2.0: A new wave of innovation for teaching and learning. *EDUCAUSE Review*, 41(2), 32–44. EDUCAUSE: Boulder, USA. Retrieved from http://www.educause.edu/ir/library/pdf/erm0621.pdf.

Casey, Michael. (2005). Working Towards a definition of Lib 2.0. *Library Crunch*. Retrieved from http://www.librarycruhch.com.

Chan, S. (2007). Tagging and Searching – Serendipity and museum collection databases. In *Proceedings of Museums and the Web 2007*, Toronto, 2007. Retrieved from http://www.archimuse.com/ mw2007/papers/chan/chan.html.

Maness, J. (2006). Lib 2.0 theory: Web 2.0 and Its Implications for Libraries. *Webology*, 3(2). Retrieved from http://www.webology.ir/2006/v3n2/a25.html.

Miller, Paul. (2005). Web 2.0: Building the New Library. *ARIADNE*, 45(Oct. 2005). Retrieved from http://www.ariadne.ac.uk/issue45/miller/ (Accessed on 03/11/2012).

Miller, Paul. 2006. *Introducing the Lib 2.0 gang*. Recorded telephone conference as part of the Talking with Talis podcast series. Jan 31, 2006. Retrieved from http://talk.talis.com/archives/2006/02/introducing_the.html

O'Reilly, T. (2005). *What is Web 2.0: Design Patterns and Business Models for the next generation of software*. O'Reilly website, 30th September 2005. O'Reilly

Media Inc. Retrieved from http://www.oreillynet.com/pub/a/oreilly/tim/news/2005/09/30/what-is-web-20.html

Xu, C., Ouyang, F., & Chu, H. (2009). The Academic library meets Web 2.0: Applications and implications. *The Journal of Academic Information officership*, 35(4), 324-31.

7

Major Online Databases Available in Social Sciences

Satwinderpal Kaur Gill

INTRODUCTION

In present scenario information environment and information needs of information seekers have been changed. Information has become one of the basic needs of human beings and it is unlimited in scope. Generally people seek information from different sources and formats for undertaking a variety of tasks. Tremendous growth in knowledge and technological advancements has led to an increased awareness of the importance of information in all aspects of life. A great amount of information is available on Internet but it has become a very time consuming job if one wants to get relevant information. Consequently some information agencies have been emerged which are acting as filter and providing relevant information to users. Database is one of such services which aims to save the valuable time of the researchers and provide them quality information.

WHAT IS A DATABASE?

A database is composed of related files that are consolidated, organized and stored together. A database can easily be accessed, managed, and updated. Databases can be classified according to types of content: bibliographic database, full-text database, numeric database, multimedia database and directory database.

Definitions of Database

David Bolton defines "A database is an application that manages data and allows fast storage and retrieval of that data." Merriam-webster dictionary defines database "a usually large collection of data organized especially for rapid search and retrieval (as by a computer)"

DATABASES IN SOCIAL SCIENCES

There are a good number of databases are available in the field of social sciences. In this paper only few of them are discussed.

1. International Political Science Abstracts (1989-present) : International Political Science Abstracts database provides abstracts and indexes from world's leading political science journals in English language. This database covers a wide range of topics like method and theory; political thinkers and ideas; political and administrative institutions; political processes (public opinion, attitudes, parties, forces, groups, and elections); international relations; and national and area studies. The abstracts are non-evaluative in nature.

2. Bibliography of Asian Studies (BAS) (1971-present) : The Bibliography of Asian Studies (BAS) database contains records on all subjects especially in the humanities and the social sciences pertaining to East, Southeast, and South Asia published worldwide. Main fields covered are Humanities, Asian Languages and Cultures, International Studies, Asian studies, Social Sciences, Anthropology and sociology. The BAS included citations to western-language periodical articles, monographs, chapters in edited volumes, conference proceedings, anthologies, and Festschriften, etc. Since 1992, newly published individual monographs are no longer being added to the database. BAS meets the needs of scholars, students, teachers, librarians, and other information seekers in Asian studies. The BAS provides various alternates for searching, displaying and downloading data. BAS fulfils the needs of scholars, students, teachers, librarians, and others seeking information in Asian studies.

3. Sociological abstracts : The Sociological Abstracts database abstract and indexes the international literature in sociology and related disciplines in the social and behavioral sciences. The database provides citations from 1963 to the present to journal articles, book reviews, books, book chapters, dissertations, and conference papers. Records for journal articles added after 1974 contain in-depth abstracts. Major areas of coverage include culture and social structure, demography and human biology, economic development, environmental interactions, evaluation research, family and social welfare, health and medicine and law, history and theory of sociology, management and complex organizations, mass phenomena and political interactions, methodology and research technology; policy, planning, forecast and speculation; radical sociology, religion and science, rural and urban sociology, social development, social differentiation, social psychology and group interaction, sociology of the arts, business, education, studies in violence and power, substance abuse and addiction, welfare services and women's studies.

4. LISA: Library and Information Science Abstracts (1969 – current) : Library and Information Science Abstracts is an abstracting and indexing service in the field of library and information science at international level. It covers library literature from 1969. LISA currently abstracts over 440 periodicals from more than 68 countries. It covers more than 20 different languages. Major areas of coverage include: Artificial intelligence, Book reviews, CD-ROMs, Computer science applications, Information centres, Information management, Information science, Information storage, Information technology, Internet technology, Knowledge management, Librarianship, Libraries and archives, Library management, Library technology, Library use and users, Medical information, Online information retrieval, Publishing and bookselling, Records management, Telecommunications, Technical services and World Wide Web.

5. Library, Information Science & Technology Abstracts (LISTA): Library, Information Science and Technology Abstracts (LISTA) indexes and abstracts more than 560 core journals, nearly 50 priority journals and nearly 125 selective journals. It also includes books, research reports and proceedings. Subjects included are library classification, catalouging, bibliometrics, online information retrieval, information management and other subjects in the scope of library science and technology.

6. Dissertation Abstracts Online : Dissertation Abstracts Online is a database providing indexes and abstracts of American dissertations accepted at an accredited institution since 1861 and it is updated monthly. Selected Masters theses have been included since 1962. Since 1988, the database includes citations for dissertations from 50 British universities that have been collected by and filmed at The British Document Supply Centre. Spring 1988, citations and abstracts from Worldwide Dissertations have also been included in the file. Abstracts are included for doctoral records from July 1980 to the present. Abstracts are included for masters theses from Spring 1988 (*Masters Abstracts*, Volume 26, Number 1) to the present. Individual, degree-granting institutions submit copies of dissertations and theses completed to University Microfilms International (UMI). Citations for these dissertations are included in the database and in University Microfilms International print publications: *Dissertation Abstracts International* (DAI), *American Doctoral Dissertations* (ADD), *Comprehensive Dissertation Index* (CDI), and *Masters Abstracts International* (MAI). The database covers almost all subjects falling under social sciences like Agriculture, Astronomy, Environmental Sciences, Business and Economics, Chemistry, Education, Engineering, Fine Arts and Music, Geography and Regional Planning, Geology, Health Sciences, History and Political Science, Language and Literature, Library and Information Science, Mathematics and Statistics, Philosophy and Religion, Physics, Psychology and Sociology.

7. Population Index : Population Index is the primary reference tool to the world's population literature. It presents an annotated bibliography of recently published books, journal articles, working papers, and other materials on population topics. This website provides a searchable and browsable database containing 46,035 abstracts of demographic literature published in Population Index.

8. DARE: International Social Sciences Directory-Institutions, Specialists, Periodicals (updated irregular) : It is an International referral database in the field of social and human sciences. The DARE database provides over 11,000 references to world wide social science research and training institutes, social science specialists, social science documentation and information services and social science periodicals since 1974 containing special references to peace, human rights and international law research institutes.

9. PsycINFO : PsycINFO is an expansive abstracting and indexing database in the behavioral sciences and mental health. It provides more than three million records devoted to peer-reviewed literature from journals, books and dissertations in the subject in question. It is a tool for scholarly research. Professional coverage beyond psychology it includes related disciplines such as medicine, law, social work, neuroscience, business, nursing, forensics, engineering and more.

10. Social Sciences Citation Index : Social Sciences Citation Index, provides quick access to the bibliographic and citation information to researchers, administrators, faculty and students they need to find research data, analyze trends, journals and researchers and share their findings. SSCI thoroughly covers 50 social sciences disciplines. It provides high-impact articles from peer-reviewed influential journals.

CONCLUSION

Online databases are an adventure of new technology. Among online depositories in social sciences these online databases are playing a vital role to provide timely and accurate information to social scientists. But it is a fact that most of such databases are designed and developed in developed countries. It is very difficult to subscribe these online resources for a user individually. So for satisfying information needs of the social scientists libraries and information centres should subscribe and provide such services to them on priority.

REFERENCES

Bolton, David (n.d.). Definition of database. Retrieved from http://cplus.about.com/od/glossar1/g/databasedefn.htm

http://databases.unesco.org/dare/form.shtml

http://library.dialog.com/bluesheets/html/b10035.html

http://thomsonreuters.com/products_services/science/science_products/az/social_sciences_citation_index/

http://www.apa.org/pubs/databases/psycinfo/index.aspx

http://www.columbia.edu/cu/lweb/eresources/databases/3015902.html

http://www.csa.com/factsheets/lisa-set-c.php

http://www.ebscohost.com/public/library-information-science-technology-abstracts-lista

http://www.lib.umich.edu/node/29175

http://www.ovid.com/webapp/wcs/stores/servlet/ProductDisplay?storeId=13051&catalogId=13151&langId=-1&partNumber=Prod-110

Merriam-Webster. Definition of database. Retrieved from http://www.merriam-webster.com/dictionary/database

Office of Population Research, Princeton University. *Population Index on the Web*. Retrieved from http://popindex.princeton.edu/

8

Evolution of Libraries in the Digital Era- From Physical to Virtual

Y. Gautam

INTRODUCTION

Libraries have gone through incredible changes over the past few years, and it seems like the cycles of change will turn even faster in the future. Academic and research libraries, hard hit by economic pressures and needing to realign strategies and operations to balance increasing reliance on electronic content and diminishing print priorities, may find some relief in this new age of automation alternatives. Public libraries need automation platforms that allow them to engage their patrons in new and creative ways and to have the flexibility to deliver services beyond the constraints of traditional ILS products and online catalogs.

The transformation of collections from print to electronic media includes increasing involvement with digitization of local library materials and the development of new services to accommodate new generations of library users. As technology rapidly transforms the way information is accessed and resources are available online in digital format, the established role of library as a physical space having racks of books looks out of step with the need of the students and researchers. For many, the current reality still is a physical visit to the library. Emergence of advanced and mobile technologies has had a great impact on all sorts of activities as costs reduce, network infrastructure becomes more robust, broadband become faster and computing power improves. Students and researchers can network and stay in touch. Technologies like blogs, wikis, podcasts, web conferencing, messaging, twitter, face book, e-book, e-journal access, semantic web computing have changed the entire scenario of information accessing and sharing.

Digitization can decrease the shelf space. Copyright law and IPR are the factors that need to be addressed along with security issues. The future library can be assumed to be a part of the networked global library comprising the physical and virtual- parallel to the decentralized world of cloud computing.

Internet has brought a dramatic change in the way libraries operate to cater to the demands of the researchers and students. The web provides a real platform for the transformation of modern libraries. Concepts like Digital Reference System, Content Enrichment System, Next Generation OPAC, are the outcomes of new technologies.

THE SIERRA PLATFORM- AN EXAMPLE

Many private vendors have joined the fray of library automation vendors launching new-generation library automation platforms. Sierra, the new system of the Innovative Interfaces, aims to offer the depth of functionality equivalent to the current Millennium ILS. This system leverages current technology architectures that include open source components, with full-featured API bundles that enable greater extensibility and flexibility in the way that libraries make use of the system.

The Sierra Platform has taken the opportunity to take advantage of technology components, architectures, and methods consistent with the times, and to anticipate what features will be popular and necessary in the future. Innovative has chosen the service-oriented architecture, open source database and indexing components, RESTful web services and APIs, and engagement with library developers as some of the key elements of its new technology strategy.

Following a service oriented architecture, the Sierra platform has been constructed in four layers. The foundation database makes use of PostgreSQL as the transactional database engine and Lucene for indexing to support search and retrieval operations. Use of these open source components stands in distinct contrast to Millennium, which uses proprietary database and indexing technologies, or the commercial Oracle database. The database layer connects to the rest of the application through a data access object layer using a component called Hibernate which lends database independence and the ability to maintain persistent transactions through workflows executed at higher levels. Since the database layer also supports standard SQL, third party tools such as Crystal Reports can be used to create reports or other data extraction or manipulation operations. Use of the open source PostgreSQL also results in significant cost savings relative to commercial database engines.

A services layer implements the business logic that represents all of the functionality of the system, including the detailed tasks and workflows involved in ILS modules such as cataloging, circulation, acquisitions, a set of services for managing electronic resources, and another others for discovery and delivery of content. The services of this layer are exposed to higher-level applications through SOAP wrappers.

Sierra aims to be more open, by making use of more open source components, but more importantly, by providing libraries access to the data through standard SQL interfaces and to higher level functionality through a full set of published APIs and RESTful web services. Libraries may use the Sierra system entirely as delivered by Innovative; others may want to create and implement their own custom applications in different areas of the system. The Innovative has indicated that Sierra will promote the establishment of library developer communities where library programmers across institutions can collaborate to create new functionality based on the Sierra APIs, share their work, and to engage with the company's own developers.

THE VIRTUAL LIBRARY

A majority of the students use the internet for research. For several years now, librarians at university libraries have been building "virtual collections", lists of links to internet sites that they consider good enough to recommend. Most university libraries now have such lists on their web sites. Most of them are well-selected, well-maintained and well-organized. Professors too have been putting together lists of links to internet sites they can recommend to their students, posting the lists on their web site syllabus pages. They are like bibliographies, or like collections of actual books in an actual library. But they are really something new, a virtual library.

When a scholar or librarian selectively collects web sites - rather than just listing every site they can find—the list becomes a screened collection. Such a list is created and maintained by a specialist, in the same way a traditional librarian collects physical books and journals. Just as a traditional librarian doesn't buy every book or journal that's published, a virtual librarian wouldn't index every web site on the internet. The ability to discriminate between worthy and unworthy work is part is the job of a librarian, traditional or virtual.

After creating the virtual collection, the virtual librarian maintains it just as a regular librarian maintains a collection of physical books. Links often disappear or move, so they need to be regularly checked. A virtual librarian selectively adds to the collection, and gradually discards the oldest and least valuable links. It's a new concept, the virtual librarian who maintains the virtual library, but it's an important service that librarians and scholars can provide in their fields of specialization. In English literature, scholars who would in the past have published print bibliographies on an author, period, or genre, could maintain a collection of links to actual articles and books that can be viewed on the internet. The internet bibliographies are, in effect libraries of articles and books selected by the bibliographer.

As good web cataloging gets underway, more and more academic journals would begin to be published directly on the web. Free online access to good analysis of works of literature will benefit scholars and students the world over, particularly those in poor and under-developed countries.

The virtual library vision of the library of the future, conjures up a variety of images to the users. To some, the virtual library connotes the ultimate fear: obsolescence of the librarian. To others, the virtual library offers the promised land: the utopia of information access to all.

The most fundamental precept of the virtual library is the universal application of advanced high-speed computing and telecommunication capabilities to the access and delivery of information resources. Carried to its ultimate end, the virtual library offers a universe of information to any user, anywhere in the world, at any time of the day or night through the power of a personal computer with telecommunication capabilities.

EVOLUTION NOT REVOLUTION

Librarians have a long history of adopting technology to enhance services. They were early users of typewriters to produce catalog cards, then they photoduplicated card sets to replace individually typed cards. OCLC introduced the exchange of cataloging data and computer-printed catalog cards, then OPACs eliminated the production of catalog cards altogether. Today, LANs, cooperative networks, and Internet access to OPACs, around the nation and the world, have provided instant access for users, who may be present anywhere around the world.

The virtual library did not arise out of the Internet, it's been evolving since the 1960s. During that period, both private and public libraries initiated innovative long-term projects to facilitate access to their continually expanding hard-copy collections. These programs integrated emerging information technologies with traditional printed materials. Libraries were among the first users of alternative media, such as microfiche and microfilm, tapes, sound recordings, and electronic files, which were the predecessors of today's online commercial database systems.

Another technology advancement involved the growth of electronic databases of subject-specific information such as ERIC (Educational Resources Information Center) and INSPEC (the Database for Physics, Electronics and Computing). These electronic databases quickly became an important information tools for libraries seeking to expand their resources beyond what they could physically house in their own collections.

But most of these databases were indexes only, leaving the users to locate copies of the actual text themselves. By the mid-1970s, full-text databases had been developed, and the legal community was quick to integrate them into their research operations. Today, proprietary full-text databases such as LEXIS and WESTLAW remain essentially unchallenged in the scope, depth, and quality of information that they provide to legal researchers.

Early technology projects focused on the creation of electronic card catalogs known as OPACs (online public access catalogs). By the 1980s, the success of these ventures resulted in OPACs replacing traditional card catalogs in many academic, public, and special libraries. They also allowed libraries to engage in further cost-effective cooperative efforts to facilitate resource sharing and expand access to become subject-specific.

The virtual library is not something to be feared, nor is it the ultimate answer. It is another step in a long evolutionary process in which librarians, publishers, the scholarly community, and others have made information available for the advancement of knowledge, the joy of learning, and the mere satisfaction of human curiosity.

Electronic information systems followed a similar evolutionary path. Mediated online searching of SDC, Dialog, and BRS complemented the long standing use of print indexes and abstracts.

Direct end-user searching in libraries started with vendor systems such as BRS After Dark and stand-alone CD-ROMs, then added tape-loaded citation databases and networked CD-ROM databases.

Computerized access to bibliographic information led to the next logical step of evolution-electronic document delivery. Full-text products on CD-ROM, such as UMI Periodicals OnDisc, and rapid delivery through telefacsimile technology and, in limited cases, electronic file transfer, utilized by such services as CARL UnCover2 and Faxon Xpress, have brought the user one step closer to the virtual library. Today, a growing body of citation, full-text, numeric, and statistical databases are available to the user without ever entering the confines of a library building.

WEAKNESSES OF THE VIRTUAL LIBRARY CONCEPT

The first weakness of the virtual library is the lack of information on how to access or find the specific information needed by the user. This is often referred to as "navigating" in the electronic world.

The second critical element to the success of the virtual library is the willingness, and probably more importantly, the ability of libraries to contribute to the shared resources and services of the virtual library. The concept of the virtual library is just that—a concept. It's resource is the network of libraries and information providers that agree to provide access to the information resources within their control. This allegiance, partnership, or cooperative constitutes the "virtual collection," which is the composite of all the information available in all the libraries of the network.

This is not an alien concept to librarians. Cooperation and resource sharing are long-standing traditions among libraries. The concept of interlibrary loan has progressed from an informal process between librarians, to ILL standards and request forms, to the OCLC ILL subsystem, with over six million transactions per year. Library resource sharing has incorporated such concepts as cooperative collection development, reciprocal borrowing, and document delivery systems within local, state, and regional networks of member libraries. The local library has long established mechanisms to provide its patrons with access to resources outside its own walls. The mechanisms have changed in some cases from mail to UPS to fax, but the principle remains the same: to meet the information needs of the clientele efficiently. The emerging virtual library is merely another step in the same direction.

Not surprisingly, the third major pitfall of the virtual library is cost. Establishing and maintaining network services involve major commitments of resources, both financial and human. Internetworking incorporates a plethora of highly complex technical issues that must be resolved through standardization, compromise, and cooperative development.

As the network is expanded from a LAN to a WAN and eventually to an NREN, its cost grows exponentially and in parallel to its benefits, a growing circle of users are provided access to this virtual collection of resources. Funding the hardware, software, maintenance, and staffing needs of the network is a major issue, but it is no different from funding the cataloging, shelving, and preservation of paper resources.

IMPLEMENTATION CHALLENGES

Most of the early computer systems in libraries were developed for librarians' use. From bibliographic utilities to computerized online searching to automated ILL systems to online acquisitions systems, the end-user was primarily librarians and library support staff. With the advent of OPACs, CD-ROMs, and campus LANs, the focus of use shifted to the patron. However, with few exceptions, the user of these systems was expected to be in the library, using library hardware and software with assistance from library personnel.

The users cannot be expected to be present in the library to ask for assistance or to be available for traditional library instruction. The delivery of services to a primarily remote group of users through a networked system will mandate a fresh look at how libraries are organized, staffed, and funded to deliver services and information.

The concept of the NREN as an "electronic superhighway" that will instantly connect users to the information they seek, regardless of its location, is a popular concept. However it overlooks a major barrier to widespread use, which is the user's ability to identify the appropriate electronic resource in this vast sea of information and then retrieve needed information from it.

The final two areas that mandate the involvement of librarians in the emerging virtual library are the intellectual content and the technical design of this electronic library. Some of the questions that need to be answered while implementing a virtual library concept are:

- Who is going to decide what resources will be included in the virtual collection?
- How will these resources be organized?
- How will they fit into an overall collection development plan within a library, a consortium, or a larger user community?
- Will profit rule the decisions, or will librarians influence the balance in electronic information sources as they have always done in developing balanced print collections, reflecting all interests of their user population?
- How will the network be configured?
- Who will decide on the appropriate system architecture?

It is imperative that librarians become involved in the technical design issues of the virtual library, otherwise the librarians and the users will pay the price of the failure.

The problems confronting the continued development of the virtual library are not insignificant, but they are also not insurmountable. The key is that librarians must assume a leadership role in this development. We cannot totally abandon the shaping of the future of information access, retrieval, and delivery to the commercial sector.

Great progress is being made in libraries around the country through innovative and round breaking projects that are attempting to define the future of the virtual library—how it will operate, what it will include, who will have access, and of critical importance, who will have control.

VIRTUAL LIBRARY PROJECTS

A brief overview of a small selection of virtual library projects will convey not only the importance of these projects and what they have achieved, but also convince the users that all must become involved in this vital process.

One of the best known of these projects is a joint effort of Carnegie Mellon University and OCLC, called the Mercury Electronic Library. Begun in 1987-88, Project Mercury is using modern distributed computing to provide users with access to a wide variety of textual databases, including citation and abstract databases, as well as basic full-text reference sources. Project Mercury is exploring the technical design issues and working to expand available content through partnerships with journal publishers such as Elsevier and IEEE.

The University of Iowa Libraries Information Arcade is focusing on how best to support the use of information technologies for research, teaching, and scholarly communication. The system incorporates text, data, software programs, graphics, music, and digital video files, as well as capabilities for electronic mail and access to other library catalogs, electronic journals, newsletters, and academic discussion lists.

Cornell University and Xerox Corporation have formed a partnership with support from the Commission on Preservation and Access. The goal of the CLASS project is to test a prototype system for recording brittle books as digital images and producing, on demand, high-quality and archivally sound paper replacements. In addition to the obvious preservation issues, the project also seeks to investigate some of the issues surrounding scanning, storing, retrieving and providing access to digital images in a network environment.

In another project, North Carolina State University, the National Agricultural Library, and eleven land grant university libraries are collaborating in the NCSU Digitized Document Transmission Project. The aim of this project is to explore techniques for electronic receipt, display, distribution and output of digitized library research materials.

These four projects represent only a small sampling of the efforts of libraries around the world to explore, enhance, and shape the future of the virtual library. They are doing what librarians do: seeking new ways of providing information to their users.

CONCLUSION

The virtual library is not the ultimate answer to everyone's information needs. It is merely another step in a dynamic and evolutionary process. The traditional print library and traditional library services will not disappear. But librarians must accept and adapt to the introduction of new techniques and systems. The enormous potential of the virtual library must be recognized to address the issues involved in its creation, and these new systems and services need to be integrated into the libraries, for the benefit of the librarians and the users.

Several years ago, the technology industry heralded the death of the book at the hands of the newest technology marvel, the CD-ROM. Libraries will continue to defy the predictions of their demise and to be a driving force in information storage and delivery long after the Internet is replaced by the next generation of information technology solution.

REFERENCES

Arms, William Y. et al. (1992). The Design of the Mercury Electronic Library. *EDUCOM Review*, 27 (November/December 1992), 38-41.

Casorso, Tracy M. (1992). NCSU Digitized Document Transmission Project: Improving Access to Agricultural Libraries. *The Electronic Library*, 10 (October 1992), 271-273.

Commission on Preservation and Access (1992). Cornell/Xerox/CPA Joint Study in Digital Preservation-Progress Report Number 2. *The Electronic Library*, 10(3), 155-163.

University of Iowa Libraries (1993). Arcade Provides Internet Access. *Information Arcade Bulletin*, 4.

9

Status of Electronic & ICT Infrastructure in Public Libraries in Chandigarh City

Parveen Kumar

INTRODUCTION

Chandigarh, the City beautiful is a very small union territory and a planned city designed by Le Corbusier, the French architecture. The city is known for its heritage collection and monuments. Obviously, one of the oldest government public library, i.e., T.S. Central State Library, Sector 17, Chandigarh is known for its structure, design and its collection. The UNESCO public library manifesto states that a public library is the local gateway to education, culture and information. With the spread of western education the public libraries concept took a shape in 19th century since 1808 when the British Government decided to register libraries, which would be given copies of books published from the funds for encouragement of literature for the use of the public. With the advent of education and culture, public libraries in India grew in numbers and also played an important role in country's struggle for independence (Banerjee, K.K.). In post independence era, the concept of library and librarianship has undergone sea changes to reach this present stage.

Today, we are living in the information age and ICT provides hope to overcome the barriers of social and geographical isolations, increase access to information and education and enable the people to participate in the making of the decisions that have an impact on their lives. Public libraries are not far from using the information and communication technology infrastructure. It has changed the way and the libraries are undergoing radical changes. Many library services and information routines are being performed with more speed, accuracy and efficiency by Information and Communication Technology. This technology has proved its success in the field of library collection, organization and distribution. Many new services have been initiated with the help of ICT.

Public libraries are challenged to provide greater information access and improved levels of service, while coping with the pace of technological change and ever increasing budget pressure. Thus, the study focuses on the current status of available information and communication technology infrastructure in public libraries in Chandigarh City.

STATEMENT OF THE PROBLEM

Information and Communication Technology is not new to a number of public libraries. Today, the current information is acquired, organized, disseminated and accessed with ICT. To have the right information at the right time one needs to have an information and communication technology infrastructure. It is also important that staff working in libraries should have necessary skill and positive attitude towards technology. The problem upon which the study is based is to know the current status of information and communication technology infrastructure that is used in these two public libraries, i.e., T.S. Central State Library (CSL) and Divisional Library, South DL(S).

OBJECTIVES OF THE STUDY

The objectives of the study include:

1. To know the current state of information technology infrastructure available in public libraries in Chandigarh.
2. To examine the status of automation of public libraries in Chandigarh City.
3. To examine the barriers in implementing Information and Communication Technology infrastructure and its application.
4. To know the skilled manpower available in public libraries in Chandigarh City.
5. To provide suggestions and recommendations for implementing ICT infrastructure.

METHODOLOGY

As mentioned previously the main objectives of the study is to determine the current status and use of information and communication technology infrastructure in public libraries. Therefore, it is an applied research and aimed at finding the solution to specific problem. In this study the questionnaire, was used to collect the data from the aforesaid public libraries. Questionnaire was designed keeping in view the objectives of the study. The collected data was analyzed and has been presented below in the form of tables.

RESULTS AND DISCUSSIONS

1. General Information of Public Libraries

Table 1 provides the general information about the two major public libraries in Chandigarh. The data shows that the CSL is the oldest library in Chandigarh, established in 1955 under the scheme of Govt. of India, "Promotion of Art and Culture",

Table 1

Public Libraries	Central State Library (CSL), Sector-17, Chd.	Divisional Library (South) [DL(S)], Sector 34, Chd.
Year of establishment	1955	1995
Name of the Library	Tirlok Singh Central State Library	Divisional Library (South)
Website Address	www.cslchd.gov.in	www.statelibrary34.gov.in
Total Number of Librarians	9	8
Total Number of Semi Professional Staff	8	8
Name of the Librarian Incharge	Mr. Suraj Parkash Nagpal	Ms. Anju Gupta

Whereas the Divisional Library (South) was established in 1995 by Chandigarh Administration to provide the library facilities to the southern sectors. The table also provides the information related to the website address, total library staff, semi professional staff along with the name of the librarians In charge.

2. Library Collection and Membership

Table 2

Collection/Membership	CSL	DL(S)
Books	2,28,651	97360
Periodicals Received (Annually)	160	81
CD-ROMs	1270	6200
Membership	38327	11560

Table 2 indicates the total library collection and membership of the public libraries. Table shows that total book collection in CSL has 2, 28,651 whereas DL (S) has 97,360. Table further reveals that CSL annually received 160 periodicals whereas DL(S) received 81. DL(S) has maximum number of CD-ROMs, i.e., 6200 whereas CSL has 1270. At present the membership of the CSL is 38327 whereas DL(S) membership is 11560.

3. Availability of Electronic Gadgets in Public Libraries

Table 3 provides the information regarding the available electronic gadgets available in the public libraries. Table shows that both the public libraries have telephone,

Table 3

Electronic Gadgets	CSL	DL(S)
Telephone	✓	✓
Fax	✓	✓
Reprographic Machine	✓	✓
Microfiche		
Barcode Scanner	✓	✓
CD Player	✓	✓
Film Projector	✓	
Scanner	✓	✓
TV	✓	✓
VCR/VCP	✓	✓
Projector	✓	✓
Bar Code Generator	✓	✓
CD-net Device		
Microfilm Machine		
Internet Connectivity	✓	✓
Multimedia System	✓	✓
Teleconferencing Device		

Table 3 provides the information regarding the available electronic gadgets available in the public libraries. Table shows that both the public libraries have telephone, fax, reprographic machine, barcode scanner, CD player, scanner, TV, VCR/VCP, projector, bar code generator, internet connectivity and multimedia system. Regarding film projector only CSL-17 have such facility. Microfilm, microfiche, CD-net device and teleconferencing device have not been found even in the single public library.

4. Hardware Facilities Available In Public Libraries

It was deemed that the availability of computers, internet and library software are

Table 4

Hardware Items	CSL Qty.	DL(S) Qty.
Server	1	1
Personal Computer	33	35
Pentinum III	6	23
Pentinum IV	27	12
OPAC Terminals for Users	2	5
Computer with CD Rom Drive	33	34
Computers with CD Writer	15	24
Computers with Combo Drive	2	10
Bar Code Scanner	3	4
UPS	2 (5KV each)	2 (5KV)

Table 4 indicates the number of computer systems available with both the public libraries. Table shows that maximum number of computer systems is available with the DL(S), i.e., 35, followed by CD writer, i.e., 24 and followed by bar code scanner, i.e., 4. CSL has a less number of computer systems as compare to DL(S).

5. Software Facility Available In Public Libraries

Software is the general term used to describe the type of programmes or lists of instructions, which are needed to enable the computer system to carry out the necessary processing. In other words software is nothing but a collection of programmes. Softwares are of two types (i) system software and (ii) application software.

The operating system is software that controls the entire operation of the computer system. The CSL has Linux and Windows operating system whereas DL(S) has Windows operating system. Besides the operating systems both the libraries are using LIBSYS software system for automating their housekeeping operations.

Table 5

Software	CSL	DL(S)
Operating System		
MS-DOS		
Windows		✓
Unix		
Linux	✓	
Software packages		
Libsys	✓	✓
Techlibplus		
Any other		

6. Status of Automated Housekeeping Operations in Public Libraries

Table 6

Name of Public Libraries	Status of Automation	Software Used for Library Automation	Automated Areas
CSL	Partly computerized	LIBSYS, VERSION 5.0 Web OPAC Enabled	Cataloguing , Circulation, Serial Control, OPAC & Web OPAC
DL(S)	Partly computerized	LIBSYS, VERSION 4.0 WEB OPAC Enabled	Cataloguing, Circulation, Stock Verification, OPAC & Web OPAC

The process of library automation in CSL was started in 1995 using the TechLib Basis plus Software. In the year 2003 due to some technical problems the CSL changed the software with LIBSYS 5.0 Version which is an integrated multi user library management system and web OPAC enabled. The LIBSYS consists of modules on acquisition, cataloguing, circulation, serials, article indexing and OPAC. Retrospective conversion of bibliographic records has been completed and more than 2, 28, 651 bibliographic records of books and 1200 CD-ROMs are available in the library which can be accessed through LIBSYS OPAC. The library is partly computerized and the automation of the other modules is under process.

The process of automation in DL(S) was started in 2003 using the LIBSYS Software 4.0 Version. The library is also partly computerized and the automated areas include cataloguing, circulation and stock verification. The automation of the other modules is also under process. Retrospective conversion of the bibliographic records has been completed and more than 65,000 bibliographic records of books and 2000 CD-ROMs can be accessed through LIBSYS OPAC.

7. Skilled ICT Trained Staff Available in Public Libraries

Table 7

ICT Trained Staff	CSL 17	DL(S) 34
Professional		
Skilled	3	2
Semi-skilled	2	6
Unskilled	12	8

Table 7 indicates that maximum number of ICT skilled staff has been found in the library of CSL, i.e., 3 whereas in DL(S) the number of skilled staff is 2. Regarding semi-skilled maximum number is found in the library of DL(S) i.e., 6, whereas in CSL the number of semi skilled staff is 2. Regarding unskilled staff maximum number has been found in the library of CSL, i.e., 12, followed by 8 in DL(S).

8. Services Provided by Public Libraries

Table 8

Services	CSL	DL (S)
Bibliographic	✓	✓
CAS/SDI	✓	
CD-Rom/DVD/VCD	✓	✓
Computer for MS word service	✓	
Guidance to Library & Information Science Students	✓	✓
Indexing	✓	✓
Infotel	✓	

Inter Library Loan	✓	✓
Internet	✓	
Library at your doorstep (for senior citizens)	✓	
Library awareness drives	✓	
Mobile library	✓	
Monthly display of books on particular topics	✓	✓
Newspaper clipping service	✓	✓
Personal assistance for Internet searchers	✓	
Reading room	✓	✓
Reference Service	✓	✓
Renewal & reservation of books of telephone	✓	
Reprographic	✓	✓
Time slot booking for internet by telephone	✓	

The table shows that maximum numbers of services are provided by the CSL-17 to their users whereas DL(S) provides very few services. CAS/SDI, MS word, Infotel, Internet, Library at your doorstep, library awareness drive, mobile library, personal assistance to internet searchers, renewal and reservation on phone services are not provided by DL(S).

9. Barriers to ICT in Public Libraries

The major barriers to ICT and its application to public libraries are the lack of professional ICT staff/system administrator and future vision. Public libraries do not lack the financial support from their parent home. Although, skilled staff is managing the Computer Servers and application software's, yet they are lacking the professionalism of ICT, which can provide more and better services to the users with the help of latest and upcoming information and communication technology infrastructure.

CONCLUSION AND SUGGESTIONS

The study indicates that there is no shortage of budget in these public libraries but they are lacking the right direction in implementing and application of ICT in their libraries. The parent body should appoint some ICT professional/ System administrator who can suggest them what to do? And how to do? The library professionals moreover and enhance should be sent for the ICT training so they can develop self skills.

REFERENCES

Banerjee, K.K. (2006). *Public libraries in India-present scenario: A statistical approach.* Paper published in National Seminar on Public Libraries Services: Yesterday, Today and Tomorrow held at Kolkata from Feb. 20-21st Feb. pp. 31.73.

Ramana, P. Venkata (2004). *Information technology applications in libraries,* New Delhi, Ess Ess Publications.

Saffady, William (1989). Library automation: An overview. *Library Trends,* 37(3), 269-81.

UNESCO. (1974). *UNESCO Public Library Manifesto.*

SECTION - II
COLLECTION DEVELOPMENT AND ACCESS OF E-RESOURCES

10

Collection Development of Electronic Resources

Anil Kumar Siwach

INTRODUCTION

Information is an invaluable resource. Libraries and Information Centres have always strived to provide the relevant information to its users in various formats. With the advancements in Information Communication Technologies (ICTs) the possibilities of instantaneous dissemination and access to information have been created. The ICT and particularly the Web have transformed the way we create, transmit, store, process and manage information. In the recent past electronic information resources have grown tremendously and their usage is gaining momentum day by day. The modern libraries are acquiring electronic resources to fulfill the requirements of different users in a better and efficient way. For achieving this, the libraries need to select, evaluate, organize and disseminate the e-resources in the best possible way.

E-RESOURCES

Electronic resources refer to those materials that require

computer access, whether through a personal computer, mainframe, or handheld mobile device. It is also referred to any electronic product that delivers a collection of data, be it text referring to full text bases, electronic journals, image collections, other multimedia products and numerical, graphical or time based, as a commercially available title that has been published with an aim to being marketed. They may either be accessed remotely via the Internet or locally. According to International Coalition of Library Consortia (ICOLC) (1998), it is a broad term that encompasses abstracting and indexing services, electronic journals and other full text materials, the offerings of information aggregators, article delivery services, etc.

E-resources can be categorized into various types. Some of the frequently encountered types include:

- E-journals
- E-books
- ETDs
- Full-text (aggregated) databases
- Indexing and abstracting databases
- Reference databases
- Numeric and statistical databases
- Free Internet resources
- E-images
- E-audio/visual resources

WHY E-RESOURCES

The reasons for actually embarking on the purchasing of electronic resources are generally accepted because of the advantages offered by these resources over the print resources. Some of the advantages of e-resources which make them obvious choice for acquiring them for the users include:

- **Multi-access :** A networked product can provide multiple points of access to multiple simultaneous users round the clock (24 hours a day, 7 days a week).

- **Speed :** An electronic resource is lot quicker to browse or search, to extract information from, to integrate that information into other material and to cross-search or reference between different publications.
- **Storage :** The drawback of physical storage inherent in traditional libraries is not a problem with e-resources due to reduction in hardware cost.
- **Interactive :** It is interactive and allows interaction between publisher and user.
- **Ease of usability :** E-resources are easy to use and search.
- **Use of multimedia :** E-resource can consist of mixed media like text, images, audio, video, animation, etc.
- **Affordability :** As compared to print resources, the resources in electronic form are less costly in the long run.
- **Up-to-date :** Updating of e-resources is easier as compared to print counterparts.

COLLECTION DEVELOPMENT

Harrod's Librarian's Glossary defines collection development as "the process of planning a stock acquisition programme not simply to cater for immediate needs but to build a coherent and reliable collection over a number of years, to meet the objectives of the services". According to Evans and Saponaro (2005) it is "the process of identifying the strengths and weaknesses of a library's materials collection in terms of patron needs and community resources, and attempting to correct existing weaknesses, if any".

It is the process of planning and acquiring a balanced collection of library materials over a period of years, based on an ongoing assessment of the information needs of the library's clientele, analysis of usage statistics, and demographic projections (Reitz, 2012).Collections are developed by librarians and library staff by buying or otherwise acquiring materials over a period, based on assessment of the information needs of the library's users. In addition to ongoing materials acquisition, library collection development includes:

- the creation of policies to guide material selection
- replacement of worn or lost materials
- removal (weeding) of materials no longer needed in the collection
- planning for new collections or collection areas
- cooperative decision-making with other libraries or within library consortia (Wikipedia, 2012)

The purpose of collection development is to find out the users information/document needs to:

- fulfill the library's obligation to the user community to provide relevant and nascent information.
- find out the users information/document needs,
- select and acquire documents that are really useful to the clientele,
- adopt systematic and judicious spending on document collection, keeping the objectives of the service in mind, and
- periodically review the collection for weeding out unwanted and outdated documents from it.

COLLECTION DEVELOPMENT POLICY

A collection development policy is a formal written statement of the principles guiding a library's selection of materials, including the criteria used in making selection and deselection decisions (fields covered, degrees of specialization, levels of difficulty, languages, formats, balance, etc.) and policies concerning gifts and exchanges. An unambiguously worded collection development policy can be very helpful in responding to challenges from pressure groups. (Reitz, 2012)

A written collection development policy for any library is necessary to guide the selection, acquisition, deselection, preservation and provision of access for electronic materials. The Washington State Library in its statement on collection development highlights the benefits of a written collection development policy as given below:

- The policy represents an agreement with the entire community of potential users of what they can or cannot expect the library to purchase and maintain in the collection.
- It corresponds to actual community needs because it incorporates the information and decisions that resulted from long-range or strategic planning.
- The policy is a primary document in defending against potential censorship. It displays the research, planning, and impartial judgment applied to selecting materials.
- It guides staff so they can continually focus on identified priorities. It moves the selection process away from individual preferences or bias. It identifies who is responsible for selection and how requests from the public will be handled.
- It balances the selection process by setting criteria or standards for selection that result in quality choices.
- It provides for continuity throughout staff and/or board changes in personnel.
- It serves as the framework for budget allocations and offers accountability for the use of funds.
- It functions as an assessment tool for determining how well the library is meeting its goals for serving the community.

BUILDING AN E-RESOURCE COLLECTION

Developing an e-resource collection over a period of time can be a daunting task. Some of the steps involved in collection development of e-resources are similar to those of print resources but there is also a certain degree of differences involved. The steps for building an e-resource collection are highlighted in the following text but these steps are not all inclusive.

Formulation of Collection Development Policy

The processes of selection, acquisition, renewal/ cancellation of e-resources in a library become easier if there is a proper collection development policy in place. Such a policy acts as a blueprint for the selectors maintain uniformity in procedures. It provides a framework for decision-making and acts as a planning tool. The collection development policy should be review and revised periodically to maintain currency.

Even though the policies will vary from library to library, there are some common components which should be a concern of each and every library while formulating a collection development policy for e-resources. These are being highlighted here briefly.

- The mission and vision of the library should be reflected in the policy of the library. These acts as guiding force for formulating the other policy issues.
- Identification of present collection's strength and weaknesses so as to help in making future decisions.
- It should describe the reader community and their needs.
- Appropriate selection tools should be identified.
- Provide selection criteria and guidelines.
- It should have general guidelines for licensing requirements.
- There should be guidelines for weeding, cancellation, deselection and preservation of resources.
- Support cooperative or collaborative collection development activities.

Establishment of Budget

A budget is the blueprint for the upcoming fiscal year. It can be defined as an allocation of financial resources to meet specific objectives (Burnette, 2008). Budgets are usually decided on an annual basis. Establishment of budgets for e-resources is similar to that of print resources but there are some budgeting issues relating to e-resources which should be kept in consideration. These include higher cost, price fluctuations, different pricing models, decision making responsibility, inflation rates, etc.

Discovery of the Resource

With the expansion and development of e-resources the

discovery, selection and evaluation of e-resources for acquisition has become a challenging work for the librarians. The discovery of e-resources is challenging due to rapid increase in the availability of resources. Some tools can help in making sound judgment regarding selection. Important tools/ methods include:

- Trial offers for a limited period
- Demonstrations from the publisher or vendor
- Suggestions by patrons
- Vendor exhibits at conferences/ seminars/ symposia
- Discussion list/ forums
- Experience of current users/ subscribers
- Publisher/ Vendor's catalogue
- Published review in various print and electronic sources

Selection and Evaluation of E-Resources

The core collection development function of any library is the selection of resources. The selection and acquisition of e-resources is similar to the selection of print resources in many ways and it differs in various aspects. But the primary objective remains the same-satisfaction of the user's needs. The factors such as quality, relevance, authority, coverage, use, cost and audience are equally relevant for e-resources as for the print resources. While selecting e-resources the librarians have to keep in consideration many more factors like easy and quick accessibility, continuous content evaluation, organization of content, interface, technological and legal issues. Each library has varied needs depending on the type of clientele, parent organisation and the kinds of services offered. Thus, having a clearly defined set of selection criteria can help guide an organization/ library through the selection and evaluation of process.

Some of the important criteria to be considered for evaluation and selection of e-resources are as described in the coming text:

Content/ Subject: The content of an e-resource varies depending upon the type of resource being considered. For content evaluation the selector assess how many titles are included in the resource, compare it to the existing subscription, evaluate its coverage, see availability of retrospective content and check the authoritativeness of the resource.

Design and usability : The overall design of the interface, its functionality, ease of use and administrative capabilities is taken into consideration. There are certain questions to be answered for this. Is it possible to do basic and advanced search? Can the searches be refined, limited, expanded, sorted, saved, exported and edited.

Currency : Another important issue is the currency of the resource. The rate at which content is added and updated effects its selection. The selector sees if there is a time lag between the print and electronic publication.

Reputation : The reputation of the publisher or the aggregator is also important factor affecting the selection process.

Technical Requirements : The technical requirements for accessing the e-resources, compatibility of the product with existing hardware and software, requirement of training in use, etc. are considered.

Accessibility : The accessibility of the e-resource through interlinking with other resources and content is necessary. The implementation of an OpenURL link resolver can help the end user to find the full text of an article and to identify other pertinent and relevant resources.

Licensing Agreement : The licensing terms affects the accessibility of the resource. It is important to see how many sites does the license permit, whether remote or off-campus access is permitted, whether the inter-library lending (ILL) of the e-resource is permitted and is the perpetual access available. The responsibilities of both vendor and the user should be highlighted in the license agreement.

Pricing : There are basically two ways of pricing e-resources-one-time purchase or an annual subscription. Another option which can be considered is the pay-per-use. Acquiring resources through consortia can be beneficial as special offers may be provided by the content providers.

Identification of Various Pricing Options

There are various pricing models provided by the content providers. It depends which one suits a particular library. The pricing model may depend on the type of the product. The products include e-journals, e-books, full-text databases, Abstracting & Indexing databases, etc. The size of the library and the number of users can also affect the price of an electronic information product. Special pricing offers are provided by the content providers for consortia. Purchasing e-resources through consortia can be a less costly affair as heavy discounts can be possible. A library opts for bundled sets or a pay-per-view option depends on the usability of the product.

Licencing of E-Resources

The contract license must be mutually acceptable to both the parties and it should be finalized after negotiation. The librarians should be able to identify the issues that need to be addressed when negotiating a contract. Some important provisions which should be kept in consideration when negotiating and reviewing contracts with vendors are as listed below:

Content : It should be clear from the contract whether the library is acquiring the content forever or purchasing the rights to access the product.

Patron Use : There must be provisions in the agreement that all patrons of the library can use the resource, including members of the public. Under exceptional circumstances a resource should be considered which limits use by password or some other device to certain members.

Cost of Access : The cost of access points and number of simultaneous users should be appropriate to the projected use of the resource.

Access : Agreements which allow access from remote networked locations such as homes or businesses with authentication through a proxy server should be given preference.

Archiving : Strong preference should be given to agreements that allow the library to have access to, or own the content of, the last-held version of the database i.e. perpetual access should be provided.

Fair Use : Fair use as defined by University and Library guidelines must be permitted within the context of any agreement. It is preferable that fair use provisions include interlibrary loan privileges.

Confidentiality : The confidentiality and privacy of all library patrons must be protected.

Contractual obligations : The obligations of both the parties should be clearly stated.

Ordering of the Electronic Resources

When the license has been negotiated, reviewed and signed, the next step is the ordering of the e-resource. Technical information like the IP address, etc. is communicated to the content provider for activating the resource. Once the access to an e-resource is activated the acquisition department communicates with other departments such as cataloguing, reference service, etc. The payment is made only after the access to the e-resource is available.

Delivery of the Electronic Resources/ Provision of Access

After the e-resource has been acquired the major priority is to provide the access to the users. The resource needs to be integrated into some system by which the reader can easily find it and access it (Lee, 2004). Sometimes the content provider offers training in the use of the resource once it is acquired by the library.

CONCLUSION

Clifford A. Lynch has written that "the impact of the transition to electronic information, and particularly to networked electronic information and communication, goes far beyond the library and promises major changes in a wide range of social, institutional, economic, legal and political structures." The fundamental role of the library has shifted from warehousing of the information resources to filtering and providing access to seemingly infinite amount of available information. The developments in ICT are changing the concept of document from print to electronic and thus the collection development policy need to be modified to include the digital content in a collection. E-resources present a number of challenges not encountered with the selection and acquisition of traditional analogue materials and it is advisable for the library to develop clear policies and processes for the selection and management of such resources. These will provide clarity to staff and ensure that e-resources within the library are developed with due consideration of cost, technical feasibility, licensing, access and preservation requirements, and constraints.

REFERENCES

Burnette, Elizabeth S. (2008). Budgeting and acquisitions. In Collins, Maria D.D. and Carr, Patrick L. (Eds). *Managing the transition from print to electronic journals and resources: A guide for library and information professionals* (pp. 3-27). New York: Routledge.

Evans, G.E. & Sapronaro, M.Z. (2005). *Developing Library and Information Center Collections* (5th ed.). Westport, CT: Libraries Unlimited.

Ferguson, Christine L. (2008). Criteria for selecting and evaluating e-resources. In Collins, Maria D.D. and Carr, Patrick L. (Eds). *Managing the transition from print to electronic journals and resources: A guide for library and information professionals* (pp. 29-44). New York: Routledge.

International Coalition of Library Consortia (1998). *Statement of current perspective and preferred practices for the selection and purchase of electronic information.* Available at:

Intner, Shiela S. (Ed). (2009). *Studies in Library and Information Science* 4V. New Delhi: Pentagon Press.

Lee, Stuart D & Boyle, Francis. (2004). *Building an electronic resource collection: A practical guide* (2nd ed.). London: Facet Publishing.

Lynch, Clifford A. (1999). Recomputerizing the lsibrary: New roles for information technology in a time of networked information. In Cheryl LaGuardia (Ed) *Recreating the Academic Library: Breaking virtual ground.* New York: Neal-Schuman.

Prytherch, Ray (1999). *Harrod's Librarians' Glossary and Reference Book: A Directory of over 9600 Terms, Organizations, Projects and Acronyms in the Areas of Information Management, Library Science, Publishing and Archive* (9th ed.). Aldershot: Gower Pub Co.

Reitz, J.M. (2012). "Online dictionary of library and information science." Retrieved from http://www.abc-clio.com/ODLIS/odlis_c.aspx

Washington State Library. Collection Development. Retrieved from http://www.sos.wa.gov/library/libraries/libDev/downloads/trustee/19-collectiondevelopment.pdf

Wikipedia (2012). *Library collection development*. Retrieved from http://en.wikipedia.org/wiki/Library_collection_development

11

Preserving the Bits for Future: Need, Objectives, Issues and Challenges

Sunder Singh Tanwar

INTRODUCTION

Preservation is a continuous process of creating, maintaining the best environment possible for the storage and use of an artifact to prevent damage or degradation and to enable it to live as long as possible. Conservation and restoration are its sub-activities, which involve specific treatments to an object to stabilize and preserve it for the future, or to restore it to a state of former glory. The digital birth of cultural content and conversion of analogue originals into bits has opened new panorama and extended horizons in every direction, providing access and opportunities for new audiences, enlightenment, entertainment and education in ways incredible a mere two decades ago. In the information age, our digital data needs to be accessible where and when we want it. To preserve digital information over the long term requires that this information remains accessible, understandable and usable by the coming generations.

The research community is cognizant that we need to preserve our most important digital collections and thus digital preservation is critical for research and education. In addition to digital research collections, many of us also care about saving digital photos, videos and the contents of our hard drives, although we may not think of this as digital preservation. Digital preservation becomes more imperative issue when it comes to preserve the national heritage and other historic and intellectual documents, manuscripts, etc.

Information and Communication Technology (ICT) is an effective tool for providing access to information 24x7x365, as needed by the information society. With availability of products and services in digital forms, major libraries and archives of the world are earmarking larger portions of their budgetary allocation for either procuring or accessing digital contents. The enduring accessibility of digital resources must be assured, in order to justify the investments in digital resources.

The librarians and preservationists are apprehensive about the digital preservation ever since the first computer was introduced and its output found its way into the libraries. They are concerned with the abiding digital preservation for traditional information materials and have recognized formal preservation programmes that include allocation of resources for preservation, precautionary measures to detain deterioration of materials, counteractive measures to restore the usability of selected traditional materials and preservation needs in the programme planning (Tanwar, 2012).

Preservation of digital information requires more constant and ongoing attention towards effort, time and money to handle rapid technological and organisation advances than preservation of the print media. Traditional forms of print media are intrinsically limited by their nature, scope and means of production, and are now being superseded by emerging digital media techniques. Indeed, while we are still able to read our written heritage created thousands of years ago, digital information created and stored on digital media merely a few years back is in hazard of being vanished. Presently, some of the archived objects like research papers, books, newspapers, government and corporate documents, etc. are in danger of becoming unreadable. This is happening due to the rapid advancement in technology day-by-day. We need to upgrade digital media from time to time and to change form of various preserved works from one form to another.

DEFINITION OF DIGITAL PRESERVATION

Digital preservation means transforming, storing, archiving various forms of media that has been transferred to a digital format and getting a long term access to it with an aim to ensure that past and present information is accessible in digital format to subsequent generations beyond the limits of media failure or technological change. These materials may be records created during the day-to-day business of an organisation; "born-digital" materials created for a specific purpose (e.g. research outputs); or the products of digitisation projects. Born digital materials are those which are not intended to have an analogue equivalent, either as the originating source or as a result of conversion to analogue form. For further details, we can consider the following definitions.

Digital preservation can be understood as a set of managed activities necessary to ensure continued access to digital materials for as long as necessary. It combines policies, strategies and actions to ensure access to reformatted and born digital content regardless of the challenges of media failure and technological change. The goal of digital preservation is the accurate rendering of authenticated content over time (Mark and Laura, 2008).

"Digital preservation combines policies, strategies and actions to ensure access to reformatted and born digital content regardless of the challenges of media failure and technological change. The goal of digital preservation is the accurate rendering of authenticated content over time." (ALA 2007:2).

"The act of maintaining information, in a correct and Independently Understandable form, over the Long Term." (CCSDS 2002: 1-11).

"All activities concerning the maintenance and care for curation of digital or electronic objects, in relation to both storage and access.

Long-term means five years or more; short-term is less than five years." (Saur, 2006).

Digital preservation is the planning, resource allocation, and application of preservation methods, tools and technologies necessary to ensure that digital information of continuing value remains accessible and usable for as long as they are needed (Tanwar, 2012).

Thus, a clear and specific definition of digital preservation refers to the series of managed activities like the planning, resource allocation, and application of preservation methods, tools and technologies necessary to ensure continued access to reformatted and born digital materials regardless of the challenges of media failure and technological change for as long as necessary.

NEED FOR DIGITAL PRESERVATION

Data is the natural resource of the information age and is fragile and needs to be preserved just like we need to take care of natural resources such as rain, forests and the environment in the physical world. Preserving valued data in the information age is to ensure that it will continue to enlighten and enrich our world for the foreseeable future.

As defined by Jones and Beagrie (2002), digital preservation refers to the series of managed activities necessary to ensure continued access to digital materials for as long as necessary. The ease with which digital information can be created, pooled with the gigantic increase in computer processing power and network bandwidth, has led to the explosion of a vast amount of 'born-digital' data, especially in science, engineering and technology, where petabytes of data are being generated by scientific instruments on a daily basis. This overwhelming data deluge has forced preservationists to address the issue of long term preservation and curation so as to ensure that data generated today can survive the changes of technology and can be accessed in the future.

OBJECTIVES OF DIGITAL PRESERVATION

The main objectives of digital preservation are as under:

- Identification and selection of material for worth preserving and metadata.
- Providing continuous access to preserved material.
- Comply with prevailing community standards and ensuring authenticity of preserved digital materials.
- Preserve physical media to avoid physical damage/deterioration by ensuring an environmental control.
- Shifting the digital information to newer and fresher format, if required.
- Achieving co-ordination of all efforts that are undertaken for preservation worldwide in order to achieve more synergy, to avoid redundancy and to reduce cost.
- Focusing stakeholders on issues that desperately need attention in area of digital preservation and the action has to be taken at outset rather than at its secondary stages.
- Requisite training to working team members for developing and operating digital archive.

EXTENDED BENEFITS OF DIGITISATION OVER TRADITIONAL APPORACH

Digitised materials have the following benefits over the traditional documents:

- To consult a printed document physically located in library, the user has to visit the library. On the contrary, the users need not to go to the library physically to consult the digitized documents.
- The paper documents are accessible to only one user at a time. Providing online access to the digitised material, people from all over the world could gain access to the same information.
- Thus, the user has to spend lot of time and money to consult the physical document and that too in the limited library hours. One can access it round the clock free of cost and that too without wasting any time.

- High-bandwidth Internet connections together with appropriate ICT equipments make it possible to preserve the original document to avoid usual wear and tear. It is not possible in case of printed documents.
- The required document may be flawlessly available at various places and centres. Which library and information centre holds the required material is not known to the users and they remain unaware of the richness of the holdings of libraries and information centres. Online accessibility to the holdings of libraries/information centres may even be improved by digitising the available resources. The user is able to use any search term belonging to the word or phrase of the entire collection. Digitised material will provide access to its resources through user friendly interface.
- The increasing proliferation of digital information, combined with the considerable challenges, detailed elsewhere in this handbook, associated with ensuring continued access to digital information, means that it is imperative that there be concerted action to overcome these challenges. While there is as yet only largely anecdotal evidence, it is certain that many potentially valuable digital materials have already been lost. Some of these may have disappeared without ever having reached a wider audience than the original creators (see note). At the very least, this constitutes failure fully to maximise the potential benefits of the investment expended in creating these digital materials.
- An exact copy of the original material can be made any number of times without any degradation in quality. This is not possible in case of printed documents.
- Whereas traditional libraries are limited by storage space, digital libraries have the potential to store much more information, simply because digital information requires very little physical space to contain them. When the library had no space for extension digitization is the only solution.
- A particular library having digitized documents can provide the

link to any other resources of other digital library very easily thus a seamlessly integrated resource sharing can be achieved.

- The cost of maintaining digitised documents is much lower than that of traditional documents. A traditional library must spend large sums of money paying for staff, book maintains, rent, and additional books. Digital libraries do away with these fees.

CORE ISSUES IN DIGITAL PRESERVATION

For digital preservationists, a prime concern is that data might be kept perfectly secure and complete in all respects which rely on the interaction between the digital preservation environment and wider organisational objectives and procedural issues. Core issues in digital preservation are Technical issues, financial and economical issues including costs and governance issues, legal obligations, collection management, auditing requirements, strategies and policies are some of the major issues in digital preservation.

1. Technical Issues

The pace of change in digital technology, its applications and file formats has accelerated in recent years. A one or two order of magnitude improvement in power, speed, efficiency, or cost per value has occurred every several years in areas such as CPU speed, memory chip density, storage device capacity, video processing rate, and data transmission rate. New standards and protocols are being defined on a regular basis for file formats, compression techniques, hardware components, and storage media etc. Technological obsolescence occurs if computer hardware, storage media, and file formats become obsolete before the useful life of the data that is stored on and in them ends.

We expect computers to get faster and more capable and the computer manufacturers have added speed and features along the way that inadvertently obsolete some fundamental characteristics of our older computer hardware. The increased capabilities of the new computer will often require the obsolescence of older one, much like

64-bit processors obsolete 32-bit processors, which in turn obsolete 16-bit processor computers, accessories and software that was designed to run on them.

Storage Media obsolescence is a direct consequence of the relentless advances of new and more capable storage devices. Computer storage media double themselves in capacity and half their access times every 18 months and their forerunner become obsolete as their successors become smaller, denser, easier to read and faster in processing speed at lower cost.

Format obsolescence is caused by its native application becoming obsolete and applies to both standard formats and vendor specific formats. In a competitive environment, a standardized and nonproprietary format will always lack the newer, proprietary features of a vendor specific format. If a file format is to be retrievable in the future exactly as it is in the present, the creating application must also be saved for the future.

Digital unstable storage media (e.g., diskettes whose life span is limited) become obsolete. Physical files must be migrated to new media; if not, they will become inaccessible and will eventually suffer from the physical deterioration of the older media. Migration changes the way the data are physically inscribed, and it may improve preservation because, for example, error detection and correction methods for physical inscription on digital media have improved over time.

Migrating to a new format is very challenging, expensive, and requires full visual and operational verification. To avoid format obsolescence the creating application must be kept from becoming obsolete or it must be made available to interact with the obsolete format. While selecting file formats for preservation, the factors like wide adoption, history of backward compatibility, good metadata support, good range of functionality but not complex, built-in error detecting and correcting, and upgradability etc. should be considered for long-term stability.

Ensuring ongoing access, therefore, requires currency with

technology changes, and moving digital objects from obsolete to current file formats, storage media, operating systems and so on. Numbers of other technical, social and legal issues add to the difficulty of the task.

2. Intellectual Property Rights (IPR) Issues

Digital rights management raises a number of research issues for preservation planning and preservation actions and need to be considered when preserving digital materials. It may be necessary to obtain permission from the rights holders for migration of digital material into new forms or emulation of the original operating environment. It has long been felt that a poor fit between technology, processes and regulations have a considerable impact on digital preservation and significantly restrain the benefits which long-term access ought to deliver.

The use of digital contents has posed certain challenges before the IPRs holders more particularly for Copyright and Trademark holders. IPR issues in digital environment have implications not only on digital contents but applies also to the containers, wrappers and formats which make the contents accessible. Laws, customs, and practices differ from country to country and operating within a complicated and evolving legal and regulatory scene, the librarians and preservationists need a clear understanding of what it is permitted to do and what are the risks within technical processes like reformatting, shifting, migration, bit replication or even emulating data. Primary among these challenges are the management, protection and evolution of intellectual property rights.

3. Copyright

Copyright applies to work that is recorded in some way such as musical and dramatic work, films, sound recordings, literary work, typographic arrangements etc. It gives the author or creator specific rights in relation to the work and prohibits unauthorized use (mainly copying or broadcasting), and allows the author to take legal action against such infringements (Deegan, M. and Tanner, S., 2008).

The issues for copyright in digital preservation are:

- Under what circumstances does the preserving organization have the right or permission to ingest the content into the preservation system or storage environment? This activity may be deemed illegal copying under copyright laws unless the permissions to store and make available have been clearly agreed, with associated written evidence.
- Especially for moving image and sound recordings, there may be many creators and copyright holders. For instance, the background music for a documentary may have different restrictions on use from the visual content, and each of these will have to be addressed.
- There may be restrictions on the separation of elements of a work or their independent use. For example, removing a sound track from the visual track or GIS data from satellite imagery.
- Under what circumstances may the content being preserved be made accessible as this may be defined as publication, performance, or broadcasting? The digital domain creates this new problem because of the naturally one-to many relationship of digital content and networked access. Dark archives may be able to address this issue of acceptable archiving but may then conflict with the initial purpose of preservation – to provide future access.
- Metadata to record and track copyright will be required to enable digital preservation and eventual use. Sufficient metadata fields and associated records must be available to record all the rights holders and their relationships with each other and the wider collection. Management of this data can be time-consuming and costly to achieve. Without it, however, the digital preservation strategy would remain open to litigation risk and continuing uncertainty in the long term.

Within the current laws of some countries, the rules for making archival copies, i.e., for archival replacement and unpublished documents, allow certain exclusions under which copyright may not apply to that activity.

4. Moral and Ethical Rights Issues

Whatever the copyright circumstances, creators have moral rights under IPR that relates to paternity and integrity. The moral right of paternity is the right to be identified as the author of the work. Unlike copyright which will eventually expire, this moral right will persist for as long as the digital item persists or the estate of the creator is prepared to pursue the issue (Deegan, M. and Tanner, S., 2008).

CHALLENGES OF DIGITAL PRESERVATION

While embodying advantages – interoperability, precise reproduction and online access – information in digital form, along with other associated technologies, bring a lot of difficulties in its access and preservation. The new standards and protocols are being defined on a regular basis for file formats, compression techniques, network interfaces, storage media, and other software and hardware devices, etc. Physical deterioration and technology obsolescence are generally regarded as the greatest technical threats to ensuring continued access to digital material. The speed of changes in technology means that the timeframe during which preservation action must be taken is very much shorter than for printed material. The challenges in maintaining access to digital resources over time are related to notable differences between digital and paper-based materials. Some of the significant challenges for preserving digital contents are as follows:

1. Digital Contents are Dynamic in Nature

The problem of dependency on rapidly changing computer hardware, peripheral devices and software seems more challenging. The innovation in the computer hardware industries continues swiftly, usually yielding smaller, denser, easier to read and faster processing speed at lower cost. A one or two order of magnitude improvement in power, speed, efficiency or cost per value has occurred every several years in area of CPU (Central Processing Unit), memory chip density, storage device capacity, data transmission rate etc.

The initial problem with digital preservation is the contents itself (Chen, 2001). Authenticity and integrity of digital information have been underlying concerns in digital preservation because of the ease of altering digital objects and the dynamic nature of digital information. Though, the digitised documents, in mostly cases, are true replica of their print counterpart, such as printed documents, manuscripts, books, reports, etc. There are other types of digital information that are frequently or continuously changed and updated and cannot be replicated in traditional print form for example programs for web archiving, web pages etc. Another concern is the inter-linking of digital documents and the long-term management of urls and other hyperlinks.

2. Formats and Styles

From a preservation standpoint, some digital file formats are better than others. The basic issue is how readable a format remains over the course of time and succeeding wave of technological change. Earlier information resources were confined to traditional formats like books, monographs, photographs, and audio and video recordings have changed their scope and available in diversity of digital formats. The emerging formats such as hypertext, hypermedia, multimedia, dynamic web pages and interactive videos. Each of these formats poses distinct challenges relating to its encoding-decoding and compression for digital preservation. The ideal format should be able to convey its content accurately regardless of advancement in hardware, software and other aspects of information technology.

3. Hardware and Software Obsolescence

Software used to create, manage or access digital content are either no longer available or are unknown or superseded by newer versions or newer generations, with more capabilities using the most current technologies. This means that even if digital objects that are copied and transferred perfectly to new storage media, may not be to accessible. Due to incompatibilities between older systems and standards and the current generation systems, it may not be possible to retrieve, or interpret these digital objects.

Thus, the born digital and disitised documents created using the previous generation hardware and software are equally vulnerable to technological obsolescence, simply because they are no longer accessible.

Media obsolescence occurs when the storage medium used (e.g., a tape or disk) is physically incompatible with the available computer hardware and therefore cannot be read. Media obsolescence seems inevitable because advances in digital storage technology have introduced changes in the way the underlying bit stream that constitutes the records is physically represented. Consequently, older storage media are incompatible with those used in the present, and those in use today are likely to be incompatible with those developed in the future.

4. Fragility of Storage Media

Besides the analog media such as acid papers, thermo fax etc., the preservationists are battling to preserve the digital storage media and hardware which are subject to physical deterioration. Various internal and external forces such as material instability; improper storage environment - temperature, humidity, light, dust; natural disaster - fire, flood or earthquake; hardware malfunction; sabotage - theft or vandalism; and overuse can damage or destroy their readability. Once deterioration starts, in most cases complete data retrieval is not possible.

Magnetic and optical storage media are inherently fragile, so their readability and longevity are more at greater risk than others. The strength of signals recorded on the magnetic particles naturally degrades or fades over time. But the rate of degradation generally increases with 1) elevated temperatures and 2) high humidity. The magnetic and optical storage media confirms the negative impact of temperatures in excess of 26° C and a relative humidity of 70 percent or more (Dollar, 1999).

5. Selection of material for preservation

Digital heritage is made up of born digital or digitised materials of enduring value that should be kept for future generations. It entail data, facts, imaginations, ideas, opinions, and cultural values in a variety of media, including print, audio-visual materials, electronic formats and digitised non-digital collection. Digital heritage emanates from different communities, industries, sectors and regions. Not all digital materials are of enduring value. Selecting materials for preservation is a challenging task of critical significance, since such selections will determine which of the documents available today will be available to readers of the future.

A more challenging task is to select the additional important information (representation information, technical metadata etc.) so that preserved data remain readable and understandable. Simple preservation of 1s and 0s without its meaning, authenticity, and accuracy, is worthless.

KEY APPROACHES TO DIGITAL PRESERVATION

There are various theories on preservation which suggest best way to preserve digital material, and a number of approaches have been proposed for the problem of digital preservation. A number of major initiatives and projects have been established to investigate or develop strategies for preserving the burgeoning amounts of digital content being produced. To date, the alternative preservation approaches have been based on emulation, migration and metadata – or some combination of these. They range from preserving the original technology on which the archival digital objects ran, to preserving only the significant properties of an object, which are defined independently of any specific hardware or software platform. Each approach has its own advantages and disadvantages.

Digital preservation does not end with the careful storage of digital objects. In order to keep these objects accessible, a continuous effort towards the development of new strategies is required. Thibodeau suggests that a digital archive should take the following four criteria into consideration when selecting a preservation strategy:

Feasibility : possession of hardware and software capable of implementing the chosen method.

Sustainability : the method should be capable of being applied indefinitely into the future; or there should be another path which will offer a sequel to the method if it ceases being sustainable.

Practicality : implementation should be within reasonable limits of difficulty and expense.

Appropriateness : the chosen approach should be appropriate for the particular types of digital objects to be preserved and the objectives of their preservation.

In particular he emphasises appropriateness and applicability as important factors in deciding on an approach:

- Decisions about appropriateness should be based on an informed evaluation of the significant properties of the object(s) to be preserved.
- Some preservation methods only apply to specific hardware or software platforms, some to individual data types or formats, while others are very general. Depending on the range and variety of digital objects to be preserved by a repository, selection of approach might be limited to methods that are optimal for this range, or (if very wide ranging) a method with broad applicability should be chosen.

In the recent decades, major libraries and archives have established many formal preservation programs for traditional materials, microform, and at some extent audio-visual formats also. Key approaches adopted by them are as under:

1. Refreshing

Refreshing is the simplest and very cost-effective strategy of transfer of digital data from one storage device to another of the same type. In refreshing the same storage medium is used to avoid bitrate changes or alteration of data. This strategy can survive until the software and hardware used for data creation and storage are available. It is often combined with migration when the software or hardware required to access it is no longer available. Refreshing is needed to avoid data loss due to deterioration of physical media.

2. Migration

Migration is the most extensively adopted strategy in libraries and archives that have established digital holdings. Migration has been defined as a set of organized tasks designed to achieve the periodic transfer of digital materials from one hardware/software configuration to another or from one generation of computer hardware/software technology to a subsequent generation. This may include conversion of resources from one file format to another to ensure that the information content can be read transform/normalize data into formats and structures that are optimal for preservation. The various forms of migration are a) Simple Version Migration b) Format Standardization c) Typed Object Model Conversion d) Rosetta Stones Translation and e) Object Interchange Format. Migration theoretically goes beyond addressing viability by including the conversion of data to avoid obsolescence not only of the physical storage medium, but of the encoding and format of the data. However, the impact of migrating complex file formats has not been widely tested.

Advantages

- Homogeneous data easier to manage, access; possible to solve preservation issues once and for all if data never has to be transformed again.
- It is generally a reliable way to preserve the intellectual content of digital objects and is particularly suited to page-based documents.
- It is a widely used strategy and procedures for simple migration are well established.
- Conversion software for some formats is readily available.

Disadvantages:

- Complex initial processes; potential loss of data; requires a unique new solution for each new format or paradigm and each type of document that is to be converted to a new form; input and output (I/O) transfer rates have not accelerated as rapidly as storage capabilities and therefore there might not be enough time to transfer all of the data to the target system before the target system itself becomes obsolete.

- It requires a large commitment of resources, both initially and over time. Migration at the point of obsolescence is labour intensive unless it can be automated, because formats evolve so rapidly; as collections grow, the work involved in migration also increases. The migration on request approach may mitigate this to some extent, in that migration is not carried out on digital objects which may not be used; standardisation of formats also makes batch migration easier.
- Some of the data or attributes (e.g. formatting) of the digital object may be lost during migration; the authenticity of the record may then be compromised. In particular, there is likely to be a significant loss of functionality in the case of complex digital objects. Migration is based on the assumption that content is more important than functionality or look and feel.
- There may be potential IPR problems if either the source or the new format is proprietary, although these are unlikely to be as prohibitive as they might be in the case of emulation.

3. Replication

In this strategy duplicate copies of data are created on one or more than one systems. Single copy of data on single computer system is highly vulnerable to software or hardware failure, intentional or accidental data loss, and environmental catastrophes like fire, flooding, etc.

Advantages:

- We can recover data in case of hardware failure, intentional or accidental loss of data.

Disadvantages

- Digital data is more likely to survive if it is replicated in several locations but this data redundancy will introduce difficulties in refreshing, migration, versioning, and access control. It will also lead to data inconsistency.

4. Emulation

Emulation requires the creation of emulator programs that mimic the hardware and software of the original data and display it in the original format. Emulation uses this emulator to translate instructions from original software to new software which executes on new platforms. It is the replicating of functionality of an obsolete system to ensure that old software can function on newer hardware platform. The old software is said to run "in emulation" on newer platforms. This method attempts to simplify digital preservation by eliminating the need to keep old hardware working. This approach has several distinct advantages over migration.

Advantages

- More cost effective because a single emulator for a particular hardware configuration could be used; no transformations of the original byte stream are necessary; look and feel preserved; no need to process original files; emulators do not have to be written for each change in hardware configurations.

Disadvantages

- Development of emulators can be costly and needs to account for application and operating system, both of which can have many variations; always some uncertainty if the emulation is completely correct.

5. Hardware preservation

Maintaining access to data by preserving the physical computing environment that runs the system, including operating systems, original application software, media drives, and peripherals. It is sometimes called the "computer museum" solution.

Advantages

- No need to purchase new hardware and software and thereby no cost needed for migration and emulation.

Disadvantages

- Hardware preservation is not an undying solution to the problem. It can extend the window of access for obsolete technology, but is ultimately a dead end, since no superseded know-how can be kept functional indefinitely and need to be constantly upgraded.

6. Encapsulation

Grouping of a digital object and metadata which describe or characterise a digital object and necessary to provide access to that object together is known as encapsulation. Apparently, the grouping process diminishes the probability that any critical component necessary to decode and render a digital object will be lost. To encapsulate with a digital object important elements of metadata include reference, representation, provenance, fixity, and context information. Encapsulation is one of the key elements of emulation.

CONCLUSION

Digital preservation requires new workflows, new skills and close co-operation across different professions ranging from traditional preservation management skills to computing science. The pressures on information providers for digital preservation and continued access will continue to intensify over time. The issues and challenges related to long-term digital preservation identified here are the priority areas where preservationists need to focus its efforts and investments.

It must be stressed that the wide deployment of institutional repositories also provides new opportunities for digital preservation and there is a need to provide mechanisms to allow people and organisations to share the burden over time. Much could be done to consider digital preservation from the outset, to involve the authors in contributing metadata during the creation and ingest process, and to embed digital preservation into the repositories workflow, which will ease the preservation tasks at later stage. This is an opportunity to move beyond just rescuing digital objects to building the infrastructure required to manage them from the start.

REFERENCES

ALA (American Library Association) (2007). *Definitions of digital preservation.* Chicago: American Library Association. Retrieved from http://www.ala.org/

ala/mgrps/divs/alcts/resources/preserv/defdigpres0408.pdf

Arora, Jagdish. (1999). Integrating network-enabled digitized collection with traditional library and information services: Brewing a heady cocktail at the IIT Delhi. In Chen. Ching-chih (Ed.) *IT and Digital Library Development*. West Newton: MicroUse Information.

CCSDS (2002). Reference model for an Open Archival Information System (OAIS). *Blue Book*, Issue 1, Washington, DC (US): CCSDS Secretariat. Retrieved from the Consultative Committee for Space Data Systems (CCSDS) website: http://public.ccsds.org/publications/archive/650x0b1.pdf

Charles M. Dollar (1999). Selecting Storage Media for Long-Term Access to Digital Records. *The Information Management Journal*, July 1999, 36-43.

Deegan, M. and Tanner, S. (2008). Some Key Issues in Digital Preservation. In Earnshaw, Rae & Vince, John (Eds.). *Digital Convergence – Libraries of the Future* (pp.219-37). London: Springer-Verlag.

Digital Preservation Coalition (2012). Digital Preservation Materials: A Handbook, Digital Preservation Coalition, York. Retrieved from http://www.dpconline.org/advice/ preservationhandbook/introduction/ definitions-and-concepts

Digital Preservation Europe (2006). *What is digital preservation?* Retrieved from http://www.digitalpreservationeurope.eu/what-is-digital-preservation/

Evans, Mark & Carter, Laura. (2008). *The Challenges of Digital Preservation.* Presentation at the Library of Parliament, Ottawa.

JISC Digital Media (2012). An Introduction to Digital Preservation: Guides. Bristol: JISC Digital Media. Retrieved from http://www.jiscdigitalmedia.ac.uk/crossmedia/advice/an-introduction-to-digital-preservation

Kenneth Thibodeau (2002). 'Overview of technological approaches to digital preservation and challenges in coming years', The State of Digital Preservation: An International Perspective, Conference proceedings (July 2002). Retrieved from http://www.clir.org/PUBS/reports/pub107/pub107.pdf

Tanwar, Sunder Singh (2012). Digital preservation- Why & how? *PEARL: A Journal of Library and Information Science*, 6(2), 83-88.

Verheul, Ingeborg. (2006). Networking *for digital preservation : Current practice in 15 National Libraries* (IFLA Publications; 119). Munchen: K.G. Saur.

12

Online Journal: Access and Delivery Models

Prakash Dongardive

INTRODUCTION

Principally, the online journals known as electronic journals 'interchangeably' because it's all aspects of preparation, referring, assembly and distribution are carried out electronically. In other hand 'every online journals are Electronic journals but every electronic journal are not online journals. Online journals being published only on the web there is no parallel publishing such as 'CD ROM and Paper Print' counterpart publish with it. In the context of maintaining the scientific communication among the faculties and researcher, online journals are playing major role. through his developed topology, which the concept online journal does not refer to one homogeneous, online journals are divided into in the four basic categories according to their distribution types; a) Pure electronic journals: These types of journals are distributed only in digital form there is no print counterpart available with this type of journal, b) Electronic - printed journals: the journal that are distributed electronically but also distributed in printed form in limited numbers. c) Printed – electronic journals: the journals are mainly distributed in printed media but also made available electronically. d) Printed + Electronic journals: these types of journals are those journals whose printed and electronic versions started in parallel distribution criteria.

'Information, which can be accessed processed, stored, retrieved, and transmitted through electronic gadgets are called electronic information resource. The term 'electronic' is referred to the media in which information is stored and retrieved. Most information is available in electronic formats such as floppy, diskettes, CD-ROMs, magnetic tapes, OPAC of a library collection, online databases, other networked information resources, and World Wide Web. Library and Information systems have developed since last two decades. The advantage and spread of electronic Information sources and services is a result of development in Information and Communication technology. The price and variety of electronic information contents are growing and expanding, because most information have been accessing electronically. In the context of the popularity of the transition to the electronic information environment "any reading of the world press, let alone of Library and information sources, makes it clear that the transition from traditional communication channels to digital channels dominates current discussion of Information.

DEFINITIONS

Electronic journal

"Electronic Journal" as strictly a journal in which all aspects of preparation, referring, assembly and distribution are carried out electronically. In other word, an electronic journal is one where writing, editing, referring and distribution of items are carried out electronically without any paper intermediaries."

Online Journal

A journal that published electronically (on the web) rather than printed on the paper some online journal are available in either print or electronic format, other are published only on the web.

A journal that provides the full text of article available in electronic form most commonly on Web of Most online journals have a print counterpart, but some are available only on web.

Virtual journal

In several scientific sub disciplines now there is 'multi journal compilations' of articles from several journals in the field. To the casual browser, the virtual journal may appear to be an "actual journal." These types of journals have not considered electronic journal. Virtual journal do not have ISSN (international standard serial number) and these types of (VJ) journals are more like databases or alerting services. User can sign up 'contents alerts' to receive virtual journal freely. User can have (VJ) in the form of the table of contents of upcoming virtual journal issue. (VJ) Virtual journals are semi monthly publication it contains articles that have appeared in one of the participating source journals (54 journals form the 15 cooperating publishers) and that fall within a number of contemporary topical areas (13 are listed) in biological physics research. The articles are primarily those that have been published in the previous month; however the direction of the editors older articles can also appear, particularly review articles. Links to other useful web resources on biological physics are also provided.

Examples of Virtual Journals

Virtual journal of Applications of superconductivity (www.vjsuper.org)

Virtual journal of Nano scale science and technology (www.vjnano.org)

Virtual journal of quantum information (www.quantuminfo.org)

Virtual journal of ultra fast science (www.vjultrafast.org)

Virtual journal of geology (www.earth.elsevier.com/geobiology)

Virtual journal of cardiovascular surgery (www.ahavj.ahajournals.org/)

Abstracting Online Journals

Abstracting journals also known as 'synoptic journals' interchangeably. It publishes summaries of articles. Abstracting journals can be considered either access tools or actual journal. Elsevier's fuel and energy abstracts, first published in 1960, and is a typical example of a well established print abstracting journal, now it is available online. Library professional included it on a list of online journals, or on a list of indexes than bibliographic databases, designed more for browsing than for searching. Current site (http://sunsite.berkeley.edu/currentcite) it is an example of a 'boom digital' abstracting journals and it has an ISSN. The Massachusetts Medical society, publisher of the New England journal of Medicine, has sponsored 11th separate journals watch 'mews letters' (www.jwatch.org) since 1987 and each of them provide current information to the important research of medical field, now it is available in both print and online. All of these abstracting online journals dependent on other journals for their existence, playing a major role in maintaining 'information over load.

FEATURES AND CHARACTERISTICS OF ELECTRONIC JOURNALS

The positive features of electronic journals as compared with print journals are as follows:

- Allow remote access;
- Can be used simultaneously by more than one user;
- Provide timely access;
- Support different searching capabilities;
- Accommodate unique features (links to related items, reference linking);
- Save physical storage space;
- Can support multimedia information;
- Do not require physical processing (receiving and binding);
- Can be environmentally valuable; and
- Can be saved digitally.

ONLINE JOURNALS ACCESS MODEL

Internet, especially its nature of technology and utility is a remote access model. Seamless access possible through linking information resources like databases and online journals distributed at various sites. Internet and its secured cousin intranet have however, thrown up different access models that fit into the convenience of libraries. There are three access models have been emerged for online journals.

1. Remote access (through internet)
2. On site at a Library
3. Access through databases (link models)

Remote Access

In this model, the publisher hosts the journals at his website. When the library subscribes to the online journals, it is provided right to access. Depending on how this right is defined, the patron of the library can have access either from a set of designated user terminals or through library's LAN or campus LAN. Publishers grant the rights to subscribing library through one of the following methods (Butler, 1999):

User ID and password

The subscriber gets a user –id and password, which can be used, from any user terminal in the library, largely restricted to one simultaneous user at a time. While access through library's LAN or internet is possible through this method, this is generally governed by publisher's policy. This method is primarily suited for dialup access users.

IP enabled (Internet)

This method is ideal for libraries, which have campus wide LAN and intranet access to Internet. The intranet saver at the library is IP enabled by the publisher. This a controlled method of access, where publisher's server site will recognize and validate the IP address of subscriber's intranet server when each time a user logs into publisher's web site for a subscribed journal through subscriber's intranet. Large publishers like American comical society and Elsevier science find this method more secured for both themselves and libraries. This method can be used by only those libraries that have an intranet based LAN in their library or campus. Some publishers required both IP and password control to ensure further security.

Combined

Some publishers offer both, either as alternative or as combined feature. The issue is largely decided by publisher's policy of how much to keep the access open and how much restrict.

On site

In this model, the library can host the online journal within its campus. This model is driven by two factors. First, the library feels more secured to maintain the journal at its end as it has paid for the journal and is used to the ownership concept, which has been practiced for over a century. Second, the local LAN certainly offer far wider and superior bandwidth for access compared to remote access through internet in the first model. Local LANs generally offer 1 to 10 mbps bandwidth these days and possibly more to each user work desk. Internet access for dial-up users is still at kbps level. ISPs like VSNL currently offer a maximum of 33.3 kbps to dial-up users, which in practice work far below 10 kbps, which is highly inadequate for online journal access. Even if campus has a dedicated high-bandwidth link to internet at say, 2 kbps, when distributed across several user workstations, the bandwidth available to each user work desk will be a few kbps more. Internet bandwidth is however increasing fast with cost coming down. In the predictable future, internet will provide more than adequate bandwidth to remote users for convenient online journal access at affordable costs. For onsite access, publishers deliver the e-journal to the subscribers through one or many of the following media

- CD-ROM
- Down-lode from the publisher's web site
- FIP option

Access through Databases

Access model offered by publishers limit the access to their journals. But the user often fined articles of their interest through databases. Over the year, the bibliographical databases have emerged as a user favorite interface for searching and locating information. The concept of seamless demands instant linking between the article reference in databases to a corresponding full-text article in an online journal. This is achieved through the link model offered by databases producers and vendors. Some of the currently popular models are briefly presented here.

SilverLinker from SilverPlatter (www.silverplatter.com)

SilverPlatter is an electronic publisher and internet based vendor of over 200 bibliographic databases. SilverPlatter is a link technology and database of article level links offered by SilverPlatter. It carries the URLaddress to the articles for over 3,000 journals offered by several publishers on there websites. Following are some of the major publishers whose journals are linked by SilverLinker

- Academic Press
- Catchword Ltd
- Elsevier Science Direct
- Kluwer Academic Publisher
- Project Muse
- Springer-Verlag
- Walter de Gruyter

SilverLinker databases acts as an interface link between several of SilverPlatter published databases like MEDLINE, BIOSIS, CAB, etc., and the online journals located in participating publisher's website listed above. See in your mind's eye or imagine that a library subscribes to silverPlatter's MEDLINE database and set of biomedical journals form Elsevier and Kluwer. The users of this library can have seamless access to articles from the subscribed journals through SilverPlatter's MEDLINE database. When a user at this library finds an article of his interest through a MEDLINE search, the SilverPlatter database working behind MEDLINE will provide automatic link to the corresponding article of Kluwer journal at publisher's website. A mouse clicks on the retrieved MEDLINE record activities the link and connects the user to the full-text of the article. SilverPlatter expand the link beyond publisher's sites to facilitate document delivery and inter-library lone transactions for designated participating libraries and document delivery agencies.

SilverLinker implementation by a library requires:

- Subscription to any of the client required SilverPlatter databases. This can be internet subscription or a subscription for a local hosting at a local library. If the library desires to host the SilverPlatter databases locally, it will require setting up SilverPlatter's ERL/webSPIRS which is SilverPlatter's intranet based local database access solution.
- Subscription to SilverPlatter databases
- Subscription to desired list of online journals that are covered in SilverPlatter's SilverLinker. The subscription arrangements will be directly between the publisher and the library and SilverPlatter does not act as subscription agent for journals.

SilverLinker can be implemented to locally hosted online journals also, if the library maintains its own online journals archive, this process involves substantial customization.

ISI's Web of Science (WoS)

ISI (http://www.isinet.com) is a world famous producer and publisher of high-quality bibliographic database. Web of science is a enhanced version of the citation Index family of ISI databases designed for web environment. WoS covers around 8,100+journals. The coverage spans 25+ years from 1974 to current. The database is available only on the web and is not available on CD-ROM. As a unique feature, WoS provides three levels of link to every bibliographic record, which is shown on every record displayed on the screen, with the number of linked records

- Link to related record
- Link to cited record (the article cited by the displayed records)

- Link to citing record (the article citing the displayed record)

ISI offers link to the e-journals sites of the following publishers. WoS currently links to about 5,400 journals from the following publishers :

- Academic press
- American Institute of Physics
- Blackwell Science
- Catchword, Ltd.
- Cambridge University Press
- Highwire Press
- John Hopkins University
- John Wiley & Sons, Inc.
- Karger
- Kluwer Academic Publisher
- OCLC
- Royal Society of publishers
- SIAM
- Springer-Verlag
- Stockton Press

IDS from Cambridge Scientific Abstracts (CSA)

CAS (http://www.csa.com) is producer of many leading databases such as METADEX, Life Sciences Collection, and Sociological Abstracts etc. Like SilverPlatter, CSA also act as an Internet based vendor for several third-party databases such as Aerospace database, NTIS, etc. IDS are Cambridge's database access model for all its databases and third party licensed databases. Cambridge offers article level link for about 3,000 journals from several publishers. The link is offered as an integral part of IDS interface. Some of the publishers covered these are following:

- Academic press
- Blackwell Science

- Catchword Ltd
- Elsevier Science Direct
- High wire press
- Information Quest (RoweCom)
- OCLC
- Kluwer Academic Publishers
- Project Muse
- Springer-Verlag

REQUIREMENT AT USER-END

Seamless access to online journals libraries requires develop IT infrastructure at their end which will eventually deliver online journal to user's desktops which is the ultimate goal digital library. If the library prefers to go for remote access model, it will have to invest in:

- Campus wide internet with ability for every user terminal to access web resources
- A reliable and high-speed internet access infrastructure with dedicated link to internet

Investment in high-bandwidth for internet will be a critical need. The bandwidth capacity could vary 64kb to 2mb and more depending on the number of users. For efficient online journal access model, it is recommended that every user workstation gets a minimum 64kb bandwidth. On site access model can avoid high-speed internet. But, it will be required-

- Campus wide intranet with ability for every user terminal to access web resources
- Reliable IT infrastructure for archiving and hosting the online journals locally (discussed in detail in the following section of archiving)

ARCHIVING

In the history of librarianship and publishing, archiving knowledge has been a long assumed mandate and responsibility successfully carried and managed by the libraries till date. In the print journal era, publisher completely stayed away from this responsibility. Many libraries stacked today many research journals since their first volume, but, there is hardly any publisher who has complete collection of his journal archived for the use of future generation or posterity. Possibly, respecting the role played by the libraries, the publishers were open-minded in the enforcement of copyright during the print journals days. Internet or online journals make the task of illegal copying and distribution easier, so it makes the task of policing very difficult. While the copy right permits only fair-use and forbids all distribution whether for or not for profit, enforcing copyrights in the electronic environment complex task for the publisher and the governments. Internet and the online journals have created new paradigm or model for archiving journals resulting in controversial or regimental discussion and throwing in new technological complexities. The actual process of delivery is being reversed in the online journal system. While the print journals were delivered to the libraries by the publishers or the subscription agents, the libraries may have to now electronically visit publishers to collect the journals. Many issues have emerged that require thought discussion and understanding to formulate effective archiving strategy by the library community, some key issues have been debated here (Stephen, 1999):

- Right
- Accumulation
- Aggregation
- Search engine
- Interface development
- Infrastructure and Maintenance
- Third party archived

Rights

Some of the publishers allow archiving rights for online journals to libraries. However, most of them are beginning to realize that they will have to permit this historically important and sensitive process as every publisher is not in a position to guarantee continuous access for his journals. Each publisher is evolving his own commercial policy and is exercising customized technical feature and controls for delivering online journals to libraries for archiving. The future is likely to settle the rights issue for archiving, which may require certain changes in copyright laws. Some publishers have double models. They offer a choice to libraries to either use publisher's remote archives or to develop their own archives.

Accumulation

The libraries always bound the journals as a means of archiving. What they did was physically accumulating the issues for a given volume or a year for which publisher published accumulative indexes at the end of a volume or a year. In the online journal model, accumulative extends beyond a year or a volume and becomes possible for all the years for which the online journal is available for access. If the libraries decide to archive a journal, they will have to carry the additional task of accumulating the index every year for the entire period of the archived journal. Without such an accumulation, access to the archive becomes difficult.

Aggregation

This is the new task, which the libraries never carried during the print archive days. Electronic archiving makes it very important that the accumulative index files of several journals are aggregated to create a common accumulative index for all the journals carried in the archive. This index will need to be refreshed for new articles as the new articles and new journals enter the archive. Indexing, accumulation policies and practices differ from publisher to publisher. This variance will make the task of building an aggregated index for all journals in the libraries archive rather a difficult and technically complex task. Aggregating index files provided by publishers may also lead to problems in retrieval. Some publishers may not provide the index to their journals. To overcome all these problems, the library may have to resort to do its own indexing for a common acceptable standard. This will lead to a major additional task of creating and updating a bibliographical database for the entire archive hold by the library. For a library that of Indian Institute of science, which subscribes 1,000 journals, this task is equivalent to building and maintaining a database of about 150,000 articles every year.

Search Engine

Most publishers who offer online journals at their website do not even make available a search engine, nor do they provide any indexes for browsing. They host their journals as simple HTML or PDF files linked through as table of content for each issue of their journals for easy browsing and downing loading by the subscribers. Archiving these journals will require licensing a search engine from a third-party software company. Some publishers offer their search engine along with the right to archive these come to additional cost to library. They will be proprietary to the journals of the respective publishers. Opting for publishers search engine where offered will result in building a collecting of several archives, each with its own search engine and interface. The solution will emerge from the library licensing a separate search engine and aggregating all journals under one common interface. It will add a new dimension to tasks and responsibilities.

Interface developing

The companies, which offer search engine normally, offer a standard interface, which may not suit the library. It should be involved developing a suitable search interface to go with the archive pattern of the library and its user's needs. So the library may required to add its own functionalities like linking the archive to the communities union catalogue, facilitating inter library linking related transactions, etc. this will be an additional software related development responsibility for the library.

Infrastructure and Maintenance

In the past archiving the journals was relatively a simple task, limited to binding and maintaining with adequate shelf space. Archiving online journals needs substantial investment in infrastructure and maintenance. Suppose a major university or research library subscribes to about 500 journals, on a five year plan basis, electronic archiving require investment on the infrastructure of the following kind,

- Server hardware and software
- Storage of approximately one terabyte (1,000 GB) and back up facility
- Archive management and search software
- Refreshing the data to new technology and formats (once in three and five years)

which can be approximately Rs. 50-60 lakhs at present cost, with additional refreshing cost of Rs. 15-20 lakhs once in three or five years, this includes the annual cost of creating and updating bibliographic database, linking them to archived article, and associated hardware-software maintenance.

Third party archiving

Electronic archiving is a big cost and an entirely new type of serious responsibly. Its functions are similar to data warehousing. If the publishers can develop an institutional model and legal framework to guarantee continuous internet access to the subscribed journals for every subscriber, the libraries need not archive. However, the need for aggregating the subscribed journals and providing a common access interface for all the journals subscribed is a prompting enough compulsion to think of independent local archiving. The geo-political factors, the frequent corporate changes at publishing organizations in term of merger, acquisitions and closures, and the frequent changes in the structure and ownership of journal became other compelling factors for the library to think of independent local archiving. Apart from the high cost of infrastructure and maintenance, it will be a substantially repetitive cost for each library in a community. If we ware to address university libraries as a community, a simple research could possibly confirm that at list25 percents of the titles are widely duplicated among 75 percent of the Universities. This leads to the feasibility of third party local archiving as means for sharing the cost. The third party organization could be an independent corporate body, which has legal and institutional framework to support the activity to ensure and insure perpetual access to the archive to participating libraries. Alternatively, it could be a cooperative task and sharing activity among the libraries in a community who can assign the responsibility to one of its members.

PRICING AND BUSINESS MODELS

The publishing, distribution, access and archiving activities of online journals is a completely IT-enabled activity involving two independent and yet integrated task: 1) content creation and development and 2) e-commerce. Because of it's extremely nature of attracting value addition opportunities through IT, different business models have emerged, these are following-

- Publishers Models
- Aggregators Models
- Subscription Agency Model
- Models emerging through library cooperative and consortia

Publishers Model

Online journal is a technological evolution form print for publishers. They will naturally expect their revenue stream to continue and increase. Scholarly and research journals always depended on subscription revenues, as advertisement revenue were not feasible due to low circulation pattern. The circulation revenue largely come from the institutions, which often subsidized individuals and members (in case of society professional journals) there are no indication that as of now, internet would change this pattern for research journals. Hence, the publishers have largely continued the pricing models of print journals and with policies leading to stricter enforcement of copyright compliances. The pricing models that have emerged such as-

- Free subscription to e-journals against print subscription
- Additional 10-25% (or more) of print price for print and –e journals

- Plus or minus 10-15% for subscription to e-journals version only

Some publishers for whom revenue is not a consideration and the publishers of a good many popular, trade and industry magazines where revenue comes primary form advertisements, have offered their e-journal free to all, completely de-linking their e-journals from print models. This practice is more in the direction of trends set by newspaper publishers. Most publishers are testing wasters in internet stream and are likely to introduce some level of fee in future. Much depends on the maturity of internet based advertising industry, which is still in transition.

Aggregators Models

This model is sphere-headed by the bibliographic databases producers and vendors who venture into building full-text databases during the early 1980s. A databases producer of journal literature always focused on aggregating literature to provide subject focus cutting across the boundaries of journals, and also to create a tool for retrospective access to print journal archive. These database producers were the first and earliest to use IT and go electronic. Some of them have successfully applied their database models to aggregate online journals also. Bibliographic records where the database producer owned the database, the e-journal will have to be licensed from the primary journal publisher, which has made the aggregation model for journals much different from their earlier business model used for bibliographic databases. The major players in this game today are companies and organization like Bell & Howel information and learning (formerly UMI), ADONIS, and Ovid. An aggregator licenses the right from the set of publishers and aggregators them into a common database. His bibliographic databases with additional functionalities like table of contents. Tools, generating current awareness acts as the interface for delivering e-journals to libraries. Following pricing models emerged by aggregators.

Publisher's price, plus

In this model, the aggregator offers the online journals at

publisher's price plus additional charges varying from 10-50 per cent or more. The aggregator offers the subscriber the choice of selection of journals. Ovid and ADONIS fall into this category. Ovid charges as much as 30-60 per cent over the publisher's price. Ovid also offers electronic-only and electronic-plus-print price option. However, they would not handle the print journal subscription but limit themselves to electronic journals only. ADONIS delivers journals on CD-ROM as a local solution for access within the library's intranet. Ovid offer both internet and local solution models. Both offer the software for local archiving, with an additional technology fee for the software.

Less than publisher's price

Bell and Howell information and learning (BHIL) and IEEE offer this kind of pricing model. BHIL's PQD (ProQuest Direct) offer access to over 3,000 plus online journals in different subject collections. Their PQD's databases collection of over 6'000 journals acts as an access and search interface for these 3'000 plus journals. The only limitation of this model is that the library will have to subscribe to all the e-journals offered in a specific subject collection. However, a significantly lowered pricing brings down the cost per journal to a uniform level and far below publisher's price. For example, the ProQuest Medical Library (PML) from BHIL offers around220 e-journals. The cost per journal works out to around US$60. If one were to subscribe to all these journals at publisher's price, it might cost, on an average, more than US$200 per journal http://www.bellhowell.infolearning.com).

Subscription Agency models

Subscription agencies focused on the commerce side of the journal business and the databases producers focused on the contents side of the business. With internet triggering opportunity for e-commerce and the journal delivery going electronic, subscription agencies have a unique opportunity to combine e-commerce and e-journal into an effective new business model. Some of the leading names like Swets, RoweCom (Information Quest) and Blackwell have effectively combined e-journal delivery with e-commerce through their gateways. They are emerging act as:

- E-commerce gateway for subscription handling, a traditional role upgraded to internet based model.
- Interface gateway for linking to publisher's e-journals site through a common password to all the journals a library subscribes through agency.
- Bibliographic database for several journals, which acts as access interface to the library for the journals they subscribe, and a search and document delivery interface for several thousands of journals.
- The third party archive for libraries desiring to maintain a remote archive for all the journals they subscribe.

Models emerging through library co-operatives and consortia

Libraries always chose co-operative acquisition and resource sharing as their favorite model in cost reduction process, to manage the tight budget. Various models are emerging as a result of this effort two interesting models are given bellow- 1) OCLC which has been leading the way in the application of IT for library networking to promote resources sharing with the respect to copyright fulfillments, offer e-journals access to over 300 journals, with a bias to social sciences. OCLC's model is similar to Ovid model but is priced almost at publisher's price level, making it the most cost-effective model, but OCLC does not offer local solution. High wire press (http://highwire.standard.edu) was a consortium originally promoted by Stanford group of libraries. It has developed an e-journal archives and access interface for over 100+science journals. Its search engine and access interface, is one of the best in features and functionalities offered. It fully uses the capabilities and advantage of web technology. The pricing models work out fairly economical, often less than the print journal price. Highwire is willing to partner with various organizations to create e-journal content, particularly to support scholarly societies and university presses. 2) Several publishers have come forward to encourage libraries to develop their own consortia to share e-journals, each with its own set of policies and pricing models. In this consortium model, the publishers treat all the journals subscribed by consortium members as one composite collection. Consortium members are allowed to access the entire collection irrespective of how many of those journals are subscribed by each library. A major limitation enforced by the publishers is that, the participating libraries should maintain their print renewals at the previous year's level (Butler, 1999).

Thus, the online journals revolution has been set in without doubt, both the compulsions and advantages of the emerging worldwide digital library scenario and the imperatives of internet economy are unlikely to leave the libraries with any choice. Managing the complexities and decision choices thrown up by the new paradigms caused by e-journals, particularly the archiving and copyright issues will prove to be the major challenge to libraries, publishers and all other involved players.

CONCLUSION

Electronic transition of information mostly in the context of online journals provide superior way of having current and concern information to academic science community, with wide opportunities to satisfy their information needs.

REFERENCES

Declan, Butler (1999). The writing on the web for science journals in print. *Nature magazine,* 397, 195-200.

Sathyanarayana, N. V. (2007). Electronic journals: access and delivery models. *Vision of future libraries and information system,* p. 165-178.

Stephen, Arnold (1999). The scholarly hothouse: Electronic journals. *Database,* 22(1) 27-33.

13

Consortia : A Back Bone for The Library Users in Electronic Era

Chandresh A. Shah

INTRODUCTION

Each and every library demand for new information and sources is unending because the change is happing thick and fast. Shortage of financial resources have resulted in inability to procure information resources to satisfy users' needs, Hence it is necessary to enter into a collaborative arrangement, which help to get savings, and the resource base expands.

A consortium could be described as a group of organization coming together to fulfill a combined objective that usefully requires co-operation and the sharing of resources. Under consortia two of more libraries cooperate together to achieve the common objectives and buy the resources together. The primary purpose of establishing a library consortium is to share resources among members. A library consortium offer much broader range of materials than any one library could possibly offer. Consortia generally help to get products at a lower cost and extend wide access to information. It also provides provision to extended services like content page service, online documents delivery etc. By consortia offering publishers gets the opportunity to sell product to a large number of users and save their marketing and administrative costs.

NEEDS OF CONSORTIUM

No library in the world possesses all the resources to meet the various needs of the users. The rapid growth of publication, shrinking resources, escalation of prices and ever increasing expecting of users are few challenges presently facing the library and information professionals .Therefore several following factors, which have influenced the libraries to come and initiate co-operative activities.

1. Variation of pricing models
2. Rising cost of journals
3. Information Explosion
4. Diminishing library budgets
5. Increasing demand of users
6. Threats from E-print archives
7. Decrease in scientific productivity
8. Population explosion
9. language barrier
10. Impossibilities of self sufficiency

DEFINITIONS OF CONSORTIA

The 'Consortia" is the plural form of 'Consortium' but is often used in the place of singular form. It is derived from the Latin Word for 'Fellowship"-the meaning emphasizes coming together of separate groups for a purpose. Synonymously the term is used as alliance, coalition, collaboration, partnership, etc .The term consortium literally means a "Temporary cooperation of a number of powers of large interests for a common purpose. It is an association of similar type of organizations who are engaged for producing and servicing the common things for providing services for a specific purpose of its users"(Arora, 2001).

"A generic term to indicate any group of libraries that are working together towards a common goal, whether to expand cooperation or traditionally library services (such as collection development)or electronics information services. It is now come together solely to achieve better pricing for purchasing electronic information (Arnold Hirson, 1999).

"A Consortium is an association of two of more individual, companies, organizations or governments with the objective of participating in a common activity or pooling their resources for achieving a common goal (Singh and Rao, 2008).

"The term "consortium" is derived from the field of economics and refers to the grouping together of different independent companies in order to bring together financial of material resources under a single meaning body for the joint performance of specific operations (Ghose, Biswas and Jeevan, 2006).

The decreasing budgets and unparallel demands of users current information available anywhere are putting increasing pressure on libraries for acquiring or accessing the online electronic web-based resources. The emerging situation is compelling the librarians to look for new ways and means to consolidate the global resources. As a result, new kinds of partnerships are emerging that have led to the development of the concepts of 'Shared subscription' or 'Consortia based subscription' (Singh and Krishan Kumar, 2005).

OBJECTIVES OF CONSORTIA

The objective of consortia are given by (Vasanth and Mudhal, 2007)

1. Rational Utilization of funds
2. develop technical skill of library staff in using electronic resources
3. Maximize the cost benefit per subscription

4. More utilization of resources
5. Develop cooperation with other institutions to reduce the subscription cost and maximize utilization of resources
6. Guarantee the information stored continuous use by present and future users.

MODELS OF CONSORTIA

The types of consortia are generally based on various models evolved in India in variety of forms depending upon participations' affiliation and funding sources.

1. Open Consortia

This type of consortia is very flexible and it is the wish of members of consortia to join and leave at any time when they please. INDEST and AICTE Consortium are examples to this.

2. Closed Group Consortia

It is within defined group either by affiliation and collaboration, among them like Cera,DAE, IIM Consortium and the formation and operation of the consortia guidelines and its administration are fairly simple and easy.

3. Centrally Funded Model

In this model, consortium will solely depend on the parent body. A few examples are INFONET by UGC, ICMR, CSIR by DSIR.

4. Shared-budget Model

In this model, the participating libraries take the lead and form the consortium. IIM is examples of this model.

5. Publisher Initiatives

The Emerald Full-Text Library published by the Emerald Publishing Group (formerly MCB University Press) is recent example. Here, consortium members will get deep discount price to the participating libraries.

INTERNATIONAL CONSORTIA

Due to budget and all other circumstances most of the area of the world are already existing and utilizing this approach to increase the purchasing power of collaborative libraries.

Some of the international consortia as under.

1.	New England Law Library consortia	(NELLCO)	(Year of Established.1983)
2.	Cape Library Cooperative	(CALICO)	(Year of Established.1992)
3.	Capital District Library Council	(CDLC)	(Year of Established. 1966)
4.	Washington Research Library Consortium	(WRLC)	(Year of Established.1987)
5.	Astronet Consortium		(Year of Established.2005)

LIBRARY CONSORTIA IN INDIA

There are several library consortia in India are functionally very well. The following consortia are established in the various fields. Some of the consortia as under.

1. DeLCON Consortium
2. CSIR Consortium
3. UGC_INFONET Journal Consortium
4. FORSA Consortium
5. IIM Consortium
6. DAE Consortium
7. ERMED Consortium
8. CeRA Consortium
9. DRDO Consortium
10. MCTT Library Consortium
11. INDEST_AICTE Consortium
12. HELINET Consortium
13. IUC-DAEF Consortia (Atomic Energy)
14. ICMR Consortia
15. TIFR Consortia

CHARACTERISTICS OF SUCCESSFUL CONSORTIA

There are certain characteristics behind the success the

consortium. There are as under.

- Centralized Staffing
- Centralized Funding
- Linkage
- Authority to take action-take Risk
- Culture of Shared Vision & Mission
- Deep Interest to Obtain Real Benefit
- Constant Support & Commitment
- Healthy Licensing & Technology Infrastructure

The above all characteristics are needed for successfully running of Consortia.

ADVANTAGES OF LIBRARY CONSORTIA

Some of the important advantages of consortia as under, given by (Helmer, 1990)

- Benefits are manifolds
- Protects for Duplication
- Sustain the Pressure
- Foster resource sharing
- Demonstrate reduced cost
- Increase financial benefit
- Enhance library services to the users
- Improves quality of library services
- Encourage for discussion, collective thinking and leadership
- Facilitates the 'change management'
- Provides training and workshop
- Enables better access
- Facilities better management
- Accelerates sustainable growth of libraries
- Constantly available(24*7)

DISADVANTAGES OF LIBRARY CONSORTIA

Some of the Disadvantages of Consortia as under, given by (Singh and Rao,2008)

- Copyright problems
- Internet access ID is necessary
- Users are not accepting e-journals as per with the printed Journals
- Unreliable telecommunication links and insufficient bandwidth
- Lake of archiving and back files availability
- Absence printed copy of the journals
- Require training of staffs in handling electronic documents
- Consortia require high initial investments in licensees and information and communication technology

CONCLUSION

Every library has such limitations like budget, staff, equipments, time, and unlimited of user's requirement services. In above all circumstances the consortia is the only solution for the every user as well as libraries for providing the require information for each user. SO, the consortia has minimized the financial burden and paved way for enormous amount of saving of time, space, money and manpower. A consortium at this juncture is only viable solution to survive.

REFERENCES

Ghose, Maitrayee, Biswas, S.C. & Jeevan, V.K.J.. (2006). Strategic Cooperation and Consortia Building for Indian Libraries'Models and Methods. *Library Review*, 55(9), 608-20.

Helmer, John F. (1999). Epidemiology of the consortial spore. *Information Technology and libraries*. 18 (3), 119-120.

Hirshon, Arnold. (1999). Libraries, consortia and change management. *Journal of Academic Librarianship*, 25(2), 124-126.

Rajput, Prabhat Singh & Naidu, G.H.S. 92008). Library Consortia and University Libraries: Model Approach. *International Library Movement*, 30(1), 14-23

Satyanarayana, N.V., Krishnan, S. & Aroroa, Jagdish (2004). *Library consortia and resource sharing initiatives in India: A white paper.* HELINET Consortium, Rajiv Gandhi University of Health Sciences, Bangalore, May 1, 2004.

Singh, Kunwar & Rao, V. Baskar. (2008). *An Overview of Library Consortia in India.* Proceddings of Sixth Convention Planner, 2008, Nagaland University, Nagaland, Nov.6-7, pp. 14-23.

Vasanth, N. & Mudhol, Mahesh V. (2007). Consortia Purchasing: Subscription for the Electronic Journals in Indian Scenario. *SRELS Journal of Information Management,* 44(3), 261-70.

SECTION - III
E-RESOURCE MANAGEMENT

14

Biometrics – Management and Use of Online Journals in Jaykar Library, University of Pune, India

Prakash Dongardive

INTRODUCTION

The purpose of this study is to examine the attitude behaviors, perceptions and preferences of the faculty members of science stream in university of Pune. The importance of present research study is useful to know the parallel and electronic methods of online journals for knowledge dissemination among users and faculty members of science stream in University of Pune. Information needed by science faculty and student is increasing exponentially in the science. Interdisciplinary research; new fields of research has increased in science field therefore scientists need always new information. With the new technologies, academics, can distribute their own material more effectively than the traditional sources. The rising cost of the general publication, coupled with the explosive growth in research and concomitant explosion of paper journal in various discipline for science libraries to maintain a comprehensive selection of literature. Significant increase in the speed of academic discourse can be achieved via electronic publication. Therefore there is a vibrant need to know the usability of online journals with their obstacle while having online journals through faculty members and research scholars. Online journals are the signal of future. Online journals in the scientific world, much like online newspaper, are an attempt to harness the power of computer-immediate communication networks to scientific communication and discourse. E-journals in the broader context of information technology and the electronic age competitive cultural perspectives form the past twenty years.

MATERIALS AND METHODS

The study was conducted on a sample of 181 full time science faculty members of University of Pune, from 17th Science Departments of which 122 responded positively. Pre-structured questionnaires were used to get the opinion about the use of online journals use and had distributed to the all of the faculty members of science stream in university of Pune.

REVIEW OF LITERATURE

Cochenour and Moothart's (2003) study present the study of a user survey which aimed in particular to determine whether all faculties, administrative professional and graduate student at Colorado state university supported canceling print subscriptions when they are duplicated by electronic equivalents. They sent a printed questionnaire in spring 2001 to a sample of 6968. The responses rate was 10.4 percent. The result of this study demonstrated that although overall, 95.6 percent supported or strongly supported dual print/ electronic subscriptions, only 74.3 percent supported canceling print subscriptions when they are duplicated by electronic equivalents; 25.7 percent opposed or strongly opposed canceling print; 77.4 percent supported the move electronic only subscriptions under the condition that the publisher guarantees perpetual access.

Atilgan and Bayram's (2006) articles reports the result of a survey on the use of e-databases at Ankara University. They surveyed faculty in 2002 to determine level of awareness of digital library resources, particularly journals articles, along with their use rate, and to evaluate the preference of the faculty for specific electronic databases. They distributed a questionnaire to a sample of 3800 researchers at Ankara University, out of which 1996 (53 percent) usable questionnaires were returned to the investigators. The main findings were that the majority of respondents (86.5 percent) indicated that they knew that digital library resources exist in Ankara University. Many of the faculty members (88 percent) use electronic databases. Full professors (53.8 percent) and research assistants (55.4 percent) place second after associate (67.8 percent) and assistant (63.4 percent) professors in the use of electronic journals although they place first in level of awareness of the Digital library. The most preferred databases have been Web of Science, Science Direct, and EBSCO. "It seems possible that there is a positive impact of newly subscribed databases on this increased in publishing. The extent to which the use of databases can influence productivity in Ankara University might be a topic for further study," they conclude.

Raza and Upadhyay's (2006) study measures the usage of e-journals by researchers at Aligarh Muslim University (AMU, Aligarh, India) They distributed a questionnaire to a sample of 72 researchers at AMU, out of which only 52 filled questionnaires were returned to the investigator. The overall response rate was 72 percent. The finding of the study, briefly, is as follows: the researchers were aware of e-journals in AMU; many research scholars access e-journals from their departmental labs and computer centre, for research and to update their own knowledge; most of the researchers used both printed journals and e-journals; a large number of researchers were storing e-journals articles by downloading them onto discs; and lack of training and slow downloading were the problems faced by the researchers while using e-journals. This study ends with the statement that e-journals will not replace the traditional print format but rather compliment it as a new medium of communication.

Borrego et al. (2007) - reports the result of a survey o the use of print and e-journals by the academic staff of the University belonging to the consortium of academic libraries of Catalonia (CBUC). Between May and June 2005, a questionnaire was distributed to the population consisting of a total of 14,855researchers mainly by post. The 2682 replies received represented a response rate of 18.05 percent. The major results can be summarized as follows: more than percent 95 of the respondents are aware of the e-journals; electronic journals are used exclusively or predominantly by 52 percent of the respondents; use of the e-journal collection shows a statistically significant relationship with the discipline, the age of the respondents and their academic status; and 76 percent of the respondents prefer the electronic format over the printed format when both formats are accessible the acceptance of the format change is also related to the discipline and age and academic states of the respondents and 53.6 percent of respondents consult e-journals for both research and teaching.

Kurata, Keiko et al. (2007) - present a study that seeks to identify changes in the place of e-journals, using factual data on Japanese researchers' usage and view of them. Their mainly focus on distinguishing between the function of scholarly journals and the electronic forms. They sent a questionnaire to 1427 physicists, 1026 chemists, and 1276 pathologists in universities and other research institute all over Japan, of whom 775 (54.3 percent), 494 (48.1 percent), and 541 (42.4 percent), respectively, supplied answers. The finding indicates that scholarly communication is gradually changing but at different speeds in different research fields. Other major finding of the study includes the following: only age was statistically significantly related with the frequency of use: about 70 percent of the respondents read articles in an electronic form; but also, 92.5 percent of the chemist and 91.6 percent of the pathologists were reader of print journals; the most frequent pattern after the introduction of e-journals was downloading and printing out PDF file (68 percent of the physicists, 60.1 percents of the chemist and 55.4

percent of the pathologists); an increase in the number of articles read was reported by 33.8 percent of the physicist, 35.9 percent of the chemists, and 41 percent of the pathologists; and semi permanent accessibility to back issues was regarded as the most important aspect of journals to be maintained in the future.

The Stanford University Library - conducted a two-year research project investigating attitudes towards electronic journals published in Internet editions by High Wire Press, the Libraries' online service bureau for scholarly publishers. This domain of online scholarly communication is poorly understood and poorly researched. Moreover, competition among the profit and non-profit scholarly journal publishers has generated various claims regarding efficacy and efficiency of communication. Little data is available to support such claims. While the study benefited in particular more than 60 scholarly societies whose publication in Internet editions are associated with High Wire Others got benefit as well. This study is to assist scholars, librarians, and administrators in higher education and research making individual and collective choices in how they contribute to scholarly communication.

Super Journal is a research project (1999) -and the main objective was to identify the features that deliver real value, and to explore the implications with stakeholders in the publishing process: readers, authors, libraries, and publishers. The research was conducted over three years (1996-1998) and the project ended in December 1998. The project aimed to use electronic journal application and made clusters of journals available to university test sites via the World Wide Web. At the start of the project readers were asked about their expectations for electronic journals. For two years their usage was recorded and analyzed. Users consider the back file to be an important feature of an electronic journal service, and most would like a back file of 5-10 years. Responses to user survey varied from 1 to 50 years, with Science users averaging 7 years, and Social Science users averaging 11 years. Users in the Social Sciences made wider use of the journals than users in the Sciences. Averaged over all journal users, the majority (82%) of Social Science users used 1-6 journals, where the majority of Science users used 1-3 journals. The survey indicates that over 90% user used journals first time. Use of journal issues in the current year was greater in the Sciences than in the Social Sciences. User's value abstracts. Most users (72%) said they would like publishers to publish abstracts in both print and electronic versions of their journals. Five of the Social Science journals included in Super Journal did not contain abstracts, and another four did not have abstracts for all articles. The Science users viewed abstracts less frequently than the Social Science users. Science users more often browsed at Table of Contents level, or went direct from the TOC to the article itself. Typically users in the Sciences were using Super Journal to get specific articles and to keep up to date with specific journals. Surveys at the end of the project suggest that listing electronic journals on the library web site is the most successful technique overall. 24.5% of repeat users and 37.1% of non-repeat users found out about Super Journal in this way.

Mounissamy and Swaroop Rani (2005) - have conducted a survey to know the usage and usability of electronic journals of National Institute of Technology, Tiruhcirapalli. The study carried out at the NIT, Tiruchirapalli revealed that 67% of students and 33% of faculty use the electronic journals. 25% of the respondents access electronic journals daily. 45.4% access once in a week. 14.8% access electronic journals once in a month and 14.8% access as and when they feel like it. 53.4% of the respondents access 1-3 journals in a month. 26.1% access 3-6 electronic journals in a month. 12.5% access 6-10 electronic journals in a month and 8% access above 10 journals.

OBJECTIVES OF THE STUDY

To carry out the present research study systematically, the investigator laid down the following objectives,

1. To find out the awareness and the use of online journals among faculty members in science stream of university of Pune.
2. To find out the opinions of science faculty members about the adequacy of available online journals on the library web portal of University of Pune.

3. To identify the features, functionality and development of electronic journals
4. To trace the problems in the use of online journals
5. To suggest ways and means to overcome problems faced by the faculty members.

RESULT AND DISCUSSION

Perceived level of computer literacy : A computer literate user is expected to benefit from effectively use online service and confidently explore the amazing world of internet. Effective use of these online databases/journals for retrieving needed information would be cumbersome without proper computing and information retrieval skill. Hence the Respondents were asked to indicate their skill in the use of compute. According to their own assessments, a majority 72% Respondents reported that they are having 'average skill' in the use of computers. 21% of the Respondents opined to have 'Above average skills' and least 7.4% Respondents stated to have 'below average skill'

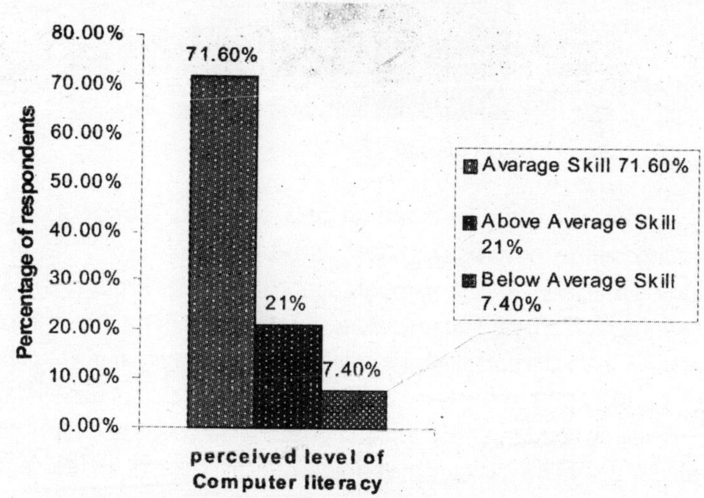

Perceived level of using the kinds of library resources : Faculty members of science stream use various library resources, in this context Respondents were asked about their preference of library resources. According to their responses the large majority of 92.62

percent Respondents reported that they use online/electronic resources, 63.93 percent of the Respondents use print resources from the library, and 24.59 percent Respondent use CD ROM resources, and 24.59 percents Respondents were using parallel resources like electronic, print, and CD ROM. In the present research study it was found that the highest 92.62 percent Respondents use online resources than those Respondents who use print and CD ROM resources.

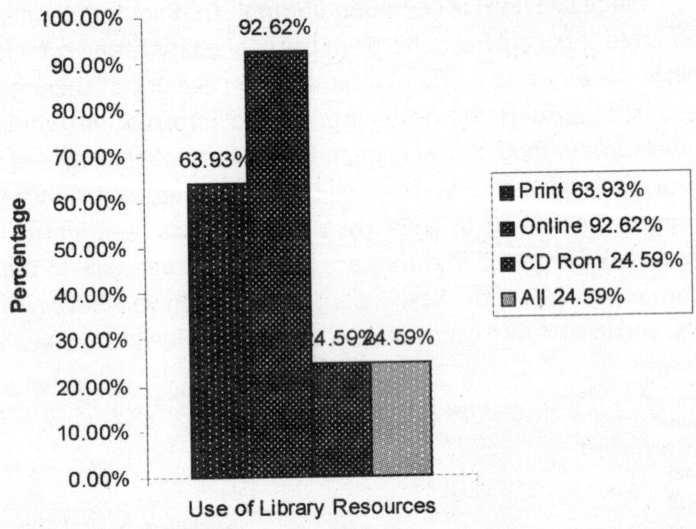

Links of online journals access : The Respondents were accessing online journals since last decade from different sites e. g. through publishers URLs, through search engine, through the link internet facility' created on university library home page. And through Jayakar library web portal which created through Jayakar library staff, on 1st august 2008 at the Jayakar library home page. It is beneficial to follow the link of every U.G.C InfoNet publisher wise full text databases for accessing online journals in various areas of subjects. In this regard Respondents were asked to give the response about accessing online journals. The result are summarized in Chart 2 that the large majority of 68.03 Respondents were access online journals through the link 'internet facility' created on the university of Pune home page, 56.55

percent responded that they were use search engine for accessing online journals, and only 43.44 percent Respondents were use Jayakar library Web Portal to access online journals and remaining 31.14 percent of the Respondents were accessing online journals through directly from publishers URLs.

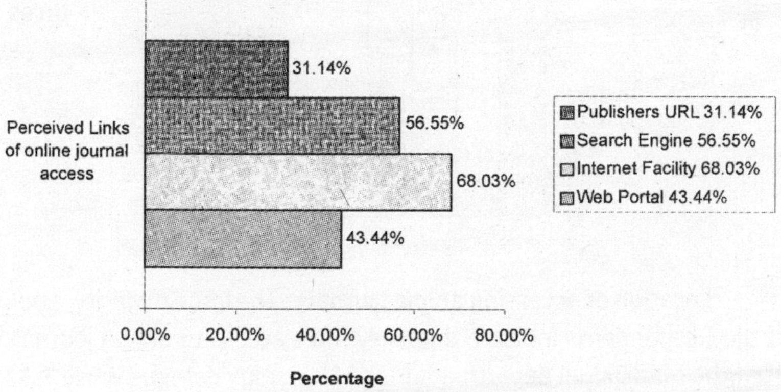

Frequency of Library Visit : The Respondents were requested to mark all the modes by which they visit library. According to their responses, the 39.34 percent Respondents opined that they were visited library once a month, 19.67 percent Respondent were visit library in twice a week as well as more 19.67 percent Respondents were visit library once a fortnight, the ratio of the daily visiting library were just 4.91 percent out of total number of Respondents. 4.09 percent Respondents were visiting library trice a week and 12.29 percent Respondents had not visited to their University library.

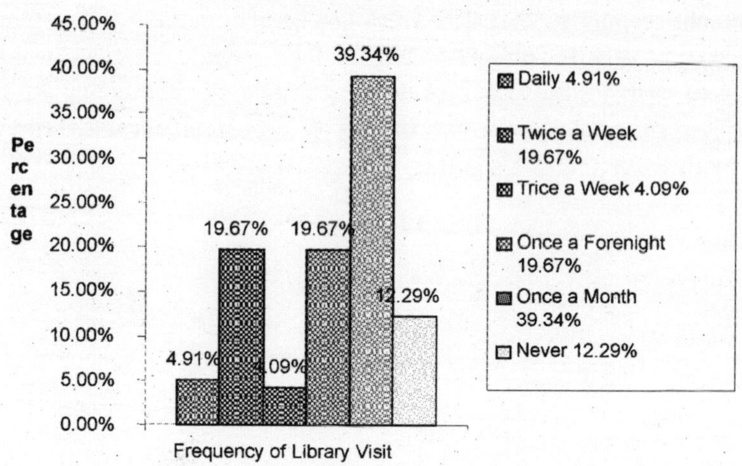

Location of accessing online journals : The large majority, 100% of the Respondents indicate that they have access to online journals from their individual department in the University campus while 7.37 percent Respondents opined that they were access online journals from their residence, and there were no response for accessing online journals from university library building out of total numbers of Respondents.

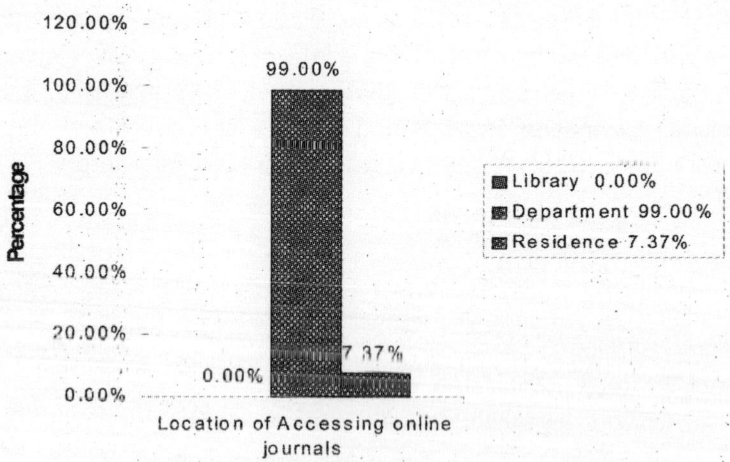

Perceived level of online journals search : Respondents were requested to mark the entire mode by which they search the online journals from library Web portal. Generally online journals are search by subject, by title, by Author, and other e.g. by publisher, ISBN no. etc. according to their responses, it was found that the large majority of 77.04 percent Respondents were search online journals by subject 62.92 percent Respondent were search the online journal by title search, 42.62 percent Respondents search their required online journals by authors search and at least 7.37 percent Respondents search their online journals by other type e. g. by publishers name and ISBN no etc.

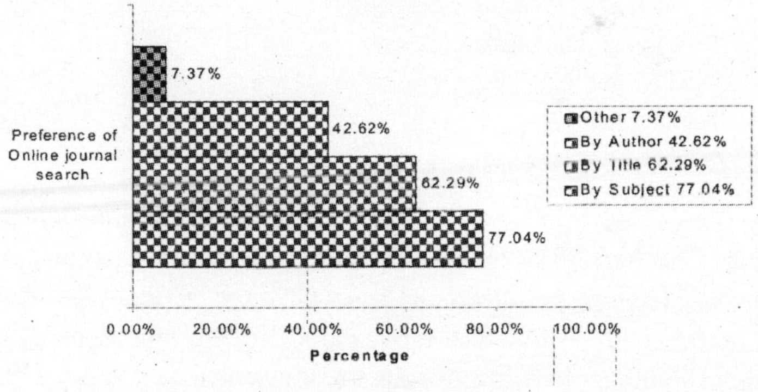

Experience of online journals use : Respondents were asked to indicate the number of years of experience they had in using the online journals. It is found that 38.52 percent respondents have been using online journals for last five years, and 26.22 percent Respondents have been using online journals for last ten year, they have ten year experience in using online journals. The chart also depicts that only 13.11 percents Respondents started using online journals since 2 years, and few 21.31 percents Respondents' have less than a year of experience. Overall, Respondents had good amount of experience to exploit optimally the electronic journals and services.

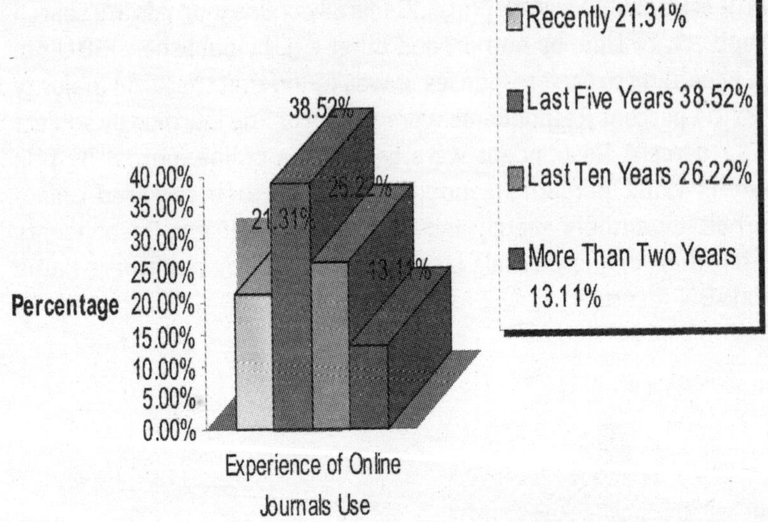

Perceived modes of archival collection for online journals access : The Respondents were asked to indicate the opinion about archival collection of electronic journals provided by university library web portal available in which mode e.g. CD ROM, online, hard copy of bound volumes/ back issue of electronic journals. According to their assessment, the large majority of 95.08% Respondents stated that archival collection of electronic journals available in online mode, 18.03%Respondents stated that the archival collection of online journal available in hard copy of bound volumes or back issue of online journals, and vary few 14.75% Respondents were stated that the archival collection of electronic journal available in both hard copy and online mode, and at least 1.63% Respondents opined that archival collection of online journals available in CD ROM mode. The majority of responses stated that online archival collection is available mostly online than CD ROM and hard copy of back issues.

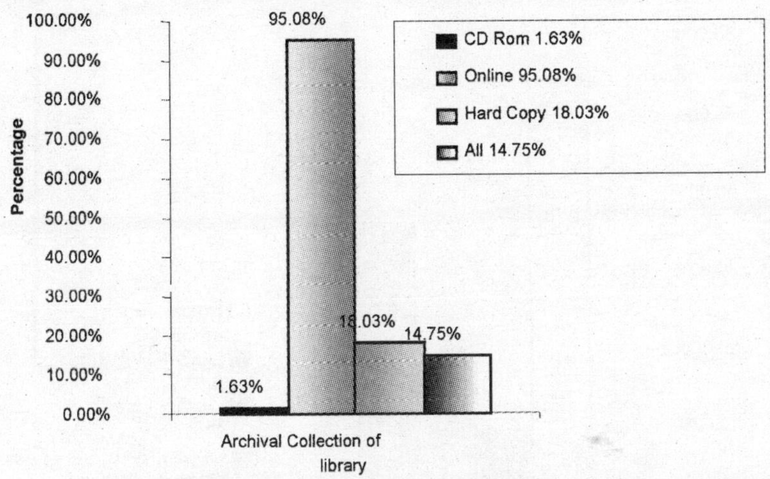

Library alerting Services : The Respondents were asked to indicate their responses about the current issue of the electronic journals because the new issues of online journals always come in the library in the print and the online form, then the faculty member should be aware about the current information, in this regard the Respondents were asked to indicate their responses about the new issue of online journals, it is found that the majority of 48.36 percent Respondents state that they come to know about know journals through email alert service (provided by library staff), 36.06% Respondents indicate that they come to know about New journals through library Web page, and very few 11.47 % Respondents indicate that they come to know about New issue through library user, and at least 9.83% of the Respondents state that they come to know about current issue through library bulletin (Internet) the majority of respondent indicate internet related alert service, those services must be update for better services through the library.

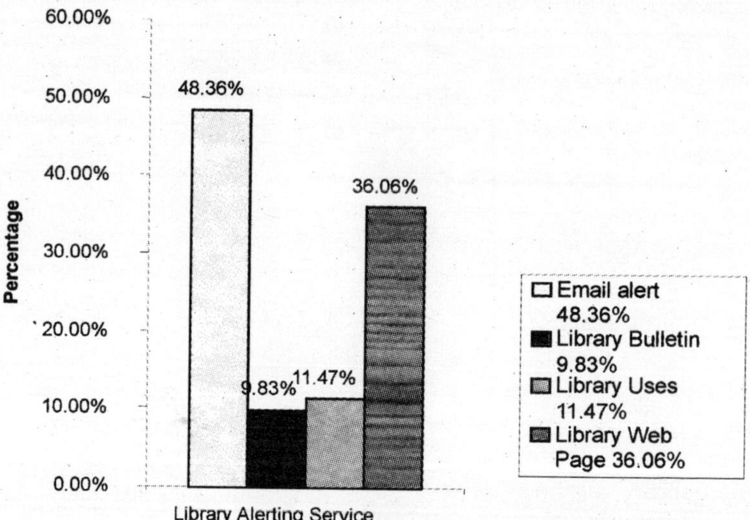

Internet Speed : Accessibility of online journals and its use rapidly depend on the internet speed. When internet speed is slow it take more time to accessing, downloading the articles then it is major problem for provision. In this regard Respondents were asked to indicate their opinions about the internet speed in the university campus; According to their assessment it was found that the large majority of 40.16% of the Respondents stated that the internet speed in the university campus was in average, 27.04% of the respondents opined that the speed was slow in University campus, 29.50% of the Respondents marked for the very slow about the speed of internet in university campus. And at least 0.81% responded that the internet speed was fast. Thus it seen that the internet speed is in average the university campus and it is a major problem in accessing online journals. The speed of internet must be increase.

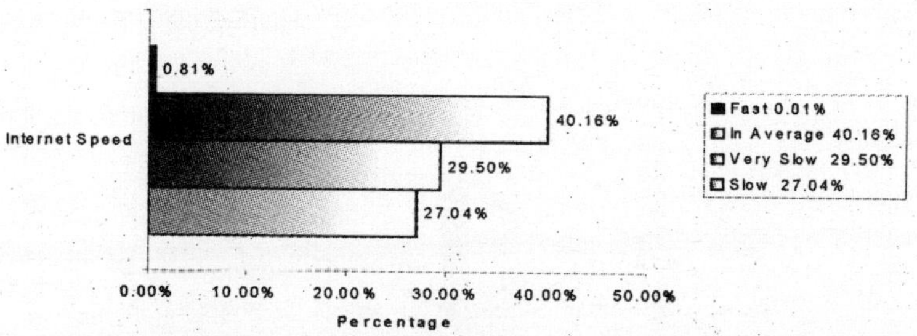

Use of UGC INFONET Publisher wise Full text databases : UGC INFONET E-journal consortia provide Full text and Full text com. Bibliographic databases to provide online journals access to 150 Universities in the country. Respondents were asked to mark about the awareness of UGC INFONET E-journals consortia according to their responses total majority of Respondents were aware about the availability of UGC INFONE E-journal consortia access at the university library and the large majority of 75.40 percent the responded that they could obtain required information from UGC INFONET journals. The percentage of Respondents about the use of publisher wise Full text databases at the Jayakar library web portal university of Pune. According to their assessment it was found that, the large majority of 89.34 percent Respondents were used Elsevier science/science direct publisher wise full text database to access online journals. 66.39 percent responded for Springer link, 42.62 percent of the Respondents indicated for Nature, 36.88 percent and 36.88 percent Respondents marked for the use of American chemical Society, and Back well publishing. 35.24 percent for Oxford University Press, 25.40 percent for Annual Review, 23.77 percent for Institute of Physics, 22.95 percent for American physical society, 20.49 percent marked for Jstor, 18.03 percent for American Institute of Physics13.11 opined for IEEE-Computer Society use, 4.09 percent for Project Euclid, 7.37 percent for EBISCO, 3.27 percent for (SIAM) Society for Industrial and Applied Mathematics, 3.27 percent for Emerald, and at least 0.81 percent and the same 0.81 percent marked for the use of Portland Press and Project Muse at the University Library.

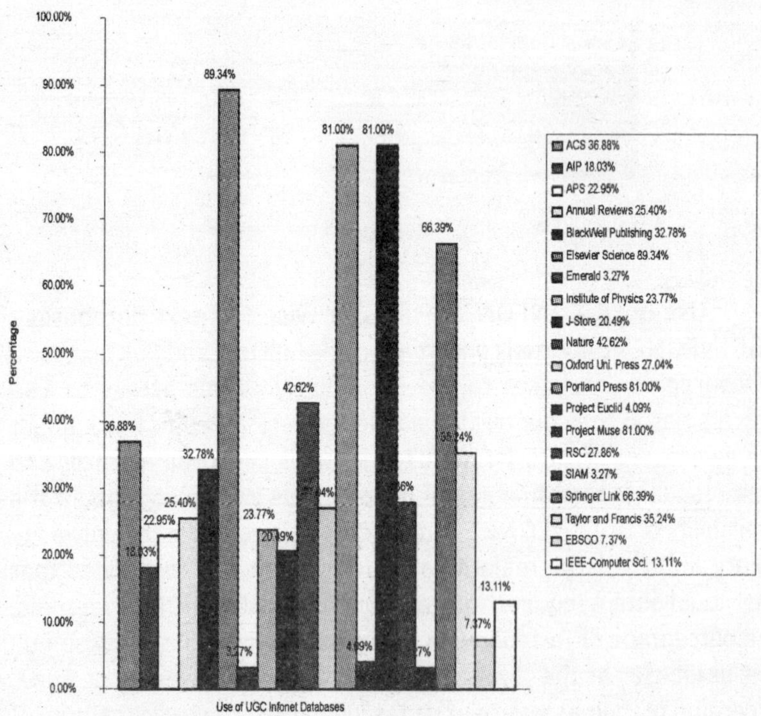

Use of Bibliographical Databases : Jayakar Library University of Pune Has subscribed some bibliographical databases for accessing online journals and other useful services. Then it must be used in this regard Respondents were asked to indicate their opinion for their assessment of the use of Bibliographical databases. According to their opinions it was found that the majority of 35.24% Respondents marked for the use of Web of Science or Web of Knowledge. 33.60% were use Sci Finder Scholar, 14.75% responded for Royal Society of Chemistry (Six databases) 9.83% marked for the use of MathSciNet, 8.19% responded for the use of JCCC, and very few 1.63% Respondents indicate their opinion for the use of ISDB (Institute for Studies in Industrial Development) this all of this Bibliographical databases are very useful for the science community for their research and teaching.

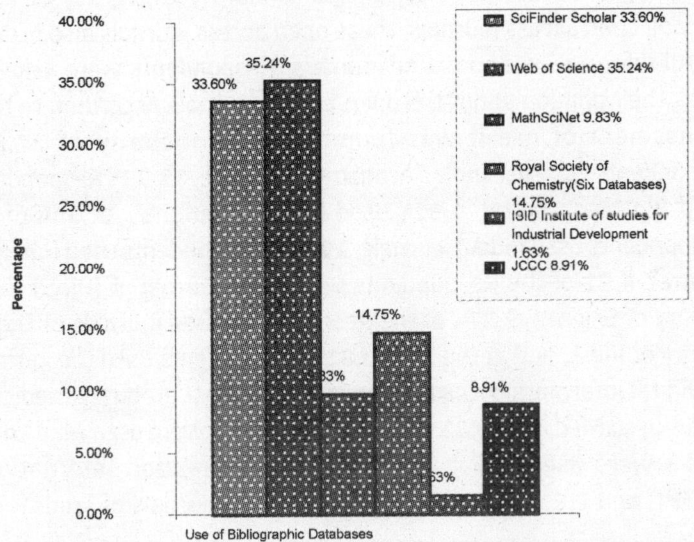

Open access Free Directories : Jayakar Library University of Pune provide open access free directory it is open for all Researcher and faculty members, it is also provider online journals. Directory of open access journals (DOAJ), Open J-gate, Free Medical Journals Provides subject wise journals, Respondents asked to indicate their responses about the use of open access free directory, it was found that the 14.75% Respondents were marked for open J-gate, 12.29% Respondents used (DOAG) Directory of open access Journals. And 4.91% of the Respondents opined that they were using Free Medical Journals.

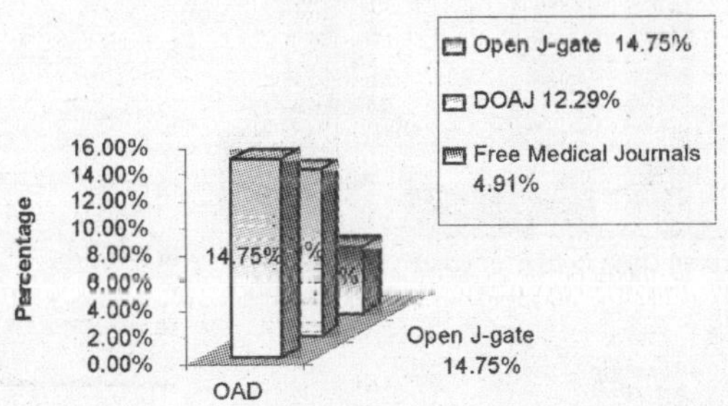

Open access Journals : Jayakar Library University of Pune Provide open access journals, these open access journals also provide useful information and online journals. Respondents were asked to mark their opinion about the open access journals According to their assessment of use it was found that the majority of 27.86% respondents were use Indian academy of Science, 13.93% Respondents used Bio Med Central, 4.91% used Bio International, 22.99% of the Respondents used Indian journals, 19.97% Respondents used Pub Med Central, 4.91 of the Respondents were used journal of (PloS) Pubic Library of Science, 3.27% of the Respondents used journals of Digital library of India, and at the least 0.81% Respondents used the journals of Digital information, 0.81% used journal of Post graduate medicine, 0.81% used Med IND, 0.81% of the Respondents were used Med know, 0.81% were used Molecular Diversity Preservation International (MDPI) and 0.81% responded that they used journals of Trials.

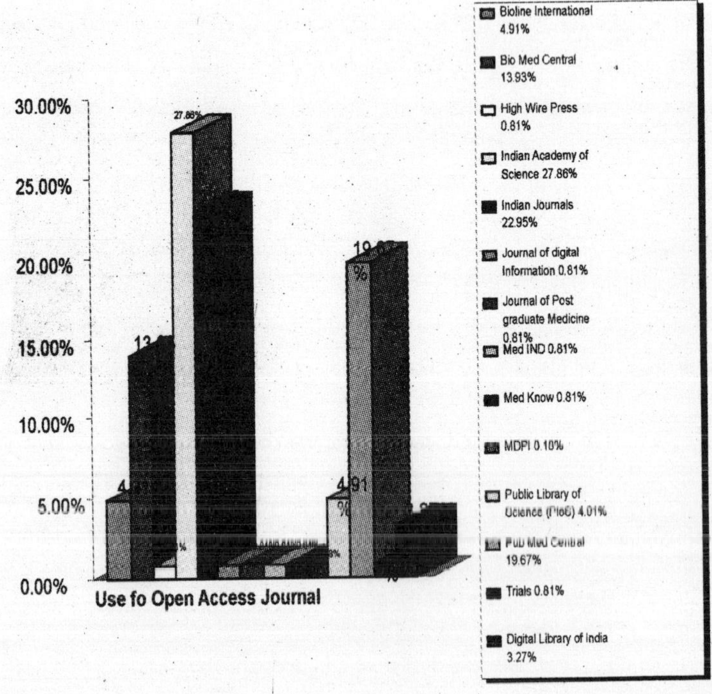

Components online journal : Respondents were asked to indicate their opined about the use of online journals components, The options 'Table of contents, Journals Abstracts, Full text, Article reference, as a online journals Components, with the Modes of use like, 'Most – A, Often – B, Sometimes – C, Somewhat – D, Least – E, were given to obtain the right perceived level of used online journal components. It was found that the Table of contents used by Respondents in different level, that the majority of 35.24% of the Respondents use mostly table of content, 20.49 responded often use of table of content, 15.57% used sometime (TOC), 3.27% marked for somewhat use of (TOC), and at least 3.37% Respondents use (TOC), Journals Abstracts. The majority of 56.55% Respondents were using Journals Abstracts Mostly, 25.40% Respondents were using journals abstract often. 4.91% of the Respondents use journals abstracts sometime about the use of journal Abstracts, 1.63% Respondents were use somewhat journal abstracts. Full text: Respondents were asked to mark their opinion about the use of Full text online journal component, after the survey it was found that the majority of 52.81% of the Respondents were using full text mostly, 36.06% Respondents responded that they used Full text often. 11.47% responded that they were using sometime full text component of online journals. Article reference: 19.67% Respondents were using the article reference mostly, 33.60% used Article reference often, and 21.31% Respondents were using Article reference sometimes, 5.73% Respondents were using article reference somewhat, and at least 1.63% of the Respondents were using article reference as a component of online journals. The following Chart shows the percentage of Respondents with their use of online journal Components;-

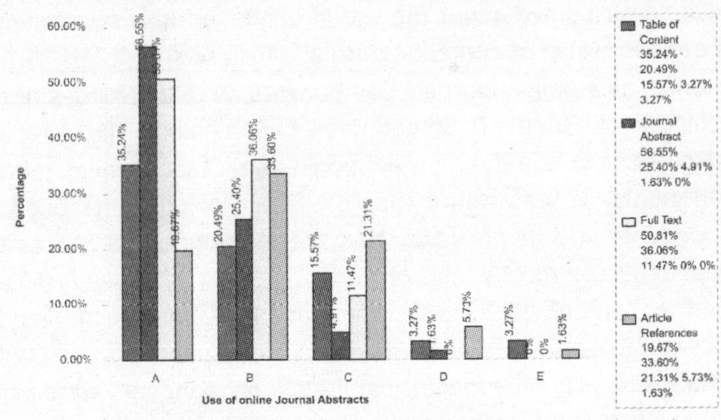

Perceived Level of using online journal Format : Online journals are published in various formats and different format provide different feature for article, thus the user use different format for their use of online journals or other purpose. Respondents were asked to give their opinions about the online journal format. Respondents were using various formats with various mode like most, often, sometime, somewhat, least. (PDF) Portable Document Format Respondents were asked to indicate their opinion about the PDF use, According to their survey it was found that the large majority of 95.90% Respondents marked for the mostly use of PDF, 4.09% Respondents marked for the often use of the PDF, (HTML) Hypertext markup language- 10.65% of the Respondents marked for the mostly use of HTML, 17.21% of the Respondents used HTML often, 18.03% of the Respondents opined for somewhat HTML format. 2.45% of the Respondents were using HTML somewhat, and 7.37% of the Respondents were using HTML at least. SGML-Standard general Markup Language- 3.27% of the Respondents were used SGML sometime, 2.45% of the Respondents marked for the use of SGML somewhat, 15.57% of the Respondents were used SGML format at least. ASCII- 3.27% of the Respondents were marked for the use of ASCII sometime, and the same 3.27% of the Respondents were use ASCII format somewhat, 15.57% opined that they using ASCII format at least. MSWord- 4.91% of the Respondents were use MS-Word mostly, 18.85% of the Respondents were using MS-Word often, 10.65% were using MS-Word sometime, 2.45% responded that they use MS-Word format somewhat, and 9.01% of the Respondents were use online format at least. Postscript- 1.63% of the Respondents were using Postscript Format mostly, 7.35% of the Respondents were use the postscript format often, and 8.19% of the Respondents using the postscript format sometimes for using online journals, 2.45% of the Respondents were using postscript format somewhat, and 13.11% of the Respondents were using postscript format at least.

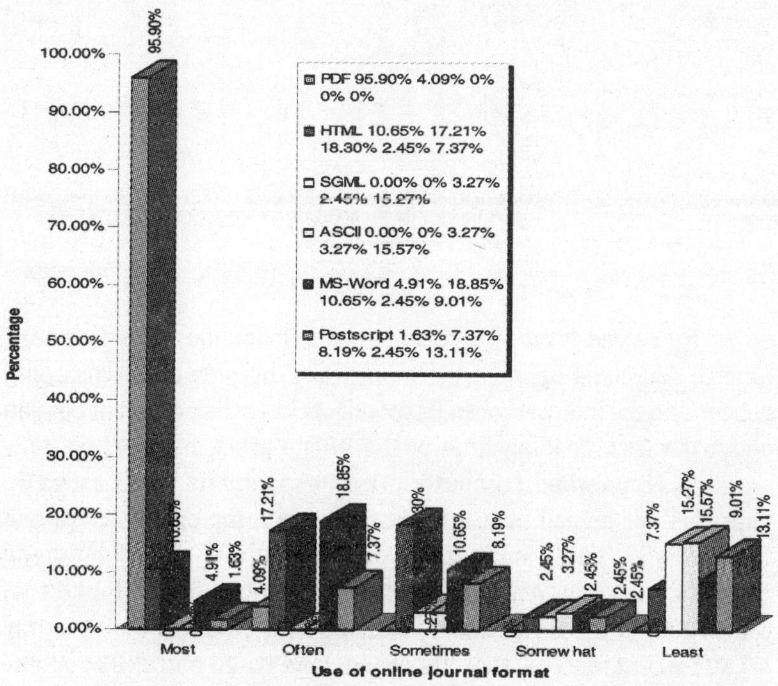

Frequencies of using online journals : Respondents were asked how frequently they used online journals. Option were Daily, weekly, Monthly, Biweekly, Bimonthly, the chart show that the large majority of 50.00% of the Respondents were accessing online journals Daily, 22.13% of the Respondents were accessing online journals weekly, 7.37% of the Respondents were accessing online journals monthly.18.03% of the Respondents were accessing online journals biweekly and 2.45% of the Respondents were accessing online journals Bimonthly.

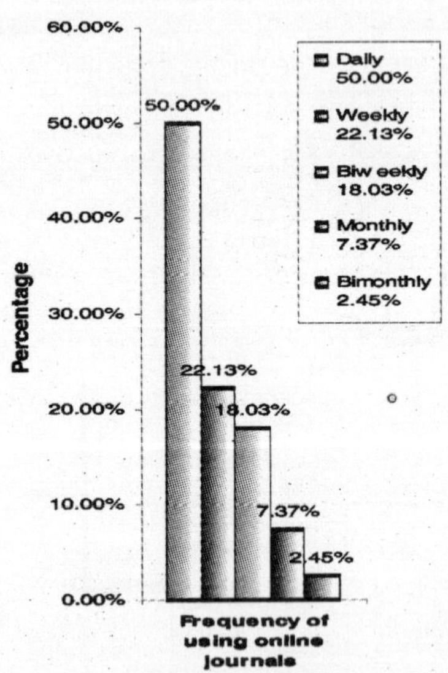

Perceived level of system speed : Online journal article taka time to download online articles generally the time of downloading depends on the internet speed Respondents have their different opinion about the downloading time of the online articles with their daily working Networked computer. The Respondents were asked to indicate their opined about the system speed; the options were less than 10 min, 10-20 min, 20-30 min, 30-40 min, 40-50 min, and more than 50 min. According to their responses, it was found that the 36.06% of the Respondents stated that it take less than 10 min, 40.98 percent reported that the system take 10-20 min, 9.83% opined that the system take 20-30 min time to download the online article, 4.91% respondent opined that it take 30-40 min to download one article, 2.45% responded that it take 40-50 min, and 2.45% of the Respondents stated that their networked computer at their Department it take more than 50 minute to download one article. Overall opinions depend on the speed of the Internet, Because of that Internet speed must be improved.

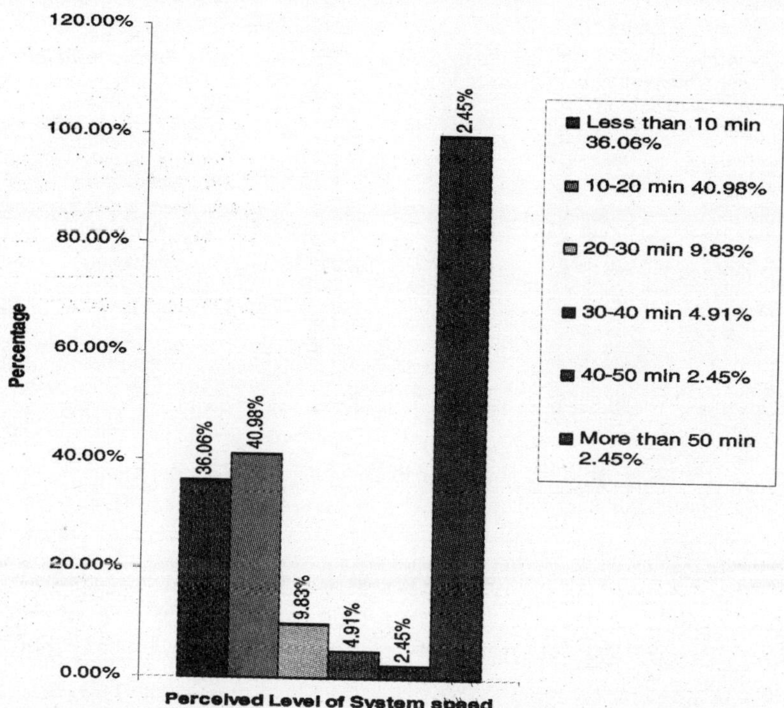

Time spent for reading online journals : Respondents were asked about the time which they spent weekly on reading online/off line journals it was found that the large majority of 43.44 percent of the Respondents state that they spent more than 120 min weekly on reading online journals. 4.91 percent spent 90-120 minute for reading online journals, 22.55 percent Respondents spent 60-90 minute, and 9.83 percent of the Respondents spent 30-60minute on reading online journals, 6.55 percent of the Respondents spent up to 30 minute on reading online journals. It was found that 50.81 percent Respondents were spent above 180 minute weekly on off line reading article. 22.95 percent of the respondent spent 120-180 minute weekly on off reading. 4.91 percent of the Respondents state that they were spent 60-120 minute on off line reading. 4.91 percent of the Respondents were reported that they were spent up to 60 minute weekly.

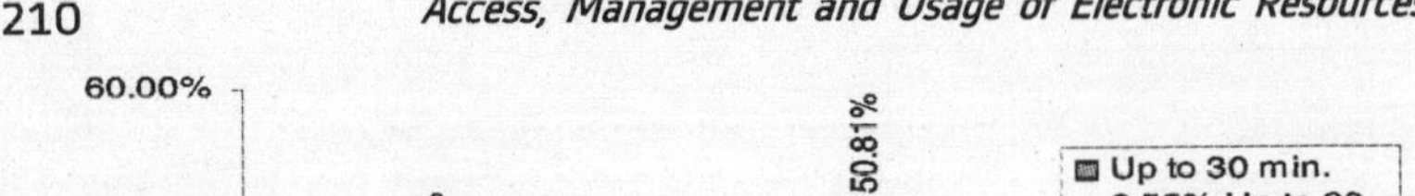

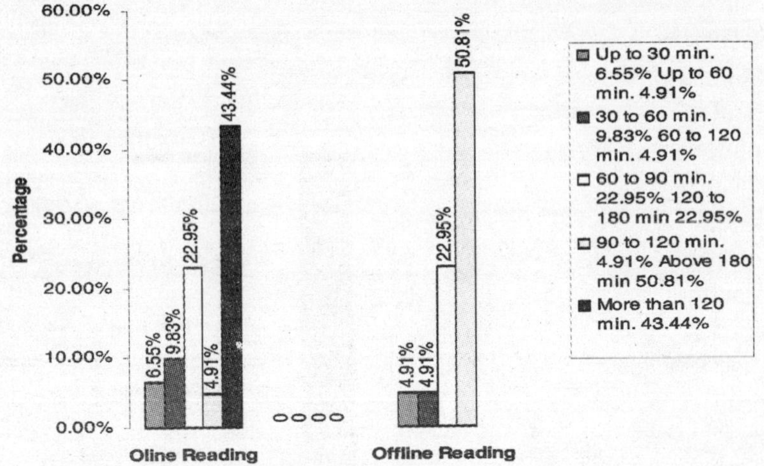

Ratio of reading online article : Respondents were asked to mark about the ratio of online article by weekly according to their assessment; it was found that the 13.93 percent of the Respondents read more than 15 articles online in a week. 13.11 percents of Respondents opined that they were read 10-15 articles in a week, 47.75 percent Respondents were read 5-10 articles in a week, and 26.2 percent of the Respondents read less than 5 articles in a week.

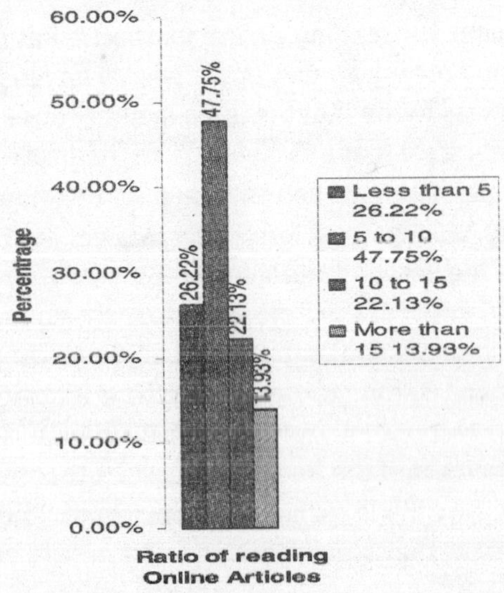

Perceived level of online reading and on print reading : Respondents were asked to reported their opinion about the reading online articles, the options were read on monitor and read on print, indifferent mode like always, often, usually, sometime, Never, It was found that the Respondents were preferred to read on the monitor and on print. Read on Monitor: it was found that the large majority of 45.08 Respondents were always read their articles on the monitor, 28.68 percent of the Respondents were often read the journal on the monitors, 13.93 percent responded that they were usually reading articles on the monitor, 18.03 percent of the were read some what their articles on the monitor, 2.45 percent of the Respondents were never read their articles on the monitor. Read on print: it was found that, the large majority of 26.22 percent Respondents were read their articles always on the print, 22.26 percent of the Respondents were read their articles often on the print. 18.03 percent Respondents were read articles usually on the print. 20.49 percent of the Respondents were read their articles sometime on the print, and 9.01 percent of the Respondents were never read the articles on print.

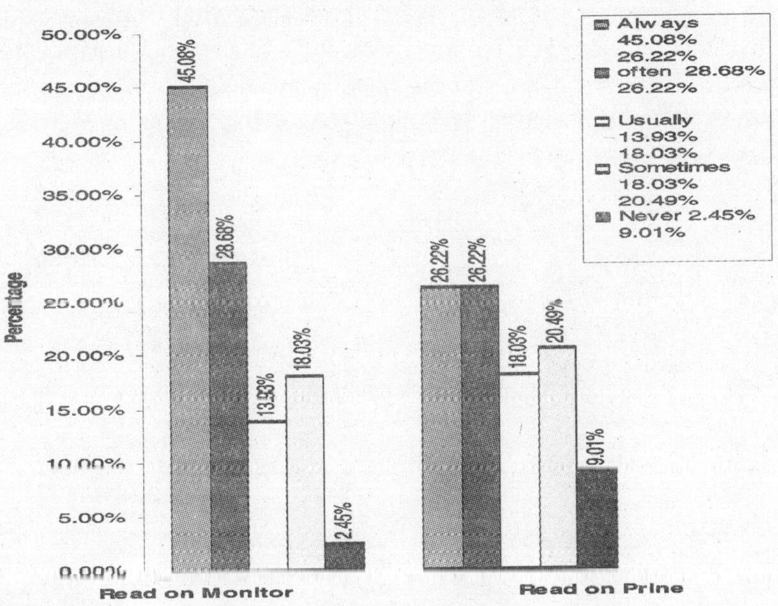

Online journals browsing features : The Respondents were asked indicate their opinions about online journals browsing features, in this regard several, specific statements were given and agreements and disagreements of the Respondents were recorded. The Chart: 22 shows that the 46.72 percent Respondents were agree strongly with the online journals browsing features, 44.26 percent were agree somewhat, 7.37 percent were disagree somewhat, about the content multimedia information as an online journal browsing feature. It was found that the large majority of 55.73 percent Respondents were Agree strongly, 41.80 percent of the Respondents were agree somewhat, 0.81 percent Respondents were disagree somewhat, and 0.81 percent of the Respondents were disagree strongly about the 'content easy to understand' a online journals browsing feature, 68.85 percent Respondents were agree strongly, 30.32 percent Respondents were agree somewhat 0.81 percent of the Respondents were disagree some somewhat, and 0.81 percent of the Respondents were disagree strongly about the 'user friendly interface' as a online journal browsing feature, as well as 40.10 percents Respondents were agree strongly, 47.54 percent Respondents were agree somewhat, 9.01 percent Respondents were disagree somewhat and 2.45 percent Respondents were disagree strongly about the 'reading on monitor' a online journal browsing feature. Overall statement shows that the online journals were very beneficial for the Respondents.

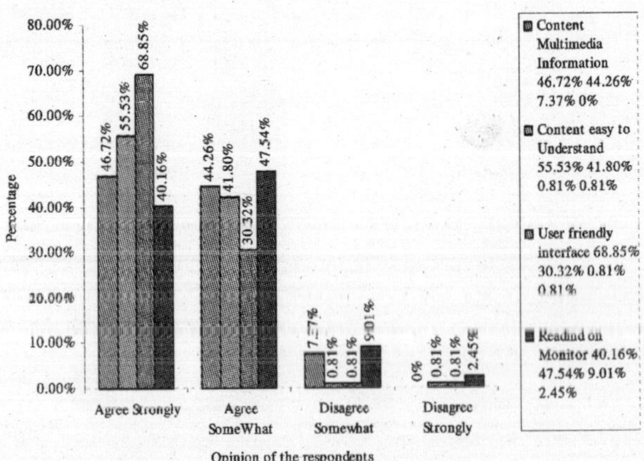

Purpose of using online journals : Respondents were asked to indicate their opinion about the purpose of using online journals, It was found that the large majority of Respondents were using online journals for the for the purpose of research need, majority of 85.24 percent Respondents were using online journals for the purpose of teaching, 79.50 percent of the Respondent were using online journals for the purpose of updating knowledge. 73.77 percent Respondents were using online journal for the purpose of preparing study materials, the most important purpose of the online journals is research reported by the majority of the Respondents.

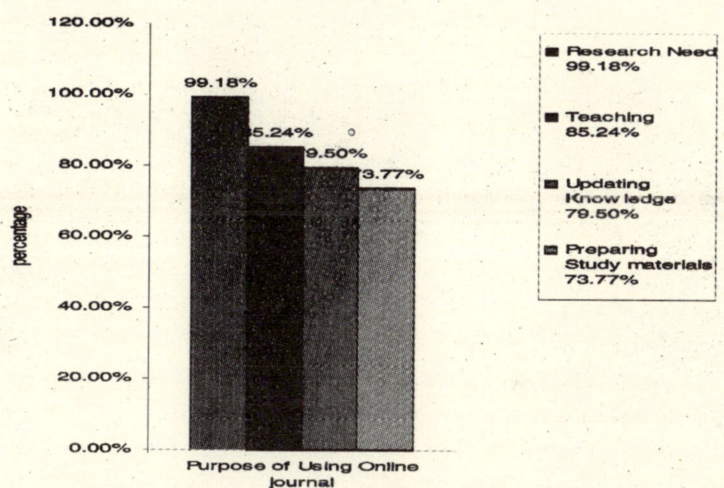

Regularly used search engines: - The Respondents were requested to provide their opinions about the regularly used search engines. It was found that the majority of 99.18 percent Respondents were using Google 19.67 percent Respondents were using SCIRUS, 4.09 percent were use Info seek, 70.49 percent Respondents use regularly Wikipedia, the free Encyclopedia, 9.83 percent Respondents were using Alta- Vista, 29.50 percent Respondents were use Yahoo search engine. The result is that about regularly using search engine among the Respondents are Google and the Wikipedia, The free Encyclopedia.

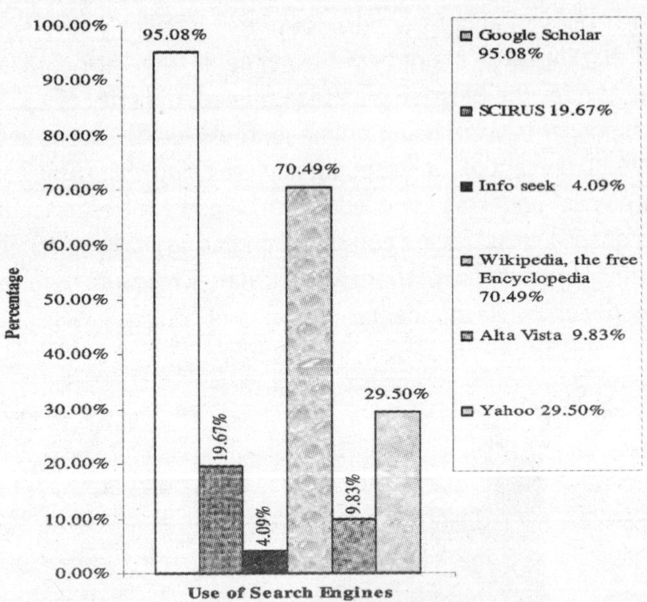

Barriers of online journals use : Respondents were asked to indicate their opined about the barriers in using online journals use, the options were lack of time, cost, unawareness of the use, lack of facilities, inadequate working hours, lack of system speed, difficulties, in accessing Non availability of Full text. According to their assessment, it was found that, the majority of 75.40 percent Respondents stated that they were facing lack of system speed, 76.22 percent of the Respondents were stated that they were facing the problem of Non availability off Full text, 37.70 percent Respondents were facing the barrier of difficulties in accessing, 36.88 percent were stated that the lack of time, 8.09 percent Respondents were facing the barrier of lack of facilities, 4.91percent and the 4.91 percent Respondents were facing the difficulty of Unawareness of use and Inadequate working hours, after considering all the problems it is seen that non availability of full text and the lack of system speed, difficulties of accessing and lack of time were the major problem in the use of online journals.

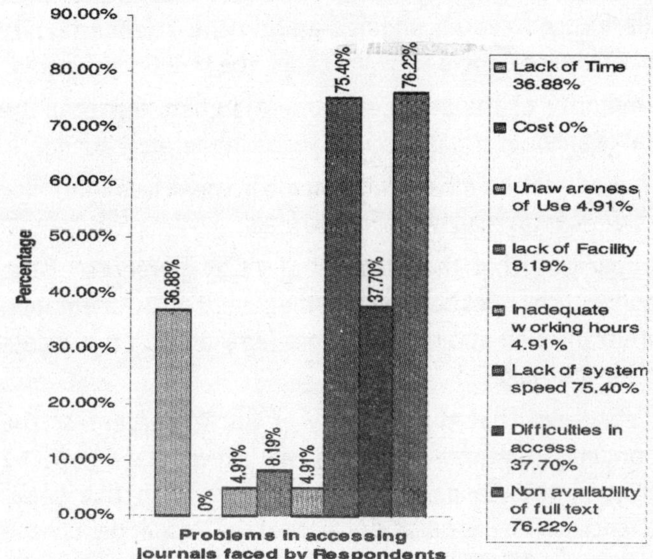

MAJOR FINDINGS

1. The majority of science faculty members use online journals for Research, teaching and for updating knowledge. The most important purpose among these is Research purpose.
2. The majority of 89.34 percent of the respondent were using science direct journals and the majority of 66.39 percent of the science faculty members responded that they access Springer link journals than other publisher wise full text databases. Thus it can be observed that the most preferred online journals of the science community are Springer journals and journals of science direct full text databases.
3. The majority of science faculty members were using Google and Wikipedia, the free Encyclopedia search engines regularly.95.08 percent of the faculty members responded that they were using Google search engine regularly and 70.49 percent responded for the use of Wikipedia, the Free

Encyclopedia search engines. The reveals that the most regularly used search engines among the science faculty members were Google and Wikipedia, the free Encyclopedia.

4. The majority of the science faculty members felt that the available online journals in science were moderately adequate.
5. The majority of science faculty member spent less than four hours weekly on reading online journals.
6. It is observed that the majority of 71.21 percents of the Respondents had not been getting the benefit of the orientation program through library staff to get familiar with the access to online journals.
7. It is observed that the majority of 26.22 percent of the Respondents have more than ten year experience and 38.52 percent of the Respondents have more than five years experience as well as 13.11 percents of the Respondents have more than two year experience and 21.31 percents or the Respondents were recently starting to access online journals.
8. It was observed that the large majority of 48.36 percents of the Respondents were using E-mail alert services to know the new issue in the library. As well as the large majority of 71.31 percent of the Respondent's state that the Jayakar library university of Pune provided services are fairly well, it is found that the faculty members opined to provide independent net connection to each faculty members PC not through D-Link.
9. A great majority of the Respondents agreed that they were getting access to more information to and able to save their time considerably in addition to improve their professional competency due to the use of online journals.
10. It is observed that 'Retrieval of Irrelevant Information' 'Poor Connectivity or Slow Access' and 'Poor databases searching skill' are the major problems identified by the Respondents in the use of online journals.
11. It was also found that the Non availability of full text, lack of time and lack of system speed were the most important factors

that hinder the use of electronic journals among the science faculty members in Pune University campus.

SUGGESTIONS

The suggestions are based on the finding of the study. The following suggestions are put forward to improve the use of online Journals among the science faculty members in University of Pune;

1. At regular intervals, the University library should organize the orientation training program so that maximum number of user can learn how to use of online journals and other electronic resources.
2. In order to eliminate the slow pace of internet connectivity it may be suggested to the to increase Bandwidth and making available computers with latest processors as terminals for online journals and other electronic information sources use.
3. More number of computer terminals with electronic information resources accessibility should be instilled and repaired of the non working computers in every department as well as each PC of faculty members should be connected through individually to internet connection not with D-Link to get proper access and save the time of faculty members.
4. The emergence of different format of online journals. Necessitate the need of help, supports and explanation of appropriate time, hence the science community of university of Pune may be provide with on-going assistance through compilation, of manual and handbooks in the use of EIS, assistance via e-mail, personal assistance and accessing quality information.
5. Also information regarding popular and latest website with their address should be displayed on the notice board on the library web page.
6. It is also suggested that university library should subscribe more useful databases e. g. 'review of scientific information,' 'ASP'- American scientific Publishers' and must be increase the

subscription of 'Web of Knowledge' and "Biological abstracts, Nature, and 'RSC' Royal society of Chemistry and science direct journals according to science community for their pursuit.

CONCLUSION

The emergence of electronic information and communication Environment has provide the academic science community of university of Pune. With wide opportunities to satisfy their information needs. The study state that the Jayakar library is switching over to electronic sources to electronic sources at on accelerated pace. Printed sources are supplemented by electronic databases, e-journals, and a variety of other media. The study state that according to the assessment of the respondents that the majority of 92.62 percent of the respondents were using online resources and the large majority of 100 % Respondents were aware about the availability of the online journals at the Jayakar library Web Portal. As well as 98.36 percents of the respondent reported that the electronic journals were supported to their research and teaching. This study has put forth result that deserves a close and a careful scrutiny. The respondents were probed about the possible constraints, retrieval of irrelevant information, poor connectivity, poor databases searching skills, figure as significant pointers to the current state of affairs. The finding of this study has provided useful insight for the library management to take necessary steps to strengthen the existing electronic information sources and services and to maximize the use of electronic journals among the faculty members of science stream in university of Pune.

BIBLIOGRAPHY

59th Annual Report (2006 – 2007), of University of Pune.

University of Pune Library web Portal. (2008). Retrieved from www.unipune.ernet.in

Angel Borrego, Liuis Anglada, Maite Barrios & Nuria Comellas. (2007). Use and Users of electronic journals at Catalan Universities: the result of a survey. *Journal of academic Librarianship,* 33, 67-75.

Baldwin, Christine (1999). *Super Journal Project.* Retrieved from: http://www.superjournal.ac.uk/sj

Cataloging Electronic Documents, University of North Dakota. Retrieved from http://www.und.edu/dept/library/Departments/abc/Catedocs.html.

Cochenour, Donnice & Moothart, Tom. (2003). E-journal acceptance at Colorado state University: A case study, *Serial Review,* 29, 16-25.

Curtis, Donnelyn. (2005). E-journals: A how-to-do-it manual for building managing, and supporting electronic journal collections. London: Facet Publishing.

Dogan Atilgan & Ozlem (Gokkurtr) Bayram. (2006). An evaluation of faculty use of the digital library at Ankara University, Turkey. *Journal of Academic librarianship,* 32, 86-93.

Hamid R. Jamali, David Nicholas & Paul Huntington (2005). The Use and the Users of the Scholarly E-journals: A Review of Log Analysis Studies. *Aslib Proceedings,* 57, 554-571.

Henk Voorbij & Hilde Ongering (2006). The use of electronic journals by Dutch Researchers: A Descriptive and Exploratory study. *Journal of academic librarianship,* 32, 223.

Hulya Dilek-Kayaoglu (2008). Use of Electronic journals by faculty at Istanbul University, Turkey: The result of a survey. *The journals of a Academic Librarianship,* 34(3), 239-247.

Keiko Kurata, Mamiko Matsubayashi, Shinji Mine, Tomohide Muranushi & Shuichi Ueda. (2007). Electronic journals and their unbundled Functions in scholarly communication: view and Utilization by scientific, Technological and Medical Researchers in Japan. *Information processing and Managemen,t* 43, 1402-15.

Lad, A. (1995). *User study of Armament Research and Development Establishment (ARDE) library.* Dissertation in M.Lib.I.Sc. Pune: University of Pune, pp.10-16.

Mounissamy, P. & Rani S. (2005). Evaluation of usage and usability of electronic journals. *SRELS Journals of Information Management,* 42(2), 189-205.

Rajeshwari, D. (2005). Use of Information sources in digital environment: A case study. In: Murthy, T. A. V (Ed) *Multilingual Computing and information Networked Digital Environment* (pp. 705-711). Proceeding of the 3rd international CALIBER INFLIBNET center, Kochi, India.

Ramesh, D. B. (2008). Emergence of electronic journals. In Nigam, B.S. & Kataria, Sanjay (eds.) *Digital Libraries* (p.259-268). New Delhi, Mahamaya Publishing House.

Raza, M. Masoom & Upadhyay, Askok Kumar. (2006). Usage of E-journals by researchers in Aligarh Muslim University: A study. *The International Information and Library Review,* 38, 170-79.

Rusch-Feja and Siebeky. (n.d.). Evaluation of usage of and Acceptance of Electronic Journals.

Sujata, H. R. and Mudhol, M. V. (2008). Use of Electronic Information sources at the college of Fisheries, Mangalore, India. *Annals of library and Information studies,* 55, 234-245.

Murty, T. A. V. & Satyabati Devi, Thiyam. (2008). Access of e-journals in the institute of higher education through UGC-Info net E-journal consortium. In Nigam, B.S. & Kataria, Sanjay (eds.) *Digital Libraries* (p.151-160). New Delhi, Mahamaya Publishing House.

Tschera Harkness Connell, Sally A. Rogers & Carol Pitts Diedrichs (2005). OhioLINK Electronic Journal Use at Ohio State University. *Portal: Libraries and the Academy,* 5, 371-390.

Vinod, D. (2005). Evaluation of the Use of Print and Electronic Journals in Central Library, I.I.T. Kharagpur. [Project Report]. I.I.T. Kharagpur, p.18-26.

Zhang, Xiaoyin & Haslam, Michaelyn. (2005). Movement toward a predominantly electronic journal collection. *Library Hi Tech,* 23(1), 82-89.

15

Electronic Resource Management: Emerging Trends and Challenging Issues

Madan Kumar Stanley

INTRODUCTION

Electronic Resource Management (ERM) is the systems and practices used to maintain information about internet-based digital information resources. These resources include e-books, e-journals, e-serial publications, citation databases, full text article databases, locally produced on-line databases, institutional repositories, CD-ROM and DVD resources. In a broad sense, e-resource is any digitally served content which is considered to be important and to which access can be provided by the libraries. Some of these are free (Open Access) while some are to be subscribed paying licensing fees.

ERM is a new concept for library professionals in the digital libraries management. As the number and modalities of accessing e-resources are increasing in number and also becoming more sophisticated, the management aspect of these is also becoming complex.

ADVANTAGES OF ERM

- Identifies potential e-resources
- Easy access to wide range of resources
- Simultaneous multi-access to several resources
- Speed & accuracy
- Work-flow can be customized for smooth and efficient working
- Multimedia files can also be included
- Document delivery will be speedier and cost-effective
- Aids in collection evaluation process
- Assigns in negotiation with vendors and aggregators regarding procurement of e-books and e-journals, databases etc.,
- Keeps the users informed about their rights and restrictions pertaining to the use of digital information resources.

STORE HOUSES TO POWER HOUSES: CHANGING SCENARIO

Conventional library collections which comprised of print form of books, journals and such other reading materials are being replaced by their digital counterparts. Gradually, traditional libraries are being transformed from mere static storehouses of print documents to dynamic power houses of information. Many commercial publishers, vendors, aggregator as well as learned societies and universities are involved in producing e-resources in a large scale. Mass digitization of scholarly material and rare documents has become a common feature.

LIBRARIES AS PUBLISHERS

Traditionally the main function of libraries has been collecting and preserving materials published by commercial houses, learned societies, centers of higher learning and also by individuals. With the advent of digital technology, the libraries are turning into publishers. Their products include Institutional Repositories, digitized manuscripts, rare books and journals from their existing print collection. Intellectual content is made available in a form that can be easily shared by the user community. The digital resources provide access to unlimited information resources via internet, 24 x 7 without any geographical limitations. The electronic content tends to be more dynamic than the static nature of print format.

CHALLENGES OF E-RESOURCES

The exponential growth of e-resources is a challenge as along with costs, the licensing models are increasing in number making it hard to have standard policies.

As e-resources are taking away a large part of library budget, many libraries pool their resources together and create consortial purchasing agreements between libraries. However, in consortial procurement what should be renewed and what should be discontinued is not an easy task for librarians.

IT-based resources are expanding rapidly and exerting increasing pressure on librarians by way of rapidly changing information needs the users. In order to meet their ever increasing demand in a digital environment, libraries have to evolve access to materials available in e-format and effectively share them as they have been sharing print resources of yester years through Inter Library Lending. According to Sadeh and Ellington (2005) the life cycle of a typical e-resource includes the stages-discovery, selection, acquisition, access and decision to renew or discontinue a particular resource.

THE FOUR C'S

Ideally, ERM helps librarian to optimize utilization of e-resources through for C's- Collect, Correct, Connect and Control.

Collect: Databases of available resources

Correct: Database must be precise, constantly updated, authority control, accurate connection and management.

Connect: Easiest and speedier connectivity for users with needed information resource.

Control: Optimizes staff and financial resources, work-flow is stream-lined enabling judicious collection development. ERM helps to keep track of on-line subscription and license agreements.

CHALLENGES OF ERM

Taking a larger perspective of the situation prevailing at present in India, the challenges of ERM can be summarized as follows:

- Inadequate financial resources
- Copyright and IPR issues
- Lack of well defined e-reference policy
- Lack of trained professional staff
- Lack of effective Information Literacy facilities
- Need for regular ICT training for professional library staff
- Archiving for future use
- Early e-publications are not compatible with revised, updated versions of softwares. Unless preservation of digital information is actively taken up, the information will become inaccessible due to changing technology platform and media instability.
- Well defined subscription policy for subscribing e-books and e-journals. Whether to go for a single-site license or a multi-site license; number of simultaneous users and remote access.
- Ever changing user information requirements.
- Identification of relevant e-resources
- Technical infrastructure such as software, hardware, internet facilities and specific physical equipments to be kept updated regularly.

CONCLUSION

The way e-resources are managed is becoming distinct. Planning, tasks and communication are giving rise to new innovative approaches. This paradigm shift is a challenge for library professionals as they are to keep themselves in step with the rapid ICT advances. Sophisticated skills for handling e-resources to meet the user information needs has gained priority.

ERM helps in centralizing the resources thereby storage of relevant resources at one point is possible. In addition, staff involved in ERM functions will become aware of recent developments. By this way a library can provide the right information resource to the appropriate user at the right time when it is critically needed. The user gets the needed information at his workstation without any loss of time.

Web sites can go out of date. Databases may be neglected when their creators move on to more green pastures or take up new projects. Digital records that are not moved out of obsolete hardware and software environments are very likely to die with them.

One of the strategies to overcome this hazard is "migration" i.e. periodic conversion of digital materials for new generation computer technology. The ability to view all information to a particular resource without referring to multiple files is the greatest advantage of ERM system.

REFERENCES

Mishra, Jyothi. (2003). Digital storage media: Its care and handling. *IASLIC Bulletin,* 48 (2), 67-70.

Sadeh, T. and Ellington, M. (2005). Electronic resource management systems: The need and the realization. *New Library World,* 106 (5/6), 1-12.

Stanley,M.K. (2012). Collection development challenges in digital environment. *Proceedings of the International Conference on Collection Development in the Digital Environment,* Chennai, Madras University Library, June 2012. pp. 127-130.

Witten, I.H., Loots, M., Trujillo, M.J. & Bainbridge, D. (2002). The promise of digital libraries in developing countries. *The Electronic Library,* 20, 7-13.

16

E-journal Management in Libraries

Seema Parmar

INTRODUCTION

With the application of Information and Communication Technology (ICT), particularly the Internet, there has been a shift from traditional resources to electronic resources (e-resources) having many advantages i.e. fast, easy, remote access , all time accessibility, cost effectiveness and obviation of storage problem. After the advent of Internet, E-resources have flourished in an explosive way and become the focus of Research and Development Institutions in recent years. It is well known that E-resources are the phenomenon of the later part of the 20th century and came in the wake of advances of computer and communication technologies. Now with the emergence of these resources the text and data is available on-line and is read on the end user's computer which is significantly different from publishing in print on the paper. It is in the digital form and does not require any intermediary medium. Information is directly accessed from the host computer. E-resources are such paperless resources which are also called skywriting, web resources and internet resources.

E-JOURNALS

E-journals are important form among e-resources as these are very much helpful in scholarly communication. E-journals can be accessed easily by multiple users at their desktops simultaneously with the support of required technology. Various researchers are getting more and more benefits of having required information from e-journals. Web based full text e-journals have naturally become the most popular tool for the users of the library for locating the desired information. As online access to scholarly scientific content is growing, e-journals are increasingly important resources for scholars and play a significant role in scholarly communication.

There is no universally accepted definition of e-journal. According to ALA Glossary "a journal is a periodical especially one containing scholarly article and/or disseminating current information on research and development in a particular subject field." If this task is done by electronic media then it may be called e-journal. If the content of a journal are produced and stored only in electronic form than it is called e-only journal. When the content of a journal produced, stored and scanned in a database and then retrieved online then same is called 'on-line' journal" (Chakraborty and Chakraborty, 2002). E-journals are vital source of information for scientific research and development. The titles of e-journals are growing three fold every 15 years and their cost is increasing 2.5 times every 10 years (Golwal etal., 2008).

The demand for e-journals is intense as they are among highly needed informational resource for scholar community. Scholarly communication serves as an input to academic research. It is important to know what other researchers in your area are doing so as to improve your own work and to avoid duplicating theirs. Hence, scholars generally want access to a broad range of academic journals.

TAXONOMY OF E-JOURNALS

Different people have categorized e-journals in a different way. Meshram (2000, pg. 18) has defined the following types of e-journals:

1. Internet Applications Electronic Journals or Classic Electronic Journals : Some of the Electronic Journals are available through internet applications, which are also called classic E- Journals. Originally they were distributed via email but now are available on the web and only alerts of new issues are distributed by email. Access to this category of E- Journals is free of cost.

2. Parallel Electronic Journals : These types of journals are published simultaneously in both print and electronic forms. The online version may include the full text of journal, only table of content, or selected articles from print versions. The website offers previews and experts view of issues. Sometimes the electronic version of the print differs from the print journal e.g. article may appear electronically before they are printed or the electronic version may have supplementary material on it.

3. Database model and software model : Another type of E-Journal is called database model and software model. Under the database model articles reside in a centralized database maintained by the publisher and subscribers are given permission to access the database to locate and download articles.

4. CD-ROM journals : Commercial publishers have also made journal titles available on CD-ROMs.

Instead of above categories, there may be another type of journals that are available only in electronic form, no counterpart likes print or CD-ROM is available of these types of journals. These types of journals are called Electronic-only-Journals.

FEATURES OF E-JORNALS

According to Sreekumar and Sunitha (2005) there are following features of e-journals:

- Allow remote access.
- They can be used simultaneously by more than one user.
- Provide timely access.
- Save Physical storage space.

- They can be saved digitally.
- Can support multimedia Information.
- Speedily Searching.
- Accommodate unique features (e.g. links to related items, reference linking).

PURPOSE OF E-JOURNAL MANAGEMENT

The chief purpose or objective of management of e-journals in a library is to explore the various challenges and issues confronted while their purchase and management and find out the feasible ways for their better purchase and maintenance that they could accessible for future use.

The following are some of the objectives of e-journals and its management in libraries:

- "Libraries can solve the ongoing Serials crisis and to share the resources among libraries.
- The main objective is to make awareness among the academicians about the on-line availability of e-journals through intra-net, internet and www.
- Libraries can provide better information service regarding the various e-journal retrieval facilities available.
- The collection of e journal documents can be maintained in libraries.
- Consortia purchasing offers for the single library the opportunity to get access to more journals than they currently have subscriptions to, thus eliminating the continuous cancellation operations.
- Document delivery processes for specific journals" (Thamaraiselvi and Kaliammal, 2011).

MANAGING E-JOURNALS IN LIBRARIES

Among all type of collection building, libraries are strengthening their e-resources specially e-journals also. The libraries therefore are finding different ways to manage this highly spent venture efficiently as this is a very challenge issue today for every library. Managing electronic journals involves various ways to selecting, acquiring, providing everlasting access for users as well as the support of library staff to keep track of them.

Thus, e-journal management has become the essential job for every librarian in the ICT era, when this special type of publication is growing rapidly to meet the ever growing demand of scholar community. As now the scholar community is increasingly adopting this speedy and nascent knowledge carrying publication it becomes the necessity of every library to make well planning for their management. For managing e-journals in better way librarians are required to welcome existing and new coming challenges, They are required be technology familiar, They should know how to deal with licensing, copyright implications and new purchasing methods such as consortia etc. archiving issues etc. In this way broadly management of e-journals involves selection, acquisition, providing access, and archiving etc.

SELECTION

The selection of print journals in a library involve various processes like need of institute community, impact factor of journals, reputation of publisher, price of journals etc. But e-journals are as different from these journals being born in electronic form their selection procedure is obvious to be different. Some important factors are considered for their selection: a) Format of files; b) Types and quality of delivery; c) Price; d) currency: e) updation policy and of conditions of use. Along with the quality of content some other technical, legal and pricing issues should also be taken in to consideration.

Technical issues : Only those libraries will move towards the selection of e-journals who have applicable technology to access them. Various factors are considered while selecting e-journals for the collection of library and they are: a) technology acquainted staff in the library and number of staff required training; b) formats of journals are compatible with the existing hardware and software; c) any technical support given by vendors etc.

Legel issues : While selecting the journals for the library a selector should consult with vendors and aggregators, to assure that all the legal needs are met before the selection decision is made. The library should carefully review licensing terms before the purchase of e-journals. Agreements often include provisions for payment and delivery of the product, warranting and limits, termination of the agreement, customer service information and responsibility of the license for the security of the product.

Pricing issues : Pricing issues of e-journals is also a challenging issue. Prices are different per the type of subscription as different for those libraries who subscribe also the print version; subscribe only e-version and different for title per access.

Different Selection Aids : While selecting e-journals for the libraries different selection aids may be used like- Product reviews, sites of commercial e-journal vendors, site of Electronic Journal access, consult e-journal aggregators.

ACQUISITION

E-journals in libraries are subscribed as per the license or agreements made and defining the periodicity of access under predetermined conditions. Negotiations between the libraries and vendors thus take more time in subscription of these journals. The journals' issues are housed in supplier's server and only accessed when retrieved by users. Access to these resources is mainly through- a) User name and password or IP Address; b) on site access; and c) Access through database. When subscription of e-journals ceases access to them ceases automatically. The problems are therefore- their perpetual access and archiving.

CATALOGUING

When a library subscribes the both version of a title then it is not difficult to maintain a record of e-journal as in the e-catalogue entry the description or link of this parallel version is normally given.

But when cataloging of only e-version requires some different procedure as some issues are involved in their cataloguing-1) The journal articles may be available in different formats such as ASCII, PDF, HTML, PostScript etc.; 2) Some journals publish articles as they are received, with the journal "issue" being compiled subsequently.; and some publishers deposit articles into database rather than maintaing them in discrete back issues.

Libraries now must decide whether or not to catalogue electronic journals. Some libraries list e-journals on their portals as an alternative to cataloguing them. No doubt it is cumbersome when dealing with large numbers of titles, and does not provide good subject access. Others do in different ways by not following the rule requirement of creating a separate cataloguing record for the electronic version, by linking to the e-journal from the records for the print journal. This is unsatisfactory when the electronic and print version differs substantially. Some solutions are being tried. OCLC s CORC (Cooperative Online Resource Cataloguing), project holds some potential for libraries to create cataloguing records for electronic resources more economically. Embedded metadata may also hold some promise. Some libraries have begun embedding metadata in HTML headers for their web pages so that software like CORC can use it to build catalog records automatically. Something similar might be possible if NSDP supplied descriptive metadata to publishers applying for ISSNs, and publishers included this on the home pages of their e-journals.

STORAGE OR PRESERVATION OF E-JOURNALS

Preservation of e-journals is a major distress for libraries. Libraries are still insecure about the transient nature of electronic journals as the publishers do not give any assurance for ever continuation of access. The individual titles may discontinue any time. Vendors or aggregators provide access to e-journals to libraries from a wide variety of. Some of publishers committed to provide perpetual access to libraries. Thus, the transient nature of electronic journals makes the preservation of e-journals a great distress and has become a vital issue which is constantly debated by librarians and publishers. The librarians and publishers are searching a choice of approaches to surmount this issue, but any suitable and trustworthy way for archiving has not been found. Various offline media like microfiche, floppy disk, ZIP disk, DVDs, CD-ROMs etc are used for preserving of e-journals and their access.

LIBRARY CONSORTIA AND E-JOURNALS

Libraries keeping in view, the increasing prices of journals and restricted budgets, are forced to resort to alternatives like Consortia. They have now stopped subscribing e-journals through intermediaries. However purchasing through consortia has become a general practice in the past few years. It can be called "mass purchase of information". A few people called it as "Big Deal". Big Deal is an agreement between libraries and publishers which benefits publishers, authors, libraries and users (Jose and Pacios, 2005, pg. 191).

Thus, consortium has played the major role in scholarly communication as it provides the resource base to Universities. Consortium is a collective activity of a group of libraries towards a common goal of sharing resources. Due to this activity Indian libraries are enriched with a huge number of scholarly resources including journals and databases. A few examples are UGC INFONET, INDEST, FORSA, CSIR, CeRA etc.

PROBLEMS IN MANAGING E-JOURNALS

- Lack of time and too much work load for the librarians.
- Lack of planning and policies on electronic journal management.
- High cost of e-journals and restricted budget.
- Communication gap between vendors and librarians.
- Inadequate personnel to handle e-tools.
- Lack of Expertise/Awareness.
- Lack of support from Faculty/academic staff in selection.
- The lack of initiatives on the part of parent institutions and the absence of action plans or priorities.

- Lack of Funding/infrastructure
- Access and security
- Copyright and Intellectual Property Right
- Internet and Intranet facilities with high bandwidth and monitor the uninterrupted access.
- Licenses varies for –IP authentication, Password authentication, –campus wide licensing, –Limited user licenses
- Access Period varies from publisher/database to another

REFERENCES

Chakraborty, H.K. & Chakraborty, Banani. (2002). *E-Journal: Coming of age*. Paper presented at Caliber Conference Proceedings, 14-16 Feb 2002 held at University of Jaipur, Rajasthan. Retrieved from http://shodhganga.inflibnet.ac.in/dxml/1944/36/browse

Evans, G Edward. (2004). *Developing Library and Information Centre Collections* (4th ed.). Colorado: Libraries Unlimited.

Faruqui, Khalid Kamal (Ed.) (1997). *Development of Collection in Libraries.* New Delhi: Anmol Publications.

Golwal, M.D, Sonawane, S & Vaishnav, A. (2008). *Use of Electronic journals in Dr. Babasaheb Ambedkar Marathwada University, Aurangabad: A Case Study.* Proceedings of the 6th International Caliber-2008, University of Allahabad, 28-29th February & 1st March 2008 .Ahemdabad INFLIBNET Centre, 2008, 700-707.

Jose, B.S. & Pacios, A. R. (2005). The impact of consortia purchasing of periodical publications on the document delivery service. *Interlending & Document Supply,* 33(4), 189-195.

Meshram, Siddharth. (2000). Electronic Journals: perspectives and issues. *Library Herald,* 38(1), 17-23.

Okoye M.O. & Ugwuanyi C.F. (2012). Management of electronic resources by cataloguers in Nigerian federal university libraries. *Library Philosophy and Practice.* Retrieved from http://unllib.unl.edu/lpp/okoye-ugwuanyi.htm

Sreekumar, M.G., & Sunitha, T. (2005). *Library capacity building through e-journal consortia: The Indian scenario.* 7th MANLIBNET Annual National Convention on Digital Libraries in Knowledge Management: Opportunities for Management Libraries, at Indian Institute of Management Kozhikode, May 5-7, (2005). Retrieved from http://hdl.handle.net/2259/249

Tenopir, Carol, et. al. (2003). *Use and users of electronic library resources: An overview and analysis of recent research studies.* Washington: Council on Library and

Information Resources. Retrieved from http://www. eslking.com/library2/ collections/librarianship/collections/e-lib_resouces/ tenopir_et_al_e-lib_resources.pdf

Thamaraiselvi & Kaliammal, A. (2005). *E-Journal Management in Academic Libraries with special reference to Indest Consortia in India.* 3rd Convention PLANNER -2005, Assam Univ., Silchar, 10-11 Nov., 2005.

17

Electronic Resource Management

Oghenovo Kelvin Onoriode

WHAT IS ELECTRONIC RESOURCE MANAGEMENT?

Electronic Information resources are information sources that are not in printed formation which are held electronically and can only be accessed through electronic devices. Electronic resources are an indispensable part of a library's collection and service offerings. Yet, as libraries subscribe to an ever-increasing array of databases, they also face a growing challenge to adequately access and manage diverse resources. Bothmann and Holmberg (2008) opined that management of the library's resources requires strategic planning. They reiterated that libraries are trying to incorporate the print resource management workflow unto the e-resources management workflow knowing that the challenge of managing e-resources is radically different. Thus electronic resource management is defined as a process of overseeing all aspects of electronic resource from pre-selection activities such as trials and initial vendor inquiries to renewal/ cancellation decisions, to the perspectives of planning, policy, and workflow issues experienced by many libraries (Bothmann & Holmberg, 2008).

In this vein, Parker, 2007 wrote that library has been a collection of information materials for ages and print media have been the bulk of the library resources. However the advent of information technology in the early 1990s led to the emergence and continuous exponential growth of digitally or electronically borne information resources. Electronic resources include CD-ROMs, e-journals, e-text or electronic books, locally loaded databases, websites and abstracting and indexing databases such as MEDLINE. According to Bothmann and Holmberg (2010), " e-resources also include products that aid in resource access for patrons such as A-Z lists, Open URL, servers, Federated search engines and resources that provide full- text content such as publishers' electronic journal content, journal content platforms such as Project Muse or Jstor and content aggregators such as EBSCOHOST's Academic Search Premier and proxy servers or other authentication tools" (Bothmann and Holmberg, 2010: 4).

An e-resource can also be "a package of e-journals or a database of abstracts and indexes that include the full text of some or all articles referenced by the indexes" (Sadeh and Ellingsen, 2005: 04). For e-resources, the interface through which it is offered should be considered because these elements are intricately linked, even though they can be licensed separately. In addition, among e-resources package, published by a publisher, a specific e-resources could be governed by a different set of license terms (Sadeh and Ellingsen, 2005).

WHY MANAGE ELECTRONIC RESOURCES

As there are diverse electronic resources in libraries and as making use of them evolves more rapidly, there is the need for articulated management through strategic planning. Management of electronic resources need to be taken more serious because of the following reason:

(a) Availability of Electronic Resources in Different Format

Coupled with development in extensible mark-up language (XML) which provides an easy way for users to extract data from XML objects that has made the management of electronic resources more challenging. As Libraries responds to the enormously increasing online resources and the users' rising demand for the resources, the acquisition, metadata organization, and system management of electronic resources become increasingly complicated due to more various types of vendor such as Database producer, publisher, and online interface provider, frequent changes in available journals and its issues within aggregated databases, and the variety in the scope of fair use for each license agreements. XML was found to be lacking and do not have the flexibility to include many of these particulars (Key & Chung, n.d).

(b) Changing library Scene and Budget

The issue of transition from acquiring print to acquiring electronic resources requires managerial ability as the need to adapt the internal organization to the new situation is indispensable. Electronic resources management is a relatively new concept. The earliest literature dates to the 1970s and 1980s (Harter and Kister 1981, Dowlin 1984). In 1984 Kenneth Dowlin (1984, p. 33) suggested that the electronic resources management has four attributes which are management of resources with a computer; the ability to link the information provider with the information seeker via electronic channels; the ability for staff to intervene in the electronic transaction when requested by the information seeker and the ability to store, organize, and transmit information to the information seeker via electronic channels(Cotter, Carroll, Hodge & Japzon, 2004).

No wonder, Gronvall (2009) emphasized that in Kenolinska Instituttet University Library, the budget for e-resources was leveraged from 45% to 96% in 2006 and a decision not to duplicate print and electronic media was enforced. For example, collection of "grey materials" was stopped as most of them are now in the Internet. Jewell, Anderson, Chandler, Farb, Parker, Riggio, and Robertson

(2004) wrote that few years ago Cornell University Libraries' strategic management plan included the bold and startling prediction of a "mostly digital environment" for that library system by 2005 Whether or not this prediction proves to be accurate for Cornell or would apply to most other libraries, it is clear trend data that spending for electronic resources has been growing much more rapidly.

(c) User Behaviour and Attitude

The use of electronic resources in increasing and the behaviour of information users in the library is showing that users are preferring electronic sources to print sources. Friedlander (2002) study suggest that user behavior and attitudes seem to have been changing even more quickly as nearly half of the undergraduates surveyed by Outsell, Inc of the scholarly information environment indicated that they used electronic resources either exclusively or almost exclusively. The same study showed that many faculty and graduate students would like to see more journals available to them electronically, but as many librarians can attest, demand for expanded access to electronic resources is growing. Many users now compare their libraries' services to those of popular Google web search engine and Amazon.com, and expect similar levels of simplicity, power and convenience from them.

(d) Changing roles of librarians

Librarians find themselves lost in a mire of spreadsheets and e-mail messages as they attempt to control their e-resources and are responsible for dealing with a variety of independent systems and data containers that are not integrated with each other. Too often, librarians rely on their memory alone to coordinate systems such as the acquisition module of their integrated library system, their alphabetic lists of electronic journals and databases, their metasearch tools, and their local link server. Much of a librarian's success at carrying out necessary tasks is based on personal experience; however, the knowledge and experience gained from dealing with e-resources is often vested in too few people-sometimes only one librarian-libraries are left at risk. Furthermore, the provision of meaningful metrics, such as detailed cost analyses and statistics on performance and usage, remains problematic, but without such metrics, managers cannot make fully informed decisions. As the spending on e-collections increases, so does the need for a better solution: "a system that supports management of the information and workflows necessary to efficiently select, evaluate, acquire, maintain, and provide informed access to electronic resources in accordance with their business and license terms" (Jewell et al., 2004).

TYPES OF E-RESOURCES

For real and proper management of e-resources, it is essential for libraries and other information managers to know the various types of e-resources. They include the following as listed by University of Chicago Library (n.d):

1. **Research Guides by Subject :** Subject guides are web resources which provide an overview of resources in a subject area. They include staff contacts, print collections, electronic resources, as well as links to other relevant Web sites. Subject guides are a good place to start when you are beginning research on a specific topic.

2. **Indexes :** An index is a reference source which provides bibliographic information about journal articles, as well as other types of materials. While indexes have long existed in print, online indexes have expanded the type of work done by researches. more options than looking for materials by subject, author or title. Online indexes allow you to look beyond subject, author, or title. They allow you to look for keywords or phrases throughout the bibliographic information—including the abstract. Sometimes people refer to indexes as "Article Databases," since they are mainly used to search for articles in journals. Many also include the full-text of an actual article online. However, it is important to realize that many indexes cover other research materials such as conference papers, book chapters, dissertations, research studies, etc.

3. **Electronic Books and Texts :** Electronic resources exist in form of E-books in libraries. Libraries provide access to a variety of electronic books, as well as the other printed works (such as essays, poems, or historical documents). Some of these electronic books and

texts are part of large, searchable databases.

4. Electronic Journals : Library also provide access and manage journal subscription to E-journal Database as part of their E-resources collection. E-journals are one of the most important component of any library's collection in that they contain much recent finding and report about topics and disciplines in every subject area.

5. Library Catalogs : Most libraries now provide access to their catalogs from their web sites. Many others provide information about their holdings into larger databases such as WorldCat or the Union Catalog.

6. Reference Sources : Many dictionaries, almanacs, encyclopedias, and other reference sources are now available online in full-text. Most of these materials are located through variety of sources such as Database Finder, the Library Catalog,

7. Statistical Sources : Online statistical sources are also part of e-resources collections. Libraries provides access to a variety of subscription databases which provide economic data or statistics. Rhese resources can be located through the sources such as Database Finder, the Library Catalog, or through many of Library's Research Guides by Subject. Though, there are many statistical sources available in print which cannot be found online.

8. Sound Recordings : There are many sound recording databases that libraries can also manage as part of their information resources. Some libraries provide access to these resources for those who want things like music online, going to Music Subject Guide for the resources which are available.

9. Image Databases (Art, Maps, Medical, etc.) : Some databases include graphics or images, such as photos, paintings or maps which are available online as electronic resources. These are mostly in art subject areas e.g the Art Subject Guide which provides extensive information about locating images.

MANAGEMENT OF E-RESOURCES IN THIS ERA

Management is an art and science which entails the allocation of scarce resources to achievement of organisational goals. Chand (1987), Stoner, Freeman and Gilbert (1995) and Peretomode (2008) wrote about the function of management as propounded by Henri Fayol (1891 – 1925). They concluded that Henri Fayol gave a breakdown of the functions of management in five broad areas, which they listed as;

(a) Planning : which is the activity that attempt to study of forecast the future and deciding today, what shall be done in the future as regard the direction of the organisation or institutions including their libraries in terms of E-resources development.

(b) Organising : which is the process of establishing roles of units and department within the library on who is to perform specific duties and function from the acquisition to use and evaluation of the e-Resources.

(c) Commanding : This involves instructing subordinates and making staff do their work in the library for effective acquisition and use of e – resources to meet organisations goals and objective.

(d) Coordinating : This refer to all efforts needed to make all staff work in synergy thereby harmonising and correlating all activities of the library towards provision of e-resources

(e) Controlling : This is making sure that everything is done in accordance with set rules and conditions and ensuring that set target are being met as regards provision of e-resources in the library.

This management thought or concept is widely applied in libraries towards providing good resources and services especially with the emergence of e-resources. Ifidon (2007), highlighted the importance of strategic management in libraries as;

1. Think ahead of the future
2. Certify goals and develop vision
3. Know what one is trying to do
4. Ensure the right direction
5. Help choose between options
6. Identify critical factors that need to be addressed

7. Make the best use of available resources like finance and personnel
8. Guide implementation
9. Achieve best result
10. Aid evaluation

Application of these management strategies will be helpful in the quest for e-resources management revolution.

In the regard, the avalanche of online resources is forcing the beginning of change on the traditional library organization. Managing of the acquired digital resource created sets of challenges for libraries that require the application of management functions. The journey to effective management of e-resources according to Parker (2007) started as a result of Digital Library Forum (DLF) held in Atlanta, Georgia, in April 2000 with a view to reviewing the shift needed to adjust from project to production perspective in digitizing efforts in libraries. This gave birth to Digital Library Federation (DLF)-Electronic Resource Management Initiative (ERMI).There were development of policies and practices and building of tools to help in the management of the over- whelming e-resources and the information therein as the structures of Library Management System (LMS) could not sustain it. "Adam Chandler of Cornell University developed a Web Hub for developing administrative metadata for electronic resource management for promoting sharing of what different individuals and libraries were building in terms of tools to support electronic resource management" (Parker, 2007 : 02).

The Electronic Resource Management Initiative Steering Committee led by Timothy Jewell of University of Washington produced a project report which collectively became a pseudo-standard for work in the area of Electronic Resources Management Systems, (ERMs). What is then Electronic Resource Management System (ERMs). Which provided an analysis of workflow: a listing of functional requirements: a wire-frame diagram providing a snapshot view of concept relationships: a definition listing of involved elements: a detailed analysis of the relationships amongst needed elements; and a hint of future XML (Extensive Mark-up Language) work to come (Jewell et al., 2004).

Thus, electronic resources management requires

(a) Planning for electronic resources

(b) Policy design for electronic resources management

(c) Electronic resources management workflow Documentation

(a) Planning for Electronic Resources Management

Planning for electronic resources is perhaps the most important and least practiced activity in libraries. Electronic resources present a number of challenges to the traditional library operations and workflow that must be addressed in order to provide smooth management. To overcome the challenges faced by many libraries, there is need for planning to tackle issues which include the number of staff assigned to electronic resource management duties, staying up-to-date with technological and vendor changes in electronic resources, budgeting limited resources for the acquisition of resources, and communication with vendors and amongst librarians and administrators. The challenges to plan for also include access issues such as management tools like openURL knowledge bases, federated searching, catalog records, and authentication.

Planning for electronic resources management also requires planning for staff that will do the job. Meeting staffing requirement for electronic resources is one the biggest challenge most libraries face as majority of libraries, regardless of total staff size, typically have only one or two professional librarians involved in electronic resource management. Paraprofessional involvement varied widely with one-third having no paraprofessional involvement, a tenth having more than five, and the rest having one to three paraprofessionals involved in the workflow. However, some libraries address the challenge of limited staffing by distributing work among existing staff, prioritizing projects according to staff availability, and emphasizing the need to invest more staff time in the electronic resource environment.

To ensure effective management of E-resources staff training, time management, implementing new technologies have to be planned for, if libraries hope to manage e-resources to meet their goals and target. other things that the library need to plan for include rapid changes in technology and e-resources, funding and budgeting as money is required to procure electronic resources.

(b) Policies for Electronic Resources Management

All e-resources management policy should be relevant and address all aspect of the e-resources management cycle which includes appropriate library user community reflecting the current needs (i.e academic community needs). Thus, the development and use of policies is critical in electronic resource management and for communicating a library's goals. Policies set guidelines of practice that aid in electronic resource management (H. White, 2005). Aside from collection development policies, libraries need policies that address issues such as types of resources to support, licensing issues, and user access. Other policy topics include how and which resources should be catalogued, placed in a content management system or subject guide, or added to an Electronic Resources Management Software (ERMS).

(c) Workflow Documentation

Work flow documentation has to do recording the work done in electronic resources management process and it closely related to planning and policy development. The documentation of the workflow is a crucial aspect of electronic resources management. Some library documented part or all of their electronic resource management workflow in order to:

1. Determine what is not getting done
2. Create consistency, particularly in terms of requests from other librarians.
3. Create comfort to other employees, even if the workflow changed and made the documentation outdated.
4. Ensure each step is completed in a particular process, to better

prepare for staff changes and leaves, or to begin a database trail.

5. Create a better understanding of what is going on and improved communication of workflow tasks to others in the library.

Many library and librarians do not see the need to document their workflow because of reasons which include; cumbersome nature of workflow in e-resources management, most electronic resource management is done on a case-by-case basis because there are too few common issues to make workflow documentation relevant, lack of time and personnel and the organizational culture which precludes the documentation process (e.g., no one documents anything; cannot use the documentation in benchmarking; turf issues). Also some librarians still believe that workflow in e-resources management is still undetermined and therefore cannot be documented.

ELECTRONIC RESOURCES MANAGEMENT LIFE CYCLE

The e-resources life cycle as written by Jena (2012) is entirely different from that of the print resources. The management of the e-Resources will become easier when the life cycle of the e-resources is completely understood. The e-Resources life cycle consists of 5 different phases and each phase of it is associated with several activities as indicated in this figure.

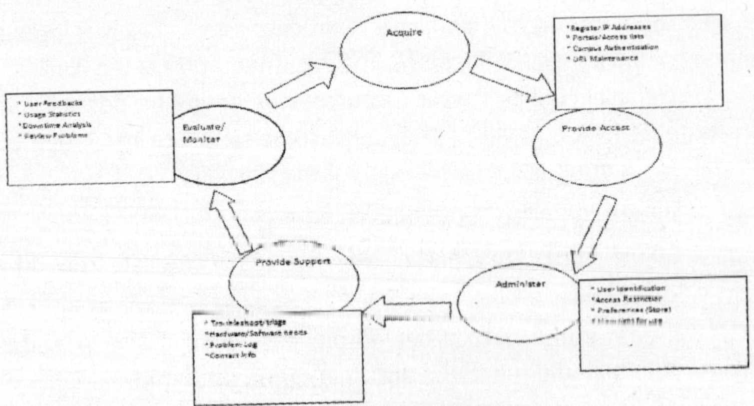

Fig. 1. E-Resources Management Cycle
Source: Jena (2012)

1. **Acquire:** E-resource is acquired by the Library;
2. **Access:** E-resource is accessed by the user;
3. **Administer:** E-resource is administered during the subscription process;
4. **Support:** User needs support in content delivery;
5. **Evaluate:** At the end of the cycle, the E-resource needs to be evaluated for considering its renewal or otherwise; several activities as associated with each phase above makes the management of the E-resources as more complex and challenging.

Jena (2012) wrote further that management of e-Resources effectively is a big challenge for library and information science professionals as these resources require special skills and expertise to build up, organize such collection. Especially now that there is exponential increase in e-Resources is likely to increase manifold in near future. With this rapid increase in production of e-resources, would result in larger collection of such resources in all the libraries. As such the management of large virtual collection would become more and more complex which would require good e-Resource management system so that e-Resources and other resources could be integrated for effective use. Moreover, every organization is going for building up institutional repository that would also need electronic resources management expertise.

MANAGEMENT ISSUES THAT ARISE IN E-RESOURCES MANAGEMENT

Electronic Resource Management System developed out of the quest to support functions which the library management system could not support fully as Parker listed the issues/functions as follows:

(i) Generating and maintaining alphabetic and subject lists of journals and/or databases.

(ii) License term negotiation, tracking, and communication processes.

(iii) Multiple staff and department involvement in selection and support of e-resources, i.e. communication and workflows.

(iv) Problem tracking and troubleshooting activities including escalating/triage support.

(v) Planned, cyclical product reviews or reviews associated with unplanned change (e.g. when a product is shifted between publishers).

(vi) Systematic usage reporting and tracking.

Therefore management of E-resources and the issues/function above require the system to do the following as enumerated by Wikipedia, (2010):

(a) Supporting acquisition and management of licensed e-resources

(b) May be integrated into other library system modules or may be standalone system

(c) May have a public interface, either separate or integrated into the OPAC.

(d) Providing descriptions of resources at the package (database) level and relate package contents (e.g. e-journals).

(e) Encoding and perhaps publicly displaying licensed rights such as e-reserves, course packs and interlibrary loan.

(f) Tracking electronic resources from point of order through licensing and final access.

(g) Providing information about data providers, consortia arrangements, and access platforms.

(h) Providing contact information for all content providers.

(i) Logging problem with resources and providers.

(j) Providing customized e-mail alerting system (e.g. notices to managers when actions are expected or required).

(k) Linking license documents to resource records.

(l) Supports retrieval of usage statistics.

SOFTWARE FOR MANAGEMENT OF E-RESOURCES

Software is set of instruction that make a computer carry out a specific task. According to Adomi (2009) software provide the means by which computer systems communicate with computer users. It is the collection of computer programs, procedure and documentation that performs different task on a computer system. William and Sawyer (2007) opined that software provide the graphical user interface (GUI) for human-computer interaction (HCI). They wrote that in time, as the interface is refined, computer may become no more difficult to use. They reiterated that for people to have smoother computing they need to know something about how software works. That software perform the function of communicating with machines (hardware) and the human user and therefore act as a bridge or intermediary as computer hardware can only understand bits and bytes (mathematical terms) and the human can only communicate only in words, speech and phrase. Parson and Oja (1998) noted that computer software determines what a computer can do. Software transforms one kind of computer to another. Library automation software tends to change a computer to a library management system. They also wrote that a computer software have legal backing in form of copyrighted software, licensed software, shrink wrap licenses, licensee for more than one user, share ware, public domain software (open source software).

According to Adomi (2009), software is categorized into programming software, system software, application software which includes utilities software such as antivirus, media player for multimedia application. A system software help the system perform its basic operating task of coordinating or managing every activities on the system. Examples of system software include operating system like windows XP, device drivers' software like the network interface card (NIC) drivers, utilities like antivirus etc. Application software on the other hand refers to software to carry out specific jobs or function which includes software like word processing such as Microsoft office, Entertainment software like games, Business software like expert software such as AutoCAD, peach tree for engineering and accounting respectively. There is also education and reference software such as library automation software like strategic library automation management software (SLAM).

Electronic resource management systems (ERMS) is the practices and software systems used by libraries to keep track of important information about electronic information resources, especially internet-based resources such as electronic journals, databases, and electronic books. The development of ERMS became necessary in the early 2000s as it became clear that traditional library catalogs and integrated library systems were not designed to handle metadata for resources as mutable as many online products are (Wikipedia, n.d).

The idea of developing electronic resource management systems emerged in 2001-2002, growing out of research by Tim Jewell at the University of Washington. The Digital Library Federation and NISO began work in May 2002 to develop standards for ERM data.[1] These standards were published in the 2004 as Electronic Resource Management: Report of the DLF ERM Initiative. Since the publication of the report, several vendors of integrated library systems have released ERMS products.

There are different ways of acquiring software for management of electronic resources. They include;

(a) E-Resources Management Software Developed in House

(b) E-Resources Management Software bought of the Shelve or through vendor

(a) E-Resources Management Software Developed in House

The cost of an annual subscription to a commercial service or the cost of purchasing an ERM system may push libraries towards an inexpensive solution. As an alternative some libraries develop e-resources management software in- house. The benefits of a in-house software include the ability to instantly update and alter the database. The library's database can be customized to the specific needs of the individual library, whereas a commercial entity must consider the needs of its customer base as a whole, as well as its profit margin, before responding to customisation requests from individual libraries. An in-house solution may integrate better with the library's website than a commercial product. On the other hand, while there have been complaints about the quality of vendor data, an in-house database requires sufficient library staffing to be able to keep up with changes to e journal access or the technical expertise necessary to maintain and improve the database. One example is the filemaker software, which can be edited either by creating more field in-house.

(b) E-Resources Management Software bought of the Shelve or through vendor

Libraries that do not use a commercial ERM system often utilize products that are bought off shelve or supplied by vendors to assist in the management of their e resources. In addition, libraries using systems that are developed in-house can look to the features offered in commercial products for inspiration. Emporia State University (ESU) is using the Registration Tracker feature of EBSCOhost to help manage e journal registration. EBSCO populates the registration tracker database with information on each journal, such as the registration instructions, access information, authentication information, and details on backfile availability. One feature of Registration Tracker allows a library staff member to create a custom note and have it e mailed to the relevant contact on a specific date. This helps to remind library staff if further action is needed to resolve an ongoing problem with e journal access. Another feature allows staff to input a note that will be displayed to library patrons as they access the journal via EBSCOhost electronic journal system (EJS).

REFERENCES

Adomi, E. E. (2009). *Library and information resources.* Benin City: Ethiope Publishing.

Bothmann, R. L. & Holmberg, M. (2008). *Strategic Planning for Electronic Resource Management.* New York: Information Science Press.

Chandan, J. S. (1987). *Management theory and practice.* Delhi: Vikas Publishing House Pvt Limited.

Cotter, G., Carroll, B. Hodge, B. & Japzon, A. (2004). *Electronic collection management and electronic information services.* Paper presented at the RTO IMC Lecture

Series on "Electronic Information Management", held in Sofia, Bulgaria, 8-10 September 2004, and published in RTO-EN-IMC-002.

Dowlin, K. (1984). *The electronic library.* New York: Neal-Schuman.

Friedlander, A. (2002). *Dimensions and use of the scholarly information environment: Introduction to a data set assembled by the Digital Library Federation and Outsell, Inc.* Washington, D.C.: Digital Library Federation and Council on Library and Information Resources. Retrieved from http://www.clir.org/pubs/reports/pub110/contents.html.

Gronvall, K. (2009). Adapting workflows for acquisition of electronic resources. *World Library and Information Congress. 75th. IFLA General Conference and Council* 23-27 August, Milan, Italy._Retrieved from http://www.ifla.org/annual-conference/ifla75/index.htm

Harter, S. & Kister, K. (1981) Online encyclopaedias: The potential. *Library Journal,* 106 (15).

Hawthorne, D. & Watson, J. (2007). *ERM on a shoestring: Betting on an alternative solution.* Presented at the annual North American Serials Interest Group meeting,

Louisville, Kentucky. (2007). House/Vendor Approach. *The Serials Librarian,* 47(4), 17 25.

Ifidon, S. E. (2007). *New directions in African library management.* Ibadan: Spectrum Books Limited.

Jena, S. K. (2012). Management of e-resources and library 2.0: Issues & challenges for LIS professionals. *Indian Journal of Information Science and Applications (IJISA), 2(1),*51.

Jewell T. D., Anderson, I., Chandler, A., Farb, S. E., Parker, K., Riggio, A. & Robertson, N.D. M. (2004). *Electronic Resource Management. Report of the DLF ERM Initiative.*

Key, S. & Chung, H. (n.d). E-resources management and user services with the YERM. Retrieved from http://www.*ohmyvocabulary.com/ifla/SunahKey.doc*

McGuigan, G. S. (2012). Addressing change in academic libraries: A review of classical organizational theory and implications for academic libraries. *Library Philosophy and Practice.* Retrieved from http://www.webpages.uidaho.edu/~mbolin/mcguigan.htm

Okoye, M.O. & Ugwuanyi, C.F. (2012).Management of electronic resources by cataloguers in Nigerian Federal University Libraries. *Library Philosophy and Practice.* Retrieved from http://unllib.unl.edu/LPP/

Parker, K. (2007). *Tools for mature management of electronic resources lifecycles in libraries.* Retrieved from http: //www.library.yale.edu/preifla2007/papers/parker.pdf.

Parson J. J. & Oja D. (1998). Computer concept (3rd ed.). Cambridge: Thompson publishing company.

Peretomode, V. F. & Peretomode, O. (2008). *Fundamentals of management and organisational behaviour*. Lagod: O. O. P. Limited.

Sadeh, T. & Ellingsen, M. (2005). Electronic resource management systems: The need and the realization. *New Library World, 106*(1212/1213), 208-218.

Stoner, J. A. F, Freeman, R. E. & Gilbert, D. R. (1995). *Management* (6th ed.). New Delhi: Pearson Education Inc.

University of Chicago Library (n.d). *Electronic resources: The university of Chicago library. www.lib.uchicago.edu/e/db/*

Wikipedia (n.d). Electronic management systems. Retrieved from http://en.wikipedia.org/wiki/Electronic_resource_management

William B. K. & Sawyer S. C. (2007). Using information technology: A practical introduction to computers and communication (7th ed.). Boston: McGraw-Hill.

Yu, H. (2008). *Electronic resources management in libraries: Research and practice*. New York: Information Science Reference.

18

Electronic Resources: Management and Access

Sandhya Aggarwal

INTRODUCTION

E-Resources are part of what we refer to as the "Invisible Web". The Invisible Web is the information accessible to us through the Internet, but not freely available to everyone on the World Wide Web, but available only to authorized users known as members or subscribers. We can use the term Internet Database, electronic products, Virtual Libraries, Clickable collections, e-libraries, Internet Resources etc. In order to cope with the present development in IT, modern libraries are now adopting various electronic resources for its collection developments to fulfill the requirements of different users in a better way. However to achieve the goals of an ideal information system there is a need to select, evaluate and organize the e-resources in the best possible way as to provide maximum ease, both to the users and the staff for its access and retrieve at all times.

SELECTION OF E-RESOURCES

The selection process should be done in relevant with the

demands of the users, committee, focus group, users' recommendation etc. Apart from this, it should take into consideration the following steps:

Users' Need : Which type of users comes in your library and collection of your library?

Content and Scope : To identify content and scope of the e-resources;

Authority : To evaluate quality of that particular resource and search capabilities and agreements to review licensing.

With the evaluation of e-resources the followings should also be considered:

- To identify the electronic version have the retrospective data
- To determine particular source of information of e-resources offer any special features which are not available in other print version
- To check the content of the e-resources with relevant to the users as well as to the collection as a whole
- To check whether the information is often updated or not;
- To identify the method of accessing of e-resources available;
- To identify the e-resources needed to maintain and redesign the library website identified;

Currency : To estimate the cost and to check either subscription based or web based when acquiring and determine the e-resources have affordable price or not though offered diverse pricing system by the publishers;

Technical Support : To evaluate the systems and technical support. To evaluate application software and installation, updated sporadically or in regular schedule and

Training : To check the facilities for educational support and training and the staffing needs for training of recruiting with the existing technology.

HOW CAN ACCESS THE E-RESOURCES

Where to start your search of the Library's ever increasing electronic resources depends on:

- What type of material you are looking for (journal articles, abstracts, or full-text?)
- Whether you are looking for a known item (particular journal title) or you want to search for whatever information might be available.

You can search for e-resources from any of the following:

E-Journals A-Z

The Library also has many more journals available in print which can be found by searching the Library Catalog. Just like that the E-journals A-Z list allows you to browse alphabetic lists of the journal titles available online.

E-Books

Access thousands of online books through databases. The majority of these books is cataloged, and can be accessed via the Library Catalog through database.

Database Finder (E-Resources A-Z)

The Library subscribes to many different types of electronic resources, from those that provide indexes of journal articles to those that aggregate full-text content from a variety of different publishers. The Database Finder provides alphabetic and subject-based lists of these electronic resources, including descriptive and coverage information to help you select the most relevant resources.

Cross-Search

Search the contents of several databases and e-journals at once.

QuickSearch

Search the contents of pre-defined sets of databases at once.

Citation Finder

Find a particular article for which you have a citation. Enter the information you know about the article, journal, or book into the form below and the Citation Linker will help you locate the full text - whether online, in the Library, or through interlibrary loan.

On-site access

If you are at any College campus and they provide the service of this type then most e-resources can be accessed directly (there is no requirement to enter a username and password).

A few e-resources do require a username and password. If so, a note in the library catalogue states "Access requires a specific username and password".

Off-site access

Most of e-resources can be accessed off-site, allowing you to work from home or from another location. There are three methods of off-site access:

- Virtual private network (VPN) - connect to the College VPN to allow you to access e-resources as if you were on-site
- Institutional login - use your College username and password to log in to e-resources
- Using the SFX link or button on Library Search, the library catalogue or A-Z lists - log in when prompted with your College username and password

MetaLib

Search up to 10 databases in one go. Save a list of your interested resources. Create information alerts and get the latest research emailed to you.

Electronic journals list

Browse the A-Z list or search by journal title.

Databases and e-books list

Browse the A-Z list or search by keyword for a database name or e-book title.

Subject guides

Your librarian produces a guide to key e-resources in your subject area.

Copyright and e-resources

Printing and downloading restrictions

Whenever we download any e-resource, one point of copyright should also be kept in mind. E-resources are all copyright material, subject to copyright law. This means that there are limits to the amount of material which can be downloaded and printed from any e-journal or e-book.

e-journals you may print up to one article or 5% from a journal issue, whichever is the greater

e-books you may print up to one chapter or 5%, whichever is the greater

There may also be additional restrictions to the level of downloading from e-books, depending on limits set by individual suppliers. Where this is the case there will usually be alerts on the supplier's website.

All license agreements prohibit the systematic downloading of material, and this is carefully monitored by suppliers, who will notify us of any problems they detect. When this arises the publisher may block access from specific ip addresses, or may suspend access to the whole service, until the problem has been resolved.

CONCLUSION

Nowadays, libraries are increasingly involved in creating and acquiring e-resources. The availability of IT based electronic resources has exerted ever-increasing pressures on libraries and there is no dough that e-resources are expanding rapidly. However, in order to meet the ever increasing demand of the user community in a digital environment, libraries have to develop ways to manage access to materials available in electronic format and to effectively share them mush as they have shared print resources for over a century through inter library lending.

REFERENCES

http://eresourcetraining.blogspot.in/2010/04/what-are-e-resources-html

http://www.lib.uchicago.edu/e/

http://www2.ebsco.com/en-us/Solutions/ejournals/Pages/index.aspx

http://www3.imperial.ac.uk/library

19

E-Journal and their Management in Libraries

Ivwighreghweta Oghenetega

DEFINITION AND MEANING OF E- JOURNAL

There is no standard accepted definition of an electronic journal. Electronic journals, also known as e-journals and electronic serials, are scholarly journals or intellectual magazines that can be accessed via electronic transmission. This, in practice, means that they are usually published on the Web. They are a specialized form of electronic document that have the purpose of providing materials for academic research and study, and they are formatted approximately like journals articles in traditional printed journals. Being in electronic form, articles usually contain metadata that can be entered into specialized databases as well as the databases and search-engines for the academic discipline concerned (Adomi, 2009).

Electronic Journals are digital version of printed journals accompanied by extensive hyper linking. They can be read both on-line and off-line. "Electronic journals" are self-defined ("e-journals" in short); those who produce such journals name them in that way. These journals are generally accessed electronically through communication devices or telephone lines. Some of these electronic serials are traditional paper journals simply made available electronically; others are sample selections, or just the table of contents of the paper journal (Thamaraiselve and Kaliammal 2011). Rusch-Feja, and Siebeky, (1999) states that "an electronic journal is a periodical – regular or irregular – and moderated unit made available in an electronic format, either on a static medium or via computer networks. According to Mudannayake (2011) Journals published in electronic format only are considered as e-journals and an electronic publication with a parallel print counter part is considered as on-line journal. Most of the electronic journals available at present are replicas of print journals. Electronic journals appear on different formats.

- Journals available on CD-ROMS (suites of e-journals can be recorded on CD-ROMS and can be distributed on subscription basis as individual or collection of titles),
- Journals available on networked systems such as Internet, Bitnet.

E-journals appear as

- Electronic only - A digital periodical that publishes on the internet or World Wide Web (WWW) which does not necessarily need a publisher and which can be managed by an editor and a scholarly community.
- Electronic version of a former print journal.
- Electronic version published simultaneously with it's counterpart in print. (Replicas of a print with papers in PDF format for easy printing).

Electronic Journals can be

- free
- paid subscription
- pay per use
- Licensed for access rights.

ADVANTAGES OF E- JOURNAL

Electronic journals carry many advantages than their counterparts in print.

Accessibility

Access to electronic journals has no limitations such as time and spatial provided with network compliances. The content pages of journals, author abstracts, and the full article can be accessed (subscribed patrons in the case of commercial publishers) before the print counterpart is appeared. Digital material can be accessed from a remote site and can be stored in a local computer. Digitized articles of journals can be browsed, searched, viewed and downloaded using a universally acceptable format the portable document format (PDF) (Mudannayake 2011).

Speed in publishing and distribution

Electronic transmission of computer readable texts reduces the time lag between writing, reviewing, printing, and mailing of journals. The speed in publishing journals electronically has attributed scholars to accept this new medium as their primary channel of communication mainly for two reasons. The fast diffusion of research findings and ideas with the ultimate goal of spreading of knowledge and professional recognition and Keeping up to date in their areas of interest (Thamaraiselvi and Kaliammal 2011).

Articles can be put on the Web as soon as they are ready, without having to wait maybe months for a space in a journal issue. The American Chemical Society's put articles on their Web site "as soon as publishable" which can be up to 11 weeks before print. This all means that the information is much more up-to-date than can be achieved with paper (Neal, 1997).

Linking

The introduction of 'hypertext' and 'hyper media' formats enables linkages from articles to external electronic resources, authors, research groups etc. making the point of access interactive. (Meadows 1997) emphasize that 'electronic-only journals have produced an advanced method of scholarly interaction in the sense that individuals can respond instantaneously to articles and their responses can be published as soon as editors receive them, this creates a more dynamic interaction than in the print journal'. Electronic Journals can carry colour graphics, motion files, and multimedia facilities.

Searchability

Searchability is one of the core advantages of a digital format. Chan (2009) argue that the easier it is to find research, the fewer duplicated experiments there will be, resulting in less wasted time. However, Missingham (1999) raises the problem of information overload. With information easier to find, there will be much more to read and keep up-to-date with. The rapid turnaround time means that articles can be read, commented on by the journal's readers, and amended much more quickly than can be done with print. The ease with which e-mail can be sent, or forms filled means that there can be much greater feedback through the Web.

Ashcroft and Langdon (1999:107,112), refer to some other advantages of electronic journals above print journals, which are listed below:

- They are easily accessible even from an individual's desktop.
- Therefore they are saving time in waiting for information.
- It is much easier to monitor the use of electronic media.
- It enables multi-user access.
- The increase in cost for keeping printed material makes electronic forms more attractive from an economic viewpoint because of economy in storage - they are space saving.
- There are no physical barriers.
- The cost is low (sometimes free).
- Authors and readers get closer.

FEATURES OF ELECTRONIC JOURNALS

Some of the important features of an e- journal according to Dish (2011) Include the following:

- Multiple accesses simultaneously are a strong feature that an e-journal provides.
- E-journals are accessible to all users regardless of geographical location through Proper compatible software and browser services.
- It does not require time-consuming printing and mailing process, therefore an e-journal take less time to publish and distribute.
- No space restriction i.e. an e-journal can publish a greater number of articles compared to the print counterpart.
- Occupy very little space if stored in a CD-ROM.
- Can include sources, video, and interactive and 3 dimensional models. E-journal can publish colour, figure and graphics at no extra cost.
- Users can access individual articles by making pay-per-view i.e. pay for the required articles, if they do not want to subscribe to the entire journal.
- Some online journals can be accessed without paying any charge.
- E-journals can be distributed more economically than the paper ones, because the main costs of preparing the text, the review process and other such procedures are not as capital-intensive as the costs of printing and mailing print copies.
- Interaction by means of letters to the editor and opinion forum is a dynamic feature of an e-journal. Some journals include at the end of every paper a forum where readers and authors can exchange opinions. An electronically published article can very easily contain a link, which facilitates e-mail communication with the author or the editor.
- E-journal can contain hyperlinks to cited articles and other information sources such as related journals or websites.
- Searching facilities in e-journals are very effective and fast. E-journals provide excellent search facilities with every issue in

which user can search articles not only by title, author, keyword but can also use Boolean operators for searching.

- E-journal is never missing from the shelf, and several people can read the same article at once from separate workstations.
- Usage statistics can be generated by using accepted standards (counter).
- Cross reference of references can be viewed.

AIMS AND OBJECTIVES OF E-JOURNAL MANAGEMENT

The main aim of the e-journal management is to explore the challenges and issues arising in purchasing and management of the e-journals in the libraries and the possible ways and means to purchase and maintain them in such a way that the e-journal resources will be accessible for use by future generations.

The following are some of the objectives of e-journals and its management in libraries:

- Libraries can solve the ongoing Serials crisis and to share the resources among libraries.
- The main objective is to make awareness among the academicians about the on-line availability of e-journals through intra-net, internet and www.
- Libraries can provide better information service regarding the various e-journal retrieval facilities available
- The collection of e journal documents can be maintained in libraries.
- Consortia purchasing offers for the single library the opportunity to get access to more journals than they currently have subscriptions to, thus eliminating the continuous cancellation operations.
- document delivery processes for specific journals (Thamaraiselvi and Kaliammal 2011)

ISSUES IN ELECTRONIC JOURNAL MANAGEMENT

As libraries build ever-larger collections of electronic resources, finding ways to manage them efficiently becomes a major challenge. The number of electronic journals, citation database and full text aggregators held by most libraries has grown rapidly. Managing these electronic resources involves providing ways to find and access them and providing library staff with the tools to keep track of them. E journals need to be selected, acquired, catalogued, archived and made available (Meadows, 1997), but presently the transition from print to electronic journals is occurring at a fast pace. E –journals must be scientifically managed to support the key mission of the institution as former being quite expensive requires an enormous financial investment. One major issue in electronic journal subscription is difficulty in developing and maintaining exclusive electronic journal holding as either the journals are subscribed in juxtaposition with the print journal or as part of aggregated title not previously held by new e journals that are available only in e journal format. E-journal management is one of the most challenging tasks that a librarian has to undertake. Nisonger (1996) has pointed out 'that there is wide diversity of electronic publications and the rapid changes they are undergoing in terms of technology what is available and the social, economic and psychological acceptance of electronic journals make planning by librarians for electronic journal management exceedingly challenging'.

E-journal management requires librarians to acquire new competencies, on technological know how, how to deal with licensing, copyright implications and new purchasing methods such as consortia etc. archiving issues etc. Management of e-journals involves selection, acquisition, providing access, and archiving.

There are two fundamental aspects of managing electronic journal effectively (Breeding, 2004). They are

- Back-end selection and acquisition task and the
- Front end delivering access.

1. Selection of Electronic Journal Title

Selection of e-journals requires judicious thinking and planning on the part of Library and Information professionals. The selection highly depends on the institution or organization's objective and the type of user community the library has to serve. Rabine and Rich (1997) have set forth some criteria for selecting open access e-journals and subscription e-journals.

Open access e-journals

- The full text of journal articles must be available directly from the Web page
- Journals must be peer reviewed or produced by academic institutions or commercial enterprises with an established reputation
- Journals must be indexed in a standard index or by an on site search engine
- Back issues must be available from the Web site
- E journal must have Web or Gopher sites. E-journals that are only available via e-mail subscription should not be considered
- Subject content must support the institution curriculum needs.

For subscription e-journals

Rabine and Rich (1997) observed that many e-journals are available via the World Wide Web for free and need nothing more than a link to the library's home page to make them accessible to the library users and that others requires subscription or registration (whether or not the subscription fee is waived) before they may make them available. According to Rabine and Rich (1997) any e-journal which requires a subscription or registration should meet the following criteria, with exceptions made on a case-by case basis.

- Accessible via the World Wide Web
- Supports curriculum or faculty research need (or needs of the user community)
- Cost is reasonable and justifiable

- Full text journals available directly from Web page.
- Peer reviewed or produced by academic institution or commercial enterprise with an established reputation.
- Back issues is available to subscribers
- English language, unless another language would be more appropriate to the curriculum/user community.
- On-site search engine and / or is indexed in a standard index
- Printing and downloading are available and easy to do
- Technology permits it to be made available to a large part of the campus population/institution
- Copyright restriction are not excessive

Selecting an e-journal involves the following actions:

- Placing a paid subscription.
- Assigning a license agreement.
- Accessing a title if required on a pay-per-use basis.
- Backup and achieves
- Determination of access through Web, CD or DVD = File Format
- Providing access through a www site / homepage. (Rabine and Rich 1997)

Selection is to be done by the Library and Information professionals through deep study regarding the relevance of the journal in context to the institution or organization and keeping in view the requirements of the users from time to time. There can be various selection procedures. Today various aggregators and vendors provide e journal access services. They are sometimes willing to let the library "try out" a product. This is one of the suitable procedures, when a library is close to taking a decision of the journals. Trial period help eliminate the guesswork in selection of the e-journal. Numerous Internet resources can assist with the identification of electronic journals on the Internet (Moller 2004).

There are a number of selection tools available in print and over the Internet. Many of the print journals already subscribed have an electronic equivalent and the access is provided free with the print subscription. Various directories for the selection of e-journals are available, like the ARL's directory of electronic journals. Internet tools like the so-called electronic journal collections on the Internet can be very useful for identification process. The micro evaluation of e-journals to determine its intrinsic quality and characteristics forms the main basis of the selection criteria. Technical compatibility with the library's hardware and software, user interface, the amount of training required, whether the journal is archived, and the e-journals data format are some criteria's to be used (Moller 2004).

Various directories and guides for the selection of e-journals are available on the Internet, some include both free and fee based including all the subjects.

- The "E-journal sites guide: A meta source" offers links to sites that collect e-journals [http :/ //www.library.ubc.ca/ejour
- CIC e-journal collection [http;//ejournals.cic.net]
- DOAJ (Directory of open Access Journals) provides about 1,385 free online journals covering all subjects and language. [http://www.doaj.org/]
- AMDECO.com [http://www.freemedicaljournals.com/] provides free medical journals over the Internet.
- With the advent of Internet many publishers and organizations are making available a sample copy of their journals on the web and anyone can access the sample copy from anywhere at any time. e.g. Major publishers who after E-journals are Tailor and Frances- SAGE, Springer and
- Kluwer, Black Well, CUP & Oxford University Press.

According to Mudannayake (2011) there is a common criticism for selection of electronic titles specially the e-only titles due to short of selecting tools. The traditional indexing services are hesitant to include e-only journals because of the ephemeral nature of the medium, lack of access to web sites, keep up with URL changes etc. When selection of e-titles for a library, the traditional factors such as subject content, language, accuracy, currency, whether it is refereed, editorial, publisher's reputation etc. have to be taken into consideration. In addition factors, which are intrinsic to electronic resources, have to be taken into account. They can be listed out as follows :

- Whether the item is in CD-ROM or networked.
- Whether the contents in post script, PDF or any other format.
- Technical compatibility with the equipment and software (the technical infrastructure needed to support access to electronic journals.
- Whether the suppliers allow users to access by IP range or requires user to register to access with IDs and passwords
- Requirements of the license that may restrict certain services (Eg: ILL, outside users)
- Effectiveness of the search engines
- The amount of training required
- The amount of maintenance required

2. Acquisition of E Journal

Acquisition is a prime activity for collection development of electronically generated journals. Present scenario is quite different from the traditional acquisition as it is possible that not even a single e- journal is owned by or housed in a library rather they are accessed through remote database. Therefore, for electronic journals acquisition refers to purchasing of access rites. Some new challenges that are to be confronted for acquisition of electronic journal include pricing models, ownership / access rights, licensing, budgeting, weeding and cancellation (Nisonger,1996). According to Mudannayake (2011) acquisition involves placing subscriptions with vendors, adopting mechanisms for accessing e- only journals which are free on the web, and other subsequent operations. Acquisition of E-journals includes various complicated issues which need to be half properly. Some of important issues which need to be addressed according to Bish (2011) include the following:

Pricing models

There are no universally accepted pricing models for electronic journals as pricing strategies varies from publishers to publishers and these are made available through the internet at varying pricing models. On the basis of the cost involved in subscribing to e journals, these broadly falls under two categories

- Free electronic journal: A number of electronic journals are available freely on public domain and are not depended on a subscription from a publisher or membership of an organization, so also described as open access journals. Open access journals also referred to as "Gold Road" to open access, are peer reviewed journals made available free of charge to the public through the internet There are literally thousand of electronic journals which offer high quality information totally free of charge (e.g. D-lib magazine, library philosophy and practice and the directories of open access journals).These are often in receipt of funding from some organizations or society and they exist to promote the free flow of information in their chosen subject area.
- Paid electronic journals also known as commercial journals. All the commercial journals require subscription to view their contents. There are many players for providing such kind of electronic journals such as traditional commercial publishers or scholarly societies or institutions of high learning.
- The other pricing models can be divided into the following categories:
  1. An annual fee for unlimited access.
  2. The price model in which the library subscribes to a journal in print format and additional fee is charged for electronic format.
  3. Library subscribes to electronic versions of journals and pays extra for the print version.
  4. Charge per connect time, which includes additional charges for downloading etc.

5. Payment per potential user, based on institution's size.
6. Payment for the article required i.e. pay per –article basis.
7. Consortia pricing, for a group of libraries.

Ownership/ Access rights

Unlike the print versions, e-journals have the problem of ownership. Print versions when discontinued, retains the previous issues before discontinuing, whereas in case of e-journals sometimes they may not be available for access or cannot be retained when discontinued. While signing the agreement library should ensure perpetual access.

Licensing : A license usually takes the form of a written contract or agreement between the library and the owner of the rights to distribute information. Typical licensing issues include method of calculating payment, restrictions on use, and what happens upon termination etc. Every library needs expert staff and an office that handles and maintains a file of license agreements. It is necessary that the professionals closely review the agreement and clear all the doubts at the time of signing the agreement (Mudannayake 2011).

The licensing issue is identified as the most complicated and time consuming part of acquisition of electronic journals. It requires the acquisition librarians to have negotiation skills and ability to develop and understand contracts. However, librarians are not educated in contract negotiation and the implications of that for patrons (Dickerson and Lamborn, 1998). Recommendations on handling licensing agreement include developing common template, common principles, a process for license review, and third party brokering of licensed products (Bosch, 1998) Various licensing guidelines have been developed to assist librarians to negotiate agreements, e.g. the guidelines prepared by Electronic Publishing Licensing Agreements Subcommittee of the Publisher/Vendor-Library Relations Committee of ALA's Association for Library Collection & Technical Services. A group of librarians and publishers in UK has also tried to work toward an agreement for a model license (Mckay, 1998).

Aggregators are taking the role of subscription agent for electronic journals. They facilitate the process of acquiring electronic journals by handling subscription, contacting with publisher, registering IP address, which will greatly reduce librarians' work. They also advise libraries on licensing terms. A potential new role may be to negotiate license agreements for librarians who lack legal and technical expertise. To take maximum advantage of these services, however, librarians need to understand what value-added service aggregators can provide to the library for electronic journals (Dickerson and Lamborn, 1998).

According to Bish (2011) aggregation has the following benefits:

- Seamless access is offered in the form of single user interface, cross journal searching and reference linking within the aggregation.
- A single license to negotiate, a single access method and a payment in a single vendor offer simplicity in maintaining single subscription.
- Through negotiation the aggregator's lowers the overall costs and at the same time provides access to larger amounts of information.
- Readership of journals is expanded and libraries access to other materials provided with subscriptions
- Aggregators offer price stability.
- One very unique feature is that through accessing their administration pages, aggregators provide sophisticated usage statistics to libraries, which helps in judging the use of e-journals.
- Provision of free e-mails and alerts of new articles to keep the users up to date with the latest research is a special feature provided by the aggregators.
- Remote users are benefited for having access to the required information.

- Archive of the e-journals subscribed during the period of the agreement is made available.

Budgeting : Most of the journals initially are free with the print journals. But in the recent times it has been seen that most of the publishers are discontinuing the print based free access. In this regard budgeting is a major issue. Moreover the proportion of e-journals that are free will inevitably decline. There are two theoretical approaches to budgeting,

1. *Subject based*: where the e-journals will be funded from the budget meant for serials.
2. Format based which implies separate budget for e-resources (Dickerson and Lamborn, 1998; Bish, 2011).

Weeding and cancellation

Weeding of e-journals could be deciding to no longer provide access i.e. the journal can be stopped. This has to be done keeping in view the user needs. If the library has a dual print and electronic subscription, then it could be decided to cancel the print version keeping in view the cost or budget and space on self. A library presumably would not wish to cancel the print subscriptions until it had confidence in archiving strategy for electronic ones. The content of electronic publications will be lost from the scholarly record if appropriate archiving strategies are not developed (Bish, 2011).

3. Access and Organization of Electronic Journals

There are so many ways a library can provide access and also organize its electronic journals collections to its users. Broadly access can be ensures either through IP ranges or login and passwords.

Multiple IP Addresses : is a group of Internet protocol (IP) addresses. Every institute and organization, libraries having its own web servers sets a single or multiple IP addresses from their internet service provider (ISP). It is also called as static IP address or group of addresses, which are unique in the Internet domain. This number or numbers provided to the publishers at the time of registration will enable the librarians to get online access which is domain restricted, in other words member can access the journals only within their organizations. Whenever the request for article is made, the server at the other end recognizes the request by IP address of the sender. Access is denied in case of mismatch.

Most of the publishers prefer to provide access through this method. However, the library not having its web server may seek access through the user name and passwords (Bish 2011).

Password Access : Accessing journals through passwords has a plus point, that the members can access the requirements from anywhere; however the misuse of passwords is a consideration. The best option for the access is through IP address. The member need not always remember the password and secondly the access is restricted only to the domain thus preventing unauthorized use (Bish 2011).

Organization of electronic journals

The following can be used to organize electronic journal in libraries for easy accessibility and retrieval of information:

Cataloguing : According to Abdus (1999: 12) it is considered necessary that e-journals should be catalogued in order to provide access to the information and instructions for effective retrieval. With some modifications, the cataloguing rules and the USMARC format can be successfully used for the cataloguing and coding of Internet resources including electronic journals. Changes have been made in the USMARC format including the definition of a new field, the 856, for "Electronic Access and Location". It includes data elements for type of access, host name, path name, file name, and similar information necessary to access or retrieve a data resource over the network (Caplan, 1993). Nancy Olson's *Cataloguing Internet Resources: A manual and practical guide* and *CONSER, the Cooperative Online Serials Program,* provide detailed guidelines on cataloguing electronic journals. Module 31 of the *CONSE'R Cataloguing Manual* is accessible via the Internet (Caplan 1993). OCLC has also developed guidelines for cataloguing Internet resources as part of its Internet Resources and InterCat projects (Dickerson and Lamborn, 1998). Several libraries have taken initiatives in cataloguing e-journals, e.g. the University of Virginia, University College London, and the North Carolina State University Libraries. But there are still problems that need to be solved in describing e-journals. The most significant problem identified is that the electronic location information is very unstable (Caplan, 1993, Abdus 1999).

Federated Search : Another major area of interest is in applications that allow users to search multiple sources simultaneously so they don't have to decide which resource might have the information they need. This approach goes by various names: federated searching, cross searching, or metasearch. A number of products with differing technological underpinnings are available in this category. The products are based on a mechanism that knows how to send a query to each individual resource behind the scenes, and then receive the results. When the user enters a search request, the system translates it into the form needed by each of the selected targets, gathers and collates results as they are returned, and then presents the orderly results. These metasearch applications typically involve presenting a set of broad subjects or a discipline, removing from the user the burden of knowing what kind of information is contained within each of the brand-name resources. As part of the configuration of the metasearch application, the library would maintain a profile of the electronic resources to which it subscribes. These are some of the major products in this category now:

- ENCompass from Endeavor Information Systems
- MetaLib from Ex Libris
- Sirsi Single Search from Sirsi (Breeding 2004; Abdus 1999).

E-Journal Locator Resources : Many libraries maintain an electronic finding aid that consists of lists of electronic databases and e-journals on their Web site apart from the main online catalog. These e-journal locaters work as good navigational tools for researchers that want a quick way to get to an e-journal without the complexities of the online catalog. These lists of e-journals may in fact be database-driven applications that also offer significant information about each e-journal, including the dates of coverage and a description of the types of material available, in addition to the title and URL. Like the online catalog, this approach takes the researcher to the e-journal itself, and not to individual articles. Keeping these journal locater applications up-to-date also requires significant effort. Rather than relying on manual work, many libraries will extract data from their online catalog or rely on an e-journal holdings service to automatically populate the e-journal locater (Breeding 2004).

Links from the Online Catalog : The online catalog provides one means for accessing electronic resources. Through title searching and subject headings, users can find any electronic journal the library subscribes to and go to that journal through the link provided. The main limitation of this approach is that it works only to find the journal itself, not the individual articles (Breeding 2004).

4. E-journal Archiving

Archiving e-journals is a major concern for libraries. There appears to be strong differences of opinion on the issue of who should do the archiving. Neavill and Sheble (1995) stated that library's role of mediating access to current information as well as the preservation of information is unique and they see little change in the importance of the library for the long- term preservation of information. They feel that there is little assurance that the files of electronic journals will be available permanently, as publishers may discontinue individual titles or go out of business. They do not think that libraries should abandon archiving and preserving functions, at least in the transitory period, before alternatives become quite stable.

Aggregators have taken e-journals from a wide variety of publishers and put them online in a common library. Some of them have also committed to provide permanent archive to libraries. For example, OCLC has made a full commitment both to archiving digital material for future scholars and to providing subscribers with access to the material they have purchased. *Net. Journal Directory* provides a listing of aggregator archival web services. Commercial document delivery and subscription services are also beginning to perform an archival role in addition to their traditional services. Luijendijk (1996) reported that EBSCO has already begun the process of archiving the electronic full text of journal articles that are available on their electronic reference products. Information Access Company, CARL Corporation, and University Microfilms International have also initiated such services. Considering these alternatives, Libraries in collaboration with consortia have also begun to selectively archive e-journals. Two examples of such consortia are CICNET (http://ejournals.cic.net) and JSTOR (http://jstor.umdl.umich.edu/). Publishers have started placing electronic copies of their e-journals in escrow at different places to ensure their continued availability. Project Muse (http://muse.jhu.edu/); Elsevier Press (http://www.elsevier.com); Blackwell Science (http:/ /www.blackwell-science.com); and Academic Press IDEAL (http:// www.idealibrary.com) are some examples. Project Muse promises archival files on CD-ROM, containing "all of the issues published online during the subscription term" and supplies a CD-ROM archival disk to its individual subscribers annually through out their subscription period (Breeding 2004).

The ephemeral nature of electronic journals makes the preservation of e-journals a great concern and has become a crucial issue which is constantly debated by librarians and publishers. Keeping track with URL changes, copyright issues and licensing also make the issue more complicated. The librarians and publishers are in the forefront of planning and experimenting various strategies to overcome this issue, but still an acceptable and reliable method for archiving of electronic journals has not been found. The common options suggested by various groups are noted below.

- Archiving to be done by original publishers.
- Creating a central archive on national or regional basis. (For an example The committee on Institutional Cooperation (CIC) an academic consortium of USA has established a cooperative archival project known as CICNet Electronic Journal collection)
- Archiving to be done by individual libraries

The general view on archiving is that the libraries should not depend on external archives. There are number of possible ways of offline archiving of electronic journals.

- Magnetic media such as tape
- Optical media
- CD-ROMS, Hard disks and floppy disks
- Micro formats
- Print (Nisonger, 1996)

The problems and issues in archiving and managing the e-journals led to a series of meetings over the past few years among publishers, librarians, and technologists sponsored by a variety of organizations, including the Society of Scholarly Publishers, the National Science Foundation, the Council on Library and Information Resources, and the Coalition for Networked Information. It was agreed that:

- Archives should be independent of publishers, and that archiving needs to be the responsibility of institutions for whom it is a core mission;
- Archiving should be based on active partnership with publishers, and that it will require a different kind of license agreement than the normal content usage license;
- Archives should address preservation over very long timeframes (100 years or more); long timeframes are likely to raise issues very different from those encountered in daily service provision;
- Archives will need to conform to standards and best practice guidelines as they evolve in the digital world and should be subject to auditing and certification

In the past two or three years, e-journals have become the largest and fastest growing segment of the digital collections for most libraries. Collections that a few years ago numbered in the few hundreds of titles now number in the thousands, and the rate of growth continues to increase. In many ways, archiving and preserving e-journals will be dramatically different from what has been done for paper based journals. In the paper era, there was large-scale redundancy in the storage of journals. Many different institutions collected the same titles. The copies of journals being saved for future generations were the same copies being read by the current generation of users. The common service model for e-journals is quite different than that for paper journals. Most e-journal access is through a single delivery system maintained either by the publisher or its agent. There is little replication, and only a few institutions actually hold copies of journals locally. Libraries can fulfill their current service requirements without facing the issues involved in the preservation of the resources. Further, in the digital realm the issues involved in day-to-day service are quite different from those involved in long-term preservation. The study by Ashcroft and Langdon (1999:108) indicated that the lack of a permanent archive is seen as a considerable disadvantage. This uncertainty of continuity of material has led some institutions to exercise extreme caution before cancelling paper subscriptions. The archiving of electronic resources raises concerns about the security of data files, search software and operating systems, remote access links, and storage costs. Assuring archival access becomes an even more critical issue for particular types of products, such as electronic journals and full-text databases. Both storing large files of data and maintaining access to them present a significant additional cost in terms of staff, time and resources. Still, users are often hesitant to rely on electronic copies of titles for fear that archival access will not be maintained (Ashcroft and Langdon 1999:108).

5. Challenges in E-journal Purchase and Management

At present, e-journals management remains considerably less efficient than the administration of print subscriptions. The full impact of electronic journals on subscription administration processes and delivery requirements is only now becoming fully clear. Although agents and publishers have been actively experimenting, both parties have yet to provide a comprehensive service portfolio that properly addresses libraries' full e-journal management needs (Thamaraiselvi and Kaliammal 2011). Some libraries have resorted to doing it themselves and in most cases libraries are moving more of their print holdings to electronic versions without any increase in their internal administration resources. The new complexities faced by librarians include:

- Knowing what e-content is available in the market;
- Tracking usage and negotiating complex licensing deals;
- Efficiently processing payments and maintaining payment records;
- Recording and complying with the unique terms and conditions of each e-journal license;
- Keeping a comprehensive listing of electronic journals holdings;
- Communicating the full list of electronic journal holdings to users; and
- Connecting users to content

Due to inefficiencies in the e-journals management chain, libraries are being forced to invest heavily in systems and tools, rather than committing their resources to acquiring content (Thamaraiseiva and Kaliammal 2011).

6. Library Consortia and Management of E-journals in Libraries

This is the process by which libraries from different institutions or university, joined together and purchasing the costly electronic products and sharing its cost creating a common infrastructure called "Consortia" that is, every member of the consortium will have electronic access not only to the journals currently subscribed to but all the journals. As we all know libraries currently subscribe only to those journals that they can afford on any specific time of date, and there will be a number of other journals of the specific publisher the library occasionally will have to inter lend as well. Such a consortium agreement will give the library, and therefore also the user, extended access —that is better service— and reduces the costs —that is staff costs and document delivery costs— in inter-lending procedures (Mudannayake 2011).

The followings are the benefit of consortia purchase of journals:

- Provide access to wider number of electronic resources at substantially lower costs.
- Research productivity of all institutions is improved with the increased access to International databases and full texts of

journals.

- Offers reduced attrition, improved income stability, incremental revenue for the publishers.
- Access to otherwise unsubscribed resources.
- Open-ended venture where Institutions can join and get the benefit of not only the lower subscription rates but also the favorable uses and conditions.
- Sharing Institutions have less pressure on space requirements for storing and managing print based e-journals.
- It provides scope for electronic archives, availability and monitoring of usage statistics.
- Effective document delivery through a single interface and access point (Bish, 2011).

7. Need for Library Consortia for Libraries

The developments in scientific publishing and the pricing policies of publishers posed new challenges and opportunities for academic libraries in purchasing and managing the serials within their restricted budget. So to solve the ongoing Serials crisis, it is essential for a common infra structure or firm to share the resources among libraries.

The continuous price increase for scientific information combined with the lack of funding for libraries has led to massive yearly cancellations of scientific journals. The exponential growth in the production of knowledge has made it more and more impossible for the individual library to purchase all the relevant information.

The rapid technological developments have resulted in a constant pressure for new hardware, software and education and training of library staff.

And finally, the overwhelming application of new technologies —especially the World Wide Web and Internet — in all media has contributed to rapid escalating user expectations in the sense that the users expect library information to be delivered just as fast as any other information they need in their daily lives.

However, precisely the same technological developments seem to include the opportunity to solve the crisis in the form of Library Consortium (Mudannayake 2011).

CONCLUSION

In this period of shrinking or stable university and library budgets, and of rising costs in serial print subscriptions, it is important for academic libraries to understand the trends and implications of the digital information revolution. Electronic journals have created unprecedented opportunities for libraries. At the same time, they have brought profound impact on the library work. The rapidly changing external environment complicates management of e-journals as far as the technology is concerned. The e-journals represent one of the largest and most exiting challenges confronting contemporary librarians. The Internet, the numbers of formats are the main concern that calls for a sound policy as regards the management issues. Library staff has to update their knowledge about the options and alternative and upgrade their skills to be able to handle e-journals effectively.

REFERENCES

Abdus S. C. (1999). Potential of Electronic Journals to Extend Library Collections. Retrieved from www.geocities.com/pakistani_librarian.

Adomi. E. (1999). Library and information resources. Benin: Ethiope Publishing Corporation.

Ashcroft, L. and Langdon, C. (1999). Electronic journals and university library collections. *Collection Building,* 18(3), 105-114. Retrieved from http://www.dlib.org/dlib/october99/rusch-feja/10rusch-feja-full-report.html

Bish, R. B (2011). Managing and handling electronic journals: some issues. Retrieved from http://www.rsbishtlbsnaa.ernet.htm

Bosch, S. (1998). Licensing information: Where can we go from here? *Library Acquisitions: Practice & Theory,* 22(1), 45-47.

Breeding. M. (2004). The many facets of managing electronic resources. Retrieved from http://staffweb.library.vanderbilt.edu/breeding

Caplan P. (1993). Cataloguing Internet resources. *The Public-Access Computer Systems Review,* 4(2), 61-66.

Chan L. (1999). Electronic journals and academic libraries. *Library Hi Tech,*17(1), 10-16.

Dickerson, E. and Lamborn, J. G. (1998). A capital idea: Electronic serials from acquisition to access: report of an institute. *Library Acquisitions: Practice and Theory,* 22(2), 167-75.

Luijendijk, W. (1996). Archiving electronic journals: The serial information provider's perspective. *IFLA Journal,* 22(3), 209-210.

Mckay, S. L. (1998). Partnering in a changing medium: The challenges of managing and delivering e-journals: The subscription agent's point of view. *Library Acquisitions: Practice* & *Theory,* 22(1), 23-27.

Meadows, J. (1996). Surveying electronic journals. *Inter lending and Document Supply,* 24(4), 32-33.

Moller,T. (2006).Open access in developing countries frontiers in Neuroscience magazine. Retrieved from http://frontierson.org/global-open-access 3.2.

Mudannaye (2011). E- Journal: A multifaceted approach with special reference to Sri Lanka. Retrieved from http://www.library.ucsb.edu/istl/96- fall/brown-duda.html

Neal, J. G. (1997). The serials revolution: Vision, innovation, tradition. *The Serials Librarian,* 30(3/4), 97-IO5.

Neavill, G. B. and Sheble, M. A. (1995). Archiving electronic journals. *Serials Review,* 21(4), 13-21.

Nisonger, T. E. (1996). Collection management issues for electronic journals. *IFLA Journal,* 22(3), 233-239.

Rabine, R & Rich, L. (1997). Managing electronic journals in times of changes. Retrieved March 2 2012 from http//www.bgsu.edu/colleges/library/infosrv/irich/acrhnd.htm

Rusch-Feja, D. and Siebeky, U. (1999) Evaluation of Usage and Acceptance of Electronic Journals: Results of an Electronic Survey of Max Planck Society Researchers including Usage Statistics from Elsevier, Springer and Academic Press (Full Report*). D-Lib Magazine,* 5(10).

Thamaraiselvi, G. and Kaliammal (2011). E-journal management in academic libraries with special reference to indest consortia in India. Retrieved from http://web.mit.edu/waynej/www/hawkins.htm

20

Electronic Information Resources Management in Academic Library in Nigeria

Olatokunbo Christopher Okiki

INTRODUCTION

University libraries in Nigeria have developed in quantity, infrastructure, personnel and services since the first university library was established at then university college now university of Ibadan over decades ago. Development of university libraries in Nigeria cannot be separated from the evolution and growth of universities in the country. The history of university library development in Nigeria dates back to pre independence, when the University of Ibadan and its library was established in 1948. As pointed out by Aguolu (1996), Government-owned university libraries are suffering from a low budgetary allocation for education. An analysis of the federal government allocation to the education sector in the last nine years is discouraging. Between 2000 and 2008, the Nigerian federal government allocated an average of only 9% of its budget to education (Mordi, 2008).

According to Parker (2007) the advent of information technology in the early 1990s had led to the emergence and continuous exponential growth of electronically borne information resources. This has tremendously transformed information resources handling and management in Nigerian academic environments, and university libraries in particular. Other factors such as provision of space economy; ease of access through numerous metadata, search engines, online catalogues, (O.P.A.Cs), and protocols; access which is not hindered by distance or boundaries and simultaneous consultation of the same e- resources by many users, provided the pre-eminence of e-resources over print format. According to Tsakonas and Papatheodorou, (2006) electronic information resources are information resources provided in electronic form, and these include CD-ROMs, resources available on the Internet such e-journals, e-print, and other computer-based electronic networks.

According to Bashiru (2010), today, "the global village is being described on the basis of ICT as information rich northern hemisphere and information poor southern hemisphere of which Nigeria is one. A major characteristic of an information poor society is Low-level ICT with minimum local content on the web for local and global consumption". Nigeria can only be part of this global movement by using ICT to bridge the gap and cross over. Frankly, EIRs have provided wider access to information in universities for teaching, learning, and research than the traditional print through the use of information and communications technologies (ICTs) by library patrons. The management of electronic resources often refers to the tools and processes used to organize administrative metadata, such as license terms, vendor contracts and usage statistics (Mitchell and Surratt, 2005).

The avalanche of online resources forced the beginning of change on the traditional library organization. Managing the acquired digital resource created sets of challenges for libraries. Electronic resources include CD-ROMs, e-journals, e-text or electronic books, locally loaded databases, websites and abstracting and indexing databases such as MEDLINE. Electronic resources also include products that aid in resource access for patrons such as A-Z lists, Open URL, servers, Federated search engines and resources that provide full- text content such as publishers' electronic journal content, journal content platforms such as Jstor and content aggregators such as EBSCOHOST's Academic Search Premier and proxy servers or other authentication tools (Pinfield, 2001, and Bothmann and Holmberg, 2010).

UNIVERSITY SYSTEM IN NIGERIA

Since 1948, when the University College Library (now Kenneth Dike Library, University of Ibadan) was established in Ibadan, it has been recognised as the intellectual heart of the university system. It is therefore, not surprising, that other university libraries established in Nigeria after 1948 imbibed the culture of ensuring that the university library is the centre of all academic activities in the universities. The Federal Government of Nigeria through her agency the National Universities Commission (NUC) initiated various programmes designed to lunch Nigerian Universities into information global society. Nok (2006) include the automation of university libraries using Management Information Systems (MIS) and Nigerian Universities Network (NUNET) with the aim of developing a viable local and wide area network in each institution as one of such programmes.

Today, there are about 124 university libraries, of which 37 are owned by the Federal Government, 37 by the states while 50 are privately owned. All these libraries are supposed to provide adequate information to their users. Libraries of tertiary institutions in Nigeria naturally display different stages of development. The development of effective information delivery systems is key component to teaching and learning processes, and modern technology greatly enhances the process.

The National Universities Commission (NUC) has made deliberate effort in the development of policies and practices and building of tools to help in the management of the over wholming o resources and the information therein as the structures of Library Management System (LMS) could not sustain it. "Adam Chandler of

Cornell University developed a Web Hub for developing administrative metadata for electronic resource management for promoting and sharing of what different individuals and libraries were building in terms of tools to support electronic resource management" (Parker, 2007).

In spite of this giant stride, many Universities in Nigeria are yet to harness the opportunities provided by these initiatives, due to inadequate facilities or lack of maintenance culture and even where these facilities are in place the potential users of these new information sources are not making use of the valuable electronic resources owing to lack of awareness or lack of skills required to navigate the modern technology. Corroborating this assertion, Abdullah (2006) noted that most users are unaware of the existence of e-books in library collections and that they are willing to discover and use them more effectively. Equally, unfriendly interfaces or usability problems tend to hinder their further use of electronic resources.

Carrigan (1995) has characterized access to information as "just-in-time" and ownership as "just-in-case". In the former, a user will only access an information material when he needs it and wherever it may be located. One only needs to pay for that access, rather than the latter, where information materials are just purchased by the library with the assumption that a user may need it at a future date. Moahi (2002) listed the advantage of "just -in-time" as saving storage space, allowing users to have remote access to library collections regardless of the location of the information source and of course, the speed of service, since if it is electronically available, will be instantaneous. This position of Moahi has firmly taken root in Nigeria universities library. Hence the purpose of this paper is proffer suggestions on how university libraries in Nigeria can manage their electronic information provision to their users.

ACCESS TO ELECTRONIC INFORMATION RESOURCES

The convergence of computers and telecommunication technology has popularised electronic publishing in the scholarly community. This is not surprising given its competitive advantage over the traditional method of publishing. For example, the cost of production and distribution is greatly reduced. The speed of production is fast and it provides instant access to (users) readers. With the advent of electronic publishing, many library and information materials are now in electronic form. The full texts of monographs, reference sources, journals, newsletters, theses and dissertations, textbooks, databases, etc are now readily produced and available electronically.

In Nigeria electronic information resources has become important to libraries because of the escalating costs of print materials. This is especially true of journals. The prices are escalating at an alarming rate. In order to fit into many library budgets, many journal titles have had to be deselected from their collection. The average cost of accessing electronic publishing has been found to be much cheaper than owning the entire issue of a journal. Other advantages are ease of accessibility, searchability and currency. In addition, many journal publishers are at various stages of discontinuing the traditional print form of their journals and are moving towards full electronic version of their journals. The implication of this is that users without access to infrastructure for digital information resources may never have access to some important journals in their fields of study or research.

In view of this, there exists debate over "access rather than holdings". This attitude amongst Nigerians may seem encouraging, considering the fact that electronic information resources tend to bring about "access", regardless of time and space. Bozimo (2010) therefore attest to this when she agreed that "contemporarily, emphasis is shifting to access to information materials rather than ownership". Jagboro (2003) is of the opinion that the prospects of electronic information resources could be outlined thus:

1. E-resources would be used unendingly in the classroom and lecture rooms of pre-primary, primary and secondary schools, and tertiary institutions respectively.
2. E-resources would likely be used to convert practically all manual system libraries to virtual libraries.

3. E-resources would be used by the Nigerian government to sensitise citizens of their programmes.
4. E-resources would be the backbone of communication.
5. E-resources would proliferate the academic, business, government, and all sectors of the Nigerian community.
6. There is even likely to be over-reliance upon e-resources.

The advent of the Internet has made electronic publishing more realizable in Nigeria universities library. This is as a result of the use of the electronic mail system of the Internet, which now allows documents of several pages to be sent electronically to several users at the same time. According to Adeogun (2003) the availability of full internet access in each library will facilitate on-line access to the world of information. Internet has become so popular in Africa that its growth in the last five years has been tremendous. According to Jensen (2002) while there were it handful of countries which had local Internet access in Africa five years ago, today, almost every capital city in Africa has Internet access.

In Nigeria in the last two decades there has been tremendous, as cyber cafes with computers fully equipped with Internet access now dot almost every corner of major cities in Nigeria. It is heartening to note that cyber cafes are usually besieged by secondary school and university students. With 45.04 million people that use the Internet, Nigeria has been named among the 20 top countries that use the Internet. According to the usage statistics on the top nations on the Internet, Internet World Stat Nigeria occupies the 11th position, just immediately after France, which has Internet population of 50.29 million. Nigeria also comes ahead of Mexico with Internet population of 42 million. This rating means that two per cent of global Internet population of 2.29 billion people is Nigerians. On a population estimate of 170.12 million people, Nigeria's Internet penetration ratio was put at 26.5 per cent. This means that 26.5 persons out of every 100 Nigerians use the Internet (http://www.internetworldstats.com/af/ng.htm).

It is obvious that Internet is now integral part of the educational culture in Nigeria. It is therefore logical that if libraries in Nigeria take the electronic route of access to information, the provision of information to their users will be strengthened. However, given the high cost of infrastructure needed for access to electronic information, it is obvious that if each individual university library decides to go through this route on its own, it will fail, so in order to ensure success, it is being proposed that all the university libraries in Nigeria should form a consortium.

TYPES OF ELECTRONIC INFORMATION RESOURCES

As technology has advanced, more and more information is available in Internet-ready format. The standard free web sources (.com, .edu, .gov, etc.) are still widely available. In Nigeria, most academic libraries subscribed to fee-based electronic databases hence accesses to unsubscribe scholarly journals are restricted and when this happens, users are often referring to the free web. Today a significant amount of scholarly research is available via the Internet. How and why you utilize these information sources depends on your research project. Resources that were once available exclusively in a print format are now available electronically. Examples of these sources are:

Non-Internet format	Internet format	Examples
Print journals	e-journals (HTML or pdf)	JSTOR,EBSCOHOST etc
Print books	e-books (HTML or pdf)	Safari Books Online, Amazon
DVDs / video tapes	streaming videos	Amazon Video etc
Radio broadcasts	Podcasting	NPR
Television broadcasts	Vcasting	Hulu, CNN, AJE

In achieving effective use of available electronic information resources libraries should provide access to information resources; expert professional support to facilitate thorough and accurate use of all library resources, access to library materials and services to the community. Aguolu and Aguolu (2002) reveal that efforts are being made worldwide to promote access to information in all formats;

they lament the attendant of underdevelopment such as power failure, machine breakdowns, and lack of spare parts and technicians, which intermittently stall the performance of the modern gadgets of information storage and transfer in developing countries.

THE ADVENT OF COMPUTERIZATION IN NIGERIAN LIBRARIES

Libraries all over the world are beginning to be more interactive than passive. The coming of computers into the library has completely changed the face of the library to more of a social networking centre. The earliest use of any technology in Nigerian libraries was the introduction of microform technology at the University of Ibadan with the purchase of three microform readers in 1948.The first instances of the usage of computers in Nigeria were when IBM set up the African Education Centre at the University of Ibadan (UI Computing Center) in 1963 and when computing services were brought to Nigeria in connection with the analysis of the 1962/63 national census.

DEPLOYMENT OF ICTS IN LIBRARIES

In Nigeria, most of the tertiary institutions strive to provide ICT, especially Internet connectivity for student use, mostly in the libraries, ICT centres, and computer pools. Many tertiary institutions' libraries in Nigeria are not computerized, and are not Internet connected, and where some ICT facilities exist they are zealously guarded (Nweke, 2006). The application of ICTs in Nigerian Tertiary Institutions shows that there is some consciousness of the significant role that ICT can play in delivering library services especially electronic information resources, even though ICT is not fully embraced by most of the higher education libraries in the country. The factors responsible for this development in the libraries vary - both in identity and strength. Generally, identifiable factors are: appreciation of ICT by the institution's Librarian, the Library Management, the University Management, relationship between the library and campus ICT units, Funding, Building, and Training for Librarianship.

APPRECIATION OF ICT BY LIBRARIAN AND LIBRARY STAFF

Libraries like those of the Universities of Ibadan, Lagos, Benin, Jos, Ife, Ahmadu Bello, Bayero University, and Abeokuta where their librarians had over the years shown some appreciation of ICT through their commitment to the deployment of ICTs in their libraries, are in the forefront. In these libraries there is significant progress in applying ICT to library services. The main application is in the area of cataloguing. Librarians and most other staff in Nigerian university libraries appear to appreciate the important role of ICT plays in today's academic endeavour.

RELATIONSHIP BETWEEN LIBRARY AND CAMPUS ICT

In most Nigeria academic libraries there is a mutual cooperation and collaboration between library and Information and communications technology unit. As John Doe once said: "No man is an island, entire of itself"; so is the environmental conditioning for ICT applications. Technicians need the users of applications, and vice-versa. These relationships include advice on specifications and type of technology to be deployed. In some cases where libraries have no technically trained ICT staff, they may have to rely on deployment of such staff to the library by the Campus ICT. Libraries like that of Ibadan, Lagos, Ife, Bayero, Jos, and Ahmadu Bello, have very good working relationships with their campus ICTs, thereby enabling good progress in their deployment of ICT (Akintunde, 2009).

FUNDING

Funding is critical to any library initiative, especially electronic information resources. E-resource is very costly in terms of hard and soft ware. Personnel are also very scarce and costly. The rate of adaptation and/or adoption of ICT to library services have, so far, been largely defined by the availability of funds in most Nigerian universities, for instance. Apart from the attitudes of Librarians and management teams, funding has been a major factor of stunted growth in the libraries. Libraries that are about making some significant changes from the manual to a fully automated library system are funded through external grants.

It is imperative therefore that Nigerian academic library must seek for alternative funding if significant progress will be made in deploying ICTs in Nigerian academic libraries. Funding by government (Federal and State) which has been the sponsor of about 75 per cent of the libraries has been dwindling and quite unreliable in the last few years. However, for private universities, there appears to be some stability as some good attention is yet given to libraries. Among Nigerian university libraries, there is no budget head yet among Federal and State universities to acquire and sustain ICT as most of the budget is barely sufficient for the payment of staff remuneration and overhead costs.

INTEGRATED LIBRARY SYSTEMS

An integrated library system (ILS) with its various modules is the core of library automation and these systems are slowly being implemented in libraries in Nigeria; most of them are in place in university. In the late 1980s several University libraries were provided with PCs and TINLIB DOS-based software by the NUC but because of lack of training, infrastructure and human capital many attempts to implement these early systems failed. The newer generations of library systems are all web-accessible and are based on MARC records and inter-operability. Examples of these systems are Millennium, VTLS, Liberty/Alice from Softlink and Koha, an open-source system developed by Katipo in New Zealand.

One topical automation project worthy of mention is the Carnegie/MacArthur funded implementation of integrated library systems for six of the government universities in Nigeria (Ahmadu Bello University, Zaria (ABU), Bayero University Kano (BUK), Obafemi Awolowo University (OAU), University of Ibadan (UI), the University of Jos (UNIJOS), and the University of Port Harcourt (UNIPORT). With the assistance of training from the Mortenson Center at the University of Illinois these university libraries have all commenced full implementation.

IMPACT OF CONSORTIUM IN MANAGING ELECTRONIC INFORMATION RESOURCES

It should be noted that efforts have been made in the past to have a sort of co-operative arrangement among libraries in Nigeria. Ubogu, et.al (1992) has presented a comprehensive review of the various efforts at forging co-operation among libraries in Nigeria. He also provided several reasons for their failures, among which are: lack of corporate or co-operative spirit, slow document delivery system, poor communication infrastructure, limited computer literacy, etc. The country has since moved away from these limitations. It has now dawned on academic libraries all over the world, including Nigeria that co-operative arrangements amongst them must work if they are to have access to unlimited amount of electronic information that can be accessed through electronic networks. The University of Lagos has a 120-seater complete computer laboratory fully furnished and donated by a mobile telecommunication giant in the country. The laboratory is an electronic reference library, and the type that should be a model for all academic libraries in Nigeria.

There has been extraordinary activity by the international community in Nigeria. Much of that activity has centered on universities, and fortunately the libraries have benefited from these efforts. The thrust of the international organization efforts has been to develop strong universities. To quote from the MacArthur Foundation on its *Global Security and Sustainability Program* for Nigeria: "One of the goals of the MacArthur Foundation in Nigeria is to help improve the country's higher education system. This pursuit is based upon the belief that strong universities and intellectual freedom are essential to developing and sustaining healthy democratic societies."

The process of strengthening universities and their libraries has revolved around two equally important activities. First, donors have focused on the development of ICT infrastructure on the campuses and in the libraries that allows users to have open and reliable access to the Internet and to the Web. Second, and most importantly for the university libraries, many donors have focused on making research materials in electronic format available to the universities. In addition, virtually all the universities in Nigeria are beneficiary of Widernet project (www.widernet.org), a non-profit project at the University of Iowa that works to improve e-resource access in developing countries.

EBSCO Information Service is a well-established aggregator of electronic journal content that offers full text access to thousands of journal titles in such diverse areas as science and technology, social sciences and humanities. The eIFL-sponsored EBSCOHost service for eIFL members can be accessed via the Internet and is also distributed via CD-ROMs, which can be loaded onto a networked hard drive. University Librarians in the last two years have consolidated the formation of a Nigerian University Library Consortium (NULIC), which was facilitated the acquisition of library materials and provide better services to patrons. The Nigerian University Library Consortium (NULIC) coordinated the payment for the renewal of license for the EBSCO Host Database which had expired after a three-year grant by the George Soros Foundation. The eIFL project provided interested Nigerian universities with three years of free access to a suite of EBSCOHost bibliographic and full-text databases.

Ironically, while the university libraries were thrilled to have access to this important resource, they simply did not have the infrastructure or equipment to take full advantage of it during the first three years when it was being offered without charge. It was only toward the end of the three years that some of the institutions began to utilize it on a regular basis and experience its value. Libraries must now pay for the access on a countrywide basis. To help libraries do this, eIFL encouraged libraries to form a consortium for cooperative purchasing and has provided several workshops on developing a consortium and using EBSCO resources.

DEVELOPMENT AND ENHANCEMENT OF SKILLS

In order to acquaint users with effective electronic information resources use in Nigeria academic libraries it is imperative to have virtually equipped librarians with appropriate skills to support scholarly research and communication. The common strategies employed is 'train the trainer' - or cascaded training - approach which encourages trainees to share their learning with others. Key areas of training include:

- Information literacy
- E-resources, including monitoring and evaluation of usage
- Library and Information Science (LIS) curriculum development
- Developing an institutional repository
- Library automation

Recognising that the changing environment demands constant re-skilling of staff (capacity building) the Nigeria government through, Nigeria Universities Commission (NUC) and other bodies such as Education Trust Fund and others have also supported libraries to improve the skills of libraries staff through continuous professional development.

CHALLENGES

Access to reliable power was and is still a real issue for most of Nigeria university campuses and of late has become relatively worse. This has hampered access to electronic resources. Also, bandwidth for the library is not sufficient to meet the needs of the users and this constitutes a major issue when the power situation is stabilized.

CONCLUSION AND RECOMMENDATIONS

It is of note that the Federal, State Government of Nigeria and International funding agencies have developed keen interested in the general development of electronic information resources in Nigerian universities. For example, the Federal Ministry of Education has embarked on the establishment of the National Virtual (Digital) Library Project. The aim of this project is to make available, in an equitable and cost effective manner, as well as enhanced access to national and international library and information resources and to share locally available resources with libraries all over the world using digital technology. The delivery of the Virtual Library is through the Internet,

CD-ROM, and Wide Area Network (WAN) and this has boosted to the development of provision of electronic resources in Nigerian educational system.

However, given the limited funding available to university libraries in Nigeria, and the growing demands of users, the National University Commission (NUC) who has been playing a leading role in the formation of a consortium should double their effort in sustaining e-resources. In addition, NUC should continue its leadership role in the newly formed consortium. Library needs to have reliable back-up power and supply, sufficient bandwidth, and access to the Internet to move forward in providing better access to its collections and e-resources.

Without robust foundational infrastructure and adequate human capital this advance in electronic information resources would not have been possible. It is very important that Nigeria move ahead with a strong national electric grid and improved Internet service provision in order for others to establish a firm foundation upon which to base an integrated electronic library system. In maintaining effective management of electronic information resources there is need to develop a strong library website to publicize as well as recreate awareness of available resources. Also, develop an outreach program for faculty and students to highlight the benefit of e-resources and provide training on their use.

REFERENCES

Abdulmumin, I. (2010). Electronic Library Use by academic staff at the University of Ilorin, Nigeria. *Journal of Library and Information Science (JOLIS),* 7(1&2), 2-5.

Adeogun, M. (2003). The digital divide and university education in Sub-Saharan Africa. African *Journal of Library, Archives and Information Science,* 3 (3), 75-81.

Akintunde, S.A. (2009). Budgeting for technical services in the era of ICT, Information Packaging in the Era of ICT: Challenges Facing Cataloguers, Classifiers and Indexers: Proceedings of Selected Papers of the Cataloguing, Classification and Indexing Section of the Nigerian Library Association, 2007-2008, Nigerian Library Association, Cataloguing, Classification and Indexing Section, Abuja, pp. 85-95.

Aguolu, I. E. (1996). Nigerian University Libraries: What Future? *The International Information & Library Review*, 28(3), 261.

Bashiru A. S. (2010). Issues and Challenges in the Creation of Institutional Repositories with Local Content: Critical Reflections. *Information, Society and Justice*, 3(1), 59-68.

Bothmann, R.L. and Holmberg, M. (2010). Strategic planning for electronic resources management. Retrieved from http://mydisk.mnsu.edu/bothmr/tenurepromotion/supportdocuments/criterion_2/e-resplanning-chapter.pdf.

Bozimo, D. (2010). Library Automation. Unpublished Lesson Note, Abraka: Department of Library and Information Science (LSE Unit), Faculty of Education, Delta State University.

Carrigan, D.P. (1995). From just-in-case to just-in-time: Limits to the Alternative Library Service Model. *Journal of Scholarly Publishing*, 26(3), 173-182.

Jagboro KO (2003). A study of Internet usage in Nigerian Universities: A case study of Obafemi Awolowo University, Ile-Ife, Nigeria. *First Monday*, 8(2). Retrieved from http://www.firstmonday.org

Jensen, M. (1996). Bridging the Gaps in Internet Development in Africa. International Development Research Center. Retrieved from http://www.idrc.ca/acacia/studies/ir-gaps.htm

MacArthur Foundation. (2005). Developing strong university libraries in Nigeria: A report. Retrieved from http://www.webpages.uidaho.edu/~mbolin/ilo-ifijeh.htm

Moahi, K.H. (2002). Issues of just-in-time (access) v. just-in-case (ownership) for libraries in developing countries: lessons to be learnt from developed countries. *Library Review*, 51 (7).

Mordi, R. (2008). Funding education in Nigeria: Surviving on a shoestring budget. *Tell Magazine*, 44, 32-34.

Mitchell, A. M. & Surratt, B.E. (2005). Cataloguing and organizing digital resources: A how-to-do-it manual for librarians. New York, Neal-Schumn Publishers.

Nigeria Internet Usage and Telecommunications Reports (2012). Retrieved from http://www.internetworldstats.com/af/ng.htm

Nok, G. (2006). The challenges of computerizing a university library in Nigeria: The Kashim Ibrahim library, Ahamadu Bello University, Zaria. *Library Philosophy and Practice* 8(2) Retrieved from http://unllib.unl.edu/LPP/nok.htm

Parker, K. (2007). Tools for mature management of electronic resources lifecycles in libraries. http: //www.library.yale.edu/preifla2007/papers/parker.pdf.

Tsakonas, G. & Papatheordorou, C (2006). Analysing and evaluating usefulness and usability in electronic information services. *Journal of Information Science*, 32(5), 400-419.

Ubogu, F.N., Okoh, M.I., Alimole, A.N. and Eyitayo, O.T. (1992). Library networks and resource sharing in Nigeria. *African Journal of Library, Archives, and Information Science*, 2(2), 99-110.

21

Management of Electronic Resources in Nigerian University Libraries

Janet Onomeh Ubogu

INTRODUCTION

Electronic Resources Management (ERM) has become a complex task when you compare it to the time when we had fewer electronic resources and we hadn't yet determined the best way to management them. As the use of electronic resources have increased, we've discovered that the simple set of tasks we used in the beginning doesn't work. The days of buying installing, training and paying for a resources are long over (Strategic Librarian, 2010).

As libraries build ever-larger collections of electronic resources, finding ways to manage them efficiently becomes a major challenge. The number of electronic journals, citations databases, and full text aggregations held by most libraries has grown rapidly. Managing these electronic resources involves providing the library's users with convenient ways to find and access them and providing library staff with the tools to keep track of them (Breeding, 2012).

Bothmann and Holnberg (2006) cited Marshall and Kawasaki (2005) Jasper and Sheble (2005) Brown, Nelson, and Wine Burgh-Freed (2005) and Robbins and Smith (2004) stated that electronic resource management may be defined in various ways. The definition may be as narrow as an A-to-Z list of serial titles, a focus on an approach to budget management or a broader concept like a content management system to create web pages, provide administrative functions, and track license agreements. This work covers various aspects of e-resources with emphasizes on evaluation, planning, policies, handling of tools and how they can be managed, having the knowledge and understanding of e-resources.

LITERATURE REVIEW

Managing a collection of electronic information resources is quite different from managing a collection of non-electronic information resources. Unlike a book, computer and networks are needed to access electronic information. More staff with different skills have to become involved. Maintenance is more complex. Patron's skills and needs are an important factor. Library choices are influenced as constrained by the marketing strategies, pricing and technology options offered by the information vendors. Different libraries making choices from the same available options can and will end up with substantially different solutions (LaMarca, Brentrup, Fark and Jargo, 1997).

The steps required for managing e-resources are more complex than those for print resources. A process that consisted of selecting, ordering, cataloguing and binding, now includes selecting, evaluating, approving, licensing, billing and registering access and is accompanied by a series of technical aspects, such as usability, performance, access technologies, public interfaces, troubleshooting and usage statistics. E-resource management is a time intensive and interactive process, often requiring more staff with a greater skill set at each stage (Kasprowski, 2006). As libraries are experiencing profound changes in terms of digital content and delivery, managers must understand what is going on in their organizations and how to best staff them. They are increasingly turning to proven business practices that allow them to evaluate and design new methods of delivery of resources and services. Process mapping has a future in libraries, especially since it allows library staff to handle complex processes such as ERM. Publication of other case studies and discussions of process mapping within the library community may lead to increased adoption of these models and methods (Afifi, 2008).

Bothmann and Holmberg(2006) cited White(2005)stated that the development and use of policies is critical in electronic resource management and for communicating a library's goals. Policies set guide lines of practice that aid in electronic resource management Aside from collection development policies, libraries need policies that address issues such as types of resources to support, licensing issues, and user access. Other policy topics include how and which resources should be catalogued, placed in a content management system or subject guide, or added to an ERMS. Also Planning for electronic resources is perhaps the most important and least practiced activity in libraries. Electronic resources present a number of challenges to the traditional library of operations and workflow that must be addressed in order to provide smooth management. The challenges faced by many libraries include operational issues such as the number of staff assigned to electronic resource management duties, staying in-step with technological and vendor changes in electronic resources, budgeting limited resources for the acquisition of resources, and communication with vendors and amongst librarians and administrators, that vendor communication is frustrating because some try to work with librarians to improve their products and services and to create win win situations, while other vendors are simply trying to earn a particular dollar amount. Publishers who are breaking into the electronic resource environment sometimes create communication problems as they lack an understanding of the access requirements libraries have (e.g., open URL,IP authentication). Couple these issues with an often-mistrustful attitude on both sides, communication becomes a big issue in electronic resource management.

Bothmann and Holmberg went further to state that staffing for electronic resources is perhaps the biggest challenge most libraries face staffing issues center on training and time. Some libraries address the challenge of limited staffing by distributing work among existing staff, prioritizing projects according to staff availability, and emphasizing the need to invest more staff time in the electronic resource environment. Other shave developed a team structure to meet the staffing need, delegating specific tasks to paraprofessionals . A lack of realistic expectations of what one electronic resource librarian can do with the large number of resources and vendors, as well as of the technological capacities of electronic resource agreement on resource needs, and assistance with the work from other staff stand as a problem to electronic resource management. Electronic resources come with demands that may also be barriers to some libraries. These demands include licensing issues and patron authentication ,bibliographic control and access questions, and overall management for purchases, renewals, and license tracking.

Joshipura,(2008)once the resource is identified, evaluation of the product is the second most critical step for selectors .Evaluation helps the selectors determine the cost, the reliability of the content provider , and most importantly the authoritativeness of the resource. A selection tool such as a trial or demonstration of the product by the provider, as well as reviews in print and electronic sources ,helps in evaluating the product and leads to sound decisions. Traditionally with print resources, the selectors consider the credentials of the author , currency, intended audience, accuracy, ease of use, reputation of the publisher, the subject it cost and the curriculum or research needs of students/faculty/patrons. They also use methods such as citation analysis, user surveys, and so forth. However, with e-resources the selector must consider additional elements such as easy access to the content, coverage, search capability and functionality of the interface; quality of technical support; method of pricing; and provisions of licensing agreements. Thus, the typical evaluation process for e-resources has many facets, and following the various selection criteria is vital for selector.

According to Poe, Bevis, Graham, Latham and Stevens (2008) management of electronic resources is a time-consuming and at times, a difficult process, although the management of electronic resources is often seen as a strictly technical services endeavor, it should been considered a multi-faceted process requiring all areas of the library. The management of electronic resources begins in the technical services area, specially, acquisitions, where the majority of the resources in the collection begin their journey.

Okoye and Ugwuanyi (2012) cited Breeding (2004) observed two fundamental aspects to managing electronic resources, back end acquisition functions and a front-end content delivery.

Front end content delivery access to users is achieved through:

(1) Provision of online catalogues

(2) Linkage and cross searching. In this scenario, 239.50 protocol is a major facility.

(3) Cross-searching alternative which engages the use of open. Archive protocol for Metadata Harvesting (OAI-PMH).

(4) Use of E-journal locator resources

(5) Linking to full text is possible through the use of digital object identifiers (DOI) that can be used to provide links to full text

(6) Open URL-Based link resolvers

Some major linking products available include:

i. SFX from Exlibris

ii. Link source from EBSCO

iii. Link finder plus from endeavour information systems

iv. Web bridge from innovative interfaces

v. Sirsi resolver from Sirsi Corp

vi. Article finder from serials solutions

vii. Icate from openly informatics (culled from Okoye and Ugwuanyi cited Breeding 2004)

(7) Federated search

This involves applications that allow users to search multiple sources simultaneously, so they do not have to decide which resource might have the information they need. This approach is also known as cross searching or metasearch. Some of the major products in this category include:

- Encompass from endeavour information systems
- Metalib from Exlibris
- Sirsi single search from Sirsi
- Webfeat prism from webfeat
- Muse search from Muse Global
- ZPORTAL from Fretwell-Dowing
- Verde from Exlibris

(Okoye and Ugwuanyi 2012 cited Breeding 2004)

They submitted that management of business details of back-end staff functions, related to acquisition payment and licensing. The traditional online catalogue approach depicts the back-end management tool for library staff. In this respect the integrated library system (ILS) is used to manage e-journals and other electronic content. However, the ILS lacks some of the needed features largely due to its orientation towards print resources. The lack falls within the parameters of licensing. With electronic resources the library signs a license for each electronic resource, be it for a simple title or more often for a large aggregation of materials such as: PROQUEST, EBSCOHOST and web of science. Licensing of e-resources involves a number of details such as the cost, the duration of the license and when it needs to be renewed, the number of simultaneous users allowed, whether the library retains access to the content, the telephone number to call for technical support and whether one is allowed to use the resource to fulfill and interlibrary loan request. These are a few of the demands of licensing e-resources. Because of the limitations of ILS, ERM was developed to overcome these limitations.

METHODOLOGY

The study examines management of e-resources in Nigerian University Libraries in South-South. Delta State University Abraka, (28) University of Benin, Benin City (42), Ambrose Alli University, Ekpoma (25), University of Calabar, Calabar (17), University of Port-Harcourt (33), River State University of Science and Technology ( ), Cross River State University (34), University of Uyo (53), Akwa Ibom State University (7), Federal University of Petroleum, Effurun (5), Niger Delta University (35), population comprised 290 librarians in these eleven universities.

Copies of twenty-item question constructed were used for data collection. 290 copies of the questionnaire were distributed and 247 copies were returned, giving (85.8%) return rate of the returned copies of the questionnaire 212 (73.1%) were found usable. Data collected were analyzed by using frequency counts and percentages.

DEMOGRAPHIC VARIABLES OF THE RESPONDENTS

Part I : The items include in this part were respondents' gender, age, educational qualification, year of experience and academic status.

Part II : The items include in this part elicited information on the management of e-resources in the university libraries in south-south, Nigeria. Simple percentage was used in analyzing the data.

Bio Data

Table 1: Gender of the respondents

Male (%)		Female (%)	
120	56.6%	92	43.3%

Table 1 above shows that majority of the respondents are male.

Table 2: Age of the respondents

Age	Frequency	Percentage
25 – 30	21	9.90%
35 – 40	95	44.8%
45 – 50	61	28.7%
55 – 60	35	16.5%

Table 2 above shows that majority of the respondents are between 35-40 years old.

Table 3: Educational qualification

Educational Qualification	Frequency	Percentage
Ph.D	15	7.07%
MSC/MLS	79	37.2%
BLS	51	24.0%
Dip	67	31.6%

Table 3 above shows that 79 (37.2%) of the respondents are MLS/ MSC Holders.

Table 4: Designation of the respondents

Designation	Frequency	Percentage
Assistant Librarian	97	45.7%
Librarian II	49	23.1%
Librarian I	36	16.9%
Senior Librarian	19	8.96%
Deputy University Librarian	09	4.24%

Table 4 above shows that majority of the respondents are assistant librarian.

Table 5: Accessing E-Resources

S/N	Access	Frequency	%age (%)	Frequency	%age (%)
1	Through ELOSS-Encyclopedia of life science	16	7.54	196	92.4
2	Through HINARI-health based	3	1.41	209	98.5
3	Through JSTOR	45	21.2	167	78.7
4	Through EBSCOHOST	115	54.2	97	45.7
5	Through BIOMEDICAL and life sciences (Medicine)	1	0.47	211	99.5
6	Through DARE	25	11.7	187	88.2
7	Through Google	201	94.8	11	5.18

Table 5 above shows that 201 (94.8%) of the respondents access e-resources through google search engine. 115 (54.2%) of them agreed that they access e-resources through ebscohost.

Table 6: Electronic Resource Management

S/N	Management	Frequency	%age (%)	Frequency	%age (%)
1	Librarians are fully involved in managing e-resources	115	54.2	97	45.7
2	Licensing e-resources are necessary	209	94.8	11	5.18
3	Managing e-resources is the same as managing print resources	81	38.2	131	61.7
4	Electronic resources are easier to manage than print resources	95	44.8	117	55.1
5	Experts are needed to manage e-resources	201	98.5	3	1.41
6	Anybody can manage e-resources	92	43.3	120	56.6
7	Management of e-resources is necessary	200	94.3	12	5.66
8	E-resources are not necessary in the library	116	54.7	96	45.2
9	In-service training is necessary	200	94.3	12	5.66
10	Parent body's input is necessary	197	92.9	15	7.07

Table 6 above shows that 209 (98.5%) of the respondents agreed that licensing of e-resources is necessary, 201 (94.8%) of them stated that experts are required in managing e-resources. Also 200(94.3%) of them stated that in-service training is necessary in managing e-resources.

Table 7: Electronic Resources Management Strategies

S/N	Strategies	Frequency	%age (%)	Frequency	%age (%)
11	Evaluation of e-resources is necessary	116	54.7	96	45.2
12	Staff training have positive effect on management of resources	191	90.0	21	9.90
13	There is need to create a committee of individuals to examine choices for a particular resource	2	0.94	210	99.0
14	Rigorous examination of staff and reassignment of duties are necessary	114	53.7	98	46.2
15	Planning and policies serve as guidelines for the management of e-resources	211	99.5	1	0.47

Table 7 above shows that 211 (99.5%) of them stated that planning and policies serve as guidelines for the management of e-resources, 191 (90.0%) of the respondents opined that staff training have positive effect on management of e-resources. While 114 (53.7%) of them stated that rigorous examination of staff and reassignment of duties are necessary.

Table 8 shows that 207 (97.6%) of the respondents agreed that communication gap between vendors and librarians is a problem to e-resource management. 198 (93.3%) of them stated that lack of personnel to handle e-tools is also a barrier to the management of e-resources. While 193 (91.0%) of them agreed that lack of planning and policies on e-resource management affects its management.

Table 8: Problems of E-Resource Management

S/N	Strategies	Frequency	%age (%)	Frequency	%age (%)
16	Lack of time and too much work load for the librarians	115	54.2	97	45.7
17	Lack of planning and policies on electronic resource management affects its management	193	91.0	19	8.96
18	High cost of e-resources	179	84.4	33	15.5
19	Communication gap between vendors and librarians	207	97.6	5	2.35
20	Inadequate personnel to handle e-tools	198	93.3	14	6.60

FINDINGS

Management of e-resources in university libraries in south-south revealed the following:

That management of e-resources is necessary, experts are required in managing e-resources. In-service training is necessary in managing e-resources, planning and policies serve as guidelines in the management of e-resources, there is need for the evaluation of e-resources, google and ebscohost are the search engines that are mostly used by the respondents, Communication gap between vendors and librarians. Lack of qualified personnel to handle e-tools are the major challenge facing e-resources management as this is supported by Bothmann and Hoberg (2010) that vendor communication is often frustrating because some try to work with librarians to improve their products and services and to create win-win situations, while other vendors are simply trying to earn a particular dollar amount. Publishers who are breaking into the electronic resource environment sometimes create problems as they lack understanding of the access requirements libraries have (e.g. open URL, IP authentication) and lack of realistic expectations of what one electronic resource librarian can do with the large number of e-resources and vendor, as well as of the technological capacities of electronic resources, agreement on resource needs and assistance with the work from other staff constitute a major problem in managing e-resources.

CONCLUSION

The importance of e-resources in the university libraries cannot be overemphasized in this digital era if we are to render quality services to our users and as well meet their desired information needs. Hence there is urgent need for the management of the university libraries investigated to employ adequate qualified personnel to manage e-resources in the libraries or on the other hand organize training for the staff on ground in order to manage these e-resources effectively. Also there should be cordial relationship between the librarian and vendor as this will bridge the communication gap between them.

RECOMMENDATION

Based on the findings the following recommendations were made.

(1) That e-resource should be given adequate attention.

(2) The management of e-resources should be handled by qualified personnel.

(3) Communication gap between librarian and vendor should be bridged for the effectiveness of e-resource management.

(4) University authorities in Nigeria should see the need to employ adequate qualify personnel to manage these e-resources.

REFERENCES

Afifi, Marianne. (2008). Process mapping for electronic resources: A lesson from business models. In Yu, Holly and Breivold, Scott (Eds.) *Electronic Resource Management in Libraries: Research and Practice* (pp. 90-104). Hersey: Information Science Reference.

Breeding, Marshall. (2012). The many facets of managing electronic resources. Retrieved from www.intotoday.com/ci/mag/jan04/breeding. shtml-cached.

Joshipura, Smita (2008). Selecting, acquiring and renewing electronic resources. In Yu, Holly and Breivold, Scott (Eds.) *Electronic Resource Management in Libraries: Research and Practice* (pp. 48-70). Hersey: Information Science Reference.

Kasprowski, Rafal. (2006). Recent developments in electronic resources management in libraries. Retrieved from http://www.asis.org/bulletin/ aug-ob/ kasprowski.html.

Lamarca, M. and Brendtrup Robbert, Fark Ronald and Jargo Lori. (1997). Managing a collection of electronic information resources. Retrieved from http:// net.educause.edu/ir/library/html/cnc9753/cnc9753.html.

Okoye M.O. and Ugwuanyi C.F. (2012). Management of electronic resources by cataloguers in Nigerian federal university libraries. *Library philosophy and practice*. retrieved from http://unllib.unl.edu/lpp/okoye-ugwuanyi.htm.

Poe, Jodi, Bevis, Mary, Graham, John-Baver, Latham, Bethany & Stevens Kimberly W. (2008). Sharing the Albatross of E-resources management workflow. In Yu, Holly and Breivold, Scott (Eds.) *Electronic Resource Management in Libraries: Research and Practice* (pp.71-89). Hersey: Information Science Reference.

Yu, Holly and Breivold, Scott (Eds.) (2008). *Electronic Resource Management in Libraries: Research and Practice*. Hersey: Information Science Reference.

Strategic Librarian (2010). Electronic resource management and agent legal in Agent legal, electronic resource management (ERM). Retrieved from http:// strategiclibrian.com/2010/12/03/electronic-resource-management-and-agentlegal.htm.

SECTION - IV
PUBLICITY, USAGE

22

Marketing of E-Resource for Academic Libraries

Sanjiv Kadyan

INTRODUCTION

Every institutions and organization needs marketing. Marketing provides an opportunity to see as to how they can offer effective and efficient services to their users or customers. The paper considers the preliminary emergence of theoretical patterns in relation to how electronic media and E-resource management can impact upon the facilitating of improved customer relationship and services by providing E-resource in academic libraries. Marketing of E-resource means transference of electronic resource to the potential users or customers. For many years, it has been noted that consumers wanted basic personalized services "they do not care how much you know until they know how much you care".

WHAT IS MARKETING?

According to KOTLER and FOX: Marketing is the analysis, planning implementation and control of carefully formulated programmes designed to bring about voluntary exchanges of values with target markets for the purpose of achieving organizations objective.

"It is a planned strategic approach of bringing together consumers and products. A Marketing oriented organization takes its marching orders from its customers; it produces Products and services based on its customers' needs, wants and levels of satisfaction. [...] Marketing is a strategic behaviour" (Keiser, 1995, p. 50).

"Marketing management is the process of planning and executing programs designed to create, build, and maintain beneficial exchange relationships with target audiences for the purposes of satisfying individual and organizational objectives" (Kotler, 1995, p. 37).

"Marketing is the management process which identifies, anticipates and supplies customer requirements efficiently and profitably" (Chartered Institute of Marketing, UK, cited by de Saez, 1993, p.1).

"A customer-centred organization is one that makes every effort to sense, serve, and satisfy the needs and wants of its clients and publics within the constraints of its budget" (Kotler, 1995, p. 43).

Similarly FOLK and LANCASTER : Marketing is a systematic process which is a combination of planning, concentrating on customer needs and his or her satisfaction.

WHAT IS E- RESOURCE?

According to AACR-2, 2005: An electronic resource is: "Material (data and / or program) encoded for manipulation by a computerized device. This material may require the use of a peripheral directly connected to computerized device (e.g.; CD-ROM drive) or connection to a computer network (e.g. the internet)."

An E-resource is an electronic information resource that can be accessed on the web, on or off campus.

WHAT IS ACADEMIC LIBRARY?

An Academic Library can be defined as a library that is an

integral part of a College, University, or other institution of Post-secondary education, administered to meet the information and research needs of its students, faculty, and staff (Online Dictionary for library and Information Science, 2002).

WHY MARKETING IN LIBRARIES?

Marketing is a useful to university libraries to improve their image and to attract more users. Marketing helps librarians improve their reputation within their organization and as profession with in society. Marketing in libraries can lead to a better understanding of users and their requirements. Effective marketing can increase the use of services, can help train customers and non-customers, can change user perceptions and ideas, and clients or customers.

REVIEW OF LITERATURE

Kim's, van Epps (2001) also looks at determine use of electronic databases but she notes that sometime usage statistics are not enough. She created a quick re-direct web-log to track the numbers of times a particular and also known as collecting click- through data.

Lee (2005) compiled an overview of library marketing resources for librarians. Her article gives a short introduction to library marketing, and the remainder is basically an annotated bibliography from where the researcher was directed to some noted library marketing resources and scholars.

Kim (2006) discussed the important talk for librarians of keeping usage statistics to justify library expenses and to help with the renewal process of subscription databases. She also mentioned the problem of making students aware of the electronic resources that are available to them.

Nevers (2007) also described the importance of promoting electronic resources from the stand point of a law library. He explains method that law libraries currently use to promote these resources, including print newsletters, formal training sessions, and advertising them in the library blog and from the library homepage.

Anson and Connell (2009) suggest libraries need to be better prepared for a future in which E-resources may be as important, as or more important than printed books.

Champeswar (2010) author emphasized that Web2.0 tools can be successfully practised by strategic planning and right exercise by the Information Professionals. The possible social network tools that can be look forward for marketing library and Information Services are Wiki, RSS feed, You Tube, Blogger, Podcast, Facebook, MYspace,Linkedin, Slidershare, Delic.io.us, Netvibes, library Thing etc.

Piyush (2012) he focussed on consumer ethnocentrism has a negative influence on the attitude towards offshore outsourcing and the perceived service quality and customer satisfaction with offshore call centres. Customer satisfaction also mediates the influences of perceived service quality on customer complaint behaviour, brand image, brand loyalty, and repeat purchase intentions.

TYPES OF E-RESOURCE IN ACADEMIC LIBRARIES

1. Databases
2 E-journals
3 E-book
4 E-news
5 E-images
6 Subject Guides
7 Web search tools e.g. Google Book search
8 Information Gateways e.g. Google scholar, Intute, Pinakes.
9 E- music and sound collections
10 Data
11 E-reference e.g. Dictionaries Translators, Directories, Glossaries,Virtual,Newspapers.

MARKETING OF E-RESOURCE IN ACADEMIC LIBRARIES

1. Library Websites: Websites are a key way to advertise. In academic libraries, it is possible to design a Website with the help of advanced technologies and computers which can be a powerful marketing tool. An effective website can be lead to mutual satisfaction for customer and librarian. Academic libraries can use the Website to help fulfil Ranganathan'laws these laws can be adapted to the present and future libraries:

- Libraries serve humanity
- Respect all forms by which knowledge is communicated
- Use technology intelligently to enhance service
- Protect free access to knowledge ; and
- Honour the past and create the future

2. Information Literacy Sessions : Information is available from many sources and in many formats, such as printed text, videos, library databases, websites and more. For maximum utilization of these resource in academic libraries Information literacy has play a very important role. "Information literacy knows when and why you need information, where to find it, and how to evaluate, use and communicate it in an ethical manner". To enhanced marketing of E-resource with the help of Information literacy sessions DULS (Delhi University Library System) conducting following activities and programs:

- E-resource orientation and programs
- Online searching techniques
- Open access/ Public domain resources
- Bibliographic citations
- One day workshops
- Hands on training Programs
- E-mail Alerts
- DULS Websites

3. OPAC (Online Public Access Catalogue) : is an online database of materials held by a library or group of libraries. "Library Catalogue is a primary source of information for the library's key resources whether access to them via OPAC or the Web" (Kennedy,

2004). A web-based Online Public Access catalogue helps home-grown Web OPACs and third generation catalogues in their competition to reach the needs. Cherry (1998) developed guidelines to evaluate OPAC display designs for web-based OPACs in Canadian academic libraries and Public libraries.

4. E-mails : E-mail is a method of exchanging digital messages from an author to one or more recipients. Where a large proportion of the users are on e-mail Information technology is an easy way of reaching them, quickly and cheaply. Email marketing is directly marketing a commercial message to a group of people using Email. E-mail marketing can be done with help of creating a database. E-mail marketing can be carried out through different types of e-mails like transactional e-mails, direct e-mails e.g. an announcement of a special offer or a catalog of products direct e-mails may be used to promotion of products in Academic libraries. Ojedokun and Owolabi (2003) reported that e-mail is the most used Internet resource by staff and students in Academic libraries.

5. Quick Response Code : QR Code is matrix barcode which requires a mobile camera Phone and specific. QR reader software to retrieve the encoded information. QR Codes are already playing a dominant role for success in marketing in Japan, European Countries and rest of the developed world. Ashford (2010) encoded about QR Codes usage in academic libraries and how the library services reached mobile users. The main objective of the QR codes is to encourage Indians librarians to apply mobile technology to their library services, to attract users, to strengthen the library usage capacity and to promote E-resource in academic libraries. Example: UC Berkeley provides QR codes for records in their catalog which contain Title, Location, availability and Call Number http://oskicat.berkeley.edu/record=b15767323~S1.

6. Word of Mouth : Word of Mouth is the sound of new ideas up to our ears in several ways such as; telling stories, dialog, conversions, shared experiences radio and etc. Word of Mouth helps us to know about what is new, and what is the latest (Sernovitz,et.al 2009) pointed out that people love to talk about products they have bought , and services they have used, also they talk about the provider of these services. Some people feel proud, however some of them provide advice to others not to think about buying a product.WOM is about earning that good conversion and key success for organisation (Lake, 2009).

7. Blogs : Blog or Weblog is a Website that contains brief entries arranged in reverse chronological order. 'Blogging' is the act of creating a blog. Blogging is also becoming a fast cornerstone tool in the online dissemination and consumptions of information (Dhiman and Sharma, 2008). Some examples of Weblogs (http://www.libdex.com/weblogs.html), St.Joseph County public library (http://homepage.mal.com/nrdtsjcpl/.) Lis News.com focuses on News for Information Professionals and is a collaborative weblog. (http://www.lisnews.com) Blogs can helps to Promoting library services, and Programmes. A great Blog requires three Ingredients: Inspiration, Motivation, and Dedication.

8. Display screens : To promote of E-resources for academic libraries linked to a collection of new books or takes the user to an RSS feed, and display screens of newly purchased library material.

9. Mobile : Vendors are beginning to provide mobile versions of their products (EBSCO Databases, RefWorks). Many users have web capable cell phones and PDA's for accessing these mobile friendly electronic resources. Creation of a mobile friendly library page with links to the available mobile friendly resources will promote these resources to mobile device using patrons. Examples University of Illinois Library,http://m.library.illinois.edu/dbs.asp. University of Wisconsin, Ebling Library for the Health Sciences http://m.ebling.library.wisc.edu/#_dbases .

10. Subject Guides : Guides targeted to a particular subject area are an excellent place for highlighting electronic resources. Librarians are including links to these resources in Research Guides, LibGuides and other formatted study guides in order to make users better aware of the resources. Example: University of Illinois-Champaign Urbana LibGuide for electronic books in the life sciences areas: http://uiuc.libguides.com/ebooks.

11. Videos and Podcasts : YouTube, Video, Teacher Tube are some examples of places to share videos that can be used to promote electronic resources. These videos can be placed on the website, blogs, wiki's and guides. Users also have the option of subscribing to your video feeds. Example: Arizona State University creates 1 minute advertisements/tutorials for their Library Channel, http://lib.asu.edu/librarychannel/category/library-minute/. Podcasts allow for audio streaming of content and can be delivered to the user via RSS feeds. Users can download and listen on their desktops, laptops and mobile devices. Podcasts are used for instruction as well as promotion of electronic resources. Example: Johns Hopkins University, Sheridan Libraries provides podcasts to "learn more about library collections, services, and people..." http://www.library.jhu.edu/podcasts/.

12. Marketing campaign : The situation on the information market is nowadays comparable all over the world. New technologies bring the effect of a connected world and libraries have to deal with information overload and the problem how to help their customers to deal with so much available information. ACRL14 and ALA developed together the national marketing campaign *"@ your library™"*, which started in 2001.But even if the main focus of this campaign lies on the promotional part, the marketing steps "behind the scenes" is also working. Thus *"@ your library™"* works together with 3M Library Systems15, an international company developing security services for libraries. 3M supports the campaign and offers on its website tips and resources for writing a marketing plan. An official logo has been developed that guides through the campaign and can be used by each participating library:

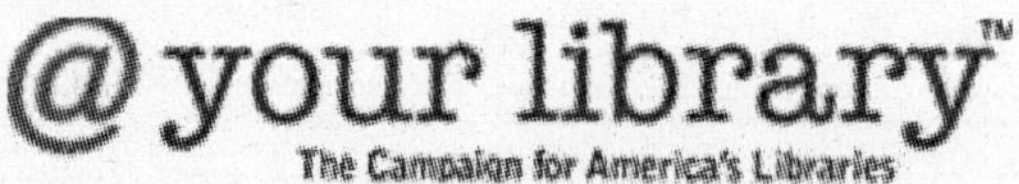

Official logo of the campaign "*@ your library™*"

(Source: ALA website)

AVAILABILITY OF E-RESOURCE THROUGH WEBSITES AND SPECIAL TOOLS

1. University of pittsburg press has made over 500 monographs available through their digital editions initiative (http:// digital.library.pitt.edu/p/pittpress/).
2. Mit press has made different individual recent publications available (http://mitpressebooks.mit.edu/)
3. Acqweb (www.acqweb.org) this site compiles information and resources relating to the practise of acquisitions. Recently redesigned, the new version features several blogs.
4. Blogdigger (http://www.blogdigger.com/index.html) and peter scott's directory of LIS weblogs (http:// www.libdex.com/ weblogs.html)
5. Aggregators e.g. Highwire press, ingenta (an online content dissemination and hosting company).
6. Thomson Reuters (Thomson corporation and Reuters is a major provider of electronic information through its west law in the UK providing legal databases, and tax and accounting information , as well as financial data).
7. Atypon systems (www.atypon.com) e.g. crossRef (a site maintained by publishers to create and manage links between scholarly content.
8. Subject- based portals e.g. SOSIG (The social science information Gateway) and EEVL (Edinburgh content licensing Engineering virtual library).
9. Marketing the library (http://star61451.tripod.com/ marketingthe library/index.html)
10. New jersey library Marketing News (http:// nancydowd.wordpress.com/)

CONCLUSION

The article has explored the approach to marketing of E-resource adopted by libraries. The role of libraries and strategic plans for library development from this perspective use all the "re" words – retool, rethink, renew, reinvent, regenerate, reposition. None of the libraries adopted a strategic approach to marketing and promotion of E-resource and some had plans for improvements in their promotion activities. In discussing marketing of E-resource library staff development and library facilities, there are more "re" words-reenergise, refresh, revitalize, refurbish, revive, renovate, revamp, rejuvenate. Effective marketing is the key to future survival followed by excellence in service delivery and library experiences which meet user expectations and requirements.

REFERENCES

Castaldo, J.C. (2008). Marketing electronic resources from the academic library homepage. Northcarolina: Chapelhill.

Gupta, D.K. (2003). Marketing of library and Information services: Building a new discipline for library and Information Science education in Asia. *Journal of Library and Information Science*, 8 (2), 95-108.

Kaushik, Anna and Arora, J. (2012). Blogs on marketing library services. *DESIDOC Journal of library and Information Technology*, 32(2), 186-192.

Madhusudhan, M. (2008). Marketing of library and information service and products in University libraries: A case study of GOA University library. *Library Philosophy and practice*, 1-6.

Madhusudhan, M. (2011). Web-based Online Public Access Catalogues of IIT libraries in India: An Evaluative Study. ICoASL (International Conference of Asian Special libraries), Branding & Marketing, & Strategic Direction, Best Practices & Performance evaluation of Special library Services. 1-25.

Nooshinfarad, F & Soorya, Z. (2011). Academic library websites as marketing tools. *Library Philosophy and practice* http:// unlib. Un/.edu/lpp/.

Prasad, M. (2012). Quick Response (QR) code to provide library services: An Introduction. *Journal of Library and Information Science*, 37(1), 1-8.

Schmidt, J. (2011). Effective Marketing of libraries in a never- better world even if it ever-was that way. World Library Information Congress. IFLA.

Sharma, Piyush. (2012). Offshore outsourcing of customer services- boon or bane? *Journal of services Marketing*, 26 (5), 352-364.

Sukula, Shiva. (2010). Electronic Resource Management: What, Why and How. New Delhi: Ess Ess Publications.

Upshall, M. (2009). Content Licensing: Buying and selling digital resources: Converting, hosting and access management. UK: Wood head Publications.

Vasileiou, M & Rowley, J. (2011). Marketing and promotion of e-books in academic libraries. *Journal of documentation*, 67 (4), 624-643.

23

E-databases With Special Reference to National Library of Veterinary Sciences, Indian Veterinary Research Institute, Izatnagar (U.P.)

S.S.Rawat
K.N.Kandpal

INTRODUCTION

An organized collection of data, typically in digital form is called e-database. The data are typically organized to model relevant aspects of reality (for example, the availability of rooms in hotels), in a way that supports processes requiring this information (for example, finding a hotel with vacancies). The database term is suitably applied to the data and their supporting data structures, but not applied to the e-database management system (DBMS). The collection of data from e-database with E-database management system is called an e-database system.

Traditional e-databases are organized by fields, records, and files in which the field is a single piece of information, record is one complete set of fields and the file is a collection of records. For example, a telephone book is analogous to a file. It contains a list of records in which each consists of three fields name, address, and telephone number. An alternative concept in e-database design is known as Hypertext. In a Hypertext e-database, any object, whether it be a piece of text, a picture, or a film, can be linked to any other object. A hypertext e-database is very useful for organizing large amounts of disparate information, but they are not designed for numerical analysis.

The term e-database system implies that the data is managed to some level of quality (measured in terms of accuracy, availability, usability, and resilience) and this in turn often implies the use of a general-purpose e-database management system (DBMS). Typically general-purpose DBMS is a complex software system that meets many usage requirements, and the e-databases that it maintains are often large and complex. The utilization of e-databases is now spread to such a wide degree that virtually every technology and product relies on e-databases and DBMSs for its development and commercialization. Also, organizations and companies, from small to large, heavily depend on e-databases for their operations (Maier et al., 1986; Shekita, 1989).

COMPONENTS OF E-DATABASES

An e-database is hence composed both of data, and of programs or software to enter and manipulate the data. Both data and software are stored within the computers which support the e-database, and the internal organization may not be obvious to the users. We will now describe some of the components that are part of e-database software.

(a) File Storage Systems : software to allocate and manage space for data kept on large computer storage devices, such as disks or tapes.

(b) File Access Methods : software to rapidly access and update data stored on those devices.

(c) Data Description Languages : means to describe data so that users and machines can refer to data elements and aggregations of similar data elements conveniently and unambiguously.

(d) Data Manipulation Languages : programs to allow the user to retrieve and process data conveniently.

To access e-database consists of several different components. Each component listed is called an *object*.

Tables: tables are where the actual data is defined and entered. Tables consist of rows (records) and columns (fields).

Queries: queries are mainly questions about the data in a e-database. A query consists of specifications indicating which fields, records, and summaries you want to see from a e-database. Queries allow you to extract data based on the criteria define by you.

Forms: forms are designed to ease the data entry process. For example, you can create a data entry form that looks exactly like a paper form. People generally prefer to enter data into a well-designed form, rather than a table.

Reports: when you want to print records from your e-database, then you need to design a report.

Pages: a data access page is a special type of Web page designed for viewing and working with data from the Internet or an intranet.

Macros: a macro is a set of one or more actions that each performs a particular operation, such as opening a form or printing a report. Macros can help you automate common tasks.

Modules: a module is a collection of Visual Basic for Applications declarations and procedures that are stored together as a unit.

In an e-database these subsystems have to be well integrated, therefore the data manipulation can 'be carried out in response to the vocabulary used in the data descriptions. Storage is allocated and rearranged as new data enter the e-database, and access to old and new data is provided as needed for manipulation. To provide the necessary reliability some redundant backup data is stored separately and appropriately identified whenever the e-database is changed. Optional software components of a e-database may provide on-line, conversational access to the e-database, help with the formulation of statistical queries, and provide printed reports on a regular schedule.

TYPES OF E-DATABASES

There are two types of databases i.e. analytical e-databases and operational e-databases.

Analytic e-databases

Analytic e-databases are primarily static, read-only e-databases which store archived, historical data used for analysis. For example, a company might store sales records over the last ten years in an analytic e-database and use that e-database to analyze marketing strategies in relationship to demographics.

On the web, you will often see analytic e-databases in the form of inventory catalogs. An inventory catalog analytical e-database usually holds descriptive information about all available products in the inventory.

Web pages are generated dynamically by querying the list of available products in the inventory against some search parameters. The dynamically-generated page will display the information about each item (such as title, author, ISBN) which is stored in the e-database.

Operational e-databases

Operational e-databases are used to manage more dynamic bits of data. These types of e-databases allow you to do more than simply view archived data. Operational e-databases allow you to modify that data means add, change or delete data.

These types of e-databases are usually used to track real-time information. For example, a company might have an operational e-database used to track warehouse/stock quantities. As customers order products from an online web store, an operational e-database can be used to keep track of how many items have been sold and when the company will need to reorder stock.

METADATA

The metadata is an ambiguous term which is used for two fundamentally different concepts. Although the expression "data about data" is often used, it does not apply to both in the same way. Structural metadata, the design and specification of data structures, cannot be about data, because at design time the application contains no data. In this case the correct description would be "data about the containers of data". Descriptive metadata, on the other hand, is about individual instances of application data, the data content. In this case, a useful description (resulting in a disambiguating neologism) would be "data about data content" or "content about content" thus metacontent. Metadata (metacontent) is traditionally found in the card catalogs of libraries. As information has become increasingly digital the metadata is also used to describe digital data using metadata standards specific to a particular discipline (Graves ,1996).

TYPES OF METADATA

The metadata application is manyfold which covering a large variety of fields of application there is nothing but specialized and well accepted models to specify types of metadata. Bretheron & Singley (1994) distinguish between two distinct classes: structural metadata and guide metadata. **Structural metadata** is used to describe the structure of computer systems such as tables, columns and indexes. **Guide metadata** is used to help humans find specific items and is usually expressed as a set of keywords in a natural language. According to Ralph Kimball metadata can be divided into 2 similar categories— Technical metadata and Business metadata. **Technical metadata** correspond to internal metadata whereas Business metadata to external metadata. Kimball adds a third category named **Process metadata.** On the other hand, NISO distinguishes between three types of metadata: descriptive, structural and administrative. **Descriptive**

metadata is the information used to search and locate an object such as title, author, subjects, keywords, publisher, the **structural metadata** gives a description of how the components of the object are organized and **administrative metadata** refers to the technical information including file type. There are also two sub-types of administrative metadata are rights management metadata and preservation metadata (The University of Melbourne, 2006).

INDIAN VETERINARY RESEARCH INSTITUTE LIBRARY

The Indian Veterinary Research Institute (IVRI) is the first premier scientific research Institute of its kind established in India as Imperial Bacteriological Laboratory at Pune in 1889. The Institute has been embarking upon extensive programmes of research in frontier areas to improve animal health and production. The IVRI Library known as National Library of Veterinary Sciences is perhaps the oldest library in this specialized area in the country. This library was started as an integral part of the Imperial Bacteriological Laboratory since its foundation on December 9, 1889 in Pune. The present library building has around 3210 sq mts. area. Area of reading room is about 826 sq mts & carpet area of stack room is 1840 sq mts. The library has been using Dewey Decimal Classification Scheme for classification of the publications. The library has seating capacity of 125 readers with two reading halls, one computer section and three stack areas.

IVRI library houses about 57454 books, 4831 theses, 3950 reports and 196145 bound volumes as well as issues of journal and other serial publications. The library remained open from 9.00 a.m. to 9.00 p.m. daily and from 8.00 am to 1.00 p.m. on holidays except National Holidays. There are 246 Scientists, 681 M.V.Sc. & Ph.D. Students and 202 other staff members as library members. The Current Display Section, Computer Section, Reading Hall (Ground Floor), Internet Room and Book Section of the Library are air-conditioned and cohesive atmosphere is being provided to the readers/ users of the library by maintaining air-conditioners. Digital Video Recording based Close Circuit TV system with 22 cameras is being used in the various sections of the library for electronic surveillance.

MAJOR SERVICES OF NLVS, IVRI

Library Automation : The library is using Libsys automation software version 4.0 on Linux based server and is being used on LAN. The books, theses, bound volumes of journals and other publications are being bar-coded. The bar-coded photo Identity cards are being provided to the library members. The circulation work is automated using laser bar-code reader.

CD-ROM Services : A CD-Mirror Hybrid Server is being used for CD-ROM services and the service is being provided on LAN. The various e-databases i.e. Agris CD, Beast CD, Biological Abstracts, Biotechnology Abstracts, FSTA, Medline Express and Vet CD databases are available on CD Mirror Server. About 182 users were trained for using the CD-ROM services themselves and about 751 users availed CD-ROM facilities per year. For smooth functioning the services the NLVS provided computer and its peripheral as a special section in NLVS.

List of CD-ROM Database and Subject area for use the database and available at National Library of veterinary sciences at IVRI

S. No	Name of E-databases	Subject	From	To
1.	Food Science and Technology Abstracts (FSTA)	Basic food science, nutrition, biotechnology, toxicology packaging and engineering.	1969	2006/04
2(a)	Medline CD (Old collection)	Microbiology, delivery of health care, nutrition pharmacology and environmental health.	1950	1965
2.(b)	Medline CD	Microbiology, delivery of health care, nutrition pharmacology and environmental health.	1966	2006/04
3.	AGRIS CD	Agriculture including forestry, animal husbandry,	1975	2005/12

		the aquatic sciences and fisheries and human nutrition.		
4.	Beast CD (Animal Production Database)	All relevant records from the CAB Abstracts database, corresponding to selections from a number of abstracts journal in the CABI rang.	1972	2009/11
5.	VET CD (Veterinary Science Databases)	All relevant veterinary sciences.	1972	2009/12
06.	Biological Abstracts(BA)	Bibliographic references with abstracts derived from life science research journals.	1972	2004
07.	Biotechnology Abstracts (BioTchA)	Genetic manipulation to biochemical engineering and fermentation.	1982	2009/12

Membership of CERA : This library is a member of CeRA, a Consortium for e-Resources in Agriculture, set up under NAIP, ICAR alongwith other institute and SAU libraries. Under CERA, Institute is getting access to about 2000 full text online journals. Necessary services are being exchanged with the member libraries under the consortium.

e-Granth Project under NAIP : This library is a consortium partner of 12 libraries of various ICAR institutes and SAUs under NAIP (Component I) on "Strengthening of Digital Library and Information Management under NARS (e-Granth)". Under this project a Union Catalogue of all the partners "AGRICAT" has been created and about 22500 records of this library are available. Further a Digital Library of Institute Depositories of National Agricultural Research System (NARS) is being created.

CONSORTIUM OF AGRICULTURE E-DATABASES

- Thesis(PhD) e-database
- CeRA database
- AGRIS e-database
- AGRICAT e-database

THESIS E-DATABASE PORTAL OF AGRICULTURAL AND VETERINARY SCIENCES

It is repository of 'Indian Agricultural Doctoral Dissertations'. KrishPrabha is a full-text electronic database of Indian Agricultural Doctoral Dissertations submitted by research scholars to the 45 State/ Deemed Agricultural University. Online submission of dissertations for continues updating the data by member library of the universities. IP based access of full-text e-database to 125 Consortia Partners and abstracts accessible to non member world over. In the e-database full-text doctoral dissertations are available from 2000 to 2009. At present about 7465 full-text doctoral dissertations are available on this e-database. The Nehru Library, CCSHAU, Hisar (Lead Centre) to facilitate accessibility of e-database full-text doctoral dissertations to the researchers, teachers and students of NARS for excellence in research (ICAR, 2011).

Contribution of NLVS, IVRI in Krishi Prabha – all soft copies Doctoral Dissertations of veterinary sciences submitted to Lead Centre (i.e. Nehru Library, CCS Haryana Agricultural University Hisar) from 2000 on words. The National Library of Veterinary Sciences is all provide online services on the IP based access of full-text dissertation e-database to their student, researcher, scientist and other users of the library. The Doctoral Dissertations broadly category as under –

S. No.	Category of Doctoral Dissertations	Records
1	Agricultural Engineering and Technology	158
2	Agriculture	4568
3	Basic Sciences	1196
4	Dairy Science	123
5	Home Science	280
6	Veterinary and Animal Sciences	1140

Doctoral Dissertations submitted to the IVRI (Deemed University) and NLVS from 2008-2011 shown in table as under –

S. No.	Year	Numbers
1	2088	45
2	2009	41
3	2010	39
4	2011	60
	Total	185

This is the screen short of home page of Krish Prabha for IP-based User and the URL : http://www.hau.ernet.in (ICAR, 2011).

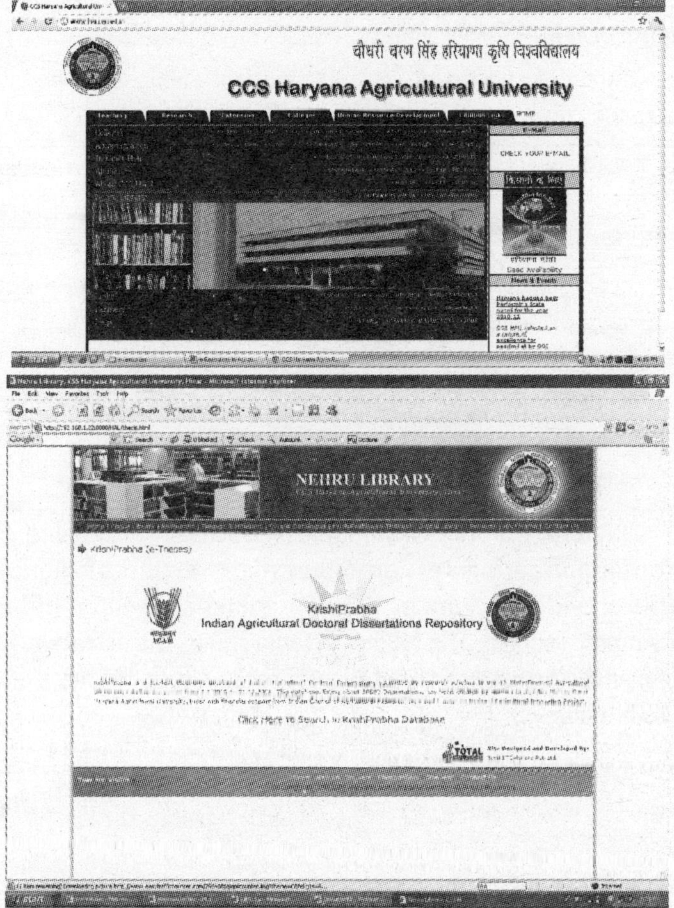

CeRA database (Consortium for e-Resources in Agriculture)

The CeRA has been updated to cover publishers being subscribed since 2008. The CeRa provide almost all reputed international journals are available online. The ICAR is having network connectivity across institute, deemed universities and state agricultural universities. These journals could be made available over the network for the use of research community. With the help of National Agricultural Innovation Project (NAIP) has funded for establishing the consortium for e-resources in agriculture (CeRA). The Indian Agricultural Research Institute (IARI), New Delhi to facilitate accessibility of scientific journals to the researchers, teachers and students of NARS for excellence in research (ICAR, 2011).

The CeRA consortium covers the main publisher-wise full text e-databases on the table as under –

S. No.	Publisher	CS Full-Text Journals
1	American Society of Agronomy	8
2	Annual Reviews Inc	22
3	CISO Publishing	8
4	Elsevier	358
5	IndianJournals. com	131
6	Oxford Journals	30
7	Springer Link (Springer-Verlay)	70
8	Taylor & Francis (Taylor & Francis Group)	1079

National Library of Veterinary Sciences (NLVS) being one of the consortium partners of Consortium for e-Resources in Agriculture (CeRA) provides document delivery online as well as offline on receiving the request. The following table shows the activity of library to deliver the articles to the students, researchers, faculty members and scientists:

S. No.	Year	No. Request for Article	Deliver	Pending	Article not available
1	2008	187	172	1*	14
2	2009	732	678	0	54
3	2010	905	736	0	169
4	2011	2845	2161	0	684
	Total	4669	3747	1*	921

* The pending shown in the table is not actually pending and the same have been delivered in that point of time but due to some problem in CeRA website the same could not be shown as delivered.

The following table shows of uses usage report on the site for NLVS, Indian Veterinary Research Institute, Izatnagar

S. No.	Year	Clicks
1	2008	N.A.
2	2009	1037
3	2010	4073
4	2011	2801
	Total	7911

This is the screen short of home page of CeRA for IP-based User and the URL : www.cera.jccc.in

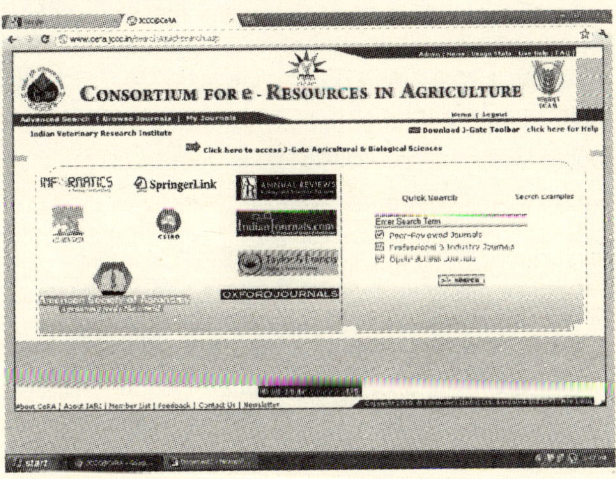

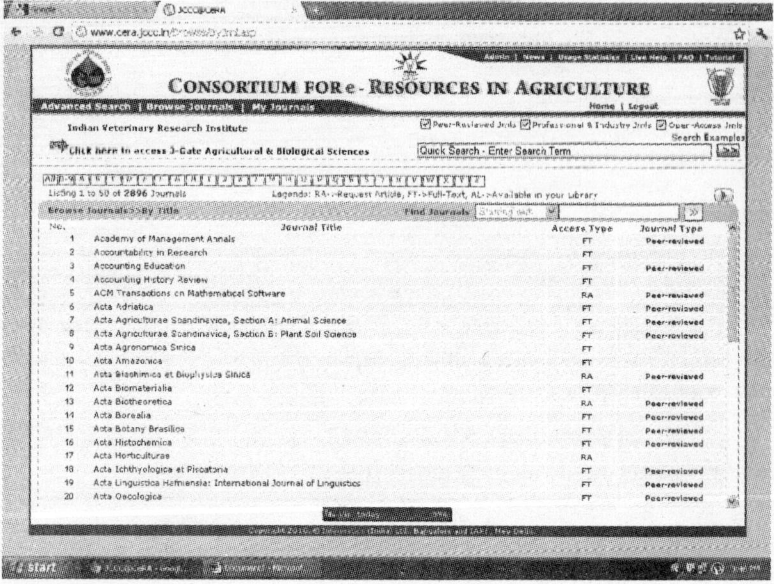

AGRIS e-Database

This project work related to the development of National Agricultural Research e-database (NARD has been stated in DIPA and two important abstracting journal have journal have been brought out from the e-database. To cover, maximum agricultural information generated by all ICAR Institutes (ICAR, 2011).

The National Library of Veterinary Sciences (NLVS), IVRI, Izatnagar to provide input from 2000 on words according to the guideline received from time to time as main centre. The NLVS provide input sheets of NARD with abstracts of following journals –

1. Indian Veterinary Journals
2. Indian Journal of Veterinary Pathology
3. Indian Journal of Veterinary Research
4. Indian Journal of Veterinary Surgery

This is the screen short of AGRIS stand alone software. Provide to input through login and password.

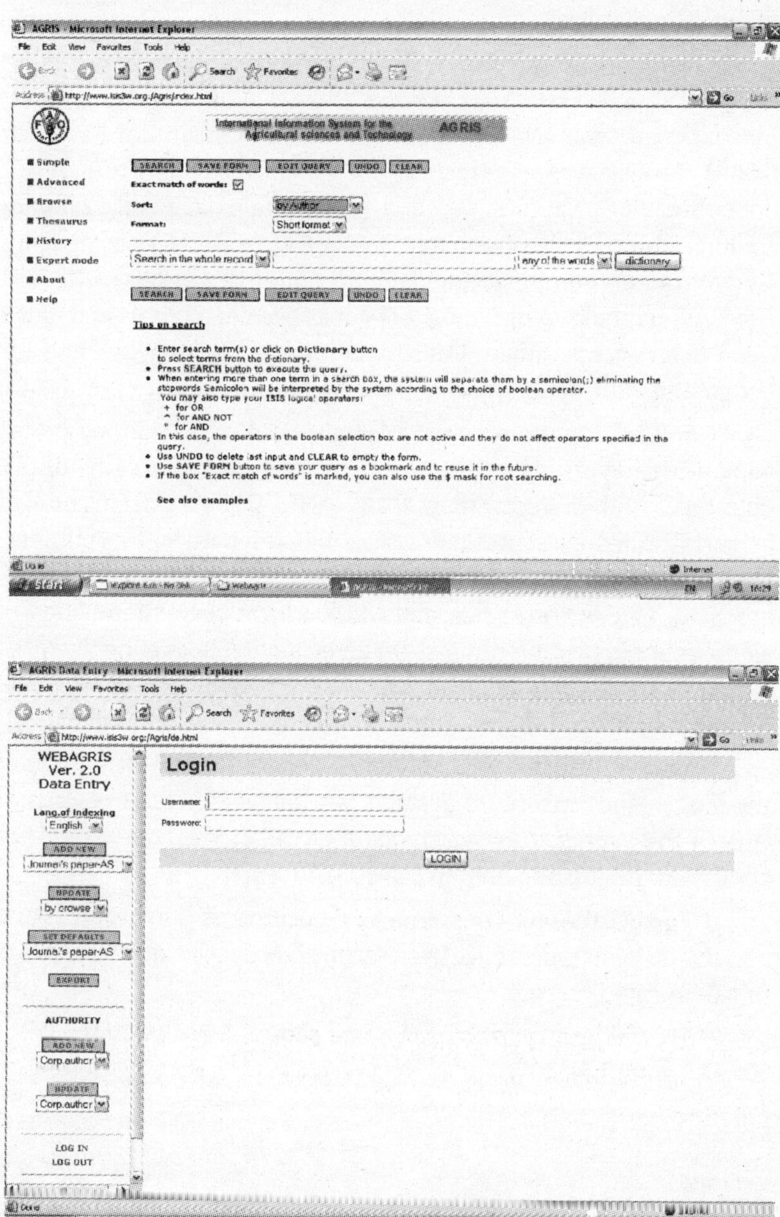
AGRIS - Microsoft Internet Explorer
File Edit View Favorites Tools Help
Search Favorites
Address http://www.isis3w.org./Agris/index.html
Go
International Information System for the Agricultural sciences and Technology
AGRIS
Simple
Advanced
Browse
Thesaurus
History
Expert mode
About
Help
SEARCH SAVE FORM EDIT QUERY UNDO CLEAR
Exact match of words:
Sort:
By Author
Format:
Short format
Search in the whole record
any of the words
dictionary
Tips on search
Enter search term(s) or click on Dictionary button to select terms from the dictionary.
Press SEARCH button to execute the query.
When entering more than one term in a search box, the system will separate them by a semicolon(;) eliminating the stopwords Semicolon will be interpreted by the system according to the choice of boolean operator.
You may also type your ISIS logical operators:
+ for OR
^ for AND NOT
* for AND
In this case, the operators in the boolean selection box are not active and they do not affect operators specified in the query.
Use UNDO to delete last input and CLEAR to empty the form.
Use SAVE FORM button to save your query as a bookmark and to reuse it in the future.
If the box "Exact match of words" is marked, you can also use the $ mask for root searching.
See also examples
Internet
start
AGRIS Data Entry - Microsoft Internet Explorer
File Edit View Favorites Tools Help
Search Favorites
Address http://www.isis3w.org:/Agris/de.html
WEBAGRIS
Ver. 2.0
Data Entry
Lang.of indexing
English
ADD NEW
Journal's paper-AS
UPDATE
by browse
SET DEFAULTS
Journal's paper-AS
EXPORT
AUTHORITY
ADD NEW
Corp.author
UPDATE
Corp.author
LOG IN
LOG OUT
Login
Username:
Password:
LOGIN
Done
start
explore.exe - No Disk
Webagris
AGRIS - Microsoft In...
AGRIS - Microsoft

AGRICAT e-database

"Strengthening of Digital Library and Information Management under NARS (e-Granth) is a project under National Agricultural Innovation Project (NAIP), Indian Council of Agricultural Research (ICAR). Its objectives – To create Online Public Access Cataloge (OPAC) under 'Indian Agricultural Research group catalogue' of all 12 library resources with Online Computer Library Centre (OCLC) partnership. To digitize important institutional repositories (limited to IARI, IVRI and UAS, Bangalore) including rare books and old journals and make them open access under NARS to strengthen capacity building for library and information management system.

Around 50,000 more records have been added to the AgriCat (Union Catalogue) and total 3,31,766 records are available in AgriCat upto the month of September, 2011. KOHA OSS has been installed in few institutes in a standalone system with test data for trial purpose. Digitization process, scanning of the old/ rare books, cleaning, cropping, PDF/A conversion and OCRing have been streamlined in all the four digitization centers. On an average 5 lakh pages/centres (Total about 20 lakh pages at four centres) have been digitized till September, 2011 [5,6]

National Library of Veterinary Sciences (NLVS) being one of the four major consortium partner, has uploaded 23903 records of IVRI in the Worldcat as per standard of OCLC. The library has also converted the existing data to MARC -21 format.

Further the work of scanning of documents is in progress and about 6.00 lakhs pages have been scanned. Action for implementation of KOHA is in progress.

This is the screen short of home page e-Granth and the URL : http://egranth.ac.in

CONCLUSION

The e-databases of Agriculture are related to multidisciplinary subjects consisting of crop sciences, animal sciences, fisheries, horticulture, forestry and fodder sciences etc. The agricultural and allied sectors of India contribute nearly 25% of Gross Domestic Product (GDP) and about 70% population of the country is dependent on agricultural for its livelihood. India is an agricultural based country.

Indian Council of Agricultural Research (ICAR) has been playing a vital role for promoting of e-databases in Institute as well as in State Agricultural Universities in India by providing financial support. Through National Agricultural Innovation Project (NAIP) sufficient budget has been provided for infrastructure and human resources development in National Agricultural Research System (NARS).

Krishi Prabha (thesis e-database), CeRA(online journals e-database), AGRIS e-database and e-Granth (developed AGRICAT e-database), all these projects are functioning smoothly in NLVS, IVRI, Izatnagar. The aim and objective of these projects are to full fill the scientific information needs of the researcher under NARS and to provide quick, accurate and timely information in agriculture through online resources. So the development of e-databases is the need of hours.

REFERENCES

Graves, R. B. & Gillman, D. W. (1996). *Standards for Management of Statistical Metadata: A Framework for Collaboration.* ISIS-96, Bratislava, Slovakia, May 21-24, 1996.

http://www.cera.jccc.in

http://www.egranth.ac.in

http://www.icar.org.in

Indian Council of Agricultural Research (2011). *ICAR Vision 2030.* New Delhi. ICAR.

Indian Council of Agricultural Research (2011). *National Agricultural Innovation Project. Half Yearly progress Report (April-September 2011) Component 1.* New Delhi: ICAR.

Maier, David et al. (1986). *Development of an object-oriented DBMS.* In Proceedings of OOPLSA '86 Conference proceedings on Object-oriented programming systems, languages and applications. (pp. 472 – 482). New York: ACM.

Shekita, Eugene J. & Carey, Michael J. (1989). *Performance enhancement through replication in an object-oriented DBMS.* In Proceedings of SIGMOD '89 Proceedings of the 1989 ACM SIGMOD international conference on Management of data (pp. 325–336). New York: ACM.

The University of Melbourne (2006). Metadata @ Melbourne. *Types of Metadata.* Retrieved from http://www.infodiv.unimelb.edu.au/metadata/add_info.html

24

Use of Electronic Resources by the Research Scholars of the Panjab University Chandigarh: A Study

Kiran Chopra
Rajveer Kaur

INTRODUCTION

Today libraries are providing electronic access to a wide variety of resources, including indexes, full-text articles, and complete journals with back files and internet/ Web resources. In fact, libraries have been moving towards an electronic environment, in which sufficient computers are necessary for patrons to access information. The array of electronic resources available in libraries today is an outgrowth of the changes in information delivery made possible through advances in both computer technologies, such as powerful personal desktop workstations, and information storage and delivery mechanisms, such as CD ROMs and user-friendly graphical user interfaces (GUIs). These advances made the ongoing efforts to replace other traditional services and processes with electronic versions attractive and economically feasible for many libraries.

The term 'e-library' refers to information accessed through electronic sources like Internet. Unlike traditional libraries, e-libraries are not limited by location of time. Libraries have changed with the emergence and application of information technology (IT). Libraries have assumed the role of educators-teaching users to find, evaluate and use information both in the library and over electronic networks. As the use of e-library continues to soar, users are expected to develop information literacy skills. These skills will enable users to make efficient and effective use of information sources.

DEFINITION OF E-RESOURCES

These are defined as online information resources including bibliographic database, electronic reference books, and search engines for full text collections, digital collections of data and data set constitute the electronic resources.

ABOUT PANJAB UNIVERSITY, CHANDIGARH

Panjab University has a long tradition of pursuing excellence in teaching and research in science and technology, humanities, social sciences, performing arts and sports. The University supports excellence and innovation in academic programmes. Promotes excellence in research, scholarship and teaching and is committed to attracting and supporting the best students and recruiting faculty who excel at teaching and research. The glorious traditions of the University established during the period of more than 129 years of its long service to the nation and since its inception in 1882 at Lahore (now in Pakistan), are a source of inspiration for the present generation of faculty members and students. By virtue of its age, experience, achievements and philosophy, the Panjab University is a University of national character and stature, in so far as it has drawn both its faculty and students from all over the country and abroad. Its faculty includes some of the most distinguished scientists and academicians in arts and humanities. The University continues to attract celebrated scholars from abroad to visit and interact with the faculty and students. Over the years the reputation of Panjab University has grown into one of innovative teaching research and community outreach. This University is accorded with grade 'Five star' status by the grading system of UGC.

The Central Library of the University is known as the A C Joshi library. The Library has five storeyed building, which is based on modern architecture setting the example of modular planned library. The library has the seating capacity to 600 readers at a time. The library has a collection around 7 lakh volumes (books, bound volumes of journals, manuscripts, etc.) and more that 650 journals are being subscribed currently by the university. The library has a digital library where readers can access to 5000 E- resources provided through UGC INFONET and INDEST consortium and also provides online access to online databases, which are subscribed by the library. The library has installed CCTV cameras for surveillance and monitoring. Library is fully automated using latest computer technology with an integrated system connected through LAN and library is using SLIM-21 digital library management software and RFID for inventory control. The library provide the services like reference, OPAC /web OPAC, Digital library, Wi-Fi connectivity, Online CAS services, Interlibrary loan facility, Online full text and bibliographical database access. There are 75 departmental libraries and AC Joshi library acts as the central point for all departmental libraries for acquiring and processing of books and journals.

STATEMENT OF THE PROBLEM

The problem of the present study is entitled, "Use of electronic resources by the research scholars of the Panjab University, Chandigarh: A Study.

OBJECTIVES

The main purpose of this study was to investigate the awareness, level of use of electronic resources, the perceived impact of use of electronic resources on the academic productivity and problems faced by researchers while using electronic resources in the Panjab University Library.

- Study the purpose and frequency of using the electronic resources and available in the library.
- To know the place from where to access the electronic resources.
- To study the use of different types of e-resources and services by the research scholars.
- Investigate whether the e-resources can replace the print resources.
- Study the impact of e-resources and services on the work of researchers.
- Know the quality of information retrieved through electronic resources.

METHODOLOGY

There are several research techniques and tools available for researchers to collect the data within the scope of the study such as questionnaire methods, Interview, pilot study and observation, etc. For this study the questionnaire and sample method have been used. The total number of 120 questionnaires was circulated among the research scholars of Humanities and science department in Panjab University out of which 90 questionnaires were return back. The data thus collected were tabulated and analysed by using statistical technique and the represents of the study are presented.

ANALYSIS OF DATA

After collecting the data from the research scholars, the data was checked and analyzed according to the objectives and hypothesis stated.

Table 1: Sample and rate of Response

Respondents	No. of questionnaire distributed	No. of questionnaire received	Total percentage
Research Scholars	120	90	75.00

The Table 1 shows that the distribution of number of questionnaires and rate responses among the study population. In total 120 questionnaires were distributed among Research Scholars, of Panjab University, out of 120 questionnaires 90 were received back and the rate of results is 75%.

Table 2: Awareness of E-Resources

Respondents	Total	Yes	No
Research Scholars	90	85(94.44)	5(5.56)

In Table 2, 94.44% research scholars were reported in the survey as being aware of e-resources. Awareness of e-resources indicated user knowledge of the availability of the resources, their services and the extent made use of them. Whereas 5.56% scholars were reported in the survey as being was not aware.

Table 3: Purpose of Use of Information resources

Purpose of use	Total Response	Total percentage
For Research	80	88.8
For knowledge	42	38.18
For current information & technology	72	80.00

Table 3 reveals that 80 (88.8%) researchers use information sources for research purpose and for current information/Technology 72 (80.00%) and for knowledge purpose (38.18%).

Table 4: Frequency of E-Resources

Respondents	Total	Usually	Sometimes	Rarely
Research Scholars	90	62(68.8)	15(13.63)	13(11.81)

Table 8 revealed that majority of scholars preferred to use e-resources in comparison to traditional resources 77 of them considered e-resources as time, 70 considered it easy to use, whereas 52 considered it more useful. The results from table 8 revealed that respondents preferred e-resources because they were more useful, time saving, easy to use, more informative and less expensive.

Table 9: Satisfaction with existing IT Infrastructures

Respondents	Total	Yes	No
Research Scholars	90	79(87.7)	11(12.2)

Table 9 indicated that 79 (87.7) of scholars were satisfied with the existing IT infrastructure. This is against 11(12.2) scholars who were not satisfied with the IT infrastructure.

Table 10: Problem in the use of E-Resources

Problems	Total Response	Total percentage
Poor connectivity	65	72.2
Limited access	81	90.0
Terminals problems	65	72.2
Retrieval of irrelevant information	43	47.7
Unawareness of information in their field	25	27.27
Poor database searching skill	27	24.54
Lack of time	61	67.77

Table 10, is a show that the limited access is the major problem facing by the research scholar i.e. 81(90.0%).65(72.2%) scholars are suffering from the poor connectivity to use the online resources. The table also shows that 65(72.2%) scholars facing the insufficient computer terminals problem, and 43(47.7%), users suffered from the retrieval of irrelevant information and 25(27.27%) face the problem due to unawareness of information in their fields, 27(24.54%) scholar facing the poor database searching skill and 61(67.77%) scholar are unable to access e-resources due to lack of time.

Table 11: Do E-resources diminish the importance of traditional resources?

Respondents	Total	Yes	No
Research Scholars	90	38(42.2)	52(57.77)

Table 11 revealed that the 52(57.77%) scholars believed that e-resources would never diminish the light of traditional resources. Whereas 38(42.2%) research scholars believe that e-resources may replace traditional source of information.

CONCLUSION AND RECOMMENDATIONS

The study showed that the uses of e-resources are very common among the research scholars of Panjab University. The result of the above study reveals that approximately all the research scholars are aware of electronic resources in the university, maximum number of scholars use and satisfied with both medium (Print/E-resource). The research scholars are using the e-resource and relies it is an important source for their research work. It is widely used by the research scholar of Panjab University for their research purposes and it plays an active role in searching of their relevant information related to research work. Some problems are faces by research scholar but overall maximum users are satisfied with the use of e-resource.

In order to improve the facilities and services for effective use of electronic resources, in the Panjab University, a number of suggestions can be made.

- User training is essential for the better use of e-resources in the library since a good number of users are searching e-literature on their own.
- Research scholars should be taught about advanced search strategies and the use of controlled vocabulary to make electronic search process much easier.
- As Research scholars are experiencing problems in gathering information, more Computer terminals and internet labs should be set up at main library and departmental libraries for

Technologies (ICTs), especially the Internet and Mobile phones has made it possible to have instant access to various types of e-resources including dictionaries. According to *Internet World Stats*, India was the third largest country among the maximum number of Internet users of the world. Our Internet users increased from 5,000,000 in the year 2000 to 121,000,000 users up to the first quarter of 2012, which covers 5.3 percent of the world's total Internet users (IWS 2012). Nevertheless, there were more than 858 million mobile phone subscribers in India up to July 2011 (Prasoon Kumar 2011). Hence, it's imperative to investigate that how much these ICTs are being utilized for academic purposes in the higher learning institutes of our country. "It has for example been noted that three mediums for dictionaries – paper, electronic gadgets, and the Internet – are now about equally popular with students" (Lan 2005, p.16). For example, an online dictionary can be accessed from the Internet and an electronic dictionary can be used offline such as in the case of CDs/ DVDs or downloaded to the computer or mobile phone also. [Since] "At the present time, the contents of online dictionaries can be as good as their traditional paper equivalents" (Lan 2005, p. 16-18), an attempt is made in the present study to investigate the usage pattern of online dictionaries among research scholars at Kurukshetra University.

Located at the holy city, Kurukshetra University was established in the year 1956. Hundreds of computers are available for use by the students at various locations viz. the Computer Laboratory / Digital Library inside the main Nehru Library; Girl Hostels; and many individual departments also have their own computer laboratories. Moreover, wi-fi access to the Internet is also available within the campus, thereby providing ample opportunities for the students to use subscribed and free e-resources.

REVIEW OF LITERATURE

Awareness of e-dictionaries among 52 social scientists (9 faculty members and 43 research scholars) at the National Social Science Documentation Centre (NASSDOC), India was found quite satisfactory as 8 out of 9 (88.89 percent) faculty members and 18 (41.86 percent) research scholars were found to be aware about these. But the frequent usage of e-dictionaries was better in the case of faculty members since 5 (55.55 percent) were using these and only 4 (9.30 percent) research scholars were using these. However, the frequency of using e-dictionaries varied a lot since most of these users were using these "either occasionally or not at all" (Haridasan & Khan 2009).

Natarajan, Suresh, Sivaraman, & Sevukan (2010) analysed the use and perception of e-resources of 117 faculty members and 108 research scholars in various faculties of Annamalai University, India. Just 32 (27.35 percent) faculty members and 29 (26.85 percent) research scholars were found to be aware of e-dictionaries. It was revealed that e-dictionaries were not frequently used since only 7 (3.11 percent) respondents did use these frequently.

Bhatti (2010) studied internet use of one hundred faculty members at the Islamia University of Bahawalpur, Pakistan, in the four faculties of Arts, Islamic Learning, Education and Science. The usage of e-dictionaries was just 21 percent with more positive response from Science faculty members.

The use of e-dictionaries by 70 social scientists in various departments of Bahauddin Zakariya University, Multan, Pakistan had also been somewhat less as just 18 (25 percent) faculty members were using these (Bhatti, Asghar, Mukhtar, & Chohan, 2011).

A study on the usage of e-dictionaries as a language-learning tool among Chinese students was conducted on 193 under-graduate and post-graduate students of the engineering and humanities faculties in four universities namely, National Cheng Kung University, Tatung University, National Taipei University of Science and Technology, and Hong Kong City University. It was found that the majority of the students (79.3 percent) had their own electronic pocket dictionaries and used these for various purposes like using Bi-Lingual dictionaries, checking spelling, pronunciation etc. However, it was also found that the ownership of the e-pocket dictionary had a negative

only from which online dictionaries cannot be used all the time. In the case of mobile phones, the use of e-dictionaries can also be limited due storage, compatibility, Internet accessibility issues etc. Moreover, while filling the questionnaire, some scholars left the usage of printed dictionaries in certain questions because the maximum questions were related to online dictionaries. Hence, the results of this study cannot imply that printed dictionaries were not used at all by the research scholars. Moreover, due to less number of M.Phil. scholars, class wise differences were not taken into consideration while testing the hypotheses, hence, hypotheses had been tested on the single variable only.

DATA ANALYSIS AND INTERPRETATION

Table 1 reveals the personal characteristics and distribution of the research scholars.

Table 1 reflects the gender and class wise distribution of the research scholars. Out of 53, there were 13 (24.5 percent) Master of Philosophy (M.Phil.) students and 40 (75.5 percent) doctorate (PhD.) level students. However, among the 38 male scholars, 10 (26.3 percent) were in M.Phil. and 28 (73.7 percent) were in the PhD. class. Out of the 15 female scholars, 3 (20 percent) were doing M.Phil. and 12 (80 percent) were doing PhD.

Table 1: Distribution of Research Scholars

Class	Gender		Total No. (%age)
	Male No. (%age)	Female No. (%age)	
M.Phil.	10 (26.3)	3 (20.0)	13 (24.5)
PhD.	28 (73.7)	12 (80.0)	40 (75.5)
Total	**38**	**15**	**53**

Faculty	Class		Total No.
	M.Phil. No. (%age)	PhD. No. (%age)	(%age)
Sciences	2 (15.4)	10 (25.0)	12 (22.6)
Social Sciences	5 (38.5)	15 (37.5)	20 (37.7)
Arts & Humanities	6 (46.2)	15 (37.5)	21 (39.6)
Total	**13**	**40**	**53**

Table 1 also shows the faculty and class wise distribution of the research scholars. There were 12 (22.6 percent) scholars in the *Sciences* faculty, of which 2 (15.4 percent) were in M.Phil. and 10 (25 percent) were in the PhD. class. However, there were 20 (37.7 percent) *Social Scientists* also, 5 (38.5 percent) in M.Phil. and 15 (37.5 percent) in PhD. Apart from this, 21 (39.6 percent) research scholars belonged to the *Arts & Humanities* faculty in this study, 6 (46.2 percent) at the M.Phil. level and 15 (37.5 percent) at the PhD. level.

Tables 2 and 3 show the usage of Internet and how frequently it's being used by the research scholars along with from where they access it.

Table 2: Internet usage among research scholars

Internet Usage(N=53)	Range	Mode	Mean
Using since (in years)	1 to 11	4	4.43
Spends time in one sitting usually (in hours)	1 to 4	1	1.4

As per Table 2, the average number of years while using the Internet by the 53 research scholars was found to be 4.43 years, but the range varied from 1 to 11 years, and the maximum (20 scholars) were using it for the last 4 years. However, the number of hours spent on the Internet by the research scholars revealed that on an average, they spent 1.4 hours in one sitting usually, with a range of 1 to 4 hours, but the maximum (35 scholars) were found to be spending 1 hour on the Internet only.

Class wise frequency of Internet usage among the research

dictionaries on a *Weekly* basis also, 2 (25 percent) in the M.Phil. class and 7 (25 percent) in the PhD. class. Just one PhD. scholar preferred *As required* to use the online dictionaries.

Table 5: Frequency and Access of online dictionaries

Aspect of Online Dictionary Use	Class		Total No. (%age)
	M.Phil. No. (%age)	PhD. No. (%age)	
	Frequency of Using Online Dictionaries		
Several times a day	-	1 (3.6)	1 (2.8)
Daily	3 (37.5)	10 (35.7)	13 (36.1)
2-3 days a week	3 (37.5)	9 (32.1)	12 (33.3)
Weekly	2 (25.0)	7 (25.0)	9 (25.0)
Other (As required)	-	1 (3.6)	1 (2.8)
Total	**8**	**28**	**36**
	Access Points		
Laptop (wi-fi network)	7 (87.5)	11 (39.3)	18 (50.0)
University or Dept. Library	-	9 (32.1)	9 (25.0)
Mobile Phone	1 (12.5)	1 (3.6)	2 (5.6)
Laptop and Mobile Phone	-	6 (21.4)	6 (16.7)
Laptop and Univ./Dept. Library	-	1 (3.6)	1 (2.8)
Total	**8**	**28**	**36**

Table 5 also reveals various access points for browsing the online dictionaries. Half of the scholars accessed these with their *Laptop* alone, 7 (87.5 percent) in the M.Phil. class and 11 (39.3 percent) in the PhD. class. 9 PhD. scholars accessed these from the *University or Departmental Library*. The scholars accessing the online dictionaries from their *Mobile Phone* only were one each in both the classes. However, 6 PhD. scholars used both their *Laptop and Mobile Phone* to access the online dictionaries, while one other PhD. scholar accessed these from own *Laptop and University or Departmental Library* also.

Table 6 reveals the type of online dictionaries used by the research scholars. There was just one scholar each in both the classes who used the *Subject* online dictionaries alone. The maximum, 27 (75 percent) scholars were using the *Language* dictionaries alone, 6 (75 percent) at the M.Phil. level and 21 (75 percent) at the PhD. level. However, 7 (19.4 percent) out of 36 research scholars were using *Both* these types of online dictionaries also, just one in the M.Phil. class and rest 6 (21.4 percent) were in the PhD. class.

But the further bifurcation in Table 6 shows that 9 (25 percent) research scholars out of 36 were using the *Subject* online dictionaries, 2 (25 percent) in M.Phil. and 7 (25 percent) in PhD. 20 (55.6 percent) scholars were using *English to English* online dictionaries, 3 (37.5 percent) of which were in the M.Phil. class and rest 17 (60.7 percent) were in the PhD. class. *English to Hindi* online dictionaries were used by the maximum number of scholars, that is, 22 (61.1 percent), 5 (62.5 percent) by M.Phil. level scholars and 17 (60.7 percent) by the PhD. level scholars. However, *Hindi to English* online dictionaries were the least used since just three PhD scholars were found to be using these.

Table 6: Types of online dictionaries used

Aspect of Online Dictionary	Class		Total No. (%age)
	M.Phil. No. (%age)	PhD. No. (%age)	
Category of Online Dictionaries			
Subject	1 (12.5)	1 (3.6)	2 (5.6)
Language	6 (75.0)	21 (75.0)	27 (75.0)
Both	1 (12.5)	6 (21.4)	7 (19.4)
Total	**8**	**28**	**36**
Type of Online Dictionaries (N=36) (multiple responses)			
Subject	2 (25.0)	7 (25.0)	9 (25.0)
English to English	3 (37.5)	17 (60.7)	20 (55.6)
English to Hindi	5 (62.5)	17 (60.7)	22 (61.1)
Hindi to English	-	3 (10.7)	3 (8.3)

Note: Due to multiple responses, the total figures and percentage doesn't equal to 100 percent. Moreover, the data of those scholars who were not using these online dictionaries is not presented here.

	Subscription of E-Dictionaries		
Free on E-mail	3 (37.5)	9 (32.1)	12 (33.3)
No (Free E-mail)	5 (62.5)	19 (67.9)	24 (66.7)
On Mobile Phone	-	-	-
Total	**8**	**28**	**36**
	Free Downloaded on (N=36) (multiple responses)		
Computers	3 (37.5)	8 (28.6)	**11 (30.6)**
Laptops	1 (12.5)	10 (35.7)	**11 (30.6)**
Mobile Phones	3 (37.5)	9 (32.1)	**12 (33.3)**

Note : Due to multiple responses, the total figures and percentage doesn't equal to 100 percent. Moreover, the data of those scholars who had not downloaded the free online dictionaries is not presented here.

It was also asked that whether they were subscribing the online dictionaries and it was found that just 12 (33.3 percent) out of the 36 scholars had subscribed the *Free on E-mail* online dictionaries, 3 (37.5 percent) of which were in M.Phil. and 9 (32.1 percent) were in PhD. But none of the research scholar had subscribed the online or e-dictionaries on the *Mobile Phone* (Table 6).

However, Table 6 also reveals that about one-third of the 36 research scholars had downloaded the free e-dictionaries on their various electronic devices. 11 (30.6 percent) had downloaded these on their *Computers*, 3 (37.5 percent) in M.Phil.and 8 (28.6 percent) in PhD. Another 11 (30.6 percent) scholars had downloaded the free e-dictionaries on their *Laptops*, of which just one was an M.Phil. student and rest 10 (35.7 percent) were PhD. students. Moreover, 12 (33.3 percent) scholars had downloaded these on their *Mobile Phones* also, 3 (37.5 percent) in M.Phil. and rest 9 (32.1 percent) in the PhD. class.

Some other aspects related to the usage of online dictionaries are presented in Table 7. To find out how many online dictionaries were usually being consulted by the research scholars for a single word, it was found that 8 (22.2 percent) consulted two online dictionaries, one an M.Phil. student and 7 (25 percent) PhD. students. 7 (19.4 percent) scholars preferred to consult three online dictionaries, 3 (37.5 percent) of which were M.Phil. scholars and 4 (14.3 percent)

PhD. scholars. However, 6 PhD. scholars were consulting four online dictionaries for a single word meaning also. Five online dictionaries were being consulted by 3 (8.3 percent) scholars, one by an M.Phil. scholar and 2 (7.1 percent) by PhD. scholars. But 12 (33.3) percent were satisfied from a single online dictionary only.

Table 7: Other aspects of online dictionary usage

Aspect of online dictionary	Class		Total No. (%age)
	M.Phil. No. (%age)	PhD. No. (%age)	
Number of Online Dictionaries used for a single word			
2 online dictionaries	1 (12.5)	7 (25.0)	8 (22.2)
3 online dictionaries	3 (37.5)	4 (14.3)	7 (19.4)
4 online dictionaries	-	6 (21.4)	6 (16.7)
5 online dictionaries	1 (12.5)	2 (7.1)	3 (8.3)
1 online dictionary only	3 (37.5)	9 (32.1)	12 (33.3)
Total	**8**	**28**	**36**
Number of Words Looked for in One Sitting Usually			
2 words	1 (12.5)	-	1 (2.8)
3 words	3 (37.5)	8 (28.6)	11 (30.6)
4 words	1 (12.5)	8 (28.6)	9 (25.0)
5 words	2 (25.0)	6 (21.4)	8 (22.2)
10 words	-	1 (3.6)	1 (2.8)
1 word only	1 (12.5)	5 (17.8)	6 (16.6)
Total	**8**	**28**	**36**

Table 7 also reveals that in one sitting usually, how many words were searched by the research scholars. One M.Phil. scholar usually searched two words on the online dictionaries. 11 (30.6 percent) scholars looked the definitions of three words, 3 (37.5 percent) of the M.Phil. class and 8 (28.6 percent) of the PhD. class. Four words were found to be searched by 9 (25 percent) scholars, just one in M.Phil. and 8 (28.6 percent) in PhD. Five words were looked by 8 (22.2 percent) scholars, of which 2 (25 percent) were M.Phil. scholars and 6 (21. 4 percent) were PhD. scholars. However, there was a doctoral level scholar who usually looked ten words also. But rest of the 6 (16.6 percent) out of the 36 scholars usually checked just a single word only.

To find out how many words were looked for by the research scholars in a week usually, Table 8 reveals this information. In the case of online dictionaries, the majority of the scholars, that is, 15 (41.7 percent) were found to be looking *Up to 5* words only, 3 (37.5 percent) M.Phil. scholars and 12 (42. 9 percent) PhD. scholars. There were 8 (22.2 percent) scholars who looked *6 to 10* words, 2 (25 percent) in the M.Phil. class and 6 (21.4 percent) in the PhD. class. However, another 8 (22.2 percent) scholars checked *11 to 15* word meanings on the online dictionaries also, 3 (37.5 percent) M.Phil. and 5 (17.9 percent) in PhD. Moreover, four PhD. scholars usually looked between *16 to 20* word meanings also on the online dictionaries. But one PhD. scholar revealed not to notice that how many words were looked in a week usually in the case of online dictionaries.

Table 8: Words looked in dictionaries in a week usually

Number of Words Looked	Class		Total No. (%age)
	M.Phil. No. (%age)	PhD. No. (%age)	
	Online Dictionaries		
Up to 5	3 (37.5)	12 (42.9)	15 (41.7)
6 to 10	2 (25.0)	6 (21.4)	8 (22.2)
11 to 15	3 (37.5)	5 (17.9)	8 (22.2)
16 to 20	-	4 (14.3)	4 (11.1)
Didn't notice this	-	1 (3.6)	1 (2.8)
Total	**8**	**28**	**36**
	Printed Dictionaries		
Up to 5	2 (25.0)	10 (35.7)	12 (33.3)
6 to 10	1 (12.5)	1 (3.6)	2 (5.6)
11 to 15	-	3 (10.7)	3 (8.3)
16 to 20	3 (37.5)	4 (14.3)	7 (19.4)

21 to 25	1 (12.5)	6 (21.4)	7 (19.4)
Didn't notice this	-	1 (3.6)	1 (2.8)
Not Answered	1 (12.5)	3 (10.7)	4 (11.1)
Total	8	28	36

Table 8 also shows that how many words the research scholars look for in the printed dictionaries in a week usually. The majority of the scholars, that is, 12 (33.3 percent) out of the 36, usually look *Up to 5* words, 2 (25 percent) in M.Phil. and 10 (35.7 percent) in PhD. There was one scholar each in both the classes who usually look *6 to 10* words. Three PhD. scholars usually check *11 to 15* words in the printed dictionaries in a week. However, there were 7 (19.4 percent) scholars who usually look *16 to 20* words in a week, 3 (37.5 percent) M.Phil. and 4 (14. 3 percent) PhD. Moreover, another 7 (19.4 percent) also check *21 to 25* words in the printed dictionaries, one of which was in M.Phil. and 6 (21.4 percent) in PhD. But one PhD. scholar didn't notice this that how many words were checked in a week usually in the case of printed dictionaries. Other four scholars didn't answer this.

Table 9 reveals the search behaviour of research scholars while searching online word meanings. 13 (36.1 percent) scholars preferred to type all their words on the search engine only, of which 5 (62.5 percent) were M.Phil. level students and 8 (28.6 percent) PhD. level students. 11 (30.6 percent) scholars initially type their first word on the search engine but look for the next words from the online dictionaries, 2 (25 percent) in M.Phil. and 9 (32.1 percent) in PhD. Another 11 (30.6 percent) scholars had showed the preference to initially search the online dictionaries on the search engine and then look their respective word meanings from the online dictionary websites, just one M.Phil. level scholar, and 10 (35.7 percent) PhD. level scholars. However, one PhD. scholar directly accessed the online dictionary websites from their respective uniform resource locators (URLs).

Table 9: Search Behaviour for online word meanings

Search Behaviour	Class		Total No. (%age)
	M.Phil. No. (%age)	PhD. No. (%age)	
How scholars search the online word meanings			
Type all words in the Search Engine only	5 (62.5)	8 (28.6)	13 (36.1)
Type first word on the search engine but look next ones from online dictionaries	2 (25.0)	9 (32.1)	11 (30.6)
First search web dictionaries on a search engine, then check meanings on the dictionary websites	1 (12.5)	10 (35.7)	11 (30.6)
Other (Directly access online dictionaries from URL)	-	1 (3.6)	1 (2.8)
Total	**8**	**28**	**36**
What they do after finding the word meanings			
Just read the definition on the computer screen	7 (87.5)	19 (67.9)	26 (72.2)
Copy the definition and Paste it in an e-file	1 (12.5)	8 (28.6)	9 (25.0)
Print the definition	-	1 (3.6)	1(2.8)
Total	**8**	**28**	**36**

Table 9 also shows that what research scholars usually do after finding the word meanings. Majority of the scholars, that is, 26 (72.2 percent) preferred to *Just read the definition on the computer screen* itself, of which 7 (87.5 percent) were M.Phil. scholars and 19 (67.9 percent) were PhD. scholars. However, 9 (25 percent) scholars also liked to *Copy the definition and Paste it in an e-file* for future use, just one in M.Phil. and 8 (28.6 percent) in the PhD. class. Moreover, there was just one PhD. scholar who preferred to *Print the definition* also.

Table 10: Can scholars name the online dictionaries used

Recall of online dictionaries names	Class		Total No. (%age)
	M.Phil. No. (%age)	Ph D. No. (%age)	
Yes	1 (12.5)	5 (17.9)	6 (16.7)
No	7 (87.5)	23 (82.1)	30 (83.3)
Total	**8**	**28**	**36**

It was also asked to the research scholars to name a few online dictionary websites they usually used. But only 6 (16.7 percent) were able to do so, just one from the M.Phil, class and 5 (17.9 percent) from the PhD. class (Table 10). However, one M.Phil. scholar and one PhD. scholar named two online dictionary websites. Two PhD. scholars named just one online dictionary website only. But one PhD. level scholar was able to remember the names of three online dictionary websites also along with one other PhD. scholar who named four online dictionary websites.

Table 11: Authenticity and Satisfaction level for free online dictionaries

Level of authenticity and satisfaction	Class		Total No. (%age)
	M.Phil. No. . (%age)	PhD. No . (%age)	
	How much authentic definitions felt		
0 to 25%	1 (12.5)	1 (3.6)	2 (5.6)
25 to 50 %	-	1 (3.6)	1 (2.8)
50 to 75%	2 (25.0)	8 (28.6)	10 (27.8)
75 to 100%	5 (62.5)	18 (64.3)	23 (63.9)
Total	**8**	**28**	**36**
	How much satisfied		
0 to 25%	1 (12.5)	1 (3.6)	2 (5.6)
25 to 50 %	-	2 (7.1)	2 (5.6)
50 to 75%	2 (25.0)	7 (25.0)	9 (25.0)
75 to 100%	5 (62.5)	18 (64.3)	23 (63.9)
Total	**8**	**28**	**36**

It was also asked to the research scholars to show their preferences for the authenticity and satisfaction regarding the free online dictionaries on a 0 to 100 percent scale with four divisions. As per Table 11, the majority of the scholars, that is, 23 (63.9 percent) out of 36, felt that the definitions in the free online dictionaries are authentic between *75 to 100%*, 5 (62.5 percent) M.Phil. scholars and 18 (64.3 percent) PhD. scholars. The other 10 (27.8 percent) considered that the definitions are authentic between *50 to 75%* only, of which 2 (25 percent) were M.Phil. level students and 8 (28.6 percent) were PhD. level students. However, one PhD. scholar felt that these definitions are authentic between *25 to 50%* only. One scholar from each class considered that the definitions available in the free online dictionaries are authentic only between *0 to 25%*.

Table 11 also shows that how much the research scholars were satisfied with the free online dictionaries. The majority of the scholars, that is, 23 (63.9 percent) out of 36 were satisfied between *75 to 100%*, 5 (62.5 percent) of the M.Phil. class and 18 (64.3 percent) of the PhD. class. 9 (25 percent) scholars were satisfied with the free online dictionaries between the range of *50 to 75%* also, 2 (25 percent) M.Phil. and 7 (25 percent) PhD. However, two PhD. scholars were satisfied between 25 to 50% only and one scholar from both these classes was satisfied between *0 to 25%* with the free online dictionaries.

The second hypothesis had been tested regarding the authenticity of the free online dictionaries as felt by the research scholars (class wise differences had not been tested). The value of Chi-Square came to 34.4 (1 df, N=36, $p < 0.001$) showing statistically significant results by which it can be said that they believe the definitions on the free online dictionaries are authentic, thereby rejecting this null hypothesis.

The third and the last hypothesis had been tested in relation to the satisfaction level of the research scholars with the free online dictionaries (without considering class wise differences). The Chi-Square value was found to be 32.6 (1 df, N=36, $p < 0.001$) and shows statistically significant results by which it can be said that they were highly satisfied with the free online dictionaries as this null hypothesis also got rejected.

Table 12: Opinion and Perception about online dictionaries

Opinion and Perception	Class		Total No. (%age)
	M.Phil. No. . (%age)	PhD. No . (%age)	
Believe that free online dictionaries are better than printed ones			
Yes	1 (12.5)	9 (32.1)	10 (27.8)
No	7 (87.5)	18 (64.3)	25 (69.4)
Can't Say	-	1 (3.6)	1 (2.8)
Total	8	28	36
Can free online dictionaries replace the printed ones			
Yes	2 (25.0)	11 (39.3)	13 (36.1)
No	6 (75.0)	16 (57.1)	22 (61.1)
Can't Say	-	1 (3.6)	1 (2.8)
Total	8	28	36

Table 12 reveals the opinion and perception of research scholars regarding online dictionaries. 10 (27.8 percent) out of 36 scholars believed that the free online dictionaries are better that the printed ones, of which 9 (32.1 percent) were the doctoral level students. However, the rest 25 (69.4 percent) didn't believe it and one PhD. scholar was unsure about it.

Moreover, about one-third, 13 scholars (36.1 percent) out of the 36 also felt that online dictionaries can replace the printed ones in the future, 2 (25 percent) M.Phil. level students and 11 (39.3 percent) PhD. level students. But the majority of them, 22 scholars (61.1 percent) refused this statement and one PhD. scholar was unsure (Table 12).

Table 13: Reasons for using and not using online dictionaries

Reason	Class		Total No. (%age)
	M.Phil. No. (%age)	PhD. No. (%age)	
Reasons for Using (multiple responses) (N=36)			
Free to use	6 (75.0)	22 (78.6)	28 (77.8)
Helps in understanding new words	2 (25.0)	10 (37.5)	12 (33.3)
Printed dictionaries are costly	-	8 (28.6)	8 (22.2)
Other	1 (12.5)	4 (14.3)	5 (13.9)
Reasons for NOT Using (multiple responses) (N=17)			
Cannot use these all the time	1 (20.0)	8 (66.7)	9 (52.9)
Wastage of time	1 (20.0)	-	1 (5.9)
Un-authentic definitions	-	1 (8.3)	1 (5.9)
Prefer own or use from library	5 (100)	8 (66.7)	13 (76.5)
Other (having own CD)	-	1 (8.3)	1 (5.9)

Note : Due to multiple responses, the total figures and percentage doesn't equal to 100 percent. Moreover, the data of those scholars who had not chosen these options is not presented here in both the above cases.

In Table 13, various reasons for using and not using the online dictionaries are depicted. The reasons to use the online dictionaries reveal that 28 (77.8 percent) scholars felt that these are *Free to use*, 6 (75 percent) M.Phil. scholars and 22 (78.6 percent) PhD. scholars. Other 12 (33.3 percent) scholars said that online dictionaries *Helps in understanding new words*, of which 2 (25 percent) were in the M.Phil. class and 10 (37.5 percent) in the PhD. class. Eight PhD. scholars told that *Printed dictionaries are costly*. Five other scholars (13. 9 percent) gave more reasons also for using the online dictionaries.

Table 13 also shows the reasons for not using the online dictionaries. 9 (52.9 percent) out of 17 scholars said that they *Cannot use these all the time*, just one M.Phil. scholar and 8 (66.7 percent) PhD. scholars. Even one M.Phil. scholar considered these as *Wastage of time* also. One PhD. scholar felt that these give *Un-authentic definitions*. But most of the scholars, that is, 13 (76.5 percent) out of

17, who were not using the online dictionaries preferred to use their own dictionaries or use the printed ones from the library. One PhD. scholar also revealed that due to the Oxford dictionary in CD format, there is no need to consult online dictionaries. However, the comments of a few scholars revealed that due to internet connectivity and networking problems, they may not be able to use the online dictionaries all the time.

Table 14: Purchased e-dictionaries in CD/DVD format

E-dictionaries(N=53)	Class		Total No. (%age)
	M.Phil. No. (%age)	PhD. No. (%age)	
English to English	-	5 (12.5)	5 (9.4)
English to Hindi	-	1 (2.5)	1 (1.9)
Not Purchased	13 (100)	34 (85.0)	47 (88.7)
Total	**13**	**40**	**53**

Out of 53, there were just 6 (11.3 percent) doctoral level research scholars who had purchased the e-dictionaries in the CD/DVD format (Table 14). However five of these had purchased *English to English* e-dictionaries and one owned an *English to Hindi* e-dictionary also.

DISCUSSION

The first hypothesis that research scholars do not use the online dictionaries had been rejected since about two-third scholars out of fifty three (Table 4) were found using these (statistically significant with Chi-Square value of 6.81, 1df, N=53, $p < 0.001$). Much usage of the online dictionaries may be consistent with others like Lan reflected that "more than 70% of students interviewed at Hong Kong Polytechnic University claim that they use e-dictionaries more often than the traditional bulky paper products..."(2005, p.16).

Though many reasons could be attributed to the much usage of online dictionaries in the present study, however, the most likely explanation could be the availability and ownership of the various

Internet access tools, since 42 scholars (79.2 percent) did have their own computers or laptops (Table 3) to get a ready access to the wi-fi Internet. Moreover, about one-fourth (N=53, 26.4 percent) scholars had access to the Internet from their mobile phones also, which enhances the usage of the online dictionaries (Table 3). Additionally, those who were found using the online dictionaries (Table 5) also showed that 50 percent (N=36) scholars accessed these from their laptops alone and other 16.7 percent accessed the online dictionaries from their laptops and mobile phones also.

This finding that ownership of the latest ICTs leads to more usage of the online dictionaries may be consistent with the Chinese study in which majority of the students (79.3 percent) had their own e-pocket dictionaries which were used for various purposes. However, the scores of the Chinese students had a negative impact with the ownership of the e-pocket dictionaries where significant differences were found between the ownership and non-ownership of electronic pocket dictionaries in relation to the English exam scores ($t=3.3$, $df=33$, $P<0.003$) that non-owners of these dictionaries had better English exam scores (Mean Score MS=77.2 percent, SD=21.1) than owners (MS=60.3 percent, SD=25.1). However, it should also be noted that the population of the Chinese study was specifically the language learners and moreover, "some students left this item [English scores] blank..." hence analysis was based on those ones only who revealed their scores but otherwise these represented a sub sample only (Jian, Sandnes, Law, Huang, & Huang, 2009).

The ownership of the latest ICTs can thus be a major factor, but it may not be the only reason for the usage of online dictionaries, as time may also play an important role here. Since, the scholars in this study were found using the Internet for the last 4.43 mean years with the maximum range up to 11 years also, this may also affect the usage of online dictionaries (Table 2). Moreover, 43.3 percent (N=53) scholars were found using the Internet *Daily* and other 17 percent *Several times a day* (Table 3), these factors (time and frequency of Internet use) also enhance the usage of the online dictionaries. Additionally, those who were actually using the online dictionaries also showed the pattern of frequent access in using these dictionaries as 36.1 percent (N=36) scholars used these *Daily*, and other 33.3 percent used the online dictionaries *2-3 days a week* (Table 5).

But those who do not own a laptop or internet enabled mobile phone do have the opportunity to access the online dictionaries from the university or departmental libraries along with those who own these latest ICTs. As 30.2 percent (N=53) were also found to access the Internet from the university or departmental library (Table 3). In the case of those scholars who were actually using the online dictionaries (Table 5), one-fourth (N=36) also accessed these from the university or departmental library. One more reason could be that many online dictionaries are available free on the Internet and 77.8 percent (N=36) research scholars also gave this reason (Table 13).

The comments provided by five other research scholars (Table 13) for using the online dictionaries could also reflect upon their usage:

An M.Phil. scholar said that "It gives more knowledge & exact meaning...".

The PhD. scholars commented that online dictionaries are:

"Easy to handle (use)";

"Easy to access in blinking of eyes";

"Some time[s] online dic[tionaries] are very useful, because if we work at online and want to search any meaning. Then there is no need to consult printed dictionary, and these are easy to use [also]";

"It helps in searching the meaning of words. Anytime anything we can search the meaning of words / terms where we can't carry the printed dictionary. But according to me printed dictionary is more authentic instead of online / non-print dictionary. But overall, it helps us."

Hence, several reasons could be attributed for the use of online dictionaries among the research scholars like, access to the Internet, owning a computer or laptop and internet enabled mobile phone, number of years, frequency of Internet use, access points for using the Internet and free availability of the online dictionaries. And of course, the population of this study is research scholars, which itself is a major factor for use the dictionaries, whether printed or online ones.

The second hypothesis that research scholars do not consider the definitions of the free online dictionaries to be authentic had been rejected (statistically significant with Chi-Square of 34.4, 1df, N=36, $p < 0.001$) since 63.9 percent (N=36) scholars felt that the definitions are authentic between *75 to 100%* and other 27.8 percent considered these to be authentic between *50 to 75%* (Table 11). This finding is consistent with the medical dictionaries usage study (Ahmad, Mansoor-ul-Haq, & Iqbal, 2011) which also showed that most of the MBBS students "(89% always and 07% nearly always)" had "faith in the definitions of the medical dictionaries." As far as the authenticity of the online dictionaries is concerned, it cannot be asserted from the findings of this study that whether those online dictionaries used by the research scholars in this study were authentic, or not authentic. Further research on this aspect can throw a light on this issue. Though statistically significant, this finding is the opinion of the research scholars only. It may be due to the usage of standardized dictionaries or just a little exaggerated positive opinion regarding the free online dictionaries. But only 16.7 percent (N=36) were able to remember the name of the online dictionaries (Table 10) and most of the scholars took the assistance of the search engines to use the online dictionaries (Table 9), hence, it cannot be asserted that all the research scholars were using the standardized online dictionaries. Moreover, this finding may also imply the lack of information literacy skills among the research scholars, especially the critical evaluation of web contents, which needs to be provided.

The third and the last hypothesis that research scholars were not satisfied with the free online dictionaries also got rejected (statistically significant with Chi-Square of 32.6, 1df, N=36, $p < 0.001$) as 63.9 percent scholars were found satisfied with these between *75 to 100%* and other 25 percent were satisfied between the range of *50 to 75%* (Table 11). The satisfaction level seems consistent with the medical dictionary study (Ahmad, Mansoor-ul-Haq, & Iqbal, 2011) in which 86 percent MBBS students were found satisfied with the subject dictionaries. The statistically significant satisfaction with the free online dictionaries of the present study may be attributed to many reasons. When many scholars consider these dictionaries to be authentic ones, satisfaction may seem to be automatically achieved. But it may be a general human tendency also to have great satisfaction with the free things in life (not made clear from this study). Moreover, much usage of the free online dictionaries implies that these were satisfying because of using these again and again, however, this cannot be made clear from this study, as the names of the free online dictionaries revealed by the research scholars were quite a few only (Table 10). As Hass had asserted in 1962 that "the perfect dictionary is one in which you can find the thing you are looking for preferably in the very first place you look" (as cited in Bergenholtz & Bothma, 2011, p. 55) and one-third (33.3 percent) scholars of the present study were found satisfied with one online dictionary only while checking a single word (Table 7), this may also be a reason for much satisfaction with the free online dictionaries among the research scholars. But the comment of Bergenholtz & Bothma regarding users that "If he/she uses a dictionary (or a lexicon or an encyclopaedia or whatever name the lexicographical tool might have), the potential dictionary user is in an 'extra-lexicographical' situation. Looking in one or more dictionaries is a 'dictionary use' situation. In some cases the use of a dictionary would be the best choice but in many others certainly not" (2011, p. 61) reflects that the users must be familiar with information search skills and having satisfaction without information literacy might seem dangerous. Nevertheless, the rest two-third scholars in the present study (Table 7) did check more than one online dictionary (ranging from two to five online dictionaries) also for single a word meaning, which again may be dependent upon the usage of standardized dictionaries, however, not made clear from this study but could be further explored in future.

Since the most of the previous studies reviewed in this paper had shown less usage of electronic dictionaries, it is recommended that more research in the area of electronic and online dictionaries is required while inferring any generalizations based on the results of this study, like comparing the relationship with the printed dictionaries. Although the present study reveals statistically significant results but the findings cannot be generalized on all types of users. Even in the case of research scholars also, it has to be ensured that Internet access tools are adequately available. For future researchers who want to study the usage pattern of online dictionaries, it is suggested that this area can be further explored only where the study is focused on the electronic and online dictionaries, rather than investigating the use of all electronic resources available under the virtual universe.

CONCLUSION

Various aspects related to the use of online dictionaries among research scholars had been investigated in the present study. Statistically significant results (with Chi-Square) had been obtained regarding the use of online dictionaries by the research scholars. In the case of the free online dictionaries, these were considered to provide highly authentic definitions and the research scholars were highly satisfied with their usage also, were both found statistically significant with Chi-Square. It had also been discussed that statistical significant results may be dependent on some other factors like the availability of the Internet access tools, frequency of access etc. It has been suggested that this area could be further explored only by specifically investigating the use of online and electronic dictionaries rather than one-shot research of all the e-resources together.

REFERENCES

Ahmad, A., Mansoor-ul-Haq, H., & Iqbal, Z. (2011). A study of behaviour of medical students towards dictionary use. *Language in India: Strength for Today and Bright Hope for Tomorrow,* 11 (4), 122-131. Retrieved from http://languageinindia.com/april2011/aliahmedmedicaldictionaryfinal.pdf

Bergenholtz, H. & Bothma, T. J. D. (2011). Needs-adapted data presentation in e-information tools. *Lexikos* 21 (AFRLIEX-reeks/series), 53-77. Retrieved from http://www.ajol.info/index.php/lex/article/viewFile/72820/61727.

Bhatti, R. (2010). Internet use among faculty members in the changing higher education environment at the Islamia University of Bahawalpur, Pakistan. *Library Philosophy and Practice.* Retrieved from http://digitalcommons.unl.edu/cgi/viewcontent.cgi?article=1393& context= libphilprac.

Bhatti, R., Asghar, M. B., Mukhtar, S., & Chohan, T. M. (2011). Internet use by social scientists at the Bahauddin Zakariya University, Multan, Pakistan: A survey. *Library Philosophy and Practice.* Retrieved from http://unllib.unl.edu/LPP/bhatti-asghar-mukhtar-chohan.htm

Dahan, H. B. A. M., & Omar, C. A. M. B. (2011). The development of e-dictionary for the use with MAHARAH AL-QIRAAH textbook at a matriculation centre in a university in Malaysia. *Turkish Online Journal of Educational Technology,* 10 (3), 255-264. Retrieved from http://www.tojet.net/articles/v10i3/10329.pdf

Haridasan, S., & Khan, M. (2009). Impact and use of e-resources by social scientists in National Social Science Documentation Centre (NASSDOC), India. *The Electronic Library,* 27 (1), 117-133. DOI 10.1108/02640470910934632

IWS (2012). *Internet World Stats: Usage and Population Statistics.* Retrieved from http://www.internetworldstats.com/top20.htm

Jian, H. L., Sandnes, F. K., Law, K. M. Y., Huang, Y. P., & Huang, Y. M. (2009). The role of electronic pocket dictionaries as an English learning tool among Chinese students. *Journal of Computer Assisted Learning,* 25, 503-514. DOI: 10.1111/j.1365-2729.2009.00325.x

Lan, L. (2005). The growing prosperity of on-line dictionaries. *English Today* 83, 21 (3 – July), 16-21. DOI: 10.1017/S0266078405003044

Natarajan, A., Suresh, B., Sivaraman, P. & Sevukan, R. (2010). Use and user perception of electronic resources in Annamalai University: A case study. *Annals of Library and Information Studies,* 57 (March), 59-64. Retrieved from http://nopr.niscair.res.in/bitstream/123456789/8285/4/ALIS%2057(1)%2059-64.pdf

Prasoon Kumar (2011). *The Mobile Indian,* New Delhi, Sept. 12, 2011. Retrieved from http://www.themobileindian.com/news/Mobile

26

Availability and Utilization of Electronic Resources by Lecturers at the Engineering & Environmental Campus of the Olabisi Onabanjo University Ogun State, Nigeria.

M. A. Adeniji

INTRODUCTION

The College of Engineering and Environmental studies, Ibogun Campus of the Olabisi Onabanjo University Ogun State Nigeria was commissioned on Thursday 27th November 2003 by the then His Excellency Otunba Gbenga Daniel the Governor of Ogun State (The News, 2007). The College has two faculties namely faculty of Engineering with the following four departments - Agricultural Engineering, Computer Engineering, Electrical & Electronics

Engineering, Mechanical Engineering, and the Faculty of Environmental Studies with the following three departments Architecture, Fine & Applied Arts and Urban & Regional Planning. In pursuance of the vision of the College as Engineering arm of the university the academic staff were employed whose duty amongst others is to instruct, carry out research and communicate research findings. This academic staff otherwise known as lecturers lives and interacts with their colleagues and other member of the academic community. Other duties of these academicians centered on the teaching and provide guidance to students who are the future professionals in Engineering and Environment Science. To perform the above function effectively therefore, they use various electronic resources either at their campuses or other place of interest for their teaching and research work. The utilization of the e-resources by the lecturers has transformed the academic institution into an information society, which is essential for a literate organization that the nations yearned for.

Table 1: No. of Academic Staff in the College

Status	No. of Lecturers
Professor	01
Reader	01
Senior Lecturer	01
Lecturer 1	02
Lecturer 11	16
Assistant Lecturer	06
Graduate Assistant	03
Total	**30**

Source: O O .U (CEES) (2011) Academic Staff Norminal Roll

ACADEMIC STAFF OF THE ENGINEERING AND ENVIRONMENTAL CAMPUS

The academic staff of the College of Engineering and Environment studies Ibogun Campus of the Olabisi Onabanjo

University, Ogun state, Nigeria is directly responsible for teaching and research of the academic programmes of the school and they form the bulk of personnel engaged in institutional services, while administrative and technical staff provide supportive service to the academicians of this citadel of learning.

The adoption of e-resources in the University helps a lot in teaching, learning and research. Ogunleye, (2008) and Panhwar, (2008) observed that the e- resources has been seen as the most cost – effective means of passing instruction to a large number of students in their various campus. Oyedun, (2007) saw electronic resources as facilities that assist lecturers to offer quick, adequate and efficient services to their students. It also serves as a booster that helps them to meet the diverse needs of the academic work at the appropriate time. Therefore, the adoption of electronic-resources in academic institutions in Nigeria assists the lecturers to perform a dual role, one to the faculty members, while the other is to the community where they offer consultancy services.

OBJECTIVE OF THE STUDY

This study looked at the electronic resources and its utilization by the lecturers of the College of Engineering and Environmental studies of the Olabisi Onabanjo University, Nigeria. This research will serve as eye opener to the people who are interested in these professionals who have a dual role as a lecturers and professional in their various disciplines that make up the College academic programmes.

METHODOLOGY

Data was collected through a site visits along with questionnaires which were administered to lecturers of the College. The population of the study consists of thirty (30) lecturers. The instrument for the study was administered by the researcher to the lecturers. The Departments use for this research work is as follows: -

1. Agricultural Engineering (AGR ENG).
2. Architecture (ARCH).

3. Computer Engineering(COM)
4. Electrical & Electronics Engineering
5. Fine and Applied Art (F. A .A)
6. Mechanical Engineering (MEC).
7. Urban and Regional Planning (U R P)

The E-Resources facilities at the College for the Lecturers utilization are shown in Table 2.

Table 2

e- resources	ARCH	AGR ENG	COM ENG	ELE/ELE	FAA	MEC ENG	URP
CD-ROM	-	-	-	-	-	-	-
VSAT Server			1	-	-	-	-
Telephone	4	5	6	5	5	6	4
Internet/e-mail	5	4	8	5	4	6	4
Cyber Café	-	-	1	-	-	-	-
Printer	3	3	4	5	4	4	3
Scanners	1	1	1	1	1	-	-
Computer	5	4	6	6	4	6	3

INTERNET

Internet is the most prominent e- resource used in Nigerian academic institutions is World Wide Web (W, W. W) or internet which Omagbemi, Akintola and Olayiwola (2004) saw as the most prominent resources that offered limitless access to global information available on net for those who can annex the benefit that the resources offered. Through it information is being updated regularly which enable users to obtain quick and efficient services at the appropriate time. Oketunji(2004) as cited by Odunewu and Omagbemi (2008) stated that these resources add value to the services that the academicians provide for the students and staff within the academic community where they are found. Making reference to the usage of internet in Olabisi Onabanjo University Adejimi(2007 saw this resource as a global information system that assist students and staff to share electronic resources in their various field of endevour, through it they obtained the needed information that aided their research work. At the ibogun Campus of the university internet as learning and teaching resources is use regularly on daily basis by almost all the academic staff of the College for their research activities and a back-up for their teaching assignment which is their primary function in academic community.

E–Mail : is the acronym for electronic mail. With internet facilities mails can be sent or received through e-mail facilities with the participants at different location. It facilitates easy communication as against the old method of postage system that exists before the evolution of email into the information industry. Referring to the use of e-mail Agbaje, (2002) avers that the messages can be sent all over the world in a matter of minutes and the cost in a few seconds. However for anyone to use the email services it requires that such a users has an e- mail box which is equivalent to the old method of mail delivery as practice in Nigeria. The users of e-mail in the College of Engineering include all the lecturers and other staff, undergraduates and people from the College community

CD-ROM : This is the latest development e-resources facilities in academic institutions in Nigeria as a storage device it can be used to store large data of information, books, periodicals; dictionaries and encyclopedia. The CD- ROM is found useful as a learning resource that the lecturer use on daily basis to get the needed information. The information stored in it cannot be changed, or overwritten or erased. They are not susceptible to viruses, as to retrieval of information from it, the software are users friendly than the on-line command language which may be complicated and require technical expertise for effective use Mosunro (1996),Oguntuase,(2004),Oduwole and Sowole (2006) all posited that CD-ROMs enable users to search bibliographical databases on their own with little or no assistance by librarians. Referring to the successful story of this information resources like encyclopedias that is available on CD-ROMs devices Okorie, (2010) observed that in future the resources will be more accepted in the university library that do not have internet facilities because it would give them the opportunity to use the CD- ROM to access an international database that are available on CD-ROM appropriate to their programme in the institutions. In Nigerian University Oketunji, (2000) highlights the benefits of CD-ROM to the students and staff of the tertiary institutions as thus:

- Storage capacity, it can store up to 660 megabytes of data, the 660 megabytes would fill more than 1,800 floppy disks or store the amount of text that fills 330,000 pages of papers.
- Durability of the device make it environmental friendly as problem associated with the environment like moisture, heat, power outage or fluctuations do not affect its performance
- Low mailing cost, the monetary value of shipping cost of CD-ROM is less expensive.
- No telecommunication is needed as CD-ROM by passes the usage of computer databases by telephone links as CD-ROM can be access directly by the computer.
- The end user can use it with little or less training in computer usage because of its user friendly nature than the online systems software. Through this CD-ROM, lecturers or other users find e-resources easy to use for their research work.

The CD-ROM is available in abundant for all the staff of the College to access for their daily information needs, presently the university main library in Ago Iwoye ,Ogun state, Nigeria which is 120 kilometers away from College has some CD-ROM facilities for various disciplines of the schools in which any interested lecturers can make request for from the University librarian or through her representative the College librarians at different geographical from the University main library.

Computer

This is an electronic device which is capable of accepting, stores and retrieves data when it is needed, Adebimpe,(2012), computer can be seen as the power house where the other e-resources mention above can be put into practical use. A computer in line with the view of Ibijola & Ade-Ibijola (2012) comprises of two main parts hardware and software, The former refers to basic electronic part of the device while the later is made up of programmes that control the working of the hardware, The advent of computer into the academic scene in Nigeria where lecturers played major role has made it possible to automate library operation which the lecturer used often in their research work. Through computer link to the internet lecturer can assist the students to carry out their research effectively. The versatility of computer can be seen in their speed, storage facilities, link resources and accuracy in record management which is the basic for student record management in academic institutions in Nigeria. This is the most common e-resources facilities available at the seven departments of the College used by the students and staff for personal and school activities. In fact, computer has been modernized into laptop and notebook that almost all the lecturers and non academic staff use to aid their routine functions.

Cyber Café : This is provision of internet services by private operators for fees. All lecturers of the College made use of Cyber café operating in their domain either at their private residence or at the Campus.

Scanner : Scanner is one of the basic resources used for digitalization of documents: The basic resources is available in only three out of seven departments that made up the College, all the staff who want to get their documents scanned can only use the three scanners available at the various departments.

Printer : A device that displayed output on paper, although people are comfortable with the information displayed on a computer screen and retained in permanent form on some type of secondary storage medium , paper continue to play an important role in our lives. Printer enables the text and graphic displayed on a computer screen to be transferred on paper. Printer has been found a useful tool in reproducing a desire documents. Almost all the lecturers of the seven departments use the printers to get the required document either for a meeting at the departmental level, or making information available to a large audience like a board of the College that want to see the activities for a particular committee or presenting a result at the senate or management of the University as a whole.

Telephone : These communication media is used for sending and receiving messages with instant response from receiver of the information. The modern way of communication through this device has give birth to internal-communication (inter- com) which is used to send message from one lecturer to the other within the College. However, the most telephone communication available to the staff of the College is the mobile phone that uses radio spectrum that do not required physical infrastructure such as road and phone cable. Almost all the lecturers of the College have one or two handset for effective communication among themselves.

VSAT Server : This resource is a network infrastructure capable of linking remote sites efficiently and effectively. The College of Engineering and Environmental Studies have VSAT to boost their e-resources connections on the internet facilities.

Table 3 : Challenges before Lecturers in utilizing the e-resources?

Challenges	Frequency
Service providers problems	01
Recurrent power outages	15
Insufficient fund	05
Inability to download information	02
Limited bandwidth	07
Total	30

The major problems identified by the users of electronic resources were categorized, with power outages with (15) topping the list of the challenges faced by them, followed by limited Bandwidth, (07), insufficient funds (05), inability to download information, (02) Service Providers problems (01)

Table 4 : Duration of Usage of electronics resources

Respondents Cadre.	Regularly	Very often	As need arise
Lecturer 11	4	2	-
Lecturer 1	6	8	2
Senior lecturer	1	3	1
Readers	1	1	-
Professor	-	1	-

From the above it is cleared that all the lecturers used the various e-resources available at their disposal regularly and very often in their daily service provision, the respondents from Lectures 1 and Senior lecturers utilized the resources as the need arise.

Table 5 : Level of e –resources facilities mostly used by the lecturers

E- Resources	Use	Not use	No responses
Political issue	26	03	1
Research topic	27	03	-
Internet with e-mail & charting	28	02	-
CD-ROM	24	04	02

Most of the lecturers used Internet/ e-mail (28) as the most online resources for their daily routine (27) of them used the e-resources for research topic, and (26) of them use e-resources for political enlightenment. The reason for using the e-resources would form the basis of frequency of its usage by these intellectuals.

CONCLUSION AND RECOMMENDATION

The evolution of e-resources has give way to a new method in service delivery in term of teaching not limited by geographical boundaries. With the availability of electronic resources to the academic institutions the academics are better informed and can use the resources to get in touch with their colleagues for research purpose as well as getting assistance in their teaching functions. For better utilization of these resources for teaching function. All the stakeholders in Education industry has one role or the others to play in order to promote effective utilization of e-resources in Nigerian Universities.

The government should provide enough resources for effective teaching and learning in Nigerian Higher institutions. The College management and the lecturers should address the constraints that hindered the usage of the e –resources in their various campuses. While, University management should invest greater part of its fund into the issue of learning resources for a better service. Individual lecturers should reciprocate the government gesture by using the e –resources for the purpose it was meant for However, with the above put been put in place the College will make a positive contribution to the development of the society and the nation at large.

REFERENCES

Adebimpe A.C. (2012). Parental and Personal Factors as Correlates of Undergraduate Usage of E-learning Facilities in Nigerian Universities. Being a paper presented at the international Conference of the Faculty of Education, Kampala International University, Tanzania. 19-22, June, 2012 Pp.2-4.

Adejimi, A. (2007). Comparing Traditional Synchronous Teaching with E-learning in Teaching of Architecture at the Olabisi Onabanjo University. *O.O.U-JET,* 1(1&2), 105-110.

Agbaje, A. (2002). Great Expectations: Serials Management and Information Technology. In Madu & Dirisu (Eds) Information Science and Technology for Library Schools in Africa. Ibadan: Evi–Coleman Publication. pp.30.

Ibijola, E. & Ade-Ibijola, A. (2006). The Computer Hardware in Information Communication and Technology (ICT) and Computer Applications edited Agagu. The University of Ado Ekiti Press, Ado- Ekiti. Pp.25-33.

Mosunro, T. (1996). CD-ROM Technology and its Application at the Kenneth Dike Library. University of Ibadan, Nigeria. *Nigerian Library and Information Science Review,* 1(2), 46-50.

Odunewu, O. and Omagbemi, C. (2008). The University Library, Information Provision, and use by Policymakers in Olabisi Onabanjo University (O.O.U), Nigeria. *Library Philosophy and Practice.* Retrieved from www.webpage.uidaho.edu/

Oduwole, A. and Sowole, A. (2006). Utilization and impact of essential Electronic Agricultural Database (TEEAL) on library Services in Nigerian Universities of Agriculture. *Electronic Library and Information systems,* 40 (2), 157 167

Ogunleye, A.O. (2008). Training Needs Assessment Study of the use of ICT and Learning in supporting the provision of Science and Engineering Education in some Nigerian Universities. A paper presented at the 2nd African Council for Distance Education (ACDE) Conference and General Assembly, Lagos, Nigeria. 8–11 July, 2008.

Oguntuase, F (2004), Penetration of new technologies into information field: A force for new service and products in University libraries. *Castalia-Ibadan Journal of Multidisciplinary Studies,* 11(1), 98-102.

Oketunji, O. (2000). Application of Information Technologies in Nigerian Libraries: Problems and Prospects in Information Technology in Library and Information Science Education in Nigeria edit. Fayose, P Ibadan: NALISE Pp.17.

Okorie, N. (2010). Utilization of Automated Electronic Information Services: A case Study at the University of Agriculture Library, Abeokuta, Nigeria. *Chinese Librarianship: an International Electronic Journa*l. Retrieved from http:www.iclc.us/clief/cl29okorie htm (Accessed on 20/10/2011).

Omagbemi, C., Akintola, B. and Olayiwola, I. (2004). Academic Libraries, the Internet and its Potential Impact on Teaching and Learning in Nigerian Tertiary Institution. *Journal of Library and Information Science,* 1(1), 35-40.

O.O.U. (CEES) (2011). Academic staff Nominal roll: A publication of the Olabisi Onabanjo University, College of Engineering & Environmental Studies. Ibogun Campus Ifo Ogun State Nigeria.

Oyedun, G (2007). Internet use in the library of federal University of Technology Minna. *Gateway library journal,* 10(1), 23-26.

Panhwar, F. (2008). E – Learning and Open and Distance Learning in Pakistan: Its Problem and Prospects. A paper presented at the 2nd African Council for Distance *Education (ACDE)Conference and General Assembly, Lagos, Nigeria. 8 – 11 July.*

The News (2007) Gov: Daniel: The long Runner. *The News Magazine,* 28(21), 33.

27

An Assessment of the Collection and Use of Electronic Resources in University Libraries in Kwara State, Nigeria

Abdulwahab Olanrewaju Issa
Shuaib Agboola Larongbe
Sunday Adebisi Oguntayo

INTRODUCTION

The library in academic institutions, like the colleges of education, polytechnics, and as well as universities, is the soul or heart of that institution; given its central and critical place and role in the realization of the core mandates of the institutions viz: teaching, research and community service. The central place of the library has never been in doubt, which explains why every such institution had its library created almost the same time with the parent institution.

In a similar vein, it follows that no programme of study in this institution is accredited without the existence of a functional and functioning library; pointing still to its critical role to its parent institution. However, the back bone of the library itself is the variety of resources in its holding, without which it cannot lay any claim to providing the services required of it. This means that the functioning and functionality of the academic library, or any library for that matter, is largely determined by the size, range, depth and currency of its collection holdings, such as books, newspapers, journals and audio-visuals (i.e. microforms). Meanwhile, the recent advances in science and technology have introduced a new dimension to library collections as well as their building process.

Though, the general principle behind the collection development process (CDP) had remained essentially the same, building the library's e-resources has certainly introduced a new perspective. The term e-resources is taken to refer to library's information bearing materials that are in electronic form, which include the electronic books (e-books); the electronic newspapers (e-newspapers); the electronic journals (e-journals) as well as the internet resources. Given the fact that the introduction of e-resources in libraries was a by-product of scientific and technological advances, libraries certainly stand to gain a lot from embracing them in their holdings for such reasons as ease and multiplication of access by the users, better, faster and more accurate services delivery by the library personnel to users, as well as greater efficiency in performance of the staff, among others. Thus, library and information resources are central to the provision of services to their users; without which libraries cannot meet their users' information needs. Our present age is characterized by the proliferation of print and non-print resources and information professionals are increasingly required to use various hardware to provide resources and services to users. This has in turn, necessitated the information professionals to possess adequate knowledge of resources, technologies and services in order to meet the attendant challenges of services provision in this age (Adomi, 2009).

Library resources are the information bearing materials

acquired, processed, and made available in the library to the users, to enable the library fulfil its aim of meeting the users; information needs. Indeed, beautiful buildings, well trained library staff and modern information storage and retrieval systems can only be appreciated if excellent services are rendered to users, services that could not be provided without live collections. Libraries now provide a broad range of resources to meet the needs of their users, collect resources in various sizes and formats over a period of time. These resources include manifestation of the printed words, audio and video recordings, microforms, visual and electronic resources, and generations of requisite equipment for accessing, viewing or listening to data stored on them. Adomi (2009) observed that library collections are changing rapidly as more and more e-resources become available, even though their proliferation does not means that print resources will disappear; as indeed, while some resources always will be best in print format; others will be in e-format. But this does pose certain challenges to librarians as to comparing similar materials in different formats and deciding which formats are best for their libraries and selecting the best materials available.

Library resources are broadly categorized into print and non-print materials where the print resources are described as those information bearing materials with characters produced either mechanically or electronically usually texts/documents in hard copies. Print resources are also grouped into reference and non-reference materials with examples such as encyclopedias, dictionaries, biographical sources, maps, atlases and gazetteers, manuals, indexes and abstracts. Some examples of non-reference materials are textbooks, periodicals, light readings, reports, theses, dissertations and ephemerals. The second broad class of information bearing resources in the library is the non-print or electronic or better still, the digitized materials, most of which required the use of equipment, such as the computers, microfilm readers, video/CD players, to access their contents. Some examples of these are video, audio, graphic materials, microforms (microfiche/microfilm), CD-ROM, DVD, e-books and e-journals as well as internet resources.

These are mainly the products of the advances that science and technology has brought onto the present age, necessitating their integration into the existing framework of library collection building. In most cases, they serve as a good complement to the printed library collections by providing for areas of patrons' needs yet to be met by the former. This is to the extent that library collections today remained largely incomplete and therefore unsatisfactory if a good number of e-resources are not included. There is also the wave of automation and/or computerization of libraries, especially the academic libraries, the world over. The justifications for this could be premised on the far-reaching benefits derivable from the trend and practice.

PROBLEM STATEMENT

Because academic libraries have remained a main forerunner in the application of modern technology to their practice worldwide, it became imperative for research attention to be directed at investigating the extent to which university libraries in the developing countries, such as Nigeria, have caught up with this positive trend. This is against the backdrop of the fact that observations have revealed that in spite of the global trend in this positive direction of automation/ computerization, some academic libraries in Nigeria have very little to show in this regard with direct implications for the building of e-resources in these libraries. To confirm or refute the above observations, therefore, this study sets to investigate the current state of the collection building of electronic resources in university libraries in Kwara State, with a view to determining their current practices in these regards. Thus, the study determines the state of their collections-print, electronic, as well as the use of these resources by their communities of users.

To achieve these set objectives, the study seeks answers to such research questions as:

(i) What is the present state of university libraries' collections in Kwara State?

(ii) What amount of print and e-resources do the libraries hold presently?

(iii) How are the e-resources acquired, organized and made accessible to users?

(iv) What challenges do e-resources posed in the above regards?

(v) What is the perception of e-resources users in these libraries?

REVIEW OF RELATED LITERATURE

Collection management is a broad term for collection development (CD) and collection building, including planning and funding, collection development, book selection, acquisitions, provision of access, use, organization, maintenance, evaluation, preservation and weeding of materials (Awoyemi, 2011). Collection management can also be conceived of as those activities traditionally associated with CD (from selection to acquisition); more all-embracing to include the systematic maintenance of library collections, covering resource allocation, technical processing, preservation and storage, weeding and discarding of stock and the monitoring and encouragement of collection use. Collection management is important because it leads to the provision of library resources for library patrons as the quality and the various types of resources, selected and acquired in the library make for effective service delivery. This is why librarians are enjoined to be more interested in collection management as a fundamental responsibility.

Today, more than ever before, economic meltdown, decreasing library budget, rising global inflation and cost of publication, information explosion, limitless scholarly information needs and government economic policies, have all had tremendous effects on the book trade with more far-reaching implications for collection management in Nigeria, as elsewhere in the world, especially in the developing countries. Moreover, today's economic climate has necessitated demands that attention be paid to the varying needs of the library in formulating the criteria for selection and the method of acquisition of relevant library resources. This must be the concern of library authorities and the collection management librarians (Awoyemi, 2011). Thus, effective book selection is now more imperative in libraries in order to match material acquisition with available funds while also making the collectors more cost effective and balanced. This remained the one sure way out of the present exponential growth in publications in all disciplines.

The advent of ICT and increasing popularity of the Internet, has made more and more information resources hitherto available only in books and journals to be available electronically. Libraries are no longer restricted to their buildings as they now have access to a wide range of databases, digitize their resources and mount them on the network thereby providing broader access to their holdings. And because e-resources operations take place mainly in an automated, computerized, digitized or even virtual library environment, they have great potentials to remove many of the constraints associated with paper library, such as the effective limitation to local collections the tendency for desired materials to be unavailable, delays in service delivery and limited opening hours. Users now have more effective, faster access to the information required.

Electronic resources refer to those materials requiring computer access, whether through microcomputer, mainframe, or other types of computers, accessible locally or from a remote location. Ibenne and Durodolu (2011) opined that the provision of e-based resources and services to library patrons has become a new duty for librarians; insisting that the virtual libraries are the only way Nigerian university libraries can meet future challenges in a world of exponentially increasing information resources output that also offers increasingly networked and digitized information. The future of virtual library service is bright for Nigerian universities due to an evolving global integration of virtual libraries, encouraging resource sharing and cooperative efforts in training and research through data connectivity. This evolution will serve as empowerment to build capacity, innovate and cultivate a new service paradigm that will affect the institutions' fundamental functions and operations of teaching, learning and research positively. This is because virtual libraries have come to stay as part of the information provision efforts in universities to support teaching, learning and research since universities thrive on the provision of the right information, to the right personal group, at the right time in the right way.

Challenges affecting collection management in Nigerian libraries include: government attitude towards library development; inadequate and mismanagement funding and personnel; high foreign exchange; poor bibliographic control; underdevelopment of publishing industry and the book trade; problem of shipping/clearing; conservation and preservation issues.

University Libraries and their Collection Usage

Information in all subjects and disciplines from different sources are available in the university libraries. Information is a vital ingredient needed by every student in all academic institutions of higher learning. The provision of relevant teaching, learning and research material in diverse formats to users is one of the major duties of the University Library. Anafulu (1992) identified some characteristics of efficient library and information services to include that it must have collections, which are appropriate for work in the subject, including the range of divisions and subdivisions within the disciplines of the faculties in the universities; providing adequate storage for the collections and access to the collection through arrangement that will facilitate easy retrieval; aside from creating strategies for access to documents and other formats not available in its collection as well as training staff to organize the services in the widest possible sense. In general, libraries are established to support the institutional objectives, through the acquisition of both information resources on their mandate, which determines the library's objectives and resources (Fagbemi, Ogunjobi and Ibe, 2011).

Parts of the objectives of academic libraries include: acquiring and making accessible a collection of electronic resources to support the instructional programs of the university, and supplementing the existing main library collections; creating an open and caring environment that encourages self-motivated and life-long learning. The university library is a repository of knowledge, but the manual library services are not adequate for processing, storage and retrieval of information in recent time due to such things as bulk growth rate of information and users as well as the difficulties in coping with updating of information. Thus, it is a must to meet up with the needed standard of efficient, effective services to users in academic libraries (Ifukor, 2012).

Access to information is no longer restricted to print resources in libraries since the advances in technology have made possible access to wide range of e-information sources and getting distant users at convenient time frame. Thus, ICT has made information access, retrieval and dissemination much easier and available irrespective of location, time, package and users. It is the most potent force that is shaping the 21st century librarianship, helping to achieve greater access to and utilization of information and knowledge. Recently, the amount of e-resources in libraries and the diversity of tools to locate and access them have increased exponentially, influencing users' information behavior. The world, including Nigeria, had continued to shift from traditional information resources to the e-based resources and services provision.

Imam, Adedoyin, Jegede and Adesanya (2008) defined library resources as the totality of acquired materials gathered together by a library for its users in print or non-print formats while electronic library resources are materials and services in e-organized format. Mostly, e-resources could only be made available to users through internet or intranet services unlike the former that are readily available to users. Thus, libraries are now being redefined as places to get unrestricted access to information in many formats and from various media. Fagbemi et al (2011) noted users' high acceptance of e-resources and unwillingness to return to print-only versions because in general Electronic Information Sources (EIS) have been rapidly adopted in academic spheres. Libraries need modern technology, tools and resources to realize their full potentials. It is now common to find various EIS in modern-day libraries, providing access to quality scientific journal articles and other information materials suitable for research.

Evans (2000) defined library collection development as the process of meeting the information needs of the people (a service population) in a timely and economical manner using information resources locally held, aside from other organizations. The collections, grouped into print and non-print, include books (text, fiction and reference), audio and/or video including microforms and transparencies, all deployed by the library to satisfy the diverse information needs of the library users. These collections are built by the library through a number of methods like purchase, subscription, exchange, and donation/gift, based on assessment of the information needs of the library users. E-books and e-periodicals are now in the forefront of library collection development concern. Given the vast resources available on the Web, librarians need to approach it deliberately and scientifically to access the resources most relevant to the needs of their users.

Studies on Library Resources Availability and Use

University libraries are indispensible agents for information gathering, organization and dissemination across the world. A university library is an academic institution that has always made information available to the academic community to support teaching, learning and research. Fasae (2011) in a study of Use of Library Resources and Services of Federal University of Technology, Akure, by postgraduate students, identified that print journals has the highest consultation (97%) followed by textbook/monographs (92%); theses and dissertations (86%), reference materials (75%), international organization publications (71%) while e-journals had (50%) followed only by conference/seminar papers (46%) and government publications (36%). Oyadonghan and Eke (2011) found that the Federal University of Technology Owerri (FUTO) library provides access to internet services, EBSCO host, e-Granary, AGORA portal, and AGORA/TEEAL while the Niger Delta University library had 18 computers with internet connectivity, which the staff and students make free use of.

Thanuskodi (2010) in a study of the use of the internet and electronic resources by the final students of the Agricultural University of Coinbatone, found that majority (52.7%) respondents use Internet, e-databases and e-journals on a weekly basis mostly. Ani and Edem (2011) found that the frequency of usage of online databases by academic staff of the University of Calabar, Nigeria, for teaching and research was low, only occasionally and the databases most highly used are Science directory, EBSCO Host, AGORA and HINARI. Okello-Obura and Ikoja-Odongo (2010) reported that Makerere University subscribed to a number of full-text databases like Emerald,, EBSCO host, AGORA, HINARI, OUP etc while their LIS students used Emerald and EBSCO host monthly even as 44% used HINARI and none using AGORA for their academic work. Lakeru (2008) found that all the libraries and information centres at ABU, Zaria subscribed to various CD-ROM and online databases like CAB abstract, Medline, Vet CD, Beast CD, AGRICOLA, AGRIS, TEEAL, AJOL and Internet portals like AGORA and HINARI. The study also found that these resources were highly used by the staff of the agricultural complex at the university.

Lwoga, E. T., Chiniwaza, G., Aronson, B & Vent, O. (2007) found that the TEEAL, AGORA, HINARI and OARE now provide free or low cost journals to developing countries to improve information access to science scholarship-African librarians and researchers. Similarly Salam and Aderibigbe (2010) found that 57.8% of academic staff of the university indicated awareness whereas 33% used it when necessary. Lwoga et al (2007) found that almost 80% of TEEAL users in Africa, Asia and Latin America indicated that this has improved their production and quality of their work. Muinde and Gorman (2009) affirmed that Kenyan research institutes' users lacked specialized information skills, so they could not manipulate ICT tools effectively to access information. Liu and Luo (2011) identified "difficulty to use (not user friendly) and no human help (reference librarians) were factors responsible for not using digital library by both undergraduate and graduate students in China. Wang and Wu (2011) found that research use of Internet ICT in China and the US by 59 Computer and Engineering Faculty is becoming more important over the last decade and they use email, web, digital library OPAC, e journals and d-bases on a daily basis and are satisfied with the EIS than print.

Oladele (2002) found that there is little awareness and little patronage of agricultural databases among agricultural researchers in Nigeria. He recommended the provision of EIS and the facilities to enhance their usage in Nigerian Agricultural Research Institutes. But Salau and Saingbe (2008) found that both the agricultural researchers and extension workers in Nasarawa State, Nigeria had over 70% usage of EIS; a position strengthen by Owolabi and Agboola (2010) who reports that majority of academic staff of University of Agriculture, Abeokuta, Nigeria use the Internet facilities for research, teaching and learning, while usage has helped to improve users' professional competencies, expedited their research activities and made them less dependent on conventional document for research and teaching. Okiki and Asiru (2011) found that 49.93% masters' programme students' use EIS, 79% used it for research and 47.8% for writing paper and completing course assignment. Obaseyi (2012) reported that in Nigeria, various EIS found in libraries include: The essential Electronic Agricultural Library (TEEAL), Internet www, Access to Global Online Research in Agriculture (AGORA), Health Internetwork Access to Research Initiative (HINARI), Online Access to Research in Environment (OARE).

METHODOLOGY

This is a survey research design focusing the case of academic libraries in Kwara State regarding their e-resources building and use. A total of four universities are involved in the study including University of Ilorin (established in 1975), Al-Hikmah University (established in 2005), Kwara State University, Malete (established in 2009) and Landmark University, Omu-Aran (established in 2011) all in Kwara State, Nigeria. Given a total of 12,100 estimated real, as against the potential users of the four libraries, constituting the population of the study, a sample of 2,500 was drawn in which the University of Ilorin contributed 100 to the sample size, while the others had 50 each, relative to their status and students' population.

While the interview schedule was used to collect data from the university librarians, the users were served with the questionnaire, which has an almost 100% return rate, on account of the physical presence of the researchers in the four places, notwithstanding the use of research assistants in all the places. The data analysis was based on the number of the completed and returned questionnaire found usable.

THE RESULTS

Table 1: Questionnaire Return Rate

University Libraries	Number Administered	Number Returned	Percentage
University of Ilorin Library	100	98	98
Al-Hikmah University Library	50	30	60
Kwara State University Library	50	48	96
Landmark University Library	50	48	96
Total	**250**	**224**	**89.6**

Table 1 presents the breakdown of the questionnaire administration in which the University of Ilorin (UI) had 100 with a return rate of 98% in comparison with the remaining three having 50 each. Aside Al-Hikmah University (AU), which returned 60%, both Kwara State University (KWASU) and Landmark University (LU) returned 96% each. Thus, of the 250% copies of the questionnaire administered, 224 copies were completed, returned and found usable for the data analysis, representing 89.6%.

DATA ANALYSIS AND PRESENTATION

Table 2: Frequency of Library Visits

Library Visits	University of Ilorin Library Library	Al-Hikmah University Library	Kwara State University Library	Landmark University Library
Daily	57(58.2)	23(76.7)	9(18.6)	9(18.6)
Weekly	31(31.6)	2(6.7)	1(2.1)	4(8.3)
Monthly	0(0.0)	3 (10.0)	33(68.8)	33(68.8)
Rarely	10(10.2)	1(3.3)	5(10.4)	1(2.1)
Not at all	0(0)	1(3.3)	1(2.1)	0(0)
Total	**98(100)**	**30(100)**	**48(100)**	**48(100)**

Table 2 provides the details of the frequency of the respondents' visit to the library in which majority (58.2%) and (31.6%) from the UI claimed daily and weekly visits respectively. However, the "not at all" claim was quite insignificant as others from KWASU and LU indicated monthly visits amounting to 68.8% each. This response pattern may be linked with new status of the two universities. This implies that respondents from these two universities do not consider library visit as central to their studies.

Table 3: Purpose of Library Visits

Information Materials	University of Ilorin Library	Al-Hikmah University Library	Kwara State University Library	Landmark University Library
Textbooks	61(62.3)	23(76.7)	33(68.8)	33(68.8)
Notebooks	33(33.7)	2(6.7)	9(18.6)	9(18.6)
Newspapers	2(2.0)	3 (10.0)	1(2.1)	4(8.3)
E-books	1(1.0)	0 (0)	5(10.4)	1(2.1)
E-journals	0(0)	1(3.3)	0(0.0)	0(0)
Accessing the Internet	1(1.0)	1(3.3)	0(0.0)	1(2.1)
Total	**98(100)**	**30(100)**	**48(100)**	**48(100)**

When asked of the purposes of their library visits, 62.3% respondents from the UI go there to read library/own textbooks and 33.7% their notebooks. Both KWASU and Landmark had 68.8% each for textbooks as their purpose of library visits even as AU had 76.7% for the same purpose. Visiting the library for purposes such as reading newspapers, e-books and journal as well as for accessing the Internet were not generally indicated by the respondents. A plausible reason for this response pattern may be the separation of the e-library or e collections from the Main Library as it is the case with the UI and KWASU as well as AU which has no e-collections. Also, the lack of visit to the library to read newspapers may not be unconnected with the general availability of Internet access on mobile phones.

This finding relates to that of Ani and Edem (2011) which found that the frequency of usage of online databases by academic staff of the University of Calabar, Nigeria, for teaching and research was low and only used occasionally. Fasae (2011) also found that print journals has the highest consultation (97%), textbook/ monographs (92%); theses and dissertations (86%), reference materials (75%), international organization publications (71%), e-journals (50%) followed only by conference/seminar papers (46%) and government publications (36%).

Table 4: What Respondents Enjoyed Most during Library Visits?

Information Materials	University of Ilorin Library	Al-Hikmah University Library	Kwara State University Library	Landmark University Library
Textbooks	57(58.2)	20(66.7)	32(66.7)	33(68.8)
Notebooks	33(33.7)	5(16.7)	13(27.0)	10(20.8)
Newspapers	4(4.0)	4(13.3)	2(4.2)	4(8.3)
E-books	1(1.0)	0 (0.0)	0(0.0)	1(2.1)
E-journals	0(0.0)	0(0.0)	0(0.0)	0(0.0)
Accessing the Internet	3(3.1)	1(3.3)	1(2.1)	0(0.0)
Total	**98(100)**	**30(100)**	**48(100)**	**48(100)**

The data presented in Table 4 sought to know what excites respondents more during library visit where their responses were very akin to that in Table 3. All the four universities had good response rate for enjoying the reading of textbooks and notebooks respectively on their library visit, as UI had 58.2%, AU (66.7%), KWASU (66.7%) and LU (68.8%) for textbooks.

Therefore, Table 5 revealed that respondents' frustration in their use of library materials tie very closely to the use of textbooks, 73.5% for the UI; 64.6% (KWASU), 56.2% (LU) and 46.7% (AU).

Table 5: My frustration whenever I visit the library relates to finding needed

Information Materials	University of Ilorin Library	Al-Hikmah University Library	Kwara State University Library	Landmark University Library
Textbooks	72(73.5)	14(46.7)	31(64.6)	27(56.2)
Notebooks	0(0.0)	0(0.0)	2(4.2)	1(2.1)
Newspapers	0(0.0)	1(3.3)	0(0.0)	3(6.3)
E-books	6(6.1)	0 (0.0)	3(6.3)	4(8.3)
E-journals	1(1.0)	1(3.3)	1(2.1)	0(0.0)
Accessing the Internet	11(11.2)	10(33.3)	8(16.6)	10(20.8)
Un-conducive library environment	8(8.2)	4(13.3)	3(6.2)	3(6.3)
Total	**98(100)**	**30(100)**	**48(100)**	**48(100)**

Table 6 : I find the library most exciting because I do always find my needed:

Information Materials	University of Ilorin Library	Al-Hikmah University Library	Kwara State University Library	Landmark University Library
Textbooks	58(59.2)	18(60.0)	38(79.1)	31(64.5)
Notebooks	16(16.3)	8(26.7)	5(10.4)	1(22.9)
Newspapers	4(4.1)	2(6.7)	2(4.2)	0(0.0)
E-books	1(1.0)	0 (0.0)	0(0.0)	3(6.3)
E-journals	1(1.0)	1(3.3)	2(4.2)	0(0.0)
Accessing the Internet	0(0.0)	1(3.3)	1(2.1)	3(6.3)
Un-conducive library environment	19(19.4)	0(0.0)	0(0.0)	0(0.0)
Total	**98(100)**	**30(100)**	**48(100)**	**48(100)**

The data presented on Table 6 were meant to crosscheck for authentication of the above by seeking their sources of excitement in the libraries as opposed to their frustration. The data thus revealed that finding and using needed textbooks constitute their primary sources of excitement with KWASU having 79.1% response, LU (64.5%), AU (60.0%) and UI (59.2%).

Table 7: The library should have more of

Information Materials	University of Ilorin Library	Al-Hikmah University Library	Kwara State University Library	Landmark University Library
Textbooks	75(76.5)	19(63.3)	37(77.0)	34(70.8)
Newspapers	2(2.0)	0(0.0)	1(2.1)	1(2.1)
Journals	1(1.0)	0(0.0)	1(2.1)	0(0.0)
e-books	1(1.0)	2 (6.7)	3(6.3)	2(4.2)
e-journals	0(0.0)	1(3.3)	0(0.0)	1(2.1)
e-newspapers	0(0.0)	0(0.0)	0(0.0)	0(0.0)
Accessing the Internet	19(19.4)	8(26.7)	6(12.5)	10(20.8)
Total	**98(100)**	**30(100)**	**48(100)**	**48(100)**

These results probably informed the data presented on Table 7, where the majority 77.0% (KWASU); 76.5% (UI); 70.8% (LU) and the 63.3% (AU) indicated their desire to have more textbooks than anything else in their respective libraries.

Table 8: How satisfied are you with the library print resources (i.e. books, newspapers and journals)?

Satisfaction Level	University of Ilorin Library	Al-Hikmah University Library	Kwara State University Library	Landmark University Library
Very satisfied	8(8.2)	15 (50.0)	7(14.6)	9(18.8)
Satisfied	67(68.4)	14(46.7)	29(60.4)	33(68.7)
Unsatisfied	23(23.4)	1(3.3)	10(20.8)	5(10.4)
Very unsatisfied	0 (0.0)	0(0.0)	2(4.2)	1(2.1)
Total	**98(100)**	**30(100)**	**48(100)**	**48(100)**

Regarding their satisfaction with their libraries' print resources, only an insignificant proportion indicated "very satisfied" even though "satisfied" represented the major response here. Even then, about a half of the respondents indicated that they are "unsatisfied" in this regard. But these results were unable to locate the non-satisfaction within a particular context such as inadequate volume, irrelevant or dated holdings. Fagbemi et al (2011) had a similar finding pointing in the direction of a high acceptance of e-resources and unwillingness to return to print-only versions by users because in general EIS have been rapidly adopted in academic spheres.

Table 9 : Satisfaction with the library's e-resources (e-books, e-newspapers, e-journals, internet access)?

Satisfaction Level	University of Ilorin Library	Al-Hikmah University Library	Kwara State University Library	Landmark University Library
Very satisfied	11(11.2)	15 (50.0)	5(10.4)	9(18.8)
Satisfied	46(47.0)	12(40.0)	15(31.3)	30(62.5)
Unsatisfied	36(36.7)	3(10.0)	21(43.7)	6(12.5)
Very unsatisfied	5 (5.1)	0(0.0)	7(14.6)	3(6.2)
Total	98(100)	30(100)	48(100)	48(100)

Surprisingly, this response patterns also reflected in the data contained in Table 9 where majority laid a similar claim for their satisfaction with the e-resources in their libraries. And just as there are for the print resources, e-resources also attracted some degree of non-satisfaction. This implied that there is a substantial room for improvements in both categories. This finding is, however not supported by Fagbemi et al (2011) as reported in Table 8.

Table 10: Suggest ways for the Improvement for the Library

Suggestions	University of Ilorin Library	Al-Hikmah University Library	Kwara State University Library	Landmark University Library
Provision of more print resources	50(51.0)	14(46.7)	22(45.8)	33(68.8)
Provision of more e-resources	4(4.1)	1(3.3)	3(6.3)	0(0.0)
Provision of steady internet access	17(17.3)	3(10.0)	15(31.3)	6(12.5)
Creating more awareness on the advantages of e-resources	1(1.0)	2(6.7)	0(0.0)	0(0.0)
Ensuring steady power supply	4(4.1)	0(0.0)	4(8.3)	0(0.0)
Others	22(22.4)	10(33.3)	4(8.3)	9(18.7)
Total	**98(100)**	**30(100)**	**48(100)**	**48(100)**

When asked to suggest ways of improvement for their libraries, respondents largely did so in the direction of provision of more print materials; 68.8% (LU); 51.0% (UI); 46.7% (AU) and 45.8% (KWASU). Other suggestions were made in the direction of more provision of steady Internet access, creating more awareness on the advantages of e-resources and the provision of more e-resources; in that order.

REPORT OF THE INTERVIEW WITH THE UNIVERSITY LIBRARY AUTHORITIES

A total of 18 questions were raised in interview schedules which were personally conducted by the researchers on the four university librarians within a range of one and a half weeks. From their responses, the four university libraries were established at times closely related to the establishment of the universities themselves viz: University of Ilorin (UI) established in 1976; Al-Hikmah University (AU) in 2005; Kwara State University (KWASU) in 2009 and Landmark University (LU) in 2011. Arising from this historical perspective, it is not surprising that only the UI is presently occupying a purposefully built accommodation. Others are in different stages of having such a desired state of accommodation. In terms of staffing, the UI has 10 professionals, and 13 each of professionals/non-professionals; followed by KWASU, 9 professionals, 1 para-professionals and 5 non-professionals. As for LU, there are 3 professionals, 2 para-professionals and 9 non-professionals, while AU has only 1 professional, 4 para-professionals and 3 non-professionals.

At the UI, professional staff members are in ranks ranging from Assistant Librarian up to the University Librarian; para-professionals ranging from Library Officers to Chief Library Officers and non-professionals ranging from Library Assistants to Assistant Library Officers. This pattern cuts across the rank composition in these libraries except for LU, which has a Director in place of the University Librarian. Their qualifications, alongside the cadres include BLS, BLIS, MLS, MLIS AND PhD for the professionals, DLS, BLS, BLIS, MLS and MLIS for the para-professionals as well as SSCE for the non-professionals. The UI however has a slightly varied situation whereby some BLIS, MLIS holders are still occupying the Library Officer cadre awaiting their appropriate upgrade.

On the advantages of e-resources in the libraries, all the interviews agreed that they save space, allowed prompt, simultaneous, remote and multiple access and retrieval and more comfort with less efforts. They are also said to be less prone to theft/mutilation and are cheaper to maintain. These agreed with the findings of Muinde and Gorman (2009) which confirmed the increased widespread realization of how useful these e-resources become in agricultural and scientific research communication, though at a slow pace owing to infrastructural problems. Similarly, Salaam (2007) found that users preferred the CD-ROM database especially TEEAL in her study on the use and the most preferred among printed journals, CD-ROM databases and online database available to researchers at the University of Agriculture, Abeokuta Library. Wang and Wu (2011) found that research use of Internet ICT in China and the US had become more important...using email, web, digital library OPAC, e-journals and d-bases on a daily basis and are satisfied with the EIS than print.

But even with these far-reaching advantages, it was found that both the UI and AU are yet to be automated. However, the UI has an e-learning platform under its digital arrangement for the two libraries which are automated, KOHA (KWASU) and Alexandria Librarian (LU) are the software in use. In terms of the size, UI has 87134 book titles and 2,458 periodical titles comprising 1836 foreign and 622 local titles. As the book collection of AU is over 9,000 and over 500 periodical titles, KWASU has 7000 books and 257 periodical titles in its collection while LU has 11,500 and 700 books and journal titles respectively. It was remarkable to find that LU holds over 30,000 e-periodical titles, which is unmatched by the other three. The UI only has an NUC subscription to such databases as EBSCOHOST, OARE, AGORA, HINARI and JSTOR. This is in line with the findings of Obaseyi (2012) who listed some of the above as part of the various EIS found in Nigerian libraries. Also, Okorie (2010) found that postgraduate students and academic staff of the university use CD-ROM databases like TEEAL, MEDLINE, CAB Abstract etc in his investigation of the use of automated electronic information services.

The e-resources in these libraries are acquired mainly through subscription, services of vendors and/or aggregators. It is only at LU that a separate budget is set aside for the acquisition of e-resources, which are organized electronically in computer memories, CD-ROM, flash drives, external hard disks even as the e-book platform is viewed from the library OPAC. Ease of access and retrieval is guaranteed by having the e-resources linked to the university websites.

Limited/non-use of e-resources, safety issues, virus attacks are some of the challenges of e-resources regarding their acquisition, organization, retrieval and use. This was in line with the report by Muinde and Gorman (2009) who affirmed that Kenyan research institutes' users lacked specialized information skills, so they could not manipulate ICT tools effectively to access information. Even Liu and Luo (2011) identified "difficulty to use (not user friendly) and no human help (reference librarians) were factors responsible for not using digital library by both undergraduate and graduate students in China.

Some of the suggested solutions to the challenges include: continuing publicity by the library authorities and lecturers who should make their students' assignments e-resources based to encourage usage; provision of standard storage facilities and appropriate back up hard copies as well as the enforcement of e-library regulations.

CONCLUSION AND RECOMMENDATIONS

On the strength of this study's findings, it is concluded that the university libraries' print and e-resources need to be strengthened for adequacy, relevance and usage so that both categories of resources could be used to complement each other for meeting the users' needs. To achieve this, the followings are recommended:

1. The two un-automated university libraries viz: UI and AU, should be automated without any further delay because it is only through an automated environment that electronic information services can be facilitated and sustained.
2. Budgets for both print and e-resources in these libraries should be separated so that the two categories could be adequately catered for in the collection building process.
3. As recommended by Okello-Obura and Ikoja-Odongo (2010), the library staff in these universities should improve their skills on e-resources searching and retrieval; given the trend that library-centered services have changed to user-centered services.
4. The library users should be adequately educated on the use of the library as a whole and especially the e-resources in these libraries for maximum advantage. Library orientation, running a documentary on use of the library (printed and/or on CD) for individual library user or running such as a tutorial on the libraries' computers are some ways of doing this.

REFERENCES

Adomi, E.E. (2009). *Library and Information Resources.* Ethiope Publishing Corporation.

Anafulu, J. C. (1992). Providing Information Service for Engineers: The Example of the Federal University of Technology Owerri, Nigeria. Workshop on Access to Service and Technology, Bauchi, February 9-13. 62-74.

Ani, O.E. & Edem, O.N. (2011). Access and Usage of Online Databases in Nigerian Universities in Teaching Research: A Case Study of Academic Staff in University of Calabar, Nigeria. Retrieved from Elsevier.conference_services.net/resources/247/.../CALX2011_0103....

Awoyemi, O.O. (2011). Challenges of Collection Management in Nigerian Libraries. *Gateway Library Journal,* 14(1), 87-96.

Evans, G. Edward (2000). *Developing Library and Information Center Collections.* Colorade: Libraries Unlimited.

Fagbemi, O.O., Ogunjobi, T.E. & Ibe, O. (2011). E-Library and Traditional Library Resources Usage: A Comparative Study in Nigeria. *Information Technology: An International Journal of Information and Communication Technology,* 8(2), 19-26.

Fasae, J. K. (2011). Use of Library Resources and Services of Federal University of Technology, Akure by Postgraduate Students. *Gateway Library Journal,* 14(1), 66-75.

Ibenne, S.K. & Durodolu, O. (2011). Imperatives of Virtual Library Services on the Quality of Teaching, Learning and Research for Students in Nigerian Universities. *Gateway Library Journal,* 14(1), 16-26.

Ifukor, M.O. (2012). The Development of E-Library at Delta State University, Library, Abraka. *The Information Technology: An International Journal of Information and Communication Technology (ICT),* 9(1), 75-82.

Imam, A., Adedoyin, S.O., Jegede, O.R. & Adesanya, O. (2008). *Library and Information Studies: An Introductory Text for Students in Tertiary Institutions.* Abeokuta. Egbe Publishers.

Lakan, E.L. (2008). Availability and Utilization of Electronic Information Databases by staff of the Agricultural Complex, Ahmadu Bello University, Zaria. *Samaru Journal of Information Studies,* (1), 44-53.

Liu, Z. & Luo, L. (2011). A Comparative Study of Digital Library Use: Factors, Perceived Influences, and Satisfaction. *The Journal of Academic Librarianship,* 37(3), 230-236.

Lwoga, E.T., Chiniwaza, G., Aronson, B. & Vent, O. (2007). Building Science Information Fluency in African Universities: How Libraries and Researchers are Benefiting from the Proceed Access to Science Scholarship. In: World

Library and Information Congress: 73rd IFLA General Conference and Council, 19-23 August, Durban, South Africa. Retrieved from http://www.ifla.org/iv/ifla73/index.htm

Muinde, F.N.N. & Gorman, G.E. (2009). Barriers to Open Access to Scientific Information in Kenya, with Particular Reference to Agricultural Information. *World Library and Information Congress.* 75th IFLA General Conference and Council, 23-27 August, 2009, Milan, Italy.

Obaseyi, L. (2012). Analysis of EIS Usage at the Nigerian Institute of Oil Palm Research Library. *The Information Technologist: An International Journal of Information and Communication Technology,* 9(1), 55-65.

Okello-Obura, C. & Ikoja-Odongo, J. R. (2010). Electronic Information Seeking among Library and Information Science Postgraduate Students at Makerere University, Uganda. *Library Philosophy and Practice.*

Okiki, O.C. & Asiru, S.M. (2011). Uses of Electronic Information Sources by Postgraduate Students in Nigeria: Influencing Factors.

Oladele, I.O.I. (2002). Information Seeking and Utilization among Agricultural Researchers in Nigeria. Retrieved from http://zonshoku.nare.affrc.go.jp/ADR/AFITA/AFIT_conf/2002/part/p.137.pdf

Owolabi, K.A. & Agboola, I.O. (2010). Availability and Use of Internet by Academic Staff in Nigerian University of Agricultural Universities: A Case Study of University of Agriculture, Abeokuta, Nigeria. *The Information Technologists: An International Journal of Information and Information and Communication Technology,* 7(1), 213-220.

Oyadonghan, J. C. & Eke, F. M. (2011). Factors Affecting Student Usage of ICT: A Comparative Study of Federal University of Technology, Owerri and Niger Delta University, Arizona. *Library Philosophy and Practice,* January 1, 2011.

Salaam, M. O. & Aderibigbe, N. A. (2010). Awareness and Utilization of the Essential Electronic Agricultural Library by Academic Staff: A Case Study of University of Agriculture, Abeokuta, Nigeria. *Chinese Librarianship: An International Electronic Journal,* 30. Retrieved from http://ww.ic\c.us/clies/c/30SA.pdf.

Salau, E.S. & Saingbe, N.D. (2008). Access and Utilization of ICTs among Agricultural Researchers and Extension Workers in Selected Institutions in Nasarawa State of Nigeria. *PAT,* 4(2), 1-11.

Thanuskodi, S. (2010). Use of Internet and Electronic Resources for Agriculture Science Information: A Case Study. *The Social Science,* 5(4), 364-367.

Wang, P. & Wu, L. (2011). Research Use of the Internet ICT by Faculty: An Interdisciplinary and Cross Cultural Comparison. Retrieved from www.cci.utk.edu/files/ul4/wang/pdf